W9-CEE-637

REIMAN MEDIA GROUP, INC. • GREENDALE, WI

■ COVER PHOTOGRAPHY
Taste of Home Photo Studio

5400 S. 60th St., Greendale WI 53129

International Standard Book Number (13):
978-1-61765-184-7

International Standard Serial Number:
1522-6603

Component Number: 117800039H

Printed in U.S.A.
1 3 5 7 9 10 8 6 4 2

Photo Credits:
• Family: Clerkenwell/the Agency Collection/Getty Images, p. 296
• Family: Jamie Grill/Getty Images, p. 297
• Woman shopping: Don Bayley/the Agency Collection/Getty Images, p. 297
• Family: Clerkenwell/the Agency Collection/Getty Images, p. 298
• Notebook: Michael Hitoshi/Getty Images, p. 298
• Woman: Blend Images/Trinette Reed/the Agency Collection/Getty Images, p. 299
• Family: Jamie Grill/Getty Images, p. 300
• Woman shopping: Don Bayley/the Agency Collection/Getty Images, p. 300
• Bag: Peter Dazeley/Getty Images, p. 300
• Spices: David Arky/Getty Image, p. 302

PICTURED ON THE FRONT COVER The King's Crowned Filets (p. 284), Peanut Butter-Chocolate Ice Cream Torte (p. 223), Asian Turkey Lettuce Wraps (p. 155), Stacked Chicken Cordon Bleu (p. 169) and Cajun Beef Casserole (p. 99).

PICTURED AT LEFT Chimichurri Monkey Bread (p. 63), Scalloped Potatoes & Ham (p. 144) and Lemon & Sage Roasted Chicken (p. 82).

contents

Introduction and Recipe Contest Winners...4
Check out the contest-winning recipes featured in this year's book, including the Grand Prize winners.

30-Minute Meals ... 8
Every meal in this chapter can be prepared in just half an hour...or less!

Give Me Five or Fewer ... 36
These easy-to-make recipes require just five ingredients but don't skimp on flavor.

Almost Homemade ... 56
Convenience products streamline preparation in these homestyle recipes.

Cooking for Kids ... 68
Kids will love these delightful dishes, from whimsical snacks to wholesome dinners.

Cook Once, Eat Twice ... 80
As the title suggests, you can prepare a hearty meal, then use the leftovers to make a second recipe that's just as delicious.

Shop Once...Eat All Week ... 94
Enjoy four weeks of dinners already planned out for you—with complete shopping lists.

Breakfast & Brunch Favorites ... 112
Your family won't be able to resist this incredible selection of tasty morning favorites.

Appetizers & Beverages ... 124
These easy-to-make starters and drinks will tide guests over until suppertime.

Speedy Sides & Salads ... 136
It's easy to find quick accompaniments to the main course with all the delicious ideas in this chapter.

Quick Soups & Sandwiches ... 150
Mix and match recipes for the perfect lunch or light dinner any day of the week.

Stovetop Dinners ... 166
Skillet meals lead to fast and easy preparation— and cleanup—for busy cooks.

Casseroles & Oven Suppers ... 182
One-dish dinners fresh from the oven are surefire family-pleasers.

Lightened-Up Delights ... 196
If you're watching what you eat by reducing calories, fat, sugar or salt from your diet, then this chapter is for you.

Delectable Desserts ... 212
Tantalizing dinner finales do not have to take all day to prepare. Here's proof!

Effortless Entertaining ... 234
These festive ideas will help make your party planning go smoothly.

Holiday & Seasonal Pleasers ... 250
Your special celebrations will be a breeze with the meals and treats in this chapter.

Easy Odds & Ends ... 278
Turn here for grilling recipes, slow cooker meals, easy-to-freeze dishes and helpful hints behind various cooking techniques.

Advice for On-the-Go Cooks ... 296
Thumb through these pages for in-depth information on menu planning, savvy shopping and expert baking tips.

General Recipe Index ... 314
Every recipe in this book is listed according to food category, major ingredient and/or cooking method.

Alphabetical Recipe Index ... 331
It's a snap to find your favorite dishes with a little help from this handy index.

Make It EASY

with 600+ family-friendly recipes & tips

Welcome to the latest edition of Quick Cooking Annual Recipes, featuring a year's worth of dishes from *Simple & Delicious* magazine.

Carefully crafted into 18 chapters based on your favorite *Simple & Delicious* columns and departments, this collection of fast-to-fix recipes is your go-to resource for no-fuss menu planning, speedy weeknight meals, hassle-free entertaining and cooking tips shared by hundreds of home cooks just like you!

HIGHLIGHTS FROM INSIDE

• Contest-Winning Recipes

Hundreds of entries are submitted for each of *S&D*'s themed recipe contests. Meet the Grand Prize winners and find the contest themes with the winning dishes on pages 5-7.

• 5 Or Fewer

Short and sweet, five-ingredient recipes are in high demand. This most-requested chapter features entrees, desserts, sides and potluck favorites that come together with just a handful of everyday items. [Editor's note: Water, salt and pepper are not counted as ingredients.]

• 4 One-Week Menu Plans

Getting in and out of the supermarket with a week's worth of dinners doesn't get any easier than this. Try all four of the week-long menus in our Shop Once...Eat All Week chapter—each menu comes complete with a grocery list.

• Freeze!

Technically, you can freeze just about anything. But not all foods maintain the same quality after a few weeks in the freezer. Recipes with a (f) have been deemed freezer-friendly by our Test Kitchen.

• Find It Fast

Two recipe indexes help you find exactly what you're looking for. The General Recipe Index is organized by food category, major ingredient and/or cooking method. The Alphabetical Index lists the recipe name alphabetically. In both, you'll find red checkmarks next to the recipes that have Nutrition Facts.

The Past Year's

RECIPE CONTESTS & THEIR WINNERS

COMPANY'S COMING

GRAND PRIZE

The King's Crowned Filets 284

1st PLACE

Pork Medallions with Brandy Cream Sauce 181

2nd PLACE

Sesame Salmon with Wasabi Mayo 193

3rd PLACE

Blue Cheese Quiche with Caramelized Pears 119

RUNNERS-UP

Stacked Chicken Cordon Bleu 169
Country Chuck Roast with Mushroom Gravy 168
Mediterranean Rack of Lamb 191
Sweet & Tender Beef Ribs 185
Pork Medallions with Raspberry-Balsamic Sauce 199
Rosemary-Orange Roasted Chicken 190
Bourbon-Glazed Ham 191
Mediterranean Shrimp Linguine 198

GRAND PRIZE

"Guests will feel like royalty when you present this tender filet with a lightly breaded horseradish topping. Best of all, it grills in just 15 minutes, giving you more time to visit."

—**TONYA BURKHARD** DAVIS, ILLINOIS

GRAND PRIZE

SWEET ON CHOCOLATE

GRAND PRIZE

Chocolate Butterscotch Tartlets 131

1st PLACE

Mocha Cappuccino Punch 130

2nd PLACE

Sacher Bars 228

3rd PLACE

Crispy Mexican Truffles 132

RUNNERS-UP

Chocolate-Peanut Butter Cup Cookies 231
Peanut Butter-Hazelnut Brownies 229
Candy-Licious Fudge 233
Chocolate Lover's Cream Pie 226
Million Dollar Pecan Bars 221
Outrageous Chocolate Mint Cookies 229
Dark Chocolate Carrot Cake 231
Triple-Layer Pretzel Brownies 221

"Tartlets are like cake pops—tiny and tasty and a tempting way to experiment with different fillings. But this prize-winning combo is too good to toy with."

—**JENNIFER LARISON** TUCSON, ARIZONA

UNDER THE SEA

GRAND PRIZE
Swordfish with Fennel and Tomatoes 286
1st PLACE
Baja Fish Tacos 175
2nd PLACE
Hot Shrimp Salad 210
3rd PLACE
Creole Shrimp Pasta 174
RUNNERS-UP
BLT Catfish Sandwiches 157
Blackened Halibut 208
Salmon with Tangy Raspberry Sauce 209
Coconut Shrimp Chowder 157
Crispy Scallops with Tarragon Cream 293
Herb-Crusted Perch Fillets with Pea Puree 175
Tropical Tilapia 209
Basil Crab Cakes 208

"Step aside, marinara. There's a new sauce in town, and it's blissfully fresh with fennel and basil. TV-inspired and husband-adored, it would be a crime not to share this one."

—**LAUREL DALZELL** MANTECA, CALIFORNIA

5-INGREDIENT FIXES

GRAND PRIZE
Balsamic-Glazed Chicken Wings 42
1st PLACE
Peppered Portobello Penne 38
2nd PLACE
Blackberry Beer Cocktail 45
3rd PLACE
Hawaiian Barbecue Beans 50
RUNNERS UP
Tomato-Basil Couscous Salad 45
Bacon-Gouda Stuffed Onions 42
Citrus-Spice Glazed Salmon 50
Pesto Portobello Pizzas 44
Garlic Chicken & Bacon Pizza 47
Frozen Lime Cake 48
Whoopie Cookies 38
Tuscan Parmesan Pork Chops 48

"Tired of the same buffalo and BBQ sauces? Try spreading your wings with a new balsamic-sugar glaze. Sweet and mildly tangy, these have a taste that will appeal to any crowd."

—**GRETCHEN WHELAN** SAN FRANCISCO, CALIFORNIA

HERBALICIOUS

GRAND PRIZE
Steakhouse Strip Steaks with Chimichurri 285
1st PLACE
Chimichurri Monkey Bread 63
2nd PLACE
Strawberry Tarragon Crumble 232
3rd PLACE
Zucchini Pesto with Shrimp and Farfalle 207
RUNNERS-UP
Fiesta Rice and Bean Salad 149
Herby Potatoes with Sour Cream 143
Bistro Herb-Rubbed Pork Tenderloin 172
Bella Basil Raspberry Tea 132
Basil-Mint Chicken Thighs 285
Garden Orzo Risotto 204
White Bean and Spinach Salads 142
Mandarin Watermelon Salad 149
Sweet & Tender Beef Ribs 185
Pork Medallions with Raspberry-Balsamic Sauce 199
Rosemary-Orange Roasted Chicken 190
Bourbon-Glazed Ham 191
Mediterranean Shrimp Linguine 198

"Chilies and lime juice give this version of chimichurri sauce a zesty Southwest flair that's dynamite with the cumin-rubbed steaks."

—**GILDA LESTER** MILLSBORO, DELAWARE

COOKIE SHORTCUTS

GRAND PRIZE
Salted Caramel Fudge Drops 272
1st PLACE
Hot Chocolate Peppermint Cookies 275
2nd PLACE
Frosted Anise Cookies 275
3rd PLACE
Honey-Nut Christmas Cookies 271
RUNNERS-UP
Chocolate Candy Cane Cookies 271
Brown Butter Spice Cookies 232
Caramel Coconut Stars 271
Cherry Cordial Cookies 218
Gingerbread Fruitcake Cookies 214
Crème de Menthe Cheesecake Cookies 271
Peppermint S'more Tassies 274
Almond Macaroons 218

"These cookies, which start with a mix, are unbelievably decadent! I like to use caramel-filled Dove chocolates. It's a nice dough to make ahead, roll into balls and freeze for up to 3 months. Then just bake the cookies as you need them."

—**CAROLE HOLT** MENDOTA HEIGHTS, MINNESOTA

30-Minute Meals

“My husband made some tweaks to the original recipe for this chicken dish to suit our tastes, and it was fabulous. Our 18-month-old son even loves it! Plus, it’s the perfect way for me to get out of cooking for a night.”

STACY KOLOJAY STREATOR, ILLINOIS
Root Beer Glazed Chicken, page 23

Spinach & Gorgonzola Salad

Here's an easily assembled side dish with a wonderful combination of flavors.

—NADINE MESCH MOUNT HEALTHY, OHIO

PREP/TOTAL TIME: 10 MIN. **MAKES:** 6 SERVINGS

- **5 cups fresh baby spinach**
- **1 cup sliced fresh strawberries**
- **⅓ cup lightly salted cashews**
- **¼ cup crumbled Gorgonzola cheese**

VINAIGRETTE

- **⅓ cup olive oil**
- **¼ cup balsamic vinegar**
- **1 tablespoon seedless raspberry jam**
- **1½ teaspoons Dijon mustard**
- **¼ teaspoon salt**
- **¼ teaspoon pepper**

1. In a large bowl, combine the spinach, strawberries, cashews and cheese. In a small bowl, whisk the remaining ingredients. Drizzle over salad; toss to coat.

Sun-Dried Tomato Garlic Bread

This fast bread tastes terrific with a variety of main courses. It comes together in minutes and is easy enough for a weekday, but special enough for a weekend meal with guests.

—NADINE MESCH MOUNT HEALTHY, OHIO

PREP/TOTAL TIME: 10 MIN. **MAKES:** 6 SERVINGS

- **¼ cup butter, softened**
- **¼ cup grated Parmesan cheese**
- **2 tablespoons chopped oil-packed sun-dried tomatoes**
- **1 to 2 garlic cloves, minced**
- **½ loaf Italian bread, halved lengthwise**

1. In a small bowl, combine the butter, cheese, tomatoes and garlic. Spread over cut sides of bread. Transfer to an ungreased baking sheet.

2. Broil 4 in. from the heat for 3-4 minutes or until golden brown. Cut into slices and serve warm.

Pasta with Shrimp & Basil

Purchasing precooked shrimp, bagged spinach and shredded cheeses from your local grocery store is a huge time-saver when you need to make this delicious pasta medley in a hurry.

—NADINE MESCH MOUNT HEALTHY, OHIO

PREP/TOTAL TIME: 25 MIN. **MAKES:** 6 SERVINGS

- **3 cups uncooked bow tie pasta**
- **2 cups sliced fresh mushrooms**
- **⅓ cup butter, cubed**
- **½ cup heavy whipping cream**
- **¾ pound peeled and deveined cooked medium shrimp**
- **1 cup fresh baby spinach**
- **½ cup pine nuts, toasted**
- **¼ cup shredded Swiss cheese**
- **¼ cup grated Parmesan cheese**
- **3 tablespoons minced fresh basil**
- **¼ teaspoon salt**
- **⅛ teaspoon pepper**

1. In a large saucepan, cook pasta according to package directions. Meanwhile, in a large skillet, saute mushrooms in butter until tender. Stir in cream. Bring to a boil over medium heat. Reduce heat; simmer, uncovered, for 2 minutes.

2. Stir in the shrimp, spinach, pine nuts, cheeses, basil, salt and pepper; cook for 1-2 minutes or until spinach is wilted. Drain pasta; add to shrimp mixture and toss to coat.

Shhh! SIMPLE SECRET

To test pasta for doneness, use a fork to remove a single piece from the boiling water. Rinse in cold water and taste. It should be tender, but with a slight bite, or "al dente." Overcooking results in a mushy texture.

Apple-Balsamic Pork Chops

When I want to get dinner on the table in a hurry, I look for recipes that meet my EFF standards—easy, fast and frugal. These sweet and delicious chops score on all three counts.

—**JAMI WELLS** BOISE, IDAHO

PREP/TOTAL TIME: 20 MIN. **MAKES:** 4 SERVINGS

- **4 boneless pork loin chops (5 ounces each)**
- **½ teaspoon salt**
- **½ teaspoon pepper**
- **2 teaspoons olive oil**
- **¼ cup apple cider or juice**
- **1 cup reduced-sodium chicken broth**
- **¼ cup apple jelly**
- **2 teaspoons balsamic vinegar**
- **1 tablespoon butter**

1. Sprinkle pork chops with salt and pepper. In a large skillet brown chops in oil. Remove and keep warm.
2. Add apple cider to the skillet, stirring to loosen browned bits from pan. Stir in the broth, jelly and vinegar. Bring to a boil; cook until liquid is reduced to ⅓ cup.
3. Return chops to the skillet. Cover and simmer for 8-10 minutes or until meat is tender, turning once. Add butter and stir until melted.

Savory Peas and Carrots

At less than 60 cents per serving, ready in 20 minutes, and prepared in one saucepan, this dish makes an ideal side. Even my husband, who doesn't like peas, eats this dish with enthusiasm.

—**MARIAN BROWN** MISSISSAUGA, ONTARIO

PREP/TOTAL TIME: 20 MIN. **MAKES:** 4 SERVINGS

- **1¼ cups fresh baby carrots, cut in half lengthwise**
- **2 cups frozen peas**
- **2 tablespoons butter**
- **2 teaspoons dried minced onion**
- **¼ teaspoon dried marjoram**
- **¼ teaspoon dried thyme**
- **⅛ teaspoon sugar**
- **⅛ teaspoon pepper**
- **Dash celery seed**

1. Place carrots in a small saucepan with enough water to cover. Bring to a boil. Cover and cook for 4-5 minutes or until crisp-tender adding the peas during the last 3 minutes of cooking; drain. Stir in the remaining ingredients until butter is melted.

Buttered Noodles

A few pantry ingredients jazz up egg noodles in this quick side they'll ask for again and again.

—**HEATHER NALLEY** EASLEY, SOUTH CAROLINA

PREP/TOTAL TIME: 20 MIN. **MAKES:** 4 SERVINGS

- **2¼ cups uncooked egg noodles**
- **¼ cup shredded part-skim mozzarella cheese**
- **2 tablespoons butter, melted**
- **2 tablespoons grated Parmesan cheese**
- **2 teaspoons minced fresh parsley**
- **¼ teaspoon salt**
- **¼ teaspoon garlic powder**
- **⅛ teaspoon pepper**

1. Cook noodles according to package directions; drain. Transfer to a serving bowl. Immediately add the remaining ingredients and toss to coat.

Italian-Style Salisbury Steaks

This is my husband's favorite entree. He loves it! If you like, you can top each serving with mozzarella or Parmesan cheese.

—**HEATHER NALLEY** EASLEY, SOUTH CAROLINA

PREP/TOTAL TIME: 20 MIN. **MAKES:** 4 SERVINGS

- **1 egg**
- **1 teaspoon Worcestershire sauce**
- **½ cup seasoned bread crumbs**
- **½ teaspoon garlic powder**
- **½ teaspoon pepper**
- **1 pound ground beef**
- **1 tablespoon canola oil**
- **1 can (14½ ounces) diced tomatoes with basil, oregano and garlic, undrained**
- **1 can (8 ounces) Italian tomato sauce**

1. In a large bowl, combine the first five ingredients. Crumble beef over mixture and mix well. Shape into four oval patties. In a large skillet, brown patties in oil on both sides. Drain.
2. In a small bowl, combine diced tomatoes and tomato sauce. Pour over patties. Bring to a boil. Reduce heat; cover and simmer for 10-15 minutes or until meat is no longer pink.

Elegant Pork Marsala

Tired of chicken? Wine and fresh mushrooms lend elegance to this simple reinvention of an Italian classic.

—**KIM GILLIS** HIGH FALLS, NEW YORK

PREP/TOTAL TIME: 30 MIN. **MAKES:** 6 SERVINGS

- **5 teaspoons cornstarch**
- **⅔ cup reduced-sodium chicken broth**
- **⅓ cup whole wheat flour**
- **½ teaspoon pepper**
- **6 boneless pork loin chops (4 ounces each)**
- **1 tablespoon olive oil**
- **2 cups sliced fresh mushrooms**
- **⅓ cup chopped onion**
- **2 turkey bacon strips, diced**
- **¼ teaspoon minced garlic**
- **1 cup Marsala wine or additional reduced-sodium chicken broth**

1. In a small bowl, combine cornstarch and broth until smooth; set aside.

2. Place flour and pepper in a large resealable plastic bag. Add pork, a few pieces at a time, and shake to coat. In a large nonstick skillet coated with cooking spray, cook chops in oil for 4-5 minutes on each side or until a meat thermometer reads 160°. Remove and keep warm.

3. In the same skillet, saute the mushrooms, onion and bacon in drippings for 3 minutes or until bacon is crisp-tender. Add garlic; cook 1 minute longer. Add wine, stirring to loosen browned bits from pan.

4. Stir cornstarch mixture; add to pan. Bring to a boil; cook and stir for 2 minutes or until slightly thickened. Serve with pork.

Cheesy Chive Potatoes

Feta makes these potatoes extra-rich, while chives add fresh flavor.

—**JEAN KOMLOS** PLYMOUTH, MICHIGAN

PREP/TOTAL TIME: 20 MIN. **MAKES:** 6 SERVINGS

- **6 medium potatoes, peeled and cubed**
- **½ cup fat-free milk**
- **½ cup crumbled feta cheese**
- **1 tablespoon butter**
- **½ teaspoon salt**
- **⅛ teaspoon pepper**
- **2 tablespoons minced chives**

1. Place potatoes in a large saucepan and cover with water. Bring to a boil. Reduce heat; cover and cook for 10-15 minutes or until tender.

2. Drain potatoes. Add the milk, cheese, butter, salt and pepper; mash. Stir in chives.

Pan-Fried Chicken Athena

The flavors of everyday pantry items ring out in perfect harmony in these savory pan-fried chicken breasts.

—**BOBBY TAYLOR** LAPORTE, INDIANA

PREP/TOTAL TIME: 30 MIN. **MAKES:** 4 SERVINGS

- **4 boneless skinless chicken breast halves (6 ounces each)**
- **2 tablespoons butter**
- **4½ teaspoons lemon juice**
- **4½ teaspoons Worcestershire sauce**
- **½ teaspoon Dijon mustard**
- **¼ teaspoon salt**
- **1 tablespoon minced chives**
- **1 tablespoon minced fresh parsley or 1 teaspoon dried parsley flakes**
- **Lemon wedges**

1. Flatten chicken breasts to ½-in. thickness. In a large skillet, cook chicken in butter over medium heat for 5-6 minutes on each side or until a meat thermometer reads 170°; remove and keep warm.

2. In the same skillet, add the lemon juice, Worcestershire sauce, mustard and salt. Bring to a boil. Remove from the heat; stir in chives and parsley. Spoon over chicken and serve with lemon wedges.

Green Beans with Shallots

Frozen green beans make these "dill-icious" beans fast and tasty.

—**LINDA RABBITT** CHARLES CITY, IOWA

PREP/TOTAL TIME: 15 MIN. **MAKES:** 4 SERVINGS

- **1 package (12 ounces) frozen Steamfresh® whole green beans**
- **1¾ cups sliced fresh mushrooms**
- **2 shallots, chopped**
- **1 tablespoon olive oil**
- **½ teaspoon salt**
- **½ teaspoon dill weed**
- **½ teaspoon pepper**

1. Cook green beans according to package directions.

2. Meanwhile, in a large skillet, saute mushrooms and shallots in oil until tender. Remove from the heat. Add the green beans, salt, dill and pepper; toss to coat.

Shrimp Piccata

I typically serve this with crusty French bread and asparagus.

—**HOLLY BAUER** WEST BEND, WISCONSIN

PREP/TOTAL TIME: 25 MIN. **MAKES:** 4 SERVINGS

- **½ pound uncooked angel hair pasta**
- **2 shallots, finely chopped**
- **2 garlic cloves, minced**
- **2 tablespoons olive oil**
- **1 pound uncooked large shrimp, peeled and deveined**
- **1 teaspoon dried oregano**
- **⅛ teaspoon salt**
- **1 cup chicken broth**
- **1 cup white wine or additional chicken broth**
- **4 teaspoons cornstarch**
- **⅓ cup lemon juice**
- **¼ cup capers, drained**
- **3 tablespoons minced fresh parsley**

1. Cook pasta according to package directions.
2. Meanwhile, in a large skillet, saute shallots and garlic in oil for 1 minute. Add the shrimp, oregano and salt; cook and stir until shrimp turn pink. In small bowl, combine the broth, wine and cornstarch; gradually stir into pan. Bring to a boil; cook and stir for 2 minutes or until thickened. Remove from the heat.
3. Drain pasta. Add the pasta, lemon juice, capers and parsley to the skillet; toss to coat.

Balsamic Broiled Asparagus

This tasty side goes well with pasta or with grilled steak, pork or even chicken.

—**HOLLY BAUER** WEST BEND, WISCONSIN

PREP/TOTAL TIME: 15 MIN. **MAKES:** 4 SERVINGS

- **1 pound fresh asparagus, trimmed**
- **3 tablespoons balsamic vinegar**
- **2 tablespoons olive oil**
- **½ teaspoon salt**
- **¼ teaspoon pepper**

1. Place asparagus in an ungreased 15-in. x 10-in. x 1-in. baking pan. In a small bowl, combine the vinegar, oil, salt and pepper. Brush half of the mixture over asparagus.
2. Broil 4 in. from the heat for 8-10 minutes or until tender, stirring occasionally. Brush with remaining mixture.

Red Pepper-Curry Chicken

The everyday ingredients in this dish are transformed into a colorful weeknight meal. The sauce beautifully coats the chicken.

—**JOHN SLIVON** MILTON, FLORIDA

PREP/TOTAL TIME: 30 MIN. **MAKES:** 4 SERVINGS

- **⅔ cup mayonnaise**
- **3 tablespoons mango chutney**
- **¾ teaspoon lemon juice**
- **¼ to ½ teaspoon cayenne pepper**
- **¼ teaspoon curry powder**
- **Dash salt**
- **4 boneless skinless chicken breasts (6 ounces each)**
- **1 medium sweet red pepper**
- **1 tablespoon olive oil**
- **¼ teaspoon pepper**
- **2 teaspoons minced fresh parsley**

1. In a small bowl, combine the first six ingredients. Set aside 1/4 cup for serving.
2. Flatten chicken slightly. Cut red pepper in half lengthwise and remove seeds. Brush with oil and sprinkle with pepper. Grill chicken and red pepper, covered, over medium heat or broil 4 in. from the heat for 6-8 minutes on each side or until a thermometer reads 170°. Baste chicken occasionally with mayonnaise mixture.
3. Chop red pepper and toss with parsley. Serve chicken with red pepper and sauce mixture.

Curry Rice Pilaf

Salted cashews add a nice crunch to this simple rice dish flavored with curry and turmeric.

—**KATIE ROSE** PEWAUKEE, WISCONSIN

PREP/TOTAL TIME: 10 MIN. **MAKES:** 5 SERVINGS

- **2 packages (8½ ounces each) ready-to-serve jasmine rice**
- **2 tablespoons butter**
- **1 cup salted whole cashews**
- **2 green onions, sliced**
- **½ teaspoon curry powder**
- **¼ teaspoon salt**
- **¼ teaspoon ground turmeric**
- **¼ teaspoon pepper**

1. Heat rice according to package directions. Meanwhile, in a small skillet, melt butter over medium heat. Add the cashews, onions and seasonings; cook and stir for 2-3 minutes or until onions are tender. Add rice; toss to coat.

Caramel Glazed Salmon

If your kids don't like fish, try a touch of sugar. My salmon entree boasts a brilliant glaze of brown sugar and Dijon mustard.

—ATHENA RUSSELL FLORENCE, SOUTH CAROLINA

PREP/TOTAL TIME: 25 MIN. **MAKES:** 4 SERVINGS

- **4 salmon fillets (6 ounces each)**
- **½ teaspoon salt**
- **⅛ teaspoon cayenne pepper**
- **¼ cup packed brown sugar**
- **2 tablespoons Dijon mustard**
- **1 tablespoon butter, melted**
- **2 teaspoons dill weed**

1. Sprinkle salmon with salt and cayenne; set aside.
2. In a small bowl, combine the brown sugar, mustard, butter and dill. Place salmon skin side down on a greased broiler pan. Broil 4-6 in. from the heat for 5 minutes. Brush half of the glaze mixture over fillets. Broil 7-10 minutes longer or until fish flakes easily with a fork, brushing occasionally with remaining glaze.

Hint of Lemon Squash Saute

A lovely hint of lemon adds refreshing tang to this super-simple veggie medley.

—TASTE OF HOME TEST KITCHEN

PREP/TOTAL TIME: 20 MIN. **MAKES:** 4 SERVINGS

- **2 medium yellow summer squash, sliced**
- **2 medium carrots, sliced**
- **1 small onion, sliced**
- **2 tablespoons olive oil**
- **1 garlic clove, minced**
- **½ teaspoon grated lemon peel**
- **¼ teaspoon dried rosemary, crushed**
- **¼ teaspoon pepper**
- **⅛ teaspoon salt**

1. In a large skillet, saute the squash, carrots and onion in oil for 5-7 minutes or until tender. Add the remaining ingredients; cook 1 minute longer.

Pork Medallions with Cranberry Sauce

Birthdays, promotions and anniversaries don't always happen on the weekend, so it's nice to have a few quick and special weeknight recipes like this one on hand. Our tasters were impressed by the tangy, smoky flavors we found in such a simple-to-prepare entree.

—CATHERINE HIGGINS BOUNTIFUL, UTAH

PREP/TOTAL TIME: 25 MIN. **MAKES:** 4 SERVINGS

- **1 pork tenderloin (1 pound), cut into 1-inch slices**
- **⅛ teaspoon salt**
- **⅛ teaspoon pepper**
- **½ cup whole-berry cranberry sauce**
- **2 tablespoons barbecue sauce**
- **1 tablespoon water**
- **2 garlic cloves, minced**
- **½ teaspoon Chinese five-spice powder**

1. Sprinkle pork with salt and pepper. In a large nonstick skillet coated with cooking spray, cook pork in batches over medium heat for 3-5 minutes on each side or until juices run clear. Remove and keep warm.
2. Add the cranberry sauce, barbecue sauce, water, garlic and five-spice powder to the skillet. Bring to a boil. Reduce heat; simmer, uncovered, for 1-2 minutes or until thickened. Serve with pork.

Parmesan Roasted Asparagus

Need a fast but upscale side? Just a few ingredients give fresh asparagus wonderful flavor.

—MARILYN BROWN POOLER, GEORGIA

PREP/TOTAL TIME: 30 MIN. **MAKES:** 4 SERVINGS

- **1 pound fresh asparagus, trimmed**
- **3 tablespoons olive oil**
- **⅓ cup shredded Parmesan cheese**
- **1 teaspoon lemon-pepper seasoning**
- **¼ teaspoon salt**

1. Place asparagus in an ungreased 15-in. x 10-in. x 1-in. baking pan. Drizzle with oil; toss to coat. Sprinkle with cheese, lemon-pepper and salt.
2. Bake at 400° for 20-25 minutes or until tender, stirring occasionally.

123 MAKE IT SIMPLE

Preheat the oven for the asparagus and prepare it right away. It will roast as you work on the pork, so everything will be ready at once. To keep the pork from sticking to the pan, make sure the skillet is good and hot.

Zippy Zucchini Pasta

Here's a colorful combination of zucchini and canned tomatoes that's scrumptious over quick-cooking angel hair pasta. We like the extra zip it gets from crushed red pepper flakes.

—**KATHLEEN TIMBERLAKE** DEARBORN HEIGHTS, MICHIGAN

PREP/TOTAL TIME: 15 MIN. **MAKES:** 3 SERVINGS

- **1 package (7 ounces) angel hair pasta or thin spaghetti**
- **2 small zucchini, cut into ¼-inch pieces**
- **2 garlic cloves, minced**
- **3 tablespoons olive oil**
- **1 can (14½ ounces) Mexican diced tomatoes, undrained**
- **¼ cup minced fresh parsley**
- **1 teaspoon dried oregano**
- **⅛ to ½ teaspoon crushed red pepper flakes**

1. Cook pasta according to package directions. Meanwhile, in a large skillet, saute zucchini and garlic in oil until zucchini is crisp-tender.

2. Add the tomatoes, parsley, oregano and pepper flakes; heat through. Drain pasta; serve with zucchini mixture.

Cheddar Bread Twists

Light and flaky, these speedy breadsticks can be served as a side dish, or with dip for an impressive appetizer.

—**TRACY TRAVERS** FAIRHAVEN, MASSACHUSETTS

PREP/TOTAL TIME: 25 MIN. **MAKES:** 10 BREADSTICKS

- **1 sheet frozen puff pastry, thawed**
- **1 egg white**
- **1 tablespoon cold water**
- **½ cup shredded cheddar cheese**
- **Dash salt**

1. Unfold puff pastry onto a lightly floured surface. In a small bowl, beat egg white and water; brush over pastry. Sprinkle with cheese and salt.

2. Cut into ten 1-in. strips; twist each strip three times. Place on a greased baking sheet. Bake at 400° for 10-13 minutes or until golden brown.

Super-Fast Corn Bread

This quick, easy and flavorful corn bread can be eaten right when it comes out of the oven.

—**BECKY BUTLER** KELLER, TEXAS

PREP/TOTAL TIME: 20 MIN. **MAKES:** 8 SERVINGS

- **1¼ cups biscuit/baking mix**
- **1¼ cups yellow cornmeal**
- **2 eggs**
- **1½ cups 2% milk**

1. Combine biscuit mix and cornmeal in a large bowl. Whisk eggs and milk; stir into dry ingredients. Transfer to a greased 9-in. oven-proof skillet.

2. Bake at 400° for 15-20 minutes or until a toothpick inserted near the center comes out clean. Cut into wedges. Serve warm.

Southern Skillet Chops

Creole seasoning adds just the right amount of kick to these pork chops. The black-eyed peas make a perfect accompaniment.

—**IRENE SULLIVAN** LAKE MILLS, WISCONSIN

PREP/TOTAL TIME: 25 MIN. **MAKES:** 4 SERVINGS

- **4 bone-in pork loin chops (8 ounces each)**
- **2 teaspoons plus ⅛ teaspoon Creole seasoning, divided**
- **2 tablespoons canola oil**
- **2 cans (14½ ounces each) diced tomatoes with mild green chilies, undrained**
- **1 can (15½ ounces) black-eyed peas, rinsed and drained**
- **Shredded cheddar cheese, optional**

1. Sprinkle pork chops with 2 teaspoons Creole seasoning. In a large skillet, brown pork chops in oil. Remove and keep warm.

2. Drain one can tomatoes; discard liquid. Add tomatoes to skillet with the remaining can of undrained tomatoes, black-eyed peas and remaining Creole seasoning, stirring to loosen browned bits from pan.

3. Bring to a boil and return chops to pan. Reduce heat; simmer, uncovered, for 2-4 minutes or until a thermometer reads 145°. Sprinkle with cheese if desired. Let stand for 5 minutes.

Editor's Note: *The following spices may be substituted for 1 teaspoon Creole seasoning: 1/4 teaspoon each salt, garlic powder and paprika; and a pinch each of dried thyme, ground cumin and cayenne pepper.*

Asian Snapper with Capers

Get the nutritional benefits of fish with this simple sauteed snapper that takes very little time and effort to prepare.

—**MARY ANN LEE** CLIFTON PARK, NEW YORK

PREP/TOTAL TIME: 20 MIN. **MAKES:** 4 SERVINGS

- **4 red snapper fillets (6 ounces each)**
- **4½ teaspoons Mongolian Fire oil or sesame oil**
- **¼ cup apple jelly**
- **3 tablespoons ketchup**
- **2 tablespoons capers, drained**
- **1 tablespoon lemon juice**
- **1 tablespoon reduced-sodium soy sauce**
- **1 teaspoon grated fresh gingerroot**

1. In a large skillet, cook fillets in oil over medium heat for 3-5 minutes on each side or until fish flakes easily with a fork; remove and keep warm.

2. Stir the jelly, ketchup, capers, lemon juice, soy sauce and ginger into the skillet. Cook and stir for 2-3 minutes or until slightly thickened; serve with red snapper.

Parsleyed Rice Pilaf

While the salmon bakes, I dress up instant rice with bouillon, minced onion and parsley for wonderful flavor.

—**KATHY PELTIER** KALISPELL, MONTANA

PREP/TOTAL TIME: 10 MIN. **MAKES:** 4 SERVINGS

- **2 cups water**
- **¼ cup dried minced onion**
- **4 teaspoons butter**
- **2 teaspoons chicken bouillon granules**
- **2 cups instant rice**
- **¼ cup minced fresh parsley**

1. In a small saucepan, bring the water, onion, butter and bouillon to a boil. Stir in rice and parsley. Remove from the heat. Cover and let stand for 5 minutes. Fluff with a fork.

Chili-Basil Tomato Soup

A co-worker shared this recipe, and my husband and I both love it! We serve it with a fresh salad and bread for a light meal.

—**PENNY LUND** FORT COLLINS, COLORADO

PREP/TOTAL TIME: 20 MIN. **MAKES:** 6 SERVINGS (2 QUARTS)

- **1 can (26 ounces) condensed tomato soup, undiluted**
- **3 cups 2% milk**
- **1 can (12 ounces) evaporated milk**
- **1 can (10 ounces) diced tomatoes and green chilies, undrained**
- **1 tablespoon minced fresh basil or 1 teaspoon dried basil**
- **½ teaspoon salt**
- **¼ teaspoon pepper**
- **Shredded Parmesan cheese, optional**

1. In a Dutch oven, combine the first seven ingredients. Cook and stir over medium heat until heated through. Garnish servings with cheese if desired.

Jalapeno Cheddar Biscuits

These tender biscuits with a cheesy richness have a nice level of heat that will appeal to all ages.

—**FLORENCE MCNULTY** MONTEBELLO, CALIFORNIA

PREP/TOTAL TIME: 25 MIN. **MAKES:** 15 BISCUITS

- **2 cups all-purpose flour**
- **3 teaspoons baking powder**
- **½ teaspoon salt**
- **½ teaspoon dried thyme**
- **½ teaspoon paprika**
- **5 tablespoons cold butter**
- **¾ cup 2% milk**
- **1 cup (4 ounces) shredded sharp cheddar cheese**
- **3 tablespoons diced pickled jalapeno slices**

1. In a large bowl, combine the flour, baking powder, salt, thyme and paprika. Cut in butter until mixture resembles coarse crumbs. Stir in the milk, cheese and jalapeno.

2. Turn onto a lightly floured surface; knead 8-10 times. Pat or roll out to ½-in. thickness; cut with a floured 2½-in. biscuit cutter. Place 2 in. apart on an ungreased baking sheet.

3. Bake at 450° for 12-14 minutes or until golden brown. Serve warm.

Editor's Note: *Wear disposable gloves when cutting hot peppers; the oils can burn skin. Avoid touching your face.*

My husband made some tweaks to the original recipe for this chicken dish to suit our tastes, and it was fabulous. Our 18-month-old son even loves it! Plus, it's the perfect way for me to get out of cooking for a night.
—**STACY KOLOJAY** STREATOR, ILLINOIS

Root Beer Glazed Chicken

PREP/TOTAL TIME: 30 MIN.
MAKES: 4 SERVINGS

- **4 boneless skinless chicken breast halves (6 ounces each)**
- **2 tablespoons canola oil**
- **1 cup root beer**
- **½ cup packed brown sugar**
- **¼ cup ketchup**
- **4 teaspoons Dijon mustard**
- **2 teaspoons grated lemon peel**

1. Flatten chicken breasts slightly. In a large skillet, cook chicken in oil for 4-6 minutes on each side or until a meat thermometer reads 170°. Remove and keep warm.
2. Stir the root beer, brown sugar, ketchup, mustard and lemon peel into the skillet. Bring to a boil. Cook and stir for 6-8 minutes or until thickened. Return chicken to skillet; heat through.

Squash and Mushroom Medley

Fresh summer veggies are the best!
—**HEATHER ESPOSITO** ROME, NEW YORK

PREP/TOTAL TIME: 20 MIN.
MAKES: 5 SERVINGS

- **1 large yellow summer squash, chopped**
- **1 large zucchini, chopped**
- **1 medium onion, chopped**
- **2 teaspoons butter**
- **1 can (7 ounces) mushroom stems and pieces, drained**
- **2 garlic cloves, minced**
- **¼ teaspoon salt**
- **⅛ teaspoon pepper**

1. In a large skillet, saute the squash, zucchini and onion in butter until tender. Add the mushrooms, garlic, salt and pepper; saute 2-3 minutes longer or until heated through.

Apricot-Honey Chicken

This tender chicken has such a short prep, you'll practically want to ring the dinner bell before you start cooking!

—**JANET PAVKOV** BARBERTON, OHIO

PREP/TOTAL TIME: 15 MIN. **MAKES:** 4 SERVINGS

- **4 boneless skinless chicken breast halves (5 ounces each)**
- **⅓ cup honey mustard**
- **3 tablespoons apricot preserves**
- **¼ teaspoon ground ginger**
- **Dash each salt and pepper**

1. Flatten chicken to ¼-in. thickness. In a small bowl, combine the mustard, apricot preserves, ginger, salt and pepper. Place the chicken on a greased foil-lined baking sheet. Spoon half of the mustard mixture over chicken.
2. Broil 4-6 in. from the heat for 4 minutes. Turn; brush with remaining mustard mixture. Broil 3-4 minutes longer or until juices run clear.

Mushroom Salad

Here's an easy and fast side dish that we often serve when my husband grills steak. It's delicious with almost any entree, and it's ready in minutes!

—**ANNA STODOLAK** VOLANT, PENNSYLVANIA

PREP/TOTAL TIME: 15 MIN. **MAKES:** 4 SERVINGS

- **½ pound sliced fresh mushrooms**
- **2 green onions, thinly sliced**
- **1 garlic clove, minced**
- **4½ teaspoons canola oil**
- **1 tablespoon minced chives**
- **1 tablespoon lemon juice**
- **1 tablespoon balsamic vinegar**
- **¾ teaspoon sugar**
- **6 cups torn mixed salad greens**
- **¾ cup salad croutons**
- **¼ cup shredded Parmesan cheese**

1. In a large skillet, saute the mushrooms, onions and garlic in oil for 3-4 minutes or until mushrooms are tender. Stir in the chives, lemon juice, vinegar and sugar.
2. Arrange salad greens on serving plates; top with mushroom mixture. Sprinkle with croutons and cheese.

Balsamic-Glazed Pork Chops

The tangy sauce, restaurant-quality flavor and appearance prompted one taste taster to say, "I wish my mom made chops like this when I was growing up!"

—**SANDY SHERMAN** CHESTER, VIRGINIA

PREP/TOTAL TIME: 30 MIN. **MAKES:** 4 SERVINGS

- **4 boneless pork loin chops (6 ounces each)**
- **¾ teaspoon salt, divided**
- **½ teaspoon pepper**
- **3 tablespoons butter, divided**
- **1 large red onion, halved and thinly sliced**
- **⅔ cup balsamic vinegar**
- **2 teaspoons brown sugar**
- **½ teaspoon dried rosemary, crushed**

1. Sprinkle pork chops with ½ teaspoon salt and pepper. In a large skillet, brown chops in 1 tablespoon butter. Remove and keep warm.
2. In the same skillet, saute onion in 1 tablespoon butter until tender. Stir in the vinegar, brown sugar, rosemary and remaining salt. Bring to a boil; cook until liquid is reduced by half.
3. Return chops to the pan; cook, uncovered, over medium heat for 4-6 minutes on each side or until a thermometer reads 145°. Remove chops to a serving plate and let stand for 5 minutes before serving. Stir remaining butter into skillet until melted. Serve with pork chops.

Broccoli with Orange Browned Butter

This no-fuss butter sauce with orange peel, salt and nutmeg will turn even broccoli haters into broccoli lovers!

—**CHRISTINE BERGMAN** SUWANEE, GEORGIA

PREP/TOTAL TIME: 15 MIN. **MAKES:** 4 SERVINGS

- **1 package (12 ounces) frozen Steamfresh® broccoli cuts**
- **2 tablespoons butter**
- **1 teaspoon grated orange peel**
- **¼ teaspoon salt**
- **Dash ground nutmeg**

1. Cook broccoli according to package directions. Meanwhile, in a small heavy saucepan, cook butter over medium heat for 3-4 minutes or until golden brown. Stir in the orange peel, salt and nutmeg.
2. Drain broccoli. Add to the saucepan and toss to coat.

Salisbury Meatballs

Saucy and so simple, these jazzed-up meatballs will help you turn out dinner in no time on any busy night.

—**MARIA REGAKIS** SOMERVILLE, MASSACHUSETTS

PREP/TOTAL TIME: 20 MIN. **MAKES:** 4 SERVINGS

- **1 large sweet onion, halved and thinly sliced**
- **1 tablespoon brown sugar**
- **3 tablespoons butter**
- **2 jars (12 ounces each) beef gravy**
- **1 package (12 ounces) frozen fully cooked homestyle meatballs, thawed**
- **Hot cooked egg noodles**

1. In a large skillet, saute onion and brown sugar in butter until onion is tender. Add gravy and meatballs. Bring to a boil. Reduce heat; simmer, uncovered, for 4-6 minutes or until meatballs are heated through, stirring occasionally. Serve with noodles.

Zucchini & Tomato Saute

In a hurry? Fresh flavors shine in this easy side that takes just minutes to make.

—**SANDRA GRIMM** PORT ORANGE, FLORIDA

PREP/TOTAL TIME: 15 MIN. **MAKES:** 4 SERVINGS

- **3 medium zucchini, sliced**
- **1 medium onion, sliced**
- **2 tablespoons butter**
- **2 medium tomatoes, cut into wedges**
- **1 teaspoon garlic salt**
- **⅛ teaspoon pepper**

1. In a large skillet, saute zucchini and onion in butter until tender. Add the tomatoes, garlic salt and pepper; saute 1-2 minutes longer or until heated through.

Sausage Alfredo

PREP/TOTAL TIME: 25 MIN.
MAKES: 6 SERVINGS

- **3½ cups uncooked spiral pasta**
- **1 pound bulk Italian sausage**
- **1 medium green pepper, chopped**
- **1 large onion, chopped**
- **1 can (4 ounces) mushroom stems and pieces, drained**
- **1 jar (15 ounces) roasted garlic Alfredo sauce**
- **¼ cup shredded Parmesan cheese**

1. Cook pasta according to package directions.
2. Meanwhile, in a large skillet, cook the sausage, green pepper, onion and mushrooms over medium heat until meat is no longer pink; drain. Stir in Alfredo sauce. Drain pasta and stir into skillet; heat through. Sprinkle with Parmesan cheese.

Herbed Corn And Carrots

Basil, parsley and onion salt dress up this simple veggie medley that goes well with a variety of entrees. It has so much flavor, you'd never guess it could be so easy!

—**HEIDI HALL** NORTH ST. PAUL, MINNESOTA

PREP/TOTAL TIME: 20 MIN.
MAKES: 4 SERVINGS

- **1 package (16 ounces) frozen corn**
- **1 large carrot, chopped**
- **2 tablespoons water**
- **3 tablespoons butter, cubed**
- **¾ teaspoon dried basil**
- **½ teaspoon onion salt**
- **½ teaspoon dried parsley flakes**
- **⅛ teaspoon pepper**

1. In a large microwave-safe bowl, combine the corn, carrot and water. Cover and microwave on high for 6-8 minutes or until vegetables are tender. Drain. Add butter and seasonings, stirring until butter is melted.

Editor's Note: *This recipe was tested in a 1,100-watt microwave.*

"I created this recipe to mimic restaurant Alfredo pasta dishes. It's half the cost and comes together almost as quickly as I could order takeout!"

—**MARLENE BAUTCH** HIXTON, WISCONSIN

Turkey Scallopini

Quick-cooking turkey breast slices make it easy to prepare a satisfying meal in minutes. I've also flattened boneless skinless chicken breast halves in place of the turkey.

—**KAREN ADAMS** CLEVELAND, TENNESSEE

PREP/TOTAL TIME: 20 MIN. **MAKES:** 4 SERVINGS

- **1 package (17.6 ounces) turkey breast cutlets**
- **¼ cup all-purpose flour**
- **⅛ teaspoon salt**
- **⅛ teaspoon pepper**
- **1 egg**
- **2 tablespoons water**
- **1 cup soft bread crumbs**
- **½ cup grated Parmesan cheese**
- **¼ cup butter, cubed**
- **Minced fresh parsley**

1. Flatten turkey to ¼-in. thickness. In a shallow bowl, combine the flour, salt and pepper. In another bowl, beat egg and water. In a third shallow bowl, combine bread crumbs and cheese.
2. Dredge turkey in flour mixture, then dip in egg mixture and coat with crumbs. Let stand for 5 minutes.
3. Melt butter in a large skillet over medium-high heat; cook turkey for 2-3 minutes on each side or until meat is no longer pink and coating is golden brown. Sprinkle with parsley.

Chicken Scallopini: *Substitute 4 boneless skinless chicken breast halves for the turkey; flatten to ¼-in. thickness and proceed as directed.*

Ribboned Vegetables

Add a splash of color to your supper table with these vivid veggie strips. Cooked in lemon and horseradish, this simple side is a light and zippy complement to a hearty cold-weather entree.

—**JULIE GWINN** HERSHEY, PENNSYLVANIA

PREP/TOTAL TIME: 25 MIN. **MAKES:** 4 SERVINGS

- **2 medium carrots**
- **2 small zucchini**
- **2 small yellow summer squash**
- **1 tablespoon butter**
- **2 teaspoons lemon juice**
- **1 teaspoon prepared horseradish**
- **½ teaspoon salt**
- **⅛ teaspoon pepper**

1. With a vegetable peeler or metal cheese slicer, cut very thin slices down the length of each carrot, zucchini and yellow squash, making long ribbons.
2. In a large skillet, saute vegetables in butter for 2 minutes. Stir in the remaining ingredients. Cook 2-4 minutes longer or until vegetables are crisp-tender, stirring occasionally.

Chicken with Rosemary Butter Sauce for 2

Just the two of you? Make it a special night with this rich and creamy chicken entree that's table-ready in no time.

—**CONNIE MCDOWELL** GREENWOOD, DELAWARE

PREP/TOTAL TIME: 20 MIN. **MAKES:** 2 SERVINGS

- **2 boneless skinless chicken breast halves (4 ounces each)**
- **2 tablespoons butter, divided**
- **¼ cup white wine or chicken broth**
- **¼ cup heavy whipping cream**
- **1½ teaspoons minced fresh rosemary**

1. In a small skillet over medium heat, cook chicken in 1 tablespoon butter for 4-5 minutes on each side or until a thermometer reads 170°. Remove and keep warm.
2. Add wine to pan; cook over medium-low heat, stirring to loosen browned bits from pan. Add cream and bring to a boil. Reduce heat; cook and stir until slightly thickened. Stir in rosemary and remaining butter until blended. Serve with chicken.

Snow Pea Medley

Even in frosty weather, I serve up garden-fresh flavor with this pretty, colorful side dish. The crisp-tender veggie combo goes with a wide variety of entrees.

—**LUCILLE MEAD** ILION, NEW YORK

PREP/TOTAL TIME: 15 MIN. **MAKES:** 2 SERVINGS

- **⅓ cup chopped red onion**
- **2 teaspoons canola oil**
- **⅓ cup julienned sweet red pepper**
- **⅓ cup julienned sweet yellow pepper**
- **½ cup fresh snow peas**
- **½ cup sliced fresh mushrooms**
- **¼ teaspoon salt**

1. In a nonstick skillet coated with cooking spray, saute onion in oil for 1-2 minutes. Add peppers; cook for 2 minutes.
2. Stir in the peas and mushrooms; saute 3-4 minutes longer or until vegetables are crisp-tender. Sprinkle with salt.

Tilapia & Lemon Sauce

This delicious yet light pairing of fish and citrus will evoke thoughts of warm, summery days—even when it's chilly outside.

—**SUSAN TAUL** BIRMINGHAM, ALABAMA

PREP/TOTAL TIME: 30 MIN. **MAKES:** 4 SERVINGS

- **¼ cup plus 1 tablespoon all-purpose flour, divided**
- **1 teaspoon salt**
- **4 tilapia fillets (4 ounces each)**
- **2 tablespoons plus 2 teaspoons butter, divided**
- **⅓ cup reduced-sodium chicken broth**
- **2 tablespoons white wine or additional reduced-sodium chicken broth**
- **1½ teaspoons lemon juice**
- **1½ teaspoons minced fresh parsley**
- **2 cups hot cooked rice**
- **¼ cup sliced almonds, toasted**

1. In a shallow bowl, combine ¼ cup flour and salt. Dip fillets in flour mixture.

2. In a large nonstick skillet coated with cooking spray, cook fillets in 2 tablespoons butter over medium-high heat for 4-5 minutes on each side or until fish flakes easily with a fork. Remove and keep warm.

3. In the same skillet, melt remaining butter. Stir in remaining flour until smooth; gradually add the broth, wine and lemon juice. Bring to a boil; cook and stir for 2 minutes or until thickened. Stir in parsley. Serve fish and sauce with rice; garnish with almonds.

Vegetable Trio

I created the recipe for this vegetable side dish with a pretty mix of garden-fresh green beans and carrots. It's a handy and colorful accompaniment to any meal.

—**MARY LOU WAYMAN** SALT LAKE CITY, UTAH

PREP/TOTAL TIME: 25 MIN. **MAKES:** 4 SERVINGS

- **4 large carrots, julienned**
- **½ pound fresh green beans, cut into 2-inch pieces**
- **1½ cups sliced fresh mushrooms**
- **1 teaspoon salt**
- **½ teaspoon dried thyme**
- **2 tablespoons butter**

1. In a large skillet, cook and stir the carrots, green beans, mushrooms, salt and thyme in butter over medium-heat for 15 minutes or until beans are crisp-tender.

Herbed Chicken and Rice

Marjoram, thyme, rosemary and sage in this main dish bring back memories of Thanksgiving. Your family will love the crunchy surprise of chopped walnuts on top.

—**CINDY REAMS** PHILIPSBURG, PENNSYLVANIA

PREP/TOTAL TIME: 30 MIN. **MAKES:** 5 SERVINGS

- **½ pound boneless skinless chicken breasts, cut into 1-inch strips**
- **1 tablespoon butter**
- **2 large carrots, shredded**
- **1 small onion, chopped**
- **2 cups hot water**
- **¼ teaspoon dried marjoram**
- **¼ teaspoon dried thyme**
- **⅛ teaspoon dried rosemary, crushed**
- **⅛ teaspoon rubbed sage**
- **2 cups uncooked instant rice**
- **½ cup chopped walnuts**

1. In a large skillet, saute chicken in butter for 3-4 minutes. Add the carrots and onion; saute until tender.

2. Add water and seasonings; bring to a boil. Stir in the rice. Cover and remove from the heat; let stand for 5 minutes. Garnish with walnuts.

Garlic Brussels Sprouts

These garlicky Brussels sprouts cooked in butter and broth are special enough for company. If you can't find fresh sprouts, try the frozen ones.

—**MYRA INNES** AUBURN, KANSAS

PREP/TOTAL TIME: 30 MIN. **MAKES:** 6 SERVINGS

- **1½ pounds fresh Brussels sprouts**
- **4 garlic cloves, chopped**
- **2 teaspoons olive oil**
- **3 teaspoons butter, divided**
- **½ cup reduced-sodium chicken broth**
- **¼ teaspoon salt**
- **⅛ teaspoon pepper**

1. Trim brussels sprouts and cut an X in the core end of each; set aside.

2. In a large saucepan, saute garlic in oil and 1 teaspoon butter for 2-3 minutes or until golden brown. Add reserved sprouts; toss to coat.

3. Stir in the broth, salt and pepper. Bring to a boil. Reduce heat; cover and simmer for 8-10 minutes or until tender. Drain; add the remaining butter and toss until melted.

Scallops with Chipotle-Orange Sauce

Tender scallops with a sprinkle of paprika and ground chipotle pepper make this recipe a surefire way to warm up dinnertime. You wouldn't know they took only 15 minutes to make!

—**JAN JUSTICE** CATLETTSBURG, KENTUCKY

PREP/TOTAL TIME: 15 MIN. **MAKES:** 2 SERVINGS

- **¾ pound sea scallops, halved**
- **¼ teaspoon paprika**
- **¼ teaspoon salt, divided**
- **2 teaspoons butter**
- **¼ cup orange juice**
- **¼ teaspoon ground chipotle pepper**
- **Hot cooked linguine, optional**
- **2 tablespoons thinly sliced green onion**

1. Sprinkle scallops with paprika and ⅛ teaspoon salt. In a nonstick skillet coated with cooking spray, melt butter over medium heat. Add scallops; cook for 3-4 minutes on each side or until firm and golden brown.
2. Add orange juice and remaining salt to the pan; bring to a boil. Remove from the heat; stir in the chipotle pepper.
3. Serve scallops and sauce over linguine if desired. Garnish with green onion.

Gingered Snow Peas

Wow your friends and family with quick-cooking, flavorful veggies without ever touching the stove. A hint of ginger makes this dish special. It's one of my favorites.

—**SUZANNE KARSTEN** WINDERMERE, FLORIDA

PREP/TOTAL TIME: 10 MIN. **MAKES:** 2 SERVINGS

- **½ pound fresh snow peas, trimmed**
- **1 tablespoon water**
- **1 tablespoon butter, melted**
- **¼ teaspoon ground ginger**
- **⅛ teaspoon salt**

1. Place peas and water in a 1-qt. microwave-safe dish. Cover and microwave on high for 3-4 minutes or until crisp-tender; drain.
2. Combine the butter, ginger and salt. Drizzle over the peas; toss to coat.

Editor's Note: *This recipe was tested in a 1,100-watt microwave.*

Rosemary Carrots

My husband and I cook with many different kinds of herbs and have found rosemary to be fantastic with carrots. This colorful side is great with chicken and potatoes but would pair well with just about any meal.

—**GRACE YASKOVIC** LAKE HIAWATHA, NEW JERSEY

PREP/TOTAL TIME: 20 MIN. **MAKES:** 6 SERVINGS

- **1½ pounds carrots, sliced**
- **1 tablespoon olive oil**
- **1 small green pepper, finely chopped**
- **1 teaspoon dried rosemary, crushed**
- **½ teaspoon salt**
- **¼ teaspoon coarsely ground pepper**

1. In a large skillet, saute carrots in oil until crisp-tender. Add green pepper; saute 5 minutes longer or until vegetables are tender. Stir in the rosemary, salt and pepper.

Chicken Strips Milano

A dear friend shared this recipe a few years ago. Since then, I've prepared the garlicky and delightful entree for both family dinners and get-togethers with friends. It's a keeper!

—**LARA PRIEST** GANSEVOORT, NEW YORK

PREP/TOTAL TIME: 20 MIN. **MAKES:** 6 SERVINGS

- **12 ounces linguine**
- **1 tablespoon minced garlic**
- **4½ teaspoons plus 2 tablespoons olive oil, divided**
- **¾ teaspoon dried parsley flakes**
- **¾ teaspoon pepper, divided**
- **¼ cup all-purpose flour**
- **1 teaspoon dried basil**
- **½ teaspoon salt**
- **2 eggs**
- **1½ pounds boneless skinless chicken breasts, cut into strips**

1. Cook linguine according to package directions.
2. Meanwhile, in a large skillet, saute garlic in 4½ teaspoons oil for 1 minute or until tender. Stir in parsley and ½ teaspoon pepper. Remove to a small bowl and set aside.
3. In a shallow bowl, combine the flour, basil, salt and remaining pepper. In another shallow bowl, whisk eggs. Dredge chicken strips in flour mixture, then dip in eggs.
4. In the same skillet, cook chicken in remaining oil over medium-high heat for 8-10 minutes or until no longer pink.
5. Drain linguine; place on a serving platter. Pour garlic mixture over linguine and toss to coat; top with chicken.

Sesame Dill Fish

Crispy fillets are a snap to make. A grocery store special on fish motivated me to adapt a recipe for pork into this quick-cooking dish.
—**LINDA HESS** CHILLIWACK, BRITISH COLUMBIA

PREP/TOTAL TIME: 15 MIN. **MAKES:** 4 SERVINGS

- **½ cup dry bread crumbs**
- **¼ cup sesame seeds**
- **½ teaspoon dill weed**
- **¼ teaspoon salt**
- **¾ cup plain yogurt**
- **1 pound catfish or other whitefish fillets**
- **¼ cup canola oil**
- **Lemon wedges, optional**

1. In a shallow bowl, combine the bread crumbs, sesame seeds, dill and salt. Place yogurt in another bowl. Dip fillets in yogurt; shake off excess, then dip in crumb mixture.
2. Heat oil in a large nonstick skillet. Fry fillets over medium-high heat for 2-3 minutes on each side or until fish flakes easily with a fork. Serve with lemon if desired.

Warm Pecan Cabbage Slaw

Slaw gets a hot new twist in this colorful side that I like to serve warm. The mild mustard flavor and pleasing blend of crisp-tender veggies and toasted pecans is a nice complement to fish or ham.
—**MARIE HATTRUP** SPARKS, NEVADA

PREP/TOTAL TIME: 20 MIN. **MAKES:** 6 SERVINGS

- **4 cups coarsely shredded cabbage**
- **½ cup shredded carrot**
- **¼ cup sliced green onions**
- **2 tablespoons water**
- **½ teaspoon salt**
- **¼ teaspoon pepper**
- **1 tablespoon butter, melted**
- **1 teaspoon Dijon mustard**
- **¼ cup chopped pecans, toasted**

1. In a large saucepan, combine the cabbage, carrot, green onions, water, salt and pepper. Cover and cook over medium heat for 5-7 minutes or until cabbage is crisp-tender. Drain, if necessary.
2. Combine butter and mustard; pour over cabbage mixture and toss to coat. Stir in pecans.

Curry Citrus Chicken

No stove or oven required! This saucy dish cooks up in a flash—and all in the microwave.
—**MARCY HALL** VISALIA, CALIFORNIA

PREP/TOTAL TIME: 20 MIN. **MAKES:** 4 SERVINGS

- **4 boneless skinless chicken thighs (4 ounces each)**
- **2 tablespoons finely chopped onion**
- **2 tablespoons lemon juice**
- **2 tablespoons orange juice**
- **2 tablespoons reduced-sodium soy sauce**
- **½ teaspoon curry powder**
- **½ teaspoon ground cumin**
- **¼ teaspoon poultry seasoning**
- **1½ teaspoons cornstarch**
- **1 tablespoon cold water**

1. Place chicken in a microwave-safe dish coated with cooking spray. Combine the onion, juices, soy sauce and seasonings; pour over chicken.
2. Cover and microwave on high for 3 minutes; turn chicken. Cover and cook 2-4 minutes longer or until chicken is no longer pink and a thermometer reads 180°. Remove chicken; let stand for 1-2 minutes.
3. Combine cornstarch and water until smooth; stir into cooking juices. Microwave, uncovered, on high for 1 to 1½ minutes or until thickened, stirring every 30 seconds. Serve with chicken.

Editor's Note: *This recipe was tested in a 1,100-watt microwave.*

Zucchini Rice Pilaf

I created this colorful rice and veggie side dish one night by combining a few ingredients I had on hand. My husband and I have been making it ever since.
—**LORI BLEVINS** DOUGLASVILLE, GEORGIA

PREP/TOTAL TIME: 25 MIN. **MAKES:** 4 SERVINGS

- **½ teaspoon dried basil**
- **2 tablespoons butter**
- **2¼ cups hot water**
- **1¼ teaspoons chicken bouillon granules**
- **1 cup uncooked long grain rice**
- **½ cup shredded carrot**
- **1 small zucchini, halved and thinly sliced**

1. In a large skillet, saute basil in butter for 2 minutes. Add water and bouillon; bring to a boil. Stir in rice and carrot. Reduce heat; cover and simmer for 10 minutes.
2. Add zucchini; cover and simmer 5 minutes longer or until rice is tender.

Give Me 5 or Fewer

"Anyone who loves coffee will adore this java-flavored cookie! If you had to play matchmaker with these treats, what hot beverage would you pair them with? There's only one answer."

KATHLEEN SPECHT CLINTON, MONTANA
Macadamia-Coffee Bean Cookies, page 52

Whoopie Cookies

I don't always have time to make whoopie pies from scratch, so I tweaked a cake mix recipe to create these. Try a bit of peanut butter in the filling, too. Whoopee for saving time!

—NUNDI HARRIS LAS VEGAS, NEVADA

PREP: 20 MIN. **BAKE:** 10 MIN./BATCH + COOLING **MAKES:** 2 DOZEN

- **1 package (18¼ ounces) devil's food cake mix**
- **¼ cup butter, softened**
- **2 eggs**
- **1 jar (7 ounces) marshmallow creme**
- **4 ounces cream cheese, softened**

1. In a large bowl, beat cake mix and butter until well combined. Beat in eggs. Shape into 1-in. balls. Place 2 in. apart on ungreased baking sheets.
2. Bake at 350° for 7-10 minutes or until tops are cracked. Cool for 2 minutes before removing to wire racks to cool completely.
3. In a large bowl beat marshmallow creme and cream cheese until light and fluffy. Spread filling on the bottoms of half of the cookies. Top with remaining cookies. Store in an airtight container in the refrigerator.

Peppered Portobello Penne

Meaty mushrooms and a kickin' hot cheese sauce take this simple pasta toss from drab to fab! My family loves that it tastes like a restaurant dish, but it's made at home.

—VERONICA CALLAGHAN
GLASTONBURY, CONNECTICUT

PREP/TOTAL TIME: 30 MIN.
MAKES: 4 SERVINGS

- **2 cups uncooked penne pasta**
- **4 large portobello mushrooms, stems removed, halved and thinly sliced**
- **2 tablespoons olive oil**
- **½ cup heavy whipping cream**
- **¾ teaspoon salt**
- **¼ teaspoon pepper**
- **1 cup (4 ounces) shredded pepper jack cheese**

1. Cook pasta according to package directions.
2. Meanwhile, in a large skillet, saute mushrooms in oil until tender. Stir in the cream, salt and pepper; heat through. Stir in cheese until melted. Drain pasta. Add to skillet and toss to coat.

Hazelnut Chocolate Mousse

This dessert is so quick and easy to make that I can surprise my family anytime of the year. It's also good using chocolate fudge-flavored pudding mix and chocolate-flavored Cool Whip instead of regular Cool Whip. I love chocolate, so it depends on how much you love chocolate. Feel free to add the toppings of your choice!

—KARLA KROHN MADISON, WISCONSIN

PREP/TOTAL TIME: 10 MIN.
MAKES: 6 SERVINGS

- **1¾ cups cold 2% milk**
- **1 package (3.9 ounces) instant chocolate pudding mix**
- **½ cup Nutella**
- **1¾ cups whipped topping**
- **Additional whipped topping**

1. Whisk milk and pudding mix in a large bowl for 2 minutes. Let stand for 2 minutes or until soft set. Whisk in Nutella until smooth. Fold in whipped topping.
2. Spoon into six dessert dishes. Chill until serving. Garnish servings with additional whipped topping.

Serve this creamy pasta as a side dish with your favorite roasted veggies and flame-grilled steak for a heavenly backyard meal.

Jazzed-Up French Bread

Fire up the grill right away for this tasty French bread. It takes seconds to prepare and then cooks away over indirect heat, giving you plenty of time to assemble the rest of the meal.

—LORI LECROY EAST TAWAS, MICHIGAN

PREP: 10 MIN. **GRILL:** 30 MIN. + STANDING **MAKES:** 10 SERVINGS

- **2 cups (8 ounces) shredded Colby-Monterey Jack cheese**
- **⅔ cup mayonnaise**
- **6 green onions, chopped**
- **1 loaf (1 pound) French bread, halved lengthwise**

1. In a small bowl, combine the cheese, mayonnaise and onions. Spread over cut sides of bread and reassemble loaf. Wrap in a double thickness of heavy-duty foil (about 28 in. x 18 in.); seal tightly.
2. Grill, covered, over indirect medium heat for 25-30 minutes or until cheese is melted, turning once. Let stand for 5 minutes before cutting into slices.

Grilled Corn Medley

Who knew a store-bought dressing could add so much flavor? This medley tastes delightful with garden-fresh veggies. Feel free to sub in your favorites and let the grill and the dressing do the rest!

—TASTE OF HOME TEST KITCHEN

PREP/TOTAL TIME: 20 MIN. **MAKES:** 8 SERVINGS

- **3 medium ears sweet corn, cut into 2-inch pieces**
- **1 medium sweet red pepper, cut into 1-inch pieces**
- **1 medium zucchini, sliced**
- **20 small fresh mushrooms**
- **¼ cup creamy Caesar salad dressing**
- **¼ teaspoon salt**
- **¼ teaspoon pepper**

1. In a large bowl, combine all ingredients; toss to coat. Transfer to a disposable foil pan. Grill, covered, over medium-hot heat for 5 minutes; stir. Grill 3-5 minutes longer or until vegetables are tender.

Chili-Beer Glazed Steaks

Bold ingredients give these tender grilled steaks a taste you won't soon forget. We loved the slightly sweet and pleasantly smoky glaze. Get ready to make mouths water!

—GEORDYTH SULLIVAN MIAMI, FLORIDA

PREP: 25 MIN. **GRILL:** 10 MIN. **MAKES:** 4 SERVINGS

- **⅔ cup chili sauce**
- **⅔ cup spicy steak sauce**
- **½ cup chopped shallots**
- **½ cup beer or nonalcoholic beer**
- **4 boneless beef top loin steaks (8 ounces each)**
- **½ teaspoon salt**
- **½ teaspoon pepper**

1. In a small saucepan, combine the chili sauce, steak sauce, shallots and beer. Bring to a boil. Reduce heat; simmer, uncovered, for 12-15 minutes or until slightly thickened. Set aside ½ cup for serving and keep warm. Sprinkle steaks with salt and pepper.
2. Moisten a paper towel with cooking oil; using long-handled tongs, lightly coat the grill rack. Grill steaks, covered, over medium heat or broil 4 in. from the heat for 4-6 minutes on each side or until meat reaches desired doneness (for medium-rare, a thermometer should read 145°; medium, 160°; well-done, 170°), basting occasionally with sauce mixture. Serve with reserved sauce.

Editor's Note: *Top loin steak may be labeled as strip steak, Kansas City steak, New York strip steak, ambassador steak or boneless club steak in your region.*

Salmon Mousse Tartlets

The Taste of Home Test Kitchen kitchen also tried these tartlets baked in the oven at 350° for 10 minutes. While they were delicious both ways, the no-bake version is easier to take to a potluck.

—DIANA DORAN PITTSBURGH, PENNSYLVANIA

PREP: 15 MIN. + CHILLING **MAKES:** 15 APPETIZERS

- **1 package (8 ounces) cream cheese, softened**
- **1½ teaspoons seafood seasoning**
- **1 teaspoon lemon juice**
- **1 pouch (6 ounces) boneless skinless pink salmon**
- **1 package (1.9 ounces) frozen miniature phyllo tart shells**
- **Fresh dill sprigs, optional**

1. In a large bowl, beat the cream cheese, seafood seasoning and lemon juice until smooth. Beat in salmon. Spoon or pipe into tart shells and garnish with dill if desired. Refrigerate for at least 20 minutes before serving.

Bacon-Gouda Stuffed Onions

Serve these tender, sweet and savory onions as a side with steak. For an added splash, drizzle everything with any leftover buttery pan juices from baking the onions. It's sooo good!

—BARB TEMPLIN NORWOOD, MINNESOTA

PREP: 10 MIN. **BAKE:** 45 MIN. **MAKES:** 4 SERVINGS

- **4 large sweet onions**
- **¼ teaspoon salt**
- **¼ teaspoon pepper**
- **5 bacon strips, cooked and crumbled**
- **½ cup shredded smoked Gouda cheese**
- **¼ cup butter, softened**
- **Minced chives**

1. Cut a ¼-in. slice from the top and bottom of each onion. Peel onions. Carefully cut and remove the center of each onion, leaving a ½-in. shell; discard removed onion or save for another use.

2. Place onions in a greased 8-in. square baking dish. Sprinkle with salt and pepper. Cover and bake at 400° for 40-45 minutes or until onions are tender. Combine the bacon, cheese and butter; spoon into onions. Bake, uncovered, 5-10 minutes longer or until cheese is melted. Sprinkle with chives.

Balsamic-Glazed Chicken Wings

Tired of the same buffalo and BBQ sauces? Try spreading your wings with a new balsamic-sugar glaze. Sweet and mildly tangy, these have a taste that will appeal to any crowd.

—GRETCHEN WHELAN SAN FRANCISCO, CALIFORNIA

PREP: 20 MIN. + MARINATING **BAKE:** 25 MIN.
MAKES: 9 SERVINGS

- **2 pounds chicken wings**
- **1½ cups balsamic vinegar**
- **2 garlic cloves, minced**
- **2 teaspoons minced fresh rosemary or ½ teaspoon dried rosemary, crushed**
- **¼ teaspoon salt**
- **¼ teaspoon pepper**
- **¼ cup packed brown sugar**

1. Cut chicken wings into three sections; discard wing tip sections. In a small bowl, combine the vinegar, garlic, rosemary, salt and pepper. Pour ½ cup marinade into a large resealable plastic bag. Add the chicken; seal bag and turn to coat. Refrigerate for 1 hour. Cover and refrigerate remaining marinade.

2. Drain and discard marinade. Place wings in a greased 15-in. x 10-in. x 1-in. baking pan. Bake at 375° for 25-30 minutes or until no longer pink, turning every 10 minutes.

3. Meanwhile, combine brown sugar and reserved marinade in a small saucepan. Bring to a boil; cook until liquid is reduced by half.

4. Place wings in a large bowl. Pour glaze over wings and toss to coat.

Editor's Note: *Uncooked chicken wing sections (wingettes) may be substituted for whole chicken wings.*

Grilled Pineapple & Maple Sundaes

This is one of our all-time favorite summer desserts. It's easy, elegant and makes a nice light treat after a big meal. You've gotta try it at your next barbecue!

—SHERALYN FRIESEN
WINNIPEG, MANITOBA

PREP: 10 MIN. + MARINATING
GRILL: 10 MIN. **MAKES:** 8 SERVINGS

- **¾ cup maple syrup**
- **2 tablespoons brown sugar**
- **¾ teaspoon ground cinnamon**
- **1 fresh pineapple, peeled, cut into 8 wedges**
- **8 scoops vanilla ice cream**

1. In a large resealable bag, combine the syrup, brown sugar and cinnamon; add pineapple. Seal bag and turn to coat. Refrigerate for 10-20 minutes. Drain, reserving syrup mixture.

2. Moisten a paper towel with cooking oil; using long-handled tongs, lightly coat the grill rack. Grill pineapple, covered, over medium heat or broil 4 in. from the heat for 8-10 minutes or until lightly browned, turning once.

3. Serve pineapple with ice cream and drizzle with reserved syrup mixture.

PERFECT PAIR

Try grilled food with a new beverage! Our staff recently tried and loved **Dry Soda** (the Vanilla Bean flavor was a favorite). The four-ingredient all-natural sodas rely less on sugar and more on fruit, flower and herbal flavors. Talk about refreshing! $12/12-pack; *amazon.com*.

Pesto Portobello Pizzas

Super-easy and delicious! Lunch, dinner or snack, we can't think of a time when these pizzas wouldn't come in handy. Serve them quartered, with toothpicks, as appetizers.
—LAURIE BARMORE WATERFORD, WISCONSIN

PREP/TOTAL TIME: 30 MIN.
MAKES: 4 SERVINGS

- **4 large portobello mushrooms (4 to 4½ inches)**
- **½ cup prepared pesto**
- **1 roma tomato, thinly sliced**
- **1 cup (4 ounces) shredded part-skim mozzarella cheese**
- **4 fresh basil leaves, thinly sliced**

1. Remove and discard stems and gills from mushrooms. Place mushrooms, stem side up, on a greased baking sheet.
2. Spoon pesto over mushrooms. Top with tomato slices and sprinkle with cheese. Bake at 400° for 15-20 minutes or until mushrooms are tender. Sprinkle with basil.

Blueberry-Lemon Ice Cream Sandwiches

For the little kid in you, try this sweet, icy treat. But make no mistake; it's definitely for adults!
—TASTE OF HOME TEST KITCHEN

PREP: 20 MIN. + FREEZING
MAKES: 4 SERVINGS

- **4 slices pound cake**
- **4 teaspoons Jeremiah Weed sweet tea vodka**
- **1 cup lemon sorbet, softened**
- **1 cup blueberry crumble ice cream, softened**
- **3 ounces white baking chocolate, melted**

1. Brush cake slices with vodka. Spread sorbet over two cake slices. Spread ice cream over remaining cake slices. Sandwich each sorbet-topped cake slice with an ice cream-topped cake slice.
2. Cut sandwiches in half. Drizzle with melted chocolate. Place on a baking sheet; freeze for at least 1 hour.

Shhh! SIMPLE SECRET

Get out! These can't get any easier, you're probably thinking. But they can if you make them ahead. Prep the pizzas up to 4 hours in advance and store in the fridge. Bake and garnish as directed.

This refreshing hard lemonade has a mild alcohol flavor; the beer adds just enough fizz to dance on your tongue as you sip!
—**GINGER SULLIVAN** CUTLER BAY, FLORIDA

Blackberry Beer Cocktail

PREP/TOTAL TIME: 10 MIN.
MAKES: 10 SERVINGS

- **4 bottles (12 ounces each) beer, chilled**
- **1 can (12 ounces) frozen raspberry lemonade concentrate, thawed**
- **¾ cup fresh or frozen blackberries, thawed**
- **½ cup vodka**
- **Ice cubes**
- **Lemon slices**

1. In a large pitcher combine the beer, lemonade concentrate, blackberries and vodka. Serve over ice and garnish with lemon slices.

Tomato-Basil Couscous Salad

It's hard to believe that tossing a few pantry ingredients with summer's best can yield such a fresh, lovely salad. Pair it with grilled lemon chicken for a light lunch.

—**SONYA LABBE**
WEST HOLLYWOOD, CALIFORNIA

PREP: 20 MIN. + CHILLING
MAKES: 8 SERVINGS

- **1½ cups water**
- **1½ cups uncooked couscous**
- **2 medium tomatoes, seeded and chopped**
- **¼ cup fresh basil leaves, thinly sliced**
- **½ cup olive oil**
- **¼ cup balsamic vinegar**
- **½ teaspoon salt**
- **¼ teaspoon pepper**

1. In a small saucepan, bring water to a boil. Stir in couscous. Remove from the heat; cover and let stand for 5-10 minutes or until water is absorbed. Fluff with a fork; cool.
2. In a large bowl, combine the couscous, tomatoes and basil. In a small bowl, whisk the oil, vinegar, salt and pepper. Pour over salad; toss to coat. Refrigerate until chilled

“I never thought I liked Brussels sprouts until I was given this very old recipe. It's delicious and may just change your mind about this nutritious veggie!”

—**KELLY WALMSLEY** LEWISTOWN, ILLINOIS

Bacon-Parmesan Brussels Sprouts

It's not a good idea to add salt to this recipe, as the bacon and Parmesan cheese are already salty enough. I've substituted broccoli and/or cauliflower for the sprouts and they're also delicious prepared in this way. The only change I make is that I generally use a microwave steamer to cook the broccoli and cauliflower.

—**KELLY WALMSLEY** LEWISTOWN, ILLINOIS

PREP/TOTAL TIME: 25 MIN.
MAKES: 4 SERVINGS

- **5 bacon strips, chopped**
- **1 package (16 ounces) frozen Brussels sprouts, thawed**
- **⅓ cup sliced onion**
- **2 tablespoons water**
- **¼ teaspoon pepper**
- **1 tablespoon grated Parmesan cheese**

1. Cook bacon in a large skillet over medium heat until crisp. Remove to paper towels; drain, reserving 1 tablespoon drippings.
2. In the same skillet, saute Brussels sprouts and onion in reserved drippings until lightly browned. Add water and pepper. Bring to a boil. Reduce heat; cover and simmer for 3-4 minutes or until Brussels sprouts are heated through. Remove from the heat. Stir in bacon and sprinkle with cheese.

Maple Baked Salmon

This recipe is special because it comes from my mom, both my children like it and it's easy to prepare.

—**DANIELLE ROTHE** GREENVILLE, NEW YORK

PREP/TOTAL TIME: 30 MIN.
MAKES: 6 SERVINGS

- **6 salmon fillets (6 ounces each)**
- **¼ cup packed brown sugar**
- **¼ cup maple syrup**
- **3 tablespoons reduced-sodium soy sauce**
- **1 tablespoon Dijon mustard**
- **¼ teaspoon pepper**
- **4 teaspoons sliced almonds, toasted, optional**

1. Place salmon fillets in a greased 13-in. x 9-in. baking dish. In a small bowl, combine the brown sugar, syrup, soy sauce, mustard and pepper. Pour over salmon.
2. Cover and bake at 425° for 10 minutes. Uncover and bake 8-10 minutes longer or until fish flakes easily with a fork. Sprinkle with almonds if desired.

Garlic Chicken & Bacon Pizza

Cooking creme is the secret to adding a lot of flavor without a lot of extra ingredients in this pizza. It's our go-to for game night. We love it; you're going to love it, too!

—**JOSEE LANZI** NEW PORT RICHEY, FLORIDA

PREP/TOTAL TIME: 20 MIN. **MAKES:** 6 SERVINGS

- **1 prebaked 12-inch pizza crust**
- **½ cup Philadelphia savory garlic cooking creme**
- **1 package (6 ounces) ready-to-use grilled chicken breast strips**
- **4 strips ready-to-serve fully cooked bacon, chopped**
- **1 cup (4 ounces) shredded part-skim mozzarella cheese**

1. Place pizza crust on a greased 14-in. pizza pan. Spread with cooking creme. Top with chicken and bacon; sprinkle with cheese.
2. Bake at 425° for 10-15 minutes or until cheese is melted.

Tuscan Parmesan Pork Chops

These pork chops are all dressed up! First they're bathed in a zesty marinade, then they're coated with crunchy nuts and cheese for a special main dish with mass appeal.

—**JEANNE HOLT** MENDOTA HEIGHTS, MINNESOTA

PREP: 10 MIN. + MARINATING **BAKE:** 15 MIN.
MAKES: 4 SERVINGS

- **¾ cup zesty Italian salad dressing**
- **2 tablespoons Dijon mustard**
- **4 bone-in pork loin chops (7 ounces each)**
- **½ teaspoon salt**
- **¼ teaspoon pepper**
- **⅔ cup shredded Parmesan cheese**
- **½ cup finely chopped hazelnuts**

1. In a large resealable plastic bag, combine salad dressing and mustard. Add the pork; seal bag and turn to coat. Refrigerate for at least 1 hour.
2. Drain and discard marinade. Sprinkle pork with salt and pepper. In a shallow bowl, combine cheese and hazelnuts. Coat chops with cheese mixture. Place on a greased 15-in. x 10-in. x 1-in. baking pan. Bake at 400° for 14-18 minutes or until a thermometer reads 145°.

Frozen Lime Cake

Block parties, cookouts or anytime you need a super-cool dessert, we've got just the thing. The crust is a snap, and the ice cream and sherbet layers are delish. Everyone loves this recipe!

—**KATHY GILLOGLY** SUN CITY, CALIFORNIA

PREP: 15 MIN. + FREEZING **MAKES:** 9 SERVINGS

- **1½ cups ground almonds**
- **¾ cup crushed gingersnap cookies (about 15 cookies)**
- **⅓ cup butter, melted**
- **2 pints pineapple coconut or vanilla ice cream, softened**
- **4 cups lime sherbet, softened**
- **Whipped topping, optional**

1. In a small bowl, combine the almonds, cookies and butter. Press onto the bottom of a 9-in. square pan. Freeze for 15 minutes.
2. Spread ice cream over crust. Cover and freeze for at least 30 minutes. Top with sherbet. Cover and freeze for 4 hours or overnight.
3. Remove from the freezer 10 minutes before serving. Garnish servings with whipped topping if desired.

SIMPLE SWAP

We tested this cake with Haagen-Dazs Pineapple Coconut ice cream. But in a pinch, you can substitute vanilla ice cream with a touch of coconut extract stirred in.

Smothered Burritos

Here's a recipe that's quick and easy and will satisfy even the pickiest of eaters! Salsa verde is spicy—you can reduce the amount to make a milder version.

—KIM KENYON GREENWOOD, MISSOURI

PREP/TOTAL TIME: 25 MIN.
MAKES: 4 SERVINGS

- **1 can (10 ounces) green enchilada sauce**
- **¾ cup salsa verde**
- **1 pound ground beef**
- **4 flour tortillas (10 inches), warmed**
- **1½ cups (6 ounces) shredded cheddar cheese**

1. Combine enchilada sauce and salsa verde in a small bowl. In a large skillet, cook beef over medium heat until no longer pink; drain. Stir in ½ cup sauce mixture.
2. Spoon ⅔ cup beef mixture off center on each tortilla; sprinkle each with 3 tablespoons cheese. Fold sides and ends over filling and roll up.
3. Transfer to a greased 11-in. x 7-in. baking dish. Pour remaining sauce mixture over burritos; sprinkle with remaining cheese. Bake, uncovered, at 375° for 10-15 minutes or until cheese is melted.

Mexican Couscous

For a quick-to-cook and colorful side dish, try this speedy recipe. Use a hotter style of salsa to add more zip.

—JOHN SLIVON MILTON, FLORIDA

PREP/TOTAL TIME: 20 MIN.
MAKES: 4 SERVINGS

- **1 cup salsa**
- **¼ cup water**
- **¾ cup uncooked couscous**
- **¾ cup black beans, rinsed and drained**
- **1 medium ripe avocado, peeled and cubed**

1. Bring salsa and water to a boil in a small saucepan; stir in couscous. Cover and remove from the heat. Let stand for 10 minutes. Fluff couscous with a fork; stir in beans. Top servings with avocado.

Citrus-Spice Glazed Salmon

Got 5 minutes? Then you've got the time to get these fillets into the oven. They're perfect for entertaining, yet simple enough for family weeknight dinners.
—**KAREN LATIMER** WINNIPEG, MANITOBA

PREP/TOTAL TIME: 20 MIN.
MAKES: 4 SERVINGS

- **4 salmon fillets (6 ounces each)**
- **2 tablespoons orange marmalade**
- **1 teaspoon reduced-sodium soy sauce**
- **¼ teaspoon Chinese five-spice powder**
- **⅛ teaspoon salt**
- **⅛ teaspoon ground ginger**

1. Line a baking sheet with foil; grease foil. Place salmon on the baking sheet.
2. Place marmalade in a small microwave-safe bowl. Microwave for 10 seconds or until warmed. Stir in the soy sauce, five-spice powder, salt and ginger. Spoon over salmon.
3. Bake, uncovered, at 350° for 15-20 minutes or until the fish flakes easily with a fork.

Hawaiian Barbecue Beans

The ingredient list is short, but creative. Guests rave and wonder about the unique flavor—fresh ginger is the tasty surprise. These beans are a hit at every barbecue.
—**HELEN REYNOLDS** QUINCY, CALIFORNIA

PREP: 10 MIN. **COOK:** 5 HOURS
MAKES: 9 SERVINGS

- **4 cans (15 ounces each) black beans, rinsed and drained**
- **1 can (20 ounces) crushed pineapple, drained**
- **1 bottle (18 ounces) barbecue sauce**
- **1½ teaspoons minced fresh gingerroot**
- **½ pound bacon strips, cooked and crumbled**

1. In a 4-qt. slow cooker, combine the beans, pineapple, barbecue sauce and ginger. Cover and cook on low for 5-6 hours. Stir in bacon before serving.

Shhh! SIMPLE SECRET

Check the fillets for doneness by inserting a fork at an angle into the thickest portion of the fish and gently parting the meat. When it flakes easily into sections, it's cooked completely.

Honey Roasted Chicken

Put chicken in a baking dish, add a few pantry staples, let it bake, and presto! You'll have a sweet, succulent main course before you know it. Add rice or potatoes and a frozen Asian veggie mix, and supper is served.

—**GWYN BRANDT** HIBBING, MINNESOTA

PREP/TOTAL TIME: 30 MIN. **MAKES:** 4 SERVINGS

- **4 boneless skinless chicken breast halves (6 ounces each)**
- **½ cup honey**
- **¼ cup reduced-sodium teriyaki sauce**
- **2 tablespoons orange juice**
- **1½ teaspoons prepared mustard**
- **½ teaspoon salt**
- **¼ teaspoon pepper**

1. Place chicken in a greased 13-in. x 9-in. baking dish. Combine the remaining ingredients; pour over chicken.
2. Bake, uncovered, at 375° for 22-26 minutes or until a thermometer reads 170°, basting occasionally.

Chocolate Chip Ice Cream Pie

I got the recipe for this pie from my mom, but I changed the crust to one made of cookie dough.

—**LETITIA LANDIS** ROCHESTER, INDIANA

PREP: 10 MIN. **BAKE:** 15 MIN. + FREEZING **MAKES:** 8 SERVINGS

- **1 tube (16½ ounces) refrigerated chocolate chip cookie dough**
- **¼ cup sour cream**
- **¼ cup chocolate syrup**
- **1 quart chocolate chip ice cream, softened**

1. Cut cookie dough in half widthwise; let one half stand at room temperature for 5-10 minutes to soften (save the other half for another use). Press dough onto the bottom and up the sides of an ungreased 9-in. deep-dish pie plate. Bake at 350° for 12-16 minutes or until lightly browned. Cool on a wire rack.
2. In a small bowl, combine sour cream and syrup. Spoon half of the ice cream into crust. Cover and freeze for 1 hour. Drizzle with ¼ cup syrup mixture. Repeat layers. Cover and freeze for 8 hours or overnight.

> "Because the crust will harden after being frozen, a great way to cut through the pie layers is to dip a knife in hot water first, wipe the knife off and then cut. Repeat the process if needed."

—**LETITIA LANDIS** ROCHESTER, INDIANA

Grilled Chicken Sausages with Harvest Rice

My husband loves chicken sausages so I am always tryng new recipes with them. I used some traditional fall flavors in this easy 5-ingredient supper idea. It's quick, inexpensive, nutritious and simply delicious!

—**PAMELA SHANK** PARKERSBURG, WEST VIRGINIA

PREP/TOTAL TIME: 25 MIN. **MAKES:** 4 SERVINGS

- **1¾ cups chicken broth**
- **2 cups instant brown rice**
- **1 package (12 ounces) frozen cooked winter squash, thawed and drained well**
- **⅓ cup dried cranberries**
- **1 package (12 ounces) fully cooked apple chicken sausage links or flavor of your choice**

1. Bring broth to a boil in a large saucepan. Stir in rice. Reduce heat; cover and simmer for 3 minutes. Add squash and simmer, uncovered, for 4-6 minutes or until liquid is absorbed. Remove from the heat. Stir in cranberries; cover and let stand for 5 minutes.
2. Grill sausages, uncovered, over medium heat or broil 4 in. from the heat for 8-10 minutes or until heated through, turning often. Slice sausages and serve with the rice mixture.

> “We prefer apple-flavored chicken sausage links in this entree, but any flavor would work well.”

—**PAMELA SHANK** PARKERSBURG, WEST VIRGINIA

Alfredo Creamed Spinach

I created this recipe for my son, who craves spinach all the time. Even my husband, who doesn't normally like spinach, tried the tasty side dish and loved it!

—**GALELYNN PETERSON**
LONG BEACH, CALIFORNIA

PREP/TOTAL TIME: 20 MIN.
MAKES: 4 SERVINGS

- **2 packages (10 ounces each) frozen chopped spinach**
- **¼ pound bacon strips, chopped**
- **1 jar (15 ounces) Alfredo sauce**
- **¾ teaspoon pepper**

1. Cook spinach according to package directions. Meanwhile, in a large skillet, cook bacon over medium heat until crisp. Remove to paper towels with a slotted spoon; drain, reserving 3 tablespoons drippings.
2. Drain spinach. In the same skillet, saute spinach in reserved drippings for 1 minute. Stir in the Alfredo sauce, pepper and bacon; heat through.

Macadamia-Coffee Bean Cookies

Anyone who loves coffee will adore this java-flavored cookie! If you had to play matchmaker with these treats, what hot beverage would you pair them with? There's only one answer.

—**KATHLEEN SPECHT** CLINTON, MONTANA

PREP: 20 MIN. **BAKE:** 10 MIN./BATCH
MAKES: ABOUT 2½ DOZEN

- **1 package (17½ ounces) double chocolate chunk cookie mix**
- **1 egg**
- **¼ cup canola oil**
- **2 tablespoons water**
- **1½ cups chocolate-covered coffee beans, finely chopped**
- **1 cup macadamia nuts, chopped**

1. In a large bowl, beat the cookie mix, egg, oil and water until blended. Stir in coffee beans and nuts.
2. Drop by tablespoonfuls 2 in. apart onto greased baking sheets. Bake at 375° for 8-10 minutes or until set. Remove to wire racks to cool. Store in an airtight container.

Baked Rigatoni & Sausage

To serve a dozen people without any extra effort, simply double this recipe and prepare two of these hearty pasta bakes.

—ELAINE NEUKIRCH GENOA, ILLINOIS

PREP/TOTAL TIME: 30 MIN.
MAKES: 6 SERVINGS

- **3¾ cups uncooked rigatoni**
- **5 Italian sausage links (4 ounces each), sliced**
- **1 jar (26 ounces) spaghetti sauce**
- **¼ cup dry red wine**
- **2 cups (8 ounces) shredded Italian cheese blend**

1. Cook rigatoni according to package directions. Meanwhile, in a Dutch oven, cook sausage over medium heat until no longer pink; drain. Add spaghetti sauce and wine.
2. Drain rigatoni; add to sausage mixture and toss to coat. Transfer to a greased 13-in. x 9-in. baking dish; sprinkle with cheese. Bake, uncovered, at 350° for 15-20 minutes or until cheese is melted.

Apple Almond Salad

Fruit by itself tends to get left alone at potlucks, unless it's whipped into a sweet, tangy and crunchy salad like this one!

—CRITINA WHEELER UPTON, KENTUCKY

PREP/TOTAL TIME: 10 MIN.
MAKES: 8 SERVINGS

- **3 large apples, chopped**
- **1 cup sliced almonds, toasted**
- **1 cup dried cranberries**
- **2½ cups whipped topping**
- **⅓ cup mayonnaise**

1. In a large bowl, combine the apples, almonds and cranberries. Combine whipped topping and mayonnaise. Add to apple mixture and toss to coat.

Italian-Style Croissants

This is one of my easiest breads. A touch of pesto and Italian seasoning quickly doctor up refrigerated crescent dough, so you're ready to roll.

—ANN MARIE BARBER OAKLAND PARK, FLORIDA

PREP/TOTAL TIME: 25 MIN. **MAKES:** 8 SERVINGS

- **1 tube (8 ounces) refrigerated crescent rolls**
- **8 teaspoons prepared pesto**
- **1 egg white, lightly beaten**
- **1½ teaspoons Italian seasoning**

1. Unroll crescent dough; separate into triangles. Spread each with 1 teaspoon pesto. Roll up from the wide end and place pointed side down 2 in. apart on ungreased baking sheets. Curve ends down to form a crescent shape.
2. Brush with egg white; sprinkle with Italian seasoning. Bake at 375° for 10-13 minutes or until lightly browned.

Almost Homemade

"The herby goodness of my favorite sauce shines in this nostalgic bread recipe that comes together quickly, thanks to refrigerated biscuits. Serve warm as an appetizer with marinara for dipping, or as a side to an Italian entree."

EDEN DRANGER LOS ANGELES, CALIFORNIA
Chimichurri Monkey Bread, page 63

Deli Roast Beef Sandwiches With Mashed Potatoes

Just like Mom or Grandma used to make—but so much quicker! Store-bought mashed potatoes, gravy and deli roast beef help you turn out this heartwarming combination before you can say, "Order up!"

—**RUTH ANN BOTT** LAKE WALES, FLORIDA

PREP/TOTAL TIME: 10 MIN. **MAKES:** 4 SERVINGS

- **1 pound sliced deli roast beef**
- **2 cans (10¼ ounces each) beef gravy**
- **1 can (4 ounces) mushroom stems and pieces, drained**
- **1 package (3¾ ounces) creamy butter instant mashed potatoes**
- **4 slices Italian bread (½ inch thick)**

1. In a 2-qt. microwave-safe bowl, combine the beef, gravy and mushrooms. Cover and microwave on high for 2-3 minutes or until heated through.
2. Meanwhile, prepare potatoes according to package directions. Divide bread among four plates. Spoon beef mixture over bread. Serve with potatoes.

Editor's Note: *This recipe was tested in a 1,100-watt microwave.*

Ham & Noodles with Veggies

A hearty, nutritious dinner has never been easier! Frozen veggies in cheese sauce with pasta make this meal super-fast.

—**JEANNIE KLUGH** LANCASTER, PENNSYLVANIA

PREP/TOTAL TIME: 20 MIN. **MAKES:** 6 SERVINGS

- **1 can (14½ ounces) chicken broth**
- **1 cup water**
- **3 cups uncooked egg noodles**
- **2 packages (24 ounces each) frozen broccoli, carrots, cauliflower and cheese sauce**
- **1 package (16 ounces) cubed fully cooked ham**

1. Bring broth and water to a boil in a large saucepan. Add pasta; return to a boil. Cook for 8-10 minutes or until pasta is tender. Meanwhile, place vegetables and cheese sauce in a Dutch oven. Cover and cook over medium heat for 13-15 minutes or until heated through, stirring occasionally.
2. Pour noodles and cooking liquid into vegetable mixture. Stir in ham and heat through.

Breadstick Pizza

Make Monday fun-day with a hassle-free homemade pizza featuring refrigerated breadsticks as the crust. Feeding kids? Slice pieces into small strips and let them dip each strip into marinara sauce. They'll love it!

—**MARY HANKINS** KANSAS CITY, MISSOURI

PREP: 25 MIN. **BAKE:** 25 MIN. **MAKES:** 12 SERVINGS

- **2 tubes (11 ounces each) refrigerated breadsticks**
- **½ pound sliced fresh mushrooms**
- **2 medium green peppers, chopped**
- **1 medium onion, chopped**
- **1½ teaspoons Italian seasoning, divided**
- **4 teaspoons olive oil, divided**
- **1½ cups (6 ounces) shredded cheddar cheese, divided**
- **5 ounces Canadian bacon, chopped**
- **1½ cups (6 ounces) shredded part-skim mozzarella cheese**
- **Marinara sauce**

1. Unroll breadsticks into a greased 15-in. x 10-in. x 1-in. baking pan. Press onto the bottom and up the sides of pan; pinch seams to seal. Bake at 350° for 6-8 minutes or until set.
2. Meanwhile, in a large skillet, saute the mushrooms, peppers, onion and 1 teaspoon Italian seasoning in 2 teaspoons oil until crisp-tender; drain.
3. Brush crust with remaining oil. Sprinkle with ¾ cup cheddar cheese; top with vegetable mixture and Canadian bacon. Combine mozzarella cheese and remaining cheddar cheese; sprinkle over top. Sprinkle with remaining Italian seasoning.
4. Bake for 20-25 minutes or until cheese is melted and crust is golden brown. Serve with marinara sauce.

Cheddar Garlic Biscuits

I get a lot of recipes from friends, and this one is no exception. Biscuit mix is combined with a little minced onion, garlic powder and shredded cheddar to create these golden drop biscuits that bake in a flash.

—**FRANCES POSTE** WALL, SOUTH DAKOTA

PREP/TOTAL TIME: 25 MIN. **MAKES:** 15 BISCUITS

- **2 cups biscuit/baking mix**
- **½ cup shredded cheddar cheese**
- **½ teaspoon dried minced onion**
- **⅔ cup 2% milk**
- **¼ cup butter, melted**
- **½ teaspoon garlic powder**

1. Combine the biscuit mix, cheese and onion in a large bowl. Stir in milk until a soft dough forms; stir 30 seconds longer.
2. Drop by rounded tablespoonfuls 2 in. apart onto ungreased baking sheets. Bake at 450° for 8-10 minutes or until golden brown. Combine butter and garlic powder; brush over biscuits. Serve warm.

Sausage Breakfast Hash

Served with "dough well-done" (toast) and "dirty water" (coffee), this diner special makes a fun breakfast-for-dinner combo.

—**JACOB KITZMAN** SEATTLE, WASHINGTON

PREP/TOTAL TIME: 30 MIN. **MAKES:** 4 SERVINGS

- **3 tablespoons butter, divided**
- **1 package (20 ounces) refrigerated diced potatoes with onion**
- **1 package (7 ounces) brown-and-serve sausage links, sliced**
- **1 small green pepper, chopped**
- **1 small sweet red pepper, chopped**
- **¼ teaspoon salt**
- **Dash cayenne pepper**
- **1 cup (4 ounces) shredded Swiss cheese**
- **8 eggs**
- **¼ teaspoon pepper**
- **Hot pepper sauce, optional**

1. In a large skillet, melt 1 tablespoon butter over medium heat; stir in the potatoes, sausage, green and red peppers, salt and cayenne. Cover and cook for 12-14 minutes or until potatoes and vegetables are tender, stirring occasionally. Stir in cheese.
2. In a large skillet, fry eggs, as desired, in remaining butter. Sprinkle with pepper. Serve with hash and pepper sauce if desired.

Diner-Speak

Impress (and maybe confuse) friends with shortcut slang popular at diners. Call salad "cow feed," milk "moo juice," sugar "yum-yum," salt and pepper shakers "Mike & Ike" and water "city juice." For two eggs and a strip of bacon, ask for "two dots and a dash." For a burger with lettuce, tomato and onion, "walk a cow through the garden!"

Pecan-Crusted Chicken Waffle Sandwiches

Chicken and waffles is a Southern tradition. I turned it into a sandwich with a sweet and spicy mustard sauce to give it a kick. My friends called it "naughty and delicious" and said they could eat it all day long!

—**ELIZABETH DUMONT** BOULDER, COLORADO

PREP/TOTAL TIME: 30 MIN. **MAKES:** 4 SERVINGS

- **4 boneless skinless chicken breast halves (5 ounces each)**
- **1 egg**
- **½ cup plus ⅓ cup maple syrup, divided**
- **1 cup finely chopped pecans**
- **⅔ cup dry bread crumbs**
- **¾ teaspoon plus ⅛ teaspoon salt, divided**
- **½ teaspoon plus ⅛ teaspoon pepper, divided**
- **¼ cup canola oil**
- **¼ cup spicy brown mustard**
- **1 tablespoon white wine vinegar**
- **8 frozen waffles, toasted**

1. Flatten chicken to ½-in. thickness. In a shallow bowl, whisk egg and ½ cup syrup. In another shallow bowl, combine the pecans, bread crumbs, ¾ teaspoon salt and ½ teaspoon pepper. Dip chicken in egg mixture, then coat with pecan mixture.
2. In a large skillet over medium heat, cook chicken in oil in batches for 5-6 minutes on each side or until no longer pink. Meanwhile, combine the mustard, vinegar and remaining syrup, salt and pepper.
3. Drizzle 1 tablespoon sauce mixture over each of four waffles; top with chicken and drizzle with remaining sauce mixture. Top with remaining waffles.

FILL 'EM UP!

ROLL UP DINNER IN NO TIME WITH THESE FAST READER RECIPES THAT START WITH REFRIGERATED DOUGH

What's the quickest way to get dinner to the table when time's tight? Three readers have the secret, and they're willing to share it! Each of these recipes starts with refrigerated bread dough—a busy cook's best friend, because it doesn't need thaw time. These warm and satisfying stuffed sandwiches take minutes to prep and bake, but look so picture perfect and taste so delicious, no one will guess your new time-saving secret!

SIMPLE SWAP

CORDON BLEU SAMMIE:
Spread dough with softened butter, then top with thinly sliced deli ham and deli chicken and shredded Swiss cheese.

ROAST BEEF AND JACK SANDWICH:
Top dough with sauteed chopped sweet orange pepper and red onion, thinly sliced deli roast beef, shredded Monterey Jack cheese, a sprinkle of Italian seasoning and garlic salt.

FONTINA CHICKEN STROMBOLI:
Spread dough with prepared pesto, then top with thinly sliced rotisserie chicken and prosciutto or deli ham, sliced fontina cheese and grated Parmesan cheese.

Spiral Stromboli

Two types of deli meat and three kinds of cheese make this satisfying sandwich the perfect filler-upper! I frequently fix this on days when I need a fast meal.

—**JEAN GRUENERT** BURLINGTON, WISCONSIN

PREP: 10 MIN. **BAKE:** 25 MIN. **MAKES:** 4 SERVINGS

- **1 tube (11 ounces) refrigerated crusty French loaf**
- **¾ cup shredded part-skim mozzarella cheese**
- **¾ cup shredded cheddar cheese**
- **¼ pound each thinly sliced deli salami and ham**
- **¼ cup chopped roasted red peppers or 1 jar (2 ounces) pimientos, drained**
- **1 tablespoon butter, melted**
- **2 tablespoons shredded Parmesan cheese**

1. Unroll the dough and pat into a 14-in. x 12-in. rectangle. Sprinkle with mozzarella and cheddar cheese to within ½ in. of edges; top with meat and red peppers. Roll up jelly-roll style, starting with a short side; seal seam and tuck ends under.
2. Place seam side down on a greased baking sheet. Brush with butter; sprinkle with Parmesan cheese. Bake at 375° for 25-30 minutes or until golden brown. Slice with a serrated knife.

Turkey-Brie Stromboli

Mango chutney and melted Brie give this stuffed sandwich a mouthwatering flavor you won't soon forget! Refrigerated pizza crust and deli turkey help it come together in a dash.

—BONNIE BUCKLEY KANSAS CITY, MISSOURI

PREP/TOTAL TIME: 30 MIN. **MAKES:** 6 SERVINGS

- **1 tube (13.8 ounces) refrigerated pizza crust**
- **3 tablespoons mayonnaise**
- **1 tablespoon mango chutney**
- **6 ounces thinly sliced deli smoked turkey**
- **4 large slices tomato**
- **1 round (8 ounces) Brie cheese, rind removed, cut into ¼-inch slices**

1. On a greased baking sheet, pat pizza crust into a 13-in. x 10-in. rectangle. In a small bowl, combine mayonnaise and chutney. Spread over crust to within ½ in. of edge. Arrange turkey slices over top; layer with tomato and cheese.
2. Fold dough over filling; pinch edges to seal. Cut four 2-in. slits in top. Bake at 400° for 20-25 minutes or until golden brown. Slice and serve warm.

Hearty Sausage-Stuffed Loaf

My family devours this every time I make it. With so few ingredients, it couldn't be simpler! The rich, hearty sausage and spinach combination is wonderful for brunch, but I often serve it with a salad at suppertime.

—JUDY LEARNED BOYERTOWN, PENNSYLVANIA

PREP: 20 MIN. **BAKE:** 20 MIN. **MAKES:** 6 SERVINGS

- **¾ pound bulk pork sausage**
- **1 tube (11 ounces) refrigerated crusty French loaf**
- **2 cups (8 ounces) shredded cheddar cheese**
- **1 package (10 ounces) frozen chopped spinach, thawed and squeezed dry**
- **1 tablespoon butter, melted**
- **1 tablespoon grated Parmesan cheese**
- **Pizza sauce, optional**

1. In a small skillet, cook sausage over medium heat until no longer pink; drain. Unroll dough and pat into a 14-in. x 12-in. rectangle. Sprinkle the sausage, cheddar cheese and spinach lengthwise down the center of the dough. Bring edges of dough to the center over filling; pinch seams to seal.
2. Place seam side down on a greased baking sheet. Brush top with butter; sprinkle with Parmesan cheese. Bake at 350° for 20-25 minutes or until golden brown. Serve warm with pizza sauce if desired.

Blushing Angel Hair Pasta with Chicken

You'll feel like you're in an upscale Italian restaurant when you serve this entree with a pleasant lemon tang and a savory garlic and herb cheese sauce. No one has to know what a cinch it is!

—PATRICIA HARMON BADEN, PENNSYLVANIA

PREP/TOTAL TIME: 30 MIN. **MAKES:** 4 SERVINGS

- **1 package (9 ounces) refrigerated angel hair pasta**
- **1 can (14½ ounces) diced tomatoes with garlic and onion, drained**
- **1½ pounds boneless skinless chicken breasts, cut into ½-inch strips**
- **¼ teaspoon pepper**
- **3 tablespoons olive oil, divided**
- **1 carton (6½ ounces) reduced-fat garlic-herb spreadable cheese**
- **1 tablespoon lemon juice**

1. Cook pasta according to package directions. Meanwhile, place tomatoes in a food processor; cover and process until pureed. Set aside.
2. Sprinkle chicken with pepper. In a large skillet, saute chicken in 2 tablespoons oil until no longer pink. Remove and keep warm.
3. Stir the spreadable cheese and pureed tomatoes into skillet. Bring to a boil over medium heat. Reduce heat; simmer, uncovered, for 2-4 minutes or until slightly thickened. Stir in lemon juice and remaining oil. Return chicken to pan; heat through. Drain pasta and serve with chicken mixture.

Baked Peanut Chicken

Here's a time-saving baked chicken recipe with delicious Thai flavor. It's nutty tasting, with a bit of spice. Add a steamed veggie and you'll have a complete meal in moments.

—BRENDA HENDRICKSON DANVILLE, KENTUCKY

PREP/TOTAL TIME: 30 MIN. **MAKES:** 4 SERVINGS

- **1 can (13.66 ounces) coconut milk**
- **1 package (3½ ounces) Thai peanut sauce mix**
- **4 boneless skinless chicken breast halves (6 ounces each)**
- **1 package (8½ ounces) ready-to-serve jasmine rice**
- **2 green onions, thinly sliced**
- **Spanish peanuts, optional**

1. Combine coconut milk and sauce mix in a small saucepan. Bring to a boil; cook and stir for 2-3 minutes or until thickened.
2. Arrange chicken in a greased 11-in. x 7-in. baking dish. Pour sauce over top. Bake, uncovered, at 350° for 20-25 minutes or until a thermometer reads 170°. Prepare rice according to package directions. Serve with chicken and sprinkle with onions and peanuts if desired.

Coconut Milk

Coconut milk isn't the naturally occurring liquid found inside a coconut but a milky-white liquid with a high oil content that is derived from mature coconuts. Coconut milk is made from grated coconut meat that is soaked in warm water and then squeezed or pressed. It usually comes in cans and also comes in lighter-calorie varieties.

The herby goodness of my favorite sauce shines in this nostalgic bread recipe that comes together quickly, thanks to refrigerated biscuits. Serve warm as an appetizer with marinara for dipping, or as a side to an Italian entree.
—**EDEN DRANGER** LOS ANGELES, CALIFORNIA

Chimichurri Monkey Bread

PREP: 20 MIN. **BAKE:** 20 MIN.
MAKES: 12 SERVINGS

- **¼ cup minced fresh parsley**
- **¼ cup olive oil**
- **2 tablespoons minced fresh oregano**
- **1 tablespoon white wine vinegar**
- **2 garlic cloves**
- **¾ teaspoon kosher salt**
- **¼ teaspoon ground cumin**
- **¼ teaspoon pepper**
- **⅛ teaspoon crushed red pepper flakes**
- **2 tubes (12 ounces each) refrigerated buttermilk biscuits**

1. In a shallow bowl, combine the first nine ingredients. Cut each biscuit in half and shape into a ball. Roll in herb mixture.
2. Place biscuit pieces in a greased 10-in. fluted tube pan. Bake at 375° for 18-22 minutes or until golden brown. Cool for 5 minutes before inverting onto a serving plate.

Spinach Salmon Bundles

Here's an elegant entree that will turn a weeknight dinner into a fancy occasion. Rich salmon and flaky golden-brown pastry will delight family and guests—and they'll think you really fussed.

—**LARISSA GEDNEY**
MYRTLE BEACH, SOUTH CAROLINA

PREP/TOTAL TIME: 30 MIN.
MAKES: 4 SERVINGS

- **2 tubes (8 ounces each) refrigerated crescent rolls**
- **4 salmon fillets (6 ounces each)**
- **¼ teaspoon salt**
- **¼ teaspoon pepper**
- **⅓ cup garlic-herb spreadable cheese**
- **1 package (10 ounces) frozen chopped spinach, thawed and squeezed dry**

1. Unroll crescent dough and separate into four rectangles; seal perforations. Place a salmon fillet in the center of each rectangle; sprinkle with salt and pepper. Spoon spreadable cheese over each; top with spinach. Fold dough over filling and pinch edges to seal.
2. Place on an ungreased baking sheet. Bake at 400° for 20-25 minutes or until golden brown.

Editor's Note: *This recipe was tested with Alouette Garlic-Herb Cheese Spread.*

Turkey Alfredo Tetrazzini

Judy speeds up her mother-in-law's tetrazzini by using jarred Alfredo sauce, canned mushrooms and onion powder. We loved the peas' pop of color, the hint of white wine and the creamy, tangy taste.

—JUDY BATSON TAMPA, FLORIDA

PREP: 20 MIN. **BAKE:** 30 MIN. **MAKES:** 4 SERVINGS

- **4 ounces thin spaghetti**
- **1 jar (15 ounces) Alfredo sauce**
- **2 cups frozen peas**
- **1½ cups cubed cooked turkey or chicken**
- **1 can (4 ounces) mushroom stems and pieces, drained**
- **¼ cup shredded Swiss cheese**
- **¼ cup shredded Parmesan cheese**
- **2 tablespoons white wine or chicken broth**
- **½ teaspoon onion powder**
- **½ cup French-fried onions**
- **½ teaspoon paprika**

1. Cook spaghetti according to package directions. Meanwhile, in a bowl, combine Alfredo sauce, peas, turkey, mushrooms, cheeses, wine and onion powder. Drain spaghetti. Add to sauce mixture; toss to coat. Transfer to a greased 8-in. square baking dish. Sprinkle with onions and paprika.
2. Cover and bake at 350° for 30-35 minutes or until heated through.

Poutine

The ultimate in French-Canadian junk food, poutine commonly features warm fries topped with cheese curds and gravy. This side dish is quick to fix with frozen potatoes and packaged gravy and has all the traditional greasy spoon comfort.

—SHELISA TERRY HENDERSON, NEVADA

PREP/TOTAL TIME: 30 MIN. **MAKES:** 4 SERVINGS

- **4 cups frozen French-fried potatoes**
- **1 envelope brown gravy mix**
- **¼ teaspoon pepper**
- **½ cup white cheddar cheese curds or cubed white cheddar cheese**

1. Prepare fries according to package directions.
2. Meanwhile, prepare gravy mix according to package directions. Stir in pepper. Place fries on a serving plate; top with cheese curds and gravy.
3. Bake at 450° for 8-10 minutes or until cheese is melted.

Philly-Style Barbecue Pizza

Wondering what to do with those leftovers you carried home in a doggie bag from the restaurant? Use them to fix this delicious pizza at home! Rich, sassy shredded meat and cream cheese are a winning combination in the ultra-easy main dish.

—TASTE OF HOME TEST KITCHEN

PREP/TOTAL TIME: 30 MIN. **MAKES:** 8 SLICES

- **1 prebaked 12-inch pizza crust**
- **4 ounces cream cheese, softened**
- **2 tablespoons creamy Italian salad dressing**
- **2 garlic cloves, minced**
- **1 cup (4 ounces) shredded Colby cheese**
- **1 cup (4 ounces) shredded provolone cheese**
- **1 cup shredded leftover meat from Famous Dave's Feast for Two**
- **1 cup sliced fresh mushrooms**
- **1 small green pepper, chopped**
- **1 small onion, chopped**
- **1 teaspoon dried oregano**

1. Place crust on an ungreased 12-in. pizza pan. Combine the cream cheese, salad dressing and garlic; spread over crust to within ½ in. of edges. Layer with cheeses, shredded meat, mushrooms, pepper and onion. Sprinkle with oregano.
2. Bake at 450° for 8-10 minutes or until cheese is melted.

Creamy Onion Pork Chops

With chops this good, you won't have to rinse the plates before putting them in the dishwasher. Wine adds delectable flavor, and the meat falls off the bone. This dish is sure to initiate family members into the clean-plate club!

—KRISTINA WYATT CATAWBA, VIRGINIA

PREP: 10 MIN. **COOK:** 8 HOURS **MAKES:** 6 SERVINGS

- **6 (bone-in pork loin chops 8 ounces each)**
- **¼ teaspoon pepper**
- **⅛ teaspoon salt**
- **1¼ cups 2% milk**
- **1 can (10¾ ounces) condensed cream of onion soup, undiluted**
- **1 can (10¾ ounces) reduced-fat reduced-sodium condensed cream of mushroom soup, undiluted**
- **⅔ cup white wine or chicken broth**
- **1 envelope ranch salad dressing mix**
- **3 tablespoons cornstarch**
- **2 tablespoons water**
- **Minced fresh parsley, optional**

1. Sprinkle chops with pepper and salt; transfer to a 4-qt. slow cooker. In a large bowl, combine the milk, soups, wine and dressing mix; pour over pork. Cover and cook on low for 8-10 hours or until pork is tender.
2. Remove pork to a serving platter and keep warm. Skim fat from cooking juices; transfer to a large saucepan. Bring liquid to a boil. Combine cornstarch and water until smooth; gradually stir into the pan. Bring to a boil; cook and stir for 2 minutes or until thickened. Serve with pork and sprinkle with parsley if desired.

Logan's Fried Catfish

Pancake mix and carbonated water are the surprising secrets to these beautifully browned catfish fillets. My grandson Logan can't get enough of them cooked this way, so I always get to go fishing for more! Serve with coleslaw or sweet potato fries, and get ready for smiles.

—JODY STRAND BAKER, MONTANA

PREP: 15 MIN. **COOK:** 5 MIN./BATCH **MAKES:** 4 SERVINGS

- **2 eggs**
- **2 tablespoons carbonated water**
- **1 cup pancake mix**
- **½ teaspoon seasoned salt**
- **¼ teaspoon pepper**
- **4 catfish fillets (6 ounces each)**
- **Oil for deep-fat frying**

1. In a shallow bowl, whisk eggs and water. In another shallow bowl, combine the pancake mix, seasoned salt and pepper. Dip fillets in egg mixture, then coat with seasoned pancake mix.
2. In an electric skillet or deep-fat fryer, heat oil to 375°. Fry fillets, a few at a time, for 2-3 minutes or until golden brown. Drain on paper towels.

Slow Cooker Hula Chicken

As long as you're cooking bacon for breakfast, save some for the slow cooker. In four hours, you'll be saying "Aloha!" to lunch.

—CINDY LUND VALLEY CENTER, CALIFORNIA

PREP: 15 MIN. **COOK:** 4 HOURS **MAKES:** 6 SERVINGS

- **6 bacon strips, divided**
- **6 boneless skinless chicken thighs (about 1½ pounds)**
- **¼ teaspoon salt**
- **⅛ teaspoon pepper**
- **½ cup chopped red onion**
- **1 cup crushed pineapple, drained**
- **¾ cup barbecue sauce**

1. Cut three bacon strips in half; cook until partially cooked but not crisp. Drain on paper towels.
2. Season chicken with salt and pepper; place in a 4- or 5-qt. slow cooker. Top each thigh with a half piece of bacon. Top with onion, pineapple and barbecue sauce.
3. Cover and cook on low for 4 hours or until a thermometer reads 180°. Cook remaining bacon until crisp; drain and crumble. Sprinkle over each serving.

Sausage Florentine Potpie

You won't find a meal like this in the freezer aisle, but you will be surprised how easy it is to make at home.

—**KENDRA DOSS** KANSAS CITY, MISSOURI

PREP: 30 MIN. **BAKE:** 25 MIN. + STANDING **MAKES:** 6 SERVINGS

- **1 pound bulk Italian sausage**
- **2½ cups sliced fresh mushrooms**
- **1 medium red onion, chopped**
- **3 garlic cloves, minced**
- **1 can (10¾ ounces) reduced-fat reduced-sodium condensed cream of mushroom soup, undiluted**
- **1 package (10 ounces) frozen chopped spinach, thawed and squeezed dry**
- **1 cup half-and-half cream**
- **1 cup shredded part-skim mozzarella cheese**
- **½ cup shredded Parmesan cheese**

TOPPING

- **5 sheets phyllo dough (14 inches x 9 inches)**
- **2 tablespoons butter, melted**
- **1 egg**
- **1 tablespoon water**

1. In a large skillet, cook sausage, mushrooms, onion and garlic over medium heat until no longer pink; drain. Stir in soup, spinach, cream and cheeses; cook and stir until cheese is melted.
2. Transfer to a greased 11-in. x 7-in. baking dish. Place a phyllo sheet over top; brush with some of the butter. Repeat with remaining phyllo dough and butter. Crimp edges of dough.
3. Whisk egg and water; brush over top. Bake, uncovered, at 350° for 25-30 minutes or until golden brown. Let stand for 10 minutes before serving.

Roast Beef Potpie

Everyone in the family will want a piece of this pie, and every home cook will appreciate a helping hand from packaged beef roast and refrigerated pie pastry!

—**PATRICIA MYERS** MARYVILLE, TENNESSEE

PREP: 30 MIN. **BAKE:** 30 MIN. **MAKES:** 6 SERVINGS

- **10 fresh baby carrots, chopped**
- **6 small red potatoes, cubed**
- **1 medium onion, chopped**
- **2 tablespoons olive oil**
- **1 package (17 ounces) refrigerated beef roast au jus, coarsely chopped**
- **2 tablespoons minced fresh cilantro**
- **¼ teaspoon salt**
- **¼ teaspoon pepper**
- **⅓ cup all-purpose flour**
- **2¼ cups reduced-sodium beef broth**
- **1 sheet refrigerated pie pastry**
- **1 egg, beaten**

1. In a large skillet, saute the carrots, potatoes and onion in oil until crisp-tender. Add the beef roast, cilantro, salt and pepper. Combine flour and broth until smooth; gradually stir into the pan. Bring to a boil; cook and stir for 2 minutes or until thickened.
2. Transfer to a 9-in. deep-dish pie plate. Place pie pastry over filling. Trim, seal and flute edges. Cut slits in pastry; brush with egg. Bake at 375° for 30-35 minutes or until golden brown.

Turkey Potpie Cups

My children always look forward to turkey or chicken leftovers since I created this recipe. Refrigerated flaky biscuits make perfect individual potpie crusts.

—**KAREN WOODARD** MUSTANG, OKLAHOMA

PREP: 25 MIN. **BAKE:** 20 MIN. **MAKES:** 8 SERVINGS

- **1 tube (16.3 ounces) large refrigerated flaky biscuits**
- **3 cups cubed cooked turkey**
- **3 cups turkey gravy**
- **2¼ cups frozen mixed vegetables**
- **½ teaspoon salt**
- **½ teaspoon pepper**
- **1 cup French-fried onions**
- **2¼ cups mashed potatoes**
- **⅓ cup 2% milk**
- **½ cup shredded cheddar cheese**

1. On a lightly floured surface, roll each biscuit into an 8-in. circle. Press onto the bottoms and up the sides of eight greased 8-oz. ramekins.
2. In a large saucepan, combine the turkey, gravy, vegetables, salt and pepper. Bring to a boil. Reduce heat; simmer, uncovered, for 5 minutes. Sprinkle onions into ramekins; top with turkey mixture. In a small bowl, combine potatoes and milk; spread over tops. Sprinkle with cheese.
3. Bake at 375° for 18-22 minutes or until golden brown.

EASY AS 1, 2, 3

BRING COMFORT TO THE TABLE WITH THREE HOMESPUN VARIATIONS ON POTPIE

The days of spending hours in the kitchen, simmering broth, roasting chicken and preparing from-scratch pastry—all in the name of getting a homemade potpie on the dinner table—aren't completely lost to us. But it's nice to have some faster options. We think the readers who sent us these recipes would agree, and we salute their homemade touches on store-bought items.

Cooking for Kids

"Tangy barbecue sauce, fluffy biscuits and cheddar cheese make these muffins real kid-pleasers! Don't hesitate to try them with ground turkey or other shredded cheeses for a change."

KAREN KENNEY HARVARD, ILLINOIS
Farmhouse Barbecue Muffins, page 73

Watermelon Shark

Take a bite out of summer boredom with this kid-friendly food project that's both fresh and flavorful.
—TASTE OF HOME TEST KITCHEN

PREP: 1 HOUR **MAKES:** 32 SERVINGS

- **1 large watermelon**
- **1 medium cantaloupe, peeled, seeded and cubed**
- **2 cups seedless red grapes**
- **2 cups fresh blueberries**
- **2 medium oranges**
- **1 jar (12 ounces) pineapple preserves**
- **Swedish Fish candies**

1. With a long sharp knife, cut a slice from one end of watermelon so that watermelon stands at an angle. For mouth, using a sharp razor blade or small knife, score the mouth opening. Using a sharp knife, cut the mouth and remove. Using a sharp knife cut out teeth. Remove rind from teeth.
2. For dorsal fin, cut a triangle from removed rind. Attach fin to shark with toothpicks. For eyes, cut one grape in half. Attach with toothpicks. Stand shark on a serving plate.
3. Remove fruit from inside the watermelon; cut into cubes. In a large bowl, combine the watermelon, cantaloupe, grapes and blueberries.
4. Finely grate the peel from oranges and squeeze juice. In a small bowl, combine the preserves, orange juice and peel; add to fruit and toss gently. Spoon into shark and arrange remaining fruit salad around the base. Garnish with fish.

All-Star Ice Cream Sandwiches

You can make these bite-sized sweet treats with only four on-hand ingredients!
—TASTE OF HOME TEST KITCHEN

PREP: 15 MIN. + FREEZING **MAKES:** 4 SERVINGS

- **½ cup chocolate chip cookie dough ice cream, softened**
- **8 Oreo cookies**
- **6 ounces milk chocolate candy coating, melted**
- **Red, white and blue sprinkles**

1. Spoon 2 tablespoons of ice cream onto half of the cookies. Top with remaining cookies. Spoon melted coating over tops. Decorate with sprinkles. Place on a baking sheet; freeze for at least 1 hour.

Candy Craze Ice Cream Sandwiches

These ice cream sandwiches have a little bit of everything in them to satisfy almost anyone's cravings.
—TASTE OF HOME TEST KITCHEN

PREP: 20 MIN. + FREEZING **MAKES:** 4 SERVINGS

- **4 scoops Whoppers ice cream**
- **12 large chocolate chip cookies**
- **4 scoops peanut butter ice cream with peanut butter cup pieces**
- **½ cup M&M's minis**
- **½ cup Reese's mini peanut butter cups**

1. Place a scoop of Whoppers ice cream on each of four cookies. Top each with another cookie and a scoop of peanut butter ice cream. Top with remaining cookies.
2. Press M&M's and peanut butter cups into sides. Wrap in plastic wrap. Place on a baking sheet; freeze for at least 1 hour.

Cereal & Milk Ice Cream Sandwiches

We turned favorite breakfast cereals into sweet treats that kids will love! As for grown-ups, what better way to satisfy your inner child?
—TASTE OF HOME TEST KITCHEN

PREP: 10 MIN. + FREEZING **MAKES:** 4 SERVINGS

- **3 tablespoons Cap'n Crunch cereal**
- **3 tablespoons Froot Loops cereal**
- **3 tablespoons Fruity Pebbles cereal**
- **4 Rice Krispies treats (3.12 ounces each), halved lengthwise**
- **1 cup dulce de leche ice cream, softened**
- **4 teaspoons hot caramel ice cream topping, warmed**

1. Combine the cereals in a shallow bowl. Spread 1/4 cup ice cream onto the bottom half of each Rice Krispies treat. Drizzle with ice cream topping. Replace top half of Rice Krispies. Roll sides in cereal mixture. Place on a baking sheet; freeze for at least 1 hour.

Super-Stuffed Mexican Potatoes

These taters are packed! Your whole family will enjoy this hearty stuffed meal idea.
—STEVE WESTPHAL WIND LAKE, WISCONSIN

PREP/TOTAL TIME: 25 MIN **MAKES:** 4 SERVINGS

- **4 large baking potatoes**
- **1 jar (16 ounces) black bean and corn salsa**
- **1 package (6 ounces) ready-to-use grilled chicken breast strips**
- **1 cup cubed process cheese (Velveeta)**
- **1 medium tomato, chopped**
- **Optional toppings: chopped green onions, sliced ripe olives and sour cream**

1. Scrub and pierce potatoes; place on a microwave-safe plate. Microwave, uncovered, on high for 15-17 minutes or until tender, turning once.
2. Meanwhile, in a large saucepan, combine salsa, chicken and cheese. Cook and stir over medium heat until cheese is melted.

3. Cut an "X" in the top of each potato; fluff pulp with a fork. Spoon salsa mixture over potatoes and sprinkle with tomato. Serve with toppings of your choice.
Editor's Note: *This recipe was tested in a 1,100-watt microwave.*

Tasty Tacos

A taco seasoning made from scratch with pantry staples jazzes up ground beef, turning a weeknight into an all-out fiesta. Add your favorite toppings, and dinner is served!
—REBECCA LEVESQUE ST. GEORGE, NEW BRUNSWICK

PREP/TOTAL TIME: 30 MIN. **MAKES:** 4 SERVINGS

- **1 pound lean ground beef (90% lean)**
- **1 medium onion, finely chopped**
- **1 garlic clove, minced**
- **½ cup water**
- **1 tablespoon chili powder**
- **1½ teaspoons ground cumin**
- **½ teaspoon salt**
- **½ teaspoon paprika**
- **½ teaspoon pepper**
- **¼ teaspoon dried oregano**
- **¼ teaspoon crushed red pepper flakes**
- **8 taco shells, warmed**
- **Optional toppings: shredded lettuce, chopped tomatoes, sliced green onions and shredded cheddar cheese**

1. In a large skillet, cook the beef, onion and garlic over medium heat until meat is no longer pink; drain. Stir in the water and seasonings. Bring to a boil. Reduce heat; simmer, uncovered, for 5-10 minutes or until thickened.
2. Spoon beef mixture into taco shells. Serve with toppings of your choice.

Teddy Bear Sandwiches

Give peanut butter and jelly a fun twist! These cute teddy bear sandwiches will especially appeal to little ones. Try making them with different cutouts and shapes, too.

—TASTE OF HOME TEST KITCHEN

PREP/TOTAL TIME: 20 MIN. **MAKES:** 4 SANDWICHES

- **4 slices bread**
- **⅔ cup creamy peanut butter**
- **2 tablespoons honey**
- **1 medium banana, thinly sliced or ¼ cup seedless strawberry jam**
- **6 raisins, halved**

1. Using a 3½-in. teddy bear cookie cutter, cut out two bear shapes from each slice of bread.
2. In a small bowl, combine peanut butter and honey. Spread over four teddy bear cutouts. Top with banana slices or spread with jam and remaining bear cutouts. Arrange three raisins on each for eyes and nose.

123 MAKE IT SIMPLE

Kids can help! Ages 3 to 7: retrieve and measure items, cut out bears, combine peanut butter and honey and arrange the raisins. Ages 8 to 12: spread peanut butter mixture and assemble sandwiches.

Italian Dipping Sticks

PREP/TOTAL TIME: 25 MIN. **MAKES:** 2 DOZEN (1¼ CUPS SAUCE)

- **1 tube (11 ounces) refrigerated breadsticks**
- **¼ cup grated Parmesan cheese**
- **½ teaspoon Italian seasoning**
- **1 cup pizza sauce**
- **¼ cup shredded part-skim mozzarella cheese**

1. Unroll breadstick dough; cut each piece in half widthwise and separate. In a large resealable plastic bag, combine Parmesan cheese and Italian seasoning. Add dough pieces, a few at a time, and shake to coat.
2. Place on an ungreased baking sheet. Bake at 375° for 10-13 minutes or until golden brown.
3. Meanwhile, place pizza sauce in a microwave-safe bowl. Cover; microwave on high for 1-2 minutes or until bubbly. Sprinkle with mozzarella cheese. Microwave 1 minute longer or until cheese is melted. Serve with breadsticks.

“The pizza-like flavors in these simple breadsticks will be a hit with all ages. They'd be terrific as an after-school snack or as sleepover treats.”

—MICHELLE REVELLE GUYTON, GEORGIA

Tangy barbecue sauce, fluffy biscuits and cheddar cheese make these muffins real kid-pleasers! Don't hesitate to try them with ground turkey or other shredded cheeses for a change. —**KAREN KENNEY** HARVARD, ILLINOIS

Farmhouse Barbecue Muffins

PREP: 20 MIN. **BAKE:** 20 MIN.
MAKES: 10 SERVINGS

- **1 tube (10 ounces) refrigerated buttermilk biscuits**
- **1 pound ground beef**
- **½ cup ketchup**
- **3 tablespoons brown sugar**
- **1 tablespoon cider vinegar**
- **½ teaspoon chili powder**
- **1 cup (4 ounces) shredded cheddar cheese**

1. Separate dough into 10 biscuits; flatten into 5-in. circles. Press each onto the bottom and up the sides of a greased muffin cup; set aside.
2. In a skillet, cook beef over medium heat until no longer pink; drain. In a small bowl, combine the ketchup, brown sugar, vinegar and chili powder; add to beef and mix well.
3. Divide the meat mixture among biscuit-lined muffins cups, using about ¼ cup for each. Sprinkle with cheese. Bake at 375° for 18-20 minutes or until golden brown. Cool for 5 minutes before serving.

Sunny Breakfast Smoothies

Tofu adds body to this peach-and-cinnamon-flavored smoothie. Your kids will love the vibrant colors and delicious blend of healthy ingredients you might not otherwise think to put together.
—TASTE OF HOME TEST KITCHEN

PREP/TOTAL TIME: 15 MIN.
MAKES: 2 SERVINGS

- **½ cup fresh baby carrots**
- **2 tablespoons water**
- **1 can (11 ounces) mandarin oranges, drained**
- **1 cup frozen unsweetened sliced peaches**
- **½ cup orange juice**
- **½ crushed ice**
- **½ cup silken firm tofu**
- **¼ teaspoon ground cinnamon**

1. Place carrots and water in a microwave-safe bowl; cover. Microwave on high for 2-3 minutes or until carrots are tender. Drain and rinse in cold water.
2. In a blender, combine the carrots, oranges, peaches, juice, ice, tofu and cinnamon; cover and process for 1 minute or until blended. Pour into chilled glasses; serve immediately.

Lion and Lamb Cupcakes

March may come in like a lion and go out like a lamb, but in the meantime, there are adorable cupcakes to be made! These sweet treats are delicious any time of year—and offer an easy project that kids can help to create.

—TASTE OF HOME TEST KITCHEN

PREP: 1 HOUR **BAKE:** 20 MIN. + COOLING **MAKES:** 2 DOZEN

1 package (18¼ ounces) cake mix of your choice
1 can (16 ounces) vanilla frosting
Orange, blue and pink paste food coloring
Assorted decorations: snack-size Mounds candy bars, jelly beans, flaked coconut, chocolate jimmies and Pull-n-Peel licorice

1. Prepare and bake cake mix according to package directions for cupcakes; cool completely. Tint desired amounts of frosting orange, blue and pink.

2. For lambs, frost cupcakes white and attach a Mounds candy bar for face. Pipe additional frosting over top of candy bar for tuft of hair between the ears. Attach jelly beans for ears, sprinkle body with coconut and pipe frosting for eyes and nose.

3. For lions, frost cupcakes with orange frosting. Sprinkle edges with jimmies and attach pieces of licorice for mane. Attach jelly beans for ears. Pipe faces with frosting.

Best-Ever Pepperoni Pizza

You'll love the cheesy surprise inside the crust and the jazzed-up sauce in this fun, from-scratch pizza.

—SCOTTIE ORR-WEDEVEN GRAND RAPIDS, MICHIGAN

PREP: 30 MIN. + STANDING **BAKE:** 10 MIN. **MAKES:** 8 SLICES

1 package (¼ ounce) quick-rise yeast
1 cup warm water (120° to 130°)
2 tablespoons sugar
½ teaspoon salt
2 tablespoons plus 2 teaspoons olive oil, divided
2½ to 3 cups all-purpose flour
4 pieces string cheese
½ teaspoon Italian seasoning

SAUCE

1 can (8 ounces) tomato sauce
1 teaspoon sugar
1 teaspoon olive oil
¼ teaspoon salt
¼ teaspoon garlic powder
¼ teaspoon dried oregano
¼ teaspoon lemon juice
⅛ teaspoon dried thyme
⅛ teaspoon dried basil
⅛ teaspoon cayenne pepper

TOPPINGS

1 package (3 ounces) sliced pepperoni
2 cups (8 ounces) shredded Italian cheese blend

1. In a large bowl, dissolve yeast in warm water. Add the sugar, salt, 2 tablespoons oil and 2½ cups flour. Beat until smooth. Stir in enough remaining flour to form a soft dough (dough will be sticky).

2. Turn onto a lightly floured surface; knead until smooth and elastic, about 6-8 minutes. Place in a greased bowl, turning once to grease the top. Cover and let rest in a warm place for 10 minutes.

3. On a lightly floured surface, roll dough into a 15-in. circle. Transfer to a greased 14-in. pizza pan, letting dough drape over the edge. Cut string cheese pieces in half lengthwise; place around edge of pan. Fold the dough over string cheese; pinch to seal.
4. Prick dough thoroughly with a fork. Brush with remaining oil; sprinkle with Italian seasoning. Bake at 425° for 10-12 minutes or until golden brown.
5. In a small saucepan, combine the sauce ingredients. Bring to a boil. Reduce heat; simmer, uncovered, for 15 minutes. Spread over crust. Arrange pepperoni over top; sprinkle with Italian cheese blend. Bake for 10-15 minutes or until cheese is melted.

Bacon Cheeseburger Rice

My husband and I thought an original skillet dish lacked pizzazz, so we created a tastier version. I've had teenage nieces and nephews request the recipe after their very first bite!

—JOYCE WHIPPS WEST DES MOINES, IOWA

PREP/TOTAL TIME: 30 MIN. **MAKES:** 4 SERVINGS

- **1 pound ground beef**
- **1¾ cups water**
- **⅔ cup barbecue sauce**
- **1 tablespoon prepared mustard**
- **2 teaspoons dried minced onion**
- **½ teaspoon pepper**
- **2 cups uncooked instant rice**
- **1 cup (4 ounces) shredded cheddar cheese**
- **⅓ cup chopped dill pickles**
- **5 bacon strips, cooked and crumbled**

1. In a large skillet over medium heat, cook beef until no longer pink; drain. Add the water, barbecue sauce, mustard, onion and pepper.
2. Bring to a boil; stir in the rice. Sprinkle with cheese. Reduce heat; cover and simmer for 5 minutes. Sprinkle with pickles and bacon.

Pizza on a Stick

PREP/TOTAL TIME: 30 MIN. **MAKES:** 5 SERVINGS

- **8 ounces Italian turkey sausage links**
- **2 cups whole fresh mushrooms**
- **2 cups cherry tomatoes**
- **1 medium onion, cut into 1-inch pieces**
- **1 large green pepper, cut into 1-inch pieces**
- **30 slices turkey pepperoni (2 ounces)**
- **1 tube (13.8 ounces) refrigerated pizza crust**
- **1½ cups (6 ounces) shredded part-skim mozzarella cheese**
- **1¼ cups pizza sauce, warmed**

1. In a large nonstick skillet, cook sausage over medium heat until no longer pink; drain. When cool enough to handle, cut sausage into 20 pieces. On 10 metal or soaked wooden skewers, alternately thread the sausage, vegetables and pepperoni.
2. Unroll pizza dough onto a lightly floured surface; cut widthwise into 1-in.-wide strips. Starting at the pointed end of a prepared skewer, pierce skewer through one end of dough strip and press dough against last ingredients on the skewer. Spiral-wrap dough strip around skewer, allowing vegetables and meats to peek through. Wrap the remaining end of dough strip around skewer above the first ingredient. Repeat with remaining dough strips and prepared skewers.
3. Arrange kabobs on a baking sheet coated with cooking spray. Bake at 400° for 10-12 minutes or until vegetables are tender and pizza crust is golden. Immediately sprinkle with cheese. Serve with pizza sauce.

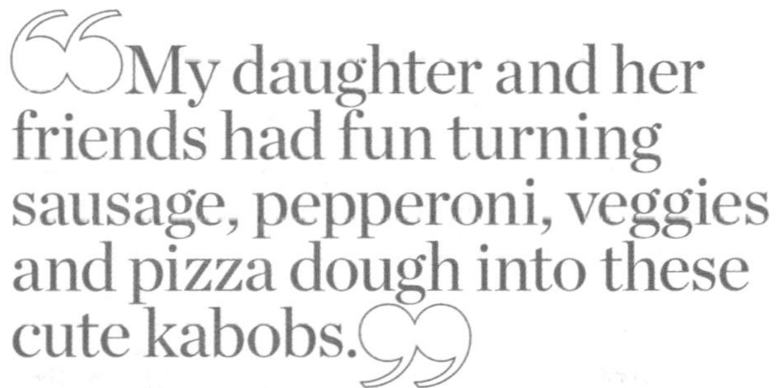

—CHARLENE WOODS NORFOLK, VIRGINIA

top tip

Homemade spaghetti sauce is great for hiding cooked veggies, such as grated carrots, chopped spinach or diced sweet potatoes.

Family-Favorite Spaghetti Sauce

Friends will rave about this recipe. Serve over pasta, and round out the meal with a simple salad and garlic bread.

—HELEN ROWE SPRING LAKE, MICHIGAN

PREP: 30 MIN. **COOK:** 6 HOURS
MAKES: 9 SERVINGS (2¼ QUARTS)

- **1 pound bulk Italian sausage**
- **½ pound ground beef**
- **1 large onion, chopped**
- **1 celery rib, chopped**
- **3 garlic cloves, minced**
- **1 tablespoon olive oil**
- **1 can (28 ounces) diced tomatoes**
- **1 can (10¾ ounces) condensed tomato soup, undiluted**
- **1 can (8 ounces) mushroom stems and pieces, drained**
- **1 can (8 ounces) tomato sauce**
- **1 can (6 ounces) tomato paste**
- **1 tablespoon sugar**
- **½ teaspoon pepper**
- **½ teaspoon dried basil**
- **¼ teaspoon dried oregano**
- **Hot cooked spaghetti**

1. In a large skillet, cook the sausage, beef, onion, celery and garlic in oil over medium heat until meat is no longer pink; drain. In a 4-qt. slow cooker, combine the diced tomatoes, tomato soup, mushrooms, tomato sauce, tomato paste, sugar and seasonings. Stir in sausage mixture.
2. Cover and cook on low for 6-8 hours or until flavors are blended. Serve with spaghetti.

Quick Crisp Snack Bars

My daughters have loved these nutritious snacks since they were in grade school. Now, both are adults and still make these bars when they want a quick treat.

—URSULA MAURER WAUWATOSA, WISCONSIN

PREP/TOTAL TIME: 30 MIN.
MAKES: 1 DOZEN

- **½ cup honey**
- **½ cup reduced-fat chunky peanut butter**
- **½ cup nonfat dry milk powder**
- **4 cups Rice Krispies**

1. In a large saucepan, combine the honey, peanut butter and milk powder. Cook and stir over low heat until blended.
2. Remove from the heat; stir in cereal. Press into an 8-in. square dish coated with cooking spray. Let stand until set. Cut into bars.

Crab Sandwiches

Feeling crabby? Beat the blues and create some happy memories of time spent together with the kids making these adorable sandwiches.

—TASTE OF HOME TEST KITCHEN

PREP/TOTAL TIME: 25 MIN. **MAKES:** 4 SERVINGS

- **2 large sweet red peppers**
- **1 small red onion**
- **2 hard-cooked eggs**
- **4 pitted ripe olives, halved**
- **4 croissants, split**
- **Fresh parsley sprigs**
- **1 package (8 ounces) flake-style imitation crabmeat**
- **¼ cup mayonnaise**
- **1 teaspoon lemon juice**

1. Chop ½ cup pepper and 2 tablespoons onion; set aside for filling. From remaining peppers, cut four sets of claws and legs. Cut four thin slices of remaining onion for mouths.
2. Cut eight thin slices of egg white. Using toothpicks, attach egg slices and olive halves to tops of croissants for eyes. Tuck in parsley for eyelashes.
3. In a small bowl, combine the crabmeat, mayonnaise, lemon juice and reserved red pepper and onion. Spoon onto croissant bottoms; replace tops. Add the claws, legs and mouths.

SIMPLE SWAP

If your children are not fond of crabmeat, then fill the sandwiches with tuna or chicken salad—or whatever deli meat they enjoy.

Peanut Butter-Graham Snack Mix

Kids of all ages will enjoy munching my richly sweet mix after school or while during homework. It's a can't-stop-munching treat!
—**DIANE SPOTTS** ELMIRA, NEW YORK

PREP: 25 MIN. + STANDING **MAKES:** 3¾ QUARTS

- **6 cups Golden Grahams**
- **4 cups raisin bran**
- **¾ cup mixed nuts**
- **¾ cup pecan halves**
- **1 cup (6 ounces) semisweet chocolate chips**
- **1 cup creamy peanut butter**
- **¼ cup butter, cubed**
- **½ teaspoon vanilla extract**
- **2½ cups confectioners' sugar**

1. Combine the cereals and nuts in a large bowl. In a large heavy saucepan over low heat, melt the chocolate chips, peanut butter and butter; stir until smooth. Remove from the heat; stir in vanilla. Pour over cereal mixture and toss gently to coat.
2. Place confectioners' sugar in a large bag; add cereal mixture. Close bag and shake to coat. Spread onto waxed paper; let stand until set. Store in airtight containers.

Strawberry Cheesecake Pops

Yum! Perfect on a summer afternoon, these cool bites taste like creamy strawberry cheesecake.
—**EMILY PAULY** HEWITT, TEXAS

PREP: 15 MIN. + FREEZING **MAKES:** 9 POPS

- **2 cups 2% milk**
- **½ cup heavy whipping cream**
- **1 package (3.4 ounces) instant cheesecake or vanilla pudding mix**
- **2 tablespoons strawberry drink mix**
- **1 cup chopped fresh strawberries**
- **Fresh mint leaves and quartered fresh strawberries**
- **9 Popsicle sticks**

1. Place the milk, cream, pudding mix and drink mix in a blender; cover and process until blended. Let stand for five minutes or until soft-set; stir in strawberries.
2. Place foil-lined muffin cups in a muffin pan; fill each liner with ⅓ cup strawberry mixture. Garnish with mint leaves and strawberries. Cover pan with foil and insert sticks in the middle of each cup; freeze. Peel off liners to serve.
Editor's Note: *This recipe was tested with Nesquik brand drink mix.*

Pinwheel Pizza Snacks

They look beautiful and taste fantastic—talk about a winning combination! My pretty pizza snacks make easy appetizers, but you could also serve them with a salad for a quick lunch.

—BONNIE HAWKINS ELKHORN, WISCONSIN

PREP/TOTAL TIME: 30 MIN. **MAKES:** 16 APPETIZERS

- **1 tube (8 ounces) refrigerated crescent rolls**
- **⅓ cup pizza sauce**
- **¼ cup grated Parmesan cheese**
- **½ cup chopped seeded tomatoes**
- **⅓ cup shredded part-skim mozzarella cheese**
- **Fresh basil leaves, thinly sliced**

1. Unroll crescent dough into one long rectangle; seal seams and perforations. Spread pizza sauce to within 1 in. of edges; sprinkle with Parmesan cheese. Roll up jelly-roll style, starting with a short side; pinch seams to seal. Cut into 16 slices.

2. Place pinwheels, cut side down, on a greased baking sheet. Top each with tomatoes and mozzarella cheese. Bake at 375° for 11-13 minutes or until golden brown and cheese is melted. Sprinkle with basil.

Alligator Cookie Pops

Our talented food styling team created these adorable cookie pops for the reptile lover in your family. They're easier to make than you might think and use everyday ingredients.

—TASTE OF HOME TEST KITCHEN

PREP: 1 HOUR + STANDING **MAKES:** 1 DOZEN

- **12 circus peanut candies**
- **14 lollipop sticks**
- **1 package (14 ounces) green Wilton candy melts**
- **12 Nutter Butter cookies**
- **24 miniature semisweet chocolate chips (about ½ teaspoon)**
- **24 semisweet chocolate chips (about 1 tablespoon)**
- **⅓ cup white baking chips, melted**
- **⅓ cup semisweet chocolate chips, melted**

1. Cut a slit in each circus peanut, forming a mouth. Using two lollipop sticks, prop mouths open. Let stand for 30 minutes.

2. In a microwave, melt candy melts; stir until smooth. Twist apart cookies. Dip the end of a lollipop stick into melted coating and place on a cookie half; replace cookie top. Repeat. Place pops on a waxed paper-lined baking sheet; refrigerate for 10 minutes or until set.

3. Meanwhile, dip a circus peanut in coating and allow excess to drip off. Place on waxed paper. Repeat with remaining circus peanuts; let stand until set.

4. Reheat candy melts if necessary; dip a cookie pop in coating and allow excess to drip off. Insert stick into a Styrofoam block to stand. While wet, position a coated circus peanut on the cookie for a head. Repeat.

5. For eyes, attach a miniature chocolate chip to each chocolate chip using melted white chips. Attach to head using melted chocolate. Using remaining melted chocolate, pipe nostrils onto faces; pipe teeth with melted white chips. Let stand until set.

Cook Once, Eat Twice

"Check your pantry; you probably have everything needed to turn these succulent ribs into a sweet, tangy, fork-tender treat."

ANNETTE THOMPSON WOODBURY, VERMONT
Slow Cooked BBQ Pork Ribs, page 93

Parmesan Chicken Couscous

Simple ingredients make clever use of leftover chicken in an innovative dish any home cook would be proud to plate. I like to serve it with a side of fresh fruit.

—**LISA ABBOTT** NEW BERLIN, WISCONSIN

PREP/TOTAL TIME: 20 MIN. **MAKES:** 4 SERVINGS

- **½ cup chopped walnuts**
- **2 teaspoons olive oil, divided**
- **3 garlic cloves, minced**
- **2 cups chopped fresh spinach**
- **1½ cups cubed cooked chicken**
- **1¼ cups water**
- **2 teaspoons dried basil**
- **¼ teaspoon pepper**
- **1 package (5.9 ounces) Parmesan couscous**
- **¼ cup grated Parmesan cheese**

1. In a large saucepan, cook walnuts over medium heat in 1 teaspoon oil for 2-3 minutes or until toasted. Remove and set aside.

2. In the same pan, saute garlic in remaining oil for 1 minute. Add the spinach, chicken, water, basil and pepper. Bring to a boil. Stir in couscous. Remove from the heat; cover and let stand for 5-10 minutes or until water is absorbed. Fluff with a fork. Stir in walnuts and sprinkle with cheese.

Lemon & Sage Roasted Chicken

Whether it's soaking in marinade or baking in the oven, this easy-to-prepare chicken allows ample hands-free time.

—**JAN VALDEZ** CHICAGO, ILLINOIS

PREP: 20 MIN. + MARINATING **BAKE:** 2¼ HOURS + STANDING
MAKES: 6 SERVINGS

- **¼ cup lemon juice**
- **¼ cup plus 3 tablespoons olive oil, divided**
- **5 garlic cloves, minced**
- **2 tablespoons minced fresh sage**
- **1 roasting chicken (6 to 7 pounds)**
- **2 tablespoons butter, softened**
- **1 medium lemon, cut into wedges**
- **8 medium potatoes, quartered**
- **2 medium onions, quartered**
- **½ teaspoon salt**
- **¼ teaspoon pepper**

1. In a 2-gallon resealable plastic bag, combine the lemon juice, 1/4 cup oil, garlic and sage. Add the chicken; seal bag and turn to coat. Refrigerate for at least 4 hours. Drain and discard marinade.

2. With fingers, carefully loosen skin from the chicken; rub butter under the skin. Fill cavity with lemon wedges. Place chicken breast side up on a rack in a roasting pan.

3. In a large bowl, combine the potatoes, onions, salt, pepper and remaining oil. Arrange around chicken. Bake, uncovered, at 350° for 2 1/4 to 2 3/4 hours or until a thermometer reads 180°. Cover loosely with foil if chicken browns too quickly. Let stand for 15 minutes before carving.

Wonderfully tender, this tasty roast with sweet onions makes the perfect comfort food at the end of a long day.
—**JEANNIE KLUGH** LANCASTER, PENNSYLVANIA

Caramelized Onion Chuck Roast

PREP: 25 MIN. **COOK:** 8 HOURS
MAKES: 4 SERVINGS PLUS LEFTOVERS

- **1 cup water**
- **1 cup beer or beef broth**
- **½ cup beef broth**
- **¼ cup packed brown sugar**
- **3 tablespoons Dijon mustard**
- **2 tablespoons cider vinegar**
- **1 boneless beef chuck roast (4 pounds), trimmed**
- **1 teaspoon onion salt**
- **1 teaspoon coarsely ground pepper**
- **1 tablespoon olive oil**
- **3 large sweet onions, halved and sliced**
- **2 tablespoons cornstarch**
- **2 tablespoons cold water**

1. In a large bowl, combine the first six ingredients; set aside. Sprinkle roast with onion salt and pepper. In a large skillet, brown meat in oil on all sides. Place onions and roast in a 5-qt. slow cooker; pour beer mixture over top. Cover and cook on low for 8-10 hours or until meat is tender.

2. Remove roast and onions and keep warm. Skim fat from cooking juices; transfer 2 cups to a small saucepan. Bring liquid to a boil. Combine cornstarch and water until smooth; gradually stir into the pan. Bring to a boil; cook and stir for 2 minutes or until thickened.

3. Serve with half of the roast and onions. Save the remaining roast, onions and cooking juices for Vegetable Beef & Barley Soup or save for another use.

Vegetable Beef & Barley Soup

Winter weather calls for steaming bowls of this hearty soup. Chuck roast leftovers add extra homemade flavor.
—**JEANNIE KLUGH** LANCASTER, PENNSYLVANIA

PREP/TOTAL TIME: 30 MIN.
MAKES: 4 SERVINGS

- **Reserved leftovers from Caramelized Onion Chuck Roast**
- **3 cups beef broth**
- **2 cups frozen mixed vegetables**
- **¼ cup quick-cooking barley**
- **1 teaspoon ground mustard**

1. In a large saucepan, combine all the ingredients. Bring to a boil. Reduce heat; simmer, uncovered, for 15-20 minutes or until barley is tender.

Honey & Spice Baked Chicken

Bring summertime flavor to the table with this moist chicken entree that will remind you of backyard barbecues. The hint of heat is tempered by sweet honey—but for pickier palates, simply decrease the cayenne pepper.

—LISA GNYP SHELBY TOWNSHIP, MICHIGAN

PREP/TOTAL TIME: 30 MIN.
MAKES: 5 SERVINGS PLUS 3 COOKED CHICKEN BREAST HALVES

- **3 teaspoons garlic powder**
- **3 teaspoons chili powder**
- **1½ teaspoons salt**
- **1½ teaspoons ground cumin**
- **1½ teaspoons paprika**
- **¾ teaspoon cayenne pepper**
- **8 boneless skinless chicken breasts (5 ounces each)**
- **6 tablespoons honey**
- **2 teaspoons cider vinegar**

1. Combine the first six ingredients; rub over chicken. Transfer to a greased 15-in. x 10-in. x 1-in. baking pan.
2. Bake at 375° for 25-30 minutes or until juices run clear. Combine honey and vinegar; baste over chicken during the last 10 minutes of cooking. Save three chicken breast halves for Chicken Chimichangas or save for another use.

Chicken Chimichangas

Crispy outside with gooey cheese inside, this homemade Mexican favorite had our testers saying, "Hello, delicious!" Pair with Spanish rice or serve with chips and salsa for a restaurant-quality meal that's table-ready in minutes.

—BRIDGET HARRISON CEDAR HILL, MISSOURI

PREP/TOTAL TIME: 20 MIN. **MAKES:** 6 SERVINGS

- **3 Honey & Spice Baked Chicken breast halves, cubed**
- **1 cup refried beans**
- **1 teaspoon chili powder**
- **½ teaspoon ground cumin**
- **¼ teaspoon garlic salt**
- **¼ teaspoon hot pepper sauce**
- **⅛ teaspoon cayenne pepper**
- **6 flour tortillas (8 inches), warmed**
- **¾ cup shredded cheddar cheese**
- **Oil for deep-fat frying**
- **Optional toppings: sour cream, salsa con queso dip, shredded lettuce, chopped tomatoes and chopped seeded jalapeno pepper**

1. In a small microwave-safe bowl, combine the first seven ingredients. Cover and microwave on high for 1½ to 2 minutes or until heated through. Spoon ⅓ cup chicken mixture off-center on each tortilla; sprinkle with cheese. Fold up edge nearest filling; fold in both sides and roll up. Secure with a toothpick.
2. In an electric skillet or deep-fat fryer, heat oil to 375°. Cook the chimichangas until golden brown, turning to cook all sides. Drain on paper towels. Serve with toppings of your choice.

Chilly Night Beef Stew

Hearty and comforting any time of the year, this nutritious slow-cooked stew is one of our favorites.

—**JANINE TALBOT** SANTAQUIN, UTAH

PREP: 30 MIN. **COOK:** 8½ HOURS **MAKES:** 10 SERVINGS

- **6 tablespoons all-purpose flour**
- **1½ teaspoons salt, divided**
- **1 teaspoon pepper, divided**
- **2 pounds beef stew meat**
- **¼ cup olive oil**
- **4 medium potatoes, peeled and cubed**
- **6 medium carrots, sliced**
- **2 medium onions, halved and sliced**
- **4 celery ribs, sliced**
- **2 cans (14½ ounces each) beef broth**
- **2 cans (11½ ounces each) V8 juice**
- **2 teaspoons Worcestershire sauce**
- **6 garlic cloves, minced**
- **2 bay leaves**
- **1 teaspoon dried thyme**
- **½ teaspoon dried basil**
- **½ teaspoon paprika**
- **6 tablespoons cornstarch**
- **½ cup cold water**

1. Combine the flour, 1 teaspoon salt and ½ teaspoon pepper in a large resealable plastic bag. Add beef, a few pieces at a time, and shake to coat.
2. Brown beef in oil in batches in a large skillet. Transfer meat and drippings to a 6-qt. slow cooker. Add the potatoes, carrots, onion and celery. Combine the broth, juice, Worcestershire sauce, garlic, bay leaf, thyme, basil, paprika and remaining salt and pepper; pour over top.
3. Cover and cook on low for 8-10 hours or until meat and vegetables are tender. Combine cornstarch and water until smooth; stir into stew. Cover and cook 30 minutes longer or until thickened. Discard bay leaves.

Layered Potato Beef Casserole

Beef stew gives a repeat performance that'll earn rave reviews. Best of all, with just a little bit of hands-on time, you'll have 50 full minutes to relax before dinner.

—**MARGIE WILLIAMS** MT. JULIET, TENNESSEE

PREP: 25 MIN. **BAKE:** 50 MIN. **MAKES:** 6 SERVINGS

- **3 tablespoons butter, divided**
- **2 tablespoons all-purpose flour**
- **¾ teaspoon dried rosemary, crushed**
- **¼ teaspoon pepper**
- **⅛ teaspoon salt**
- **2 cups 2% milk**
- **2 cups (8 ounces) shredded sharp cheddar cheese**
- **4 cups leftover beef stew**
- **4 medium Yukon potatoes, thinly sliced**
- **⅓ cup crushed butter-flavored crackers (about 8 crackers)**
- **1 tablespoon dried parsley flakes**
- **¼ teaspoon garlic powder**

1. Melt 2 tablespoons butter in a large saucepan. Stir in the flour, rosemary, pepper and salt until blended; gradually add milk. Bring to a boil; cook and stir for 2 minutes or until thickened. Remove from the heat; stir in cheese until melted.
2. Spoon 2 cups stew into a greased 2½ qt. baking dish. Layer with half of the potatoes and sauce mixture. Layer with remaining stew, potatoes and sauce.
3. Cover and bake at 400° for 45-50 minutes or until potatoes are tender. In a microwave, melt the remaining butter. Stir in the crackers, parsley and garlic powder. Sprinkle over casserole. Bake, uncovered, 5-10 minutes longer or until bubbly and topping is golden brown. Let stand for 10 minutes before serving.

Heavenly Citrus Ham

This recipe is special because it's based on the ham my grandma and mom used to make for holidays. Leftovers can be frozen up to 3 months, and thawed before using. You'll want to remember this recipe for Easter!

—PENNY HAWKINS MEBANE, NORTH CAROLINA

PREP: 15 MIN. **BAKE:** 1 HOUR 50 MIN. + STANDING
MAKES: 9 SERVINGS PLUS LEFTOVERS

- **1 fully cooked bone-in ham (6 to 8 pounds)**
- **Whole cloves**
- **1¼ cups orange soda**
- **1¼ cups orange marmalade**
- **½ cup packed brown sugar**
- **¼ cup Dijon mustard**

1. Place ham on a rack in a shallow roasting pan. Score the surface of the ham, making diamond shapes ½ in. deep; insert a clove in the center of each diamond. Loosely cover ham with foil. Bake at 325° for 1½ hours.
2. In a small saucepan, combine the soda, marmalade and brown sugar. Bring to a boil; cook until liquid is reduced by half, about 15 minutes. Stir in mustard.
3. Brush ham with some of the glaze; bake 20-30 minutes longer or until a thermometer reads 140°, basting occasionally with remaining glaze. Let stand 10 minutes before slicing.
4. Slice and cube 2 cups ham; save for Ham & Noodle Bake. Slice and serve remaining ham.

Ham & Noodle Bake

Bored by leftovers? Time to stir things up! Toss extra cooked ham, Mexican cheese and green chilies into a rich sauce. With oodles of noodles and lots of crunch, it's a party for your mouth.

—GLENDA WATTS TACOMA, WASHINGTON

PREP: 20 MIN. **BAKE:** 15 MIN. **MAKES:** 5 SERVINGS

- **5⅓ cups uncooked egg noodles**
- **2 cups cubed Heavenly Citrus Ham**
- **2 cups (8 ounces) shredded Mexican cheese blend**
- **1 can (10¾ ounces) condensed cream of mushroom soup, undiluted**
- **1 cup frozen peas**
- **½ cup sour cream**
- **1 can (4 ounces) chopped green chilies**
- **⅓ cup heavy whipping cream**
- **¼ teaspoon pepper**
- **1 can (6 ounces) French-fried onions, divided**

1. Cook noodles according to package directions. Meanwhile, in a large saucepan, combine the ham, cheese, soup, peas, sour cream, chilies, cream and pepper. Cook and stir over medium heat until cheese is melted. Drain noodles. Add noodles and half of the onions to ham mixture.
2. Transfer to a greased 13-in. x 9-in. baking dish. Sprinkle remaining onions over the top. Bake, uncovered, at 375° for 15-20 minutes or until golden brown.

Shhh! SIMPLE SECRET

To carve a bone-in ham, place it fat side up on a carving board. Using a meat fork to anchor the ham, make a horizontal cut with a carving knife from the one side of the ham to the bone. Position the cut in about the middle of the ham along the natural break between the muscles. Make a second cut from the top of the ham to the first cut. Remove the large meaty area of the ham from the bone. Remove the two remaining large meaty sections in the same manner. Place the ham pieces cut side down on a cutting board and cut into slices.

Buttery, colorful and flaky, this rich and impressive salmon will be a family favorite the first time around. Five smart ingredients, and you'll have just the leftovers you need for tomorrow night's pasta dish.
—**SONYA LABBE** WEST HOLLYWOOD, CALIFORNIA

Pesto Grilled Salmon

PREP/TOTAL TIME: 30 MIN
MAKES: 12 SERVINGS

- **1 salmon fillet (3 pounds)**
- **½ cup prepared pesto**
- **2 green onions, finely chopped**
- **¼ cup lemon juice**
- **2 garlic cloves, minced**

1. Using long-handled tongs, moisten a paper towel with cooking oil and lightly coat the grill rack. Place salmon skin side down on grill rack. Grill, covered, over medium heat or broil 4 in. from the heat for 5 minutes.

2. In a small bowl, combine the pesto, onions, lemon juice and garlic. Carefully spoon some of the pesto mixture over salmon. Grill 15-20 minutes longer or until fish flakes easily with a fork, basting occasionally with remaining pesto mixture.

Creamy Salmon Linguine

Extra Pesto Grilled Salmon gives this creamy pasta toss a luxurious taste and texture. We love it as is, but you could easily sub in any veggies you have on hand for the broccoli.
—**JACOB KITZMAN** SEATTLE, WASHINGTON

PREP/TOTAL TIME: 25 MIN.
MAKES: 4 SERVINGS

- **8 ounces uncooked linguine**
- **1 bunch broccoli, cut into florets**
- **2 garlic cloves, minced**
- **2 tablespoons butter**
- **2 cups heavy whipping cream**
- **2 tablespoons lemon juice**
- **1 pound fully cooked salmon, flaked**
- **¼ teaspoon salt**
- **¼ teaspoon pepper**
- **1 cup shredded Parmesan cheese**
- **3 tablespoons minced fresh basil or 1 tablespoon dried basil**
- **2 tablespoons capers, drained**
- **2 teaspoons grated lemon peel**

1. Cook linguine according to package directions, adding the broccoli during the last 5 minutes of cooking.

2. Meanwhile, in a large skillet, saute garlic in butter for 1 minute. Stir in cream and lemon juice. Bring to a boil. Reduce heat; simmer, uncovered, for 2-3 minutes or until slightly thickened, stirring constantly.

3. Add the salmon, salt and pepper; heat through. Drain linguine and broccoli; add to the skillet. Stir in the cheese, basil, capers and lemon peel.

Walsh Family Grilled Pork Tenderloins

Here's a favorite recipe from a dear friend. It's absolutely delicious, easy to make and a hit with both her family and mine!
—LISA FINNEGAN FORKED RIVER, NEW JERSEY

PREP: 10 MIN. + MARINATING **GRILL:** 20 MIN. **MAKES:** 8 SERVINGS

- **⅓ cup water**
- **⅓ cup molasses**
- **⅓ cup reduced-sodium soy sauce**
- **2 tablespoons minced fresh gingerroot**
- **2 garlic cloves, minced**
- **¼ teaspoon salt**
- **¼ teaspoon pepper**
- **2 pork tenderloin (1 pound each)**

1. Combine the first seven ingredients in a large resealable plastic bag. Add the pork; seal bag and turn to coat. Refrigerate for at least 8 hours or overnight.
2. Drain and discard marinade. Moisten a paper towel with cooking oil; using long-handled tongs, lightly coat the grill rack. Grill pork, covered, over indirect medium-hot heat for 20-25 minutes or until a thermometer reads 145°. Let stand for 5 minutes before slicing.

BETTER FOR YOU

Walsh Family Grilled Pork Tenderloins are delicious and healthy. A 3 oz. serving has only 143 calories, 4 grams of fat, 1 gram saturated fat and 165 milligrams sodium. And for those following a diabetic diet, this serving size has an exchange of 3 lean meat.

Ginger-Peach Pork Skillet

Leftover grilled pork, packaged rice and a jazzed-up frozen stir-fry blend speed up this saucy, sweet skillet dish with a little kick.
—ELIZABETH PERKINS SOUTH RIDING, VIRGINIA

PREP/TOTAL TIME: 25 MIN. **MAKES:** 4 SERVINGS

- **1 package (16 ounces) frozen stir-fry vegetable blend**
- **1 tablespoon canola oil**
- **½ cup peach preserves**
- **3 tablespoons reduced-sodium teriyaki sauce**
- **¾ teaspoon ground ginger**
- **¼ teaspoon salt**
- **¼ teaspoon garlic powder**
- **¼ teaspoon crushed red pepper flakes**
- **1 can (14½ ounces) reduced-sodium chicken broth**
- **3 tablespoons cornstarch**
- **2 packages (8½ ounces each) ready-to-serve whole grain brown and wild rice medley**
- **1 can (8½ ounces) sliced peaches, drained and coarsely chopped**
- **2¾ cups sliced grilled pork tenderloin**

1. Stir-fry vegetable blend in oil in a large skillet or wok, until vegetables are crisp-tender, about 4 minutes. Stir in the preserves, teriyaki sauce, ginger, salt, garlic powder and pepper flakes.
2. Whisk broth and cornstarch until smooth. Gradually stir into skillet. Bring to a boil; cook and stir for 2 minutes or until thickened.
3. Meanwhile, prepare rice according to package directions. Stir peaches and pork into the skillet and heat through. Serve with rice.

Mexican Tater-Topped Casserole

Tater Tots, cheese and a mouthwatering ground beef mixture: What's not to love in this delicious casserole one tester called "the ultimate comfort food?"

—TASTE OF HOME TEST KITCHEN

PREP: 30 MIN. **BAKE:** 40 MIN. **MAKES:** 8 SERVINGS

- **1 package (14 ounces) frozen pepper strips**
- **1 can (11 ounces) Mexicorn, drained**
- **1 can (11 ounces) condensed beefy mushroom soup, undiluted**
- **1 can (10¾ ounces) condensed cream of celery soup, undiluted**
- **⅔ cup 2% milk**
- **2 teaspoons ground cumin**
- **½ teaspoon dried oregano**
- **4 cups reserved mixture from Cajun Beef and Beans**
- **1 package (32 ounces) frozen Tater Tots**
- **2 cups (8 ounces) shredded Mexican cheese blend**
- **2 green onions, thinly sliced**

1. In a large skillet, combine the first seven ingredients. Stir in meat mixture. Bring to a boil.

2. Transfer to a greased 13-in. x 9-in. baking dish. Top with Tater Tots. Cover and bake at 350° for 30 minutes. Sprinkle with cheese and green onions. Bake, uncovered, 10-15 minutes longer or until bubbly and cheese is melted.

Cajun Beef and Beans

Here's just the hearty, stick-to-your-ribs dinner you've been looking for! Fire-roasted tomatoes, Cajun seasoning and chili powder add a nice hit of heat to this crowd-pleaser.

—SHELISA TERRY HENDERSON, NEVADA

PREP: 15 MIN. **COOK:** 45 MIN. **MAKES:** 8 SERVINGS

- **3 pounds ground beef**
- **2 medium onions, chopped**
- **2 medium green peppers, chopped**
- **3 celery ribs, chopped**
- **3 tablespoons Cajun seasoning**
- **2 tablespoons chili powder**
- **1¼ teaspoons salt**
- **½ teaspoon pepper**
- **2 cans (16 ounces each) kidney beans, rinsed and drained**
- **2 cans (14½ ounces each) fire-roasted diced tomatoes, undrained**
- **1 can (10¾ ounces) condensed tomato soup, undiluted**
- **Hot cooked rice**

1. In a Dutch oven, cook the beef, onions, peppers and celery over medium heat until meat is no longer pink; drain. Stir in the Cajun seasoning, chili powder, salt and pepper; cook 2 minutes longer.

2. Save 4 cups for Mexican Tater-Topped Casserole or save for another use. Stir the beans, tomatoes and soup into the remaining mixture. Bring to a boil. Reduce heat; simmer, uncovered, for 15 minutes. Serve with rice.

TURN THIS!

Old-World Pizza Meat Loaf

Good food and memories are made in the kitchen. A recipe like this one, that's been passed down through generations, is worth its weight in gold. In fact, this was my grandma's recipe; we all love it.

—NICHOLAS KING DULUTH, MINNESOTA

PREP: 20 MIN. **BAKE:** 55 MIN. + STANDING
MAKES: 6 SERVINGS PLUS LEFTOVERS

- **1 egg, lightly beaten**
- **1½ cups seasoned bread crumbs**
- **1 can (4¼ ounces) chopped ripe olives, drained**
- **1 can (4 ounces) mushroom stems and pieces, drained**
- **1 cup (4 ounces) shredded part-skim mozzarella cheese**
- **1 small green pepper, chopped**
- **1 small onion, chopped**
- **2 tablespoons onion soup mix**
- **1 cup pizza sauce, divided**
- **2 pounds ground beef**
- **¼ cup grated Parmesan cheese**

1. In a large bowl, combine the egg, bread crumbs, olives, mushrooms, mozzarella cheese, pepper, onion, soup mix and 1/2 cup pizza sauce. Crumble beef over mixture and mix well. Shape into a 10-in. x 6-in. rectangle and place in a greased 15-in. x 10-in. x 1-in. baking pan; Spoon remaining pizza sauce over top.
2. Bake, uncovered, at 350° for 45 minutes. Sprinkle with Parmesan cheese. Bake 10-15 minutes longer or until no pink remains and a thermometer reads 160°. Let stand 10 minutes before slicing.
3. Reserve 2 slices meat loaf for Next Day Meat Loaf Pie. Serve the remaining meat loaf.

Next Day Meat Loaf Pie

When I want to make an easy dinner that satisfies my appetite for meat and potatoes, this is my first choice. To amp up the homemade taste, sub in from-scratch or warmed refrigerated mashed potatoes.

—JANET CHEN ANN ARBOR, MICHIGAN

PREP: 15 MIN. **BAKE:** 30 MIN. **MAKES:** 4 SERVINGS

- **1⅓ cups water**
- **⅓ cup 2% milk**
- **2 tablespoons butter**
- **½ teaspoon salt**
- **1⅓ cups mashed potato flakes**
- **1 can (11 ounces) whole kernel corn, drained**
- **1 can (10¾ ounces) condensed cream of mushroom soup, undiluted**
- **2 slices Old-World Pizza Meat Loaf, cubed**
- **¼ cup shredded cheddar cheese**
- **2 tablespoons thinly sliced green onions**

1. In a large saucepan, combine the water, milk, butter and salt; bring to a boil. Stir in potato flakes. Remove from the heat; cover and let stand for 5 minutes.
2. Meanwhile, in a large bowl, combine the corn and condensed soup; gently fold in meat loaf. Transfer to a greased 8-in. square baking dish. Stir cheese and green onions into potatoes; spread over top.
3. Bake, uncovered, at 350° for 30-35 minutes or until heated through and edges are golden brown.

INTO THIS!

It's not luck; it's just an amazing Irish recipe! With this in the slow cooker by sunrise, you can bet you'll fill seats at the dinner table by sundown. —HEATHER PARRAZ ROCHESTER, WASHINGTON

Slow-Cooked Corned Beef

PREP 20 MIN. COOK: 9 HOURS
MAKES: 5 SERVINGS PLUS LEFTOVERS

- **6 medium red potatoes, quartered**
- **2 medium carrots, cut into chunks**
- **1 large onion, sliced**
- **2 corned beef briskets with spice packets (3 pounds each)**
- **¼ cup packed brown sugar**
- **2 tablespoons sugar**
- **2 tablespoons coriander seeds**
- **2 tablespoons whole peppercorns**
- **4 cups water**

1. In a 6-qt. slow cooker, combine the potatoes, carrots and onion. Add briskets (discard spice packets from corned beef or save for another use). Sprinkle the brown sugar, sugar, coriander and peppercorns over meat. Pour water over top.
2. Cover and cook on low for 9-11 hours or until meat and vegetables are tender.
3. Remove meat and vegetables to a serving platter. Thinly slice one brisket across the grain and serve with vegetables. Save the remaining brisket for Reuben Strata or save for another use.

Reuben Strata

Sure, you could turn last night's corned beef into a Reuben sandwich, but strata is more fun—and just as simple.

—PATTERSON WATKINS
PHILADELPHIA, PENNSYLVANIA

PREP: 15 MIN. **BAKE:** 45 MIN. + STANDING
MAKES: 12 SERVINGS

- **1 loaf (1 pound) day old pumpernickel bread, cubed**
- **1 Slow-Cooked Corned Beef brisket, cubed**
- **1¾ cups sauerkraut, rinsed and well drained**
- **8 eggs, beaten**
- **3 cups heavy whipping cream**
- **½ cup Thousand Island salad dressing**
- **1 cup (4 ounces) shredded Swiss cheese**

1. In a large bowl, combine the bread, corned beef and sauerkraut. In another bowl, whisk the eggs, cream and salad dressing; pour over bread mixture and toss to coat. Transfer to a greased 13-in. x 9-in. baking dish. Let stand 5 minutes.
2. Cover and bake at 375° for 40 minutes. Uncover; sprinkle with cheese and bake 5-10 minutes longer or until a knife inserted near the center comes out clean. Let stand for 10 minutes before cutting.

Grilled Ribeyes with Blue Cheese Butter

Fire up the grill for steaks that just melt in your mouth. They're garlic-infused, and the grill flavor is off the charts. With this recipe on hand, weeknight menus sizzle!

—**JIM MOODY** WICHITA, KANSAS

PREP/TOTAL TIME: 25 MIN. **MAKES:** 8 SERVINGS

- **8 beef ribeye steaks (10 ounces each)**
- **12 garlic cloves, sliced**
- **¼ cup olive oil**
- **1 teaspoon salt**
- **¾ teaspoon cayenne pepper**
- **½ teaspoon pepper**
- **½ cup crumbled blue cheese**
- **¼ cup butter, softened**

1. Cut slits into each steak; insert garlic slices. Brush with oil and sprinkle with salt, cayenne and pepper.
2. Grill, covered, over medium heat or broil 4 in. from the heat for 4-6 minutes on each side or until meat reaches desired doneness (for medium-rare, a thermometer should read 145°; medium, 160°; well-done, 170°).
3. Combine blue cheese and butter. Serve with steaks.

If you have extra blue cheese butter from the Grilled Ribeyes, use the savory butter on baked potatoes or toss with noodles.

Orange Beef and Asparagus Stir-Fry

Take your go-to Asian restaurant off speed dial; this is hands down better than takeout! Leftover grilled steak, fresh veggies and a sweet orange glaze—see what we mean?

—**CINDY JOHNSON** COLORADO SPRINGS, COLORADO

PREP/TOTAL TIME: 30 MIN. **MAKES:** 4 SERVINGS

- **4 teaspoons cornstarch**
- **¾ cup orange juice**
- **4 green onions, thinly sliced**
- **3 tablespoons reduced-sodium soy sauce**
- **3 tablespoons honey**
- **2 teaspoons minced fresh gingerroot**
- **1 garlic clove, minced**
- **2 cups cut fresh asparagus (1-inch pieces)**
- **1 medium sweet red pepper, sliced**
- **1 cup julienned carrots**
- **1 tablespoon canola oil**
- **¾ pound leftover grilled steaks, thinly sliced**
- **½ cup honey-roasted peanuts**
- **Hot cooked rice**

1. In a small bowl, whisk the cornstarch, orange juice, onions, soy sauce, honey, ginger and garlic until blended; set aside.
2. In a large skillet or wok, stir-fry the asparagus, pepper and carrots in oil for 2-3 minutes or until vegetables are crisp-tender.
3. Stir cornstarch mixture and add to the pan. Bring to a boil; cook and stir for 2 minutes or until thickened. Add beef; heat through. Sprinkle with peanuts. Serve with rice.

Slow Cooked BBQ Pork Ribs

Check your pantry; you probably have everything needed to turn these succulent ribs into a sweet, tangy, fork-tender treat.

—ANNETTE THOMPSON WOODBURY, VERMONT

PREP: 20 MIN. **COOK:** 7 HOURS **MAKES:** 8 SERVINGS

- **4 pounds boneless country-style pork ribs**
- **2 cups ketchup**
- **¼ cup packed brown sugar**
- **¼ cup maple syrup**
- **¼ cup prepared mustard**
- **¼ cup reduced-sodium soy sauce**
- **2 tablespoons lemon juice**
- **2 teaspoons dried minced garlic**
- **⅛ teaspoon pepper**

1. Place ribs in a 5- or 6-qt. slow cooker. Combine the remaining ingredients; pour over top. Cover and cook on low for 7-9 hours or until meat is tender.
2. Remove ribs and keep warm. Skim fat from cooking juices; serve with ribs.

To soften brown sugar quickly, microwave on high for 20-30 seconds. Repeat if necessary until the brown sugar softens, but watch carefully, because the sugar will begin to melt. Always store brown sugar in an airtight container.

Queso Pork Enchiladas

My husband took these to work, and now the guys always ask for them. They're restaurant-style, rich and spicy, and you can prepare them with cooked chicken or beef, too.

—ANNA RODRIGUEZ BETHPAGE, NEW YORK

PREP: 30 MIN. **BAKE:** 30 MIN. **MAKES:** 6 SERVINGS

- **1 jar (15½ ounces) salsa con queso dip, divided**
- **1 can (10 ounces) enchilada sauce, divided**
- **1 can (4 ounces) chopped green chilies**
- **⅓ cup water**
- **2 tablespoons reduced-sodium taco seasoning**
- **4 cups cubed cooked country-style pork ribs**
- **12 flour tortillas (6 inches), warmed**
- **2½ cups (10 ounces) shredded Mexican cheese blend, divided**
- **Shredded lettuce and chopped tomatoes, optional**

1. In a large skillet, combine ¾ cup queso dip, ½ cup enchilada sauce, green chilies, water and taco seasoning. Bring to a boil. Reduce heat; simmer, uncovered, for 3 minutes.
2. Spread ⅔ cup sauce mixture into a greased 13-in. x 9-in. baking dish. Stir pork into remaining sauce mixture. Place ⅓ cup pork mixture down the center of each tortilla; top with 2 tablespoons cheese. Roll up and place seam side down in prepared dish. Combine remaining queso dip and enchilada sauce; pour over enchiladas.
3. Cover and bake at 350° for 20 minutes. Uncover; sprinkle with remaining cheese; bake 10-15 minutes longer or until heated through. Serve with lettuce and tomatoes if desired.

Shop Once... Eat All Week

"Skip the marinara and serve noodles an elegant new way! Not only is our easy balsamic-infused entree a meal in itself, it's a different twist on an Italian classic."

—TASTE OF HOME TEST KITCHEN
Balsamic Chicken Fettuccine, page 99

WEEK #1 Pantry List

Choose recipes from pp. 96-99, then check to see which staples you already have. Shop for what you'll need with this list. Visit *tasteofhome.com/simple* to print (December/January 2012).

REFRIGERATED

- ☐ **boneless pork loin chops** ____ (amount you need)
- ☐ **boneless skinless chicken breasts** ____
- ☐ **butter** ____
- ☐ **green onions** ____
- ☐ **ground beef** ____
- ☐ **medium pears** ____
- ☐ **medium sweet red pepper** ____
- ☐ **shredded cheddar cheese** ____
- ☐ **sliced fresh mushrooms** ____

FROZEN

- ☐ **frozen broccoli florets** ____
- ☐ **frozen mixed vegetables** ____

Pantry Staples

BOTTLES, CANS AND JARS

- ☐ **balsamic vinaigrette** ____
- ☐ **canned condensed nacho cheese soup** ____
- ☐ **canned diced tomatoes** ____
- ☐ **canned Mexicorn** ____
- ☐ **canned pinto beans** ____
- ☐ **canned tomato paste** ____
- ☐ **jarred Alfredo sauce** ____
- ☐ **olive oil** ____

BAGS, BOXES AND PACKAGES

- ☐ **corn bread/muffin mix** ____
- ☐ **corn bread stuffing mix** ____
- ☐ **fettuccine** ____
- ☐ **medium red onions** ____
- ☐ **pouched boneless skinless pink salmon** ____
- ☐ **ready-to-serve long grain and wild rice** ____
- ☐ **ready-to-serve long grain rice** ____
- ☐ **taco shells** ____

SPICES/SEASONINGS

- ☐ **brown sugar** ____
- ☐ **Cajun seasoning** ____
- ☐ **chili powder** ____
- ☐ **dried basil** ____
- ☐ **dried thyme** ____
- ☐ **garlic cloves** ____
- ☐ **garlic powder** ____
- ☐ **Italian seasoning** ____
- ☐ **pepper** ____
- ☐ **salt** ____

Stuffed Alfredo Pork Chops

Picture this: It's Monday night, dinner's done and you have time to put your feet up and relax. A few ingredients, 15 minutes of prep and hands-free bake time make this smarty-pants main dish a busy cook's ideal weeknight meal.

—TASTE OF HOME TEST KITCHEN

PREP: 15 MIN. **BAKE:** 25 MIN. **MAKES:** 4 SERVINGS

- **1 package (8.8 ounces) ready-to-serve long grain rice**
- **1 package (10 ounces) frozen mixed vegetables**
- **¾ teaspoon garlic powder, divided**
- **¾ teaspoon Italian seasoning, divided**
- **4 boneless pork loin chops (6 ounces each)**
- **2 tablespoons butter**
- **1 jar (15 ounces) Alfredo sauce**

1. Cook rice and vegetables according to package directions. In a small microwave-safe bowl, combine the vegetables, rice, ½ teaspoon garlic powder and ½ teaspoon Italian seasoning.

2. Using a sharp knife, cut a pocket in each pork chop. Fill each chop with about ⅓ cup rice mixture; secure with toothpicks if necessary. Set aside remaining rice mixture.

3. In a large skillet, brown chops in butter on both sides. Transfer to a greased 8-in. square baking dish. Cover and bake at 350° for 25-30 minutes or until a thermometer reads 160°.

4. Meanwhile, in a small saucepan, combine the Alfredo sauce and remaining garlic powder and Italian seasoning; heat through. Cover and microwave remaining rice mixture on high for 30-45 seconds or until heated through. Serve with chops and sauce mixture.

Beef & Bean Tacos

Food won't go to waste when you serve this satisfying taco that puts canned goods to use. Even better, the creamy, not soggy, filling keeps the shell crunchy.
—TASTE OF HOME TEST KITCHEN

PREP/TOTAL TIME: 25 MIN. **MAKES:** 6 SERVINGS

- **1 pound ground beef**
- **1 can (15 ounces) pinto beans, rinsed and drained**
- **1 can (14½ ounces) diced tomatoes, undrained**
- **1 can (11 ounces) Mexicorn, drained**
- **1 can (10¾ ounces) condensed nacho cheese soup, undiluted**
- **¼ cup water**
- **2 teaspoons chili powder**
- **12 taco shells, warmed**
- **Optional toppings: chopped sweet red pepper, thinly sliced green onions and shredded cheddar cheese**

1. In a large skillet, cook the beef over medium heat until meat is no longer pink; drain. Stir in the beans, tomatoes, Mexicorn, soup, water and chili powder. Bring to a boil. Reduce heat; simmer, uncovered, for 5 minutes.
2. Spoon beef mixture into taco shells; serve with toppings of your choice.

SIMPLE SWAP

Serve the beef and bean mixture on a green salad, a baked potato or tortilla chips instead of in taco shells.

Deconstructed Pear Pork Chops

"I could eat this straight out of the pan!," one tester said after sampling this sweet and savory main dish with all the delicious flavors of a stuffed pork chop.
—TASTE OF HOME TEST KITCHEN

PREP/TOTAL TIME: 30 MIN.
MAKES: 4 SERVINGS

- **1 package (6 ounces) corn bread stuffing mix**
- **4 boneless pork loin chops (6 ounces each)**
- **½ teaspoon pepper**
- **¼ teaspoon salt**
- **2 tablespoons butter**
- **2 medium pears, chopped**
- **1 medium sweet red pepper, chopped**
- **2 green onions, thinly sliced**

1. Prepare stuffing mix according to package directions. Meanwhile, sprinkle chops with pepper and salt. In a large skillet, brown pork chops in butter. Sprinkle with pears and red pepper.
2. Top with stuffing and onions. Cook, uncovered, over medium heat for 8-10 minutes or until a thermometer reads 160°.

Salmon Fettuccine Alfredo

Alfredo sauce and salmon are a palate-pleasing pair in this creamy pasta toss with crisp vegetables. We love the simple flavors as they are, but you could also fix this with tuna, shrimp or chicken.

—TASTE OF HOME TEST KITCHEN

PREP/TOTAL TIME: 20 MIN.
MAKES: 4 SERVINGS

- **8 ounces uncooked fettuccine**
- **1 medium sweet red pepper, chopped**
- **1 tablespoon olive oil**
- **2 garlic cloves, minced**
- **2 jars (15 ounces each) Alfredo sauce**
- **2 cups frozen broccoli florets**
- **2 pouches (6 ounces each) boneless skinless pink salmon**
- **½ teaspoon dried basil**

1. Cook fettuccine according to package directions. Meanwhile, in a large skillet, saute pepper in oil until tender. Add garlic; cook 1 minute longer.

2. Stir in the Alfredo sauce, broccoli, salmon and basil. Cook, uncovered, over medium heat for 5-7 minutes or until heated through. Drain fettuccine. Add to skillet; toss to coat.

Chicken with Caramelized Pears

Tender chicken gets an upscale treatment in this simple entree with sweetened pears. Remember this idea—it also works with pork loin chops and thinly sliced apples.

—TASTE OF HOME TEST KITCHEN

PREP/TOTAL TIME: 30 MIN. **MAKES:** 4 SERVINGS

- **4 boneless skinless chicken breast halves (6 ounces each)**
- **½ teaspoon salt**
- **½ teaspoon pepper**
- **3 tablespoons butter**
- **1 medium red onion, halved and thinly sliced**
- **2 medium pears, thinly sliced**
- **2 teaspoons brown sugar**
- **½ cup balsamic vinaigrette**
- **½ teaspoon dried thyme**
- **2 packages (8.8 ounces each) ready-to-serve long grain and wild rice**

1. Sprinkle chicken with salt and pepper. In a large skillet, brown chicken in butter; remove and keep warm. In the same skillet, saute onion until tender. Add pears and brown sugar; cook 3 minutes longer. Stir in vinaigrette and thyme.

1. Return chicken to skillet. Bring to a boil. Reduce heat; simmer, uncovered, for 4-6 minutes or until chicken juices run clear. Meanwhile, cook rice according to package directions. Serve with chicken.

Cajun Beef Casserole

Do you have little ones who won't eat veggies? They won't complain one bit when you bring this cheesy casserole with a corn bread crust to the table. For picky eaters, try using less Cajun seasoning.

—TASTE OF HOME TEST KITCHEN

PREP: 15 MIN. **BAKE:** 25 MIN. **MAKES:** 6 SERVINGS

- **1 package (8½ ounces) corn bread/muffin mix**
- **1 pound ground beef**
- **2 cans (14½ ounces each) diced tomatoes, drained**
- **2 cups frozen mixed vegetables, thawed**
- **1 can (6 ounces) tomato paste**
- **1 to 2 teaspoons Cajun seasoning**
- **1 cup (4 ounces) shredded cheddar cheese**
- **2 green onions, thinly sliced**

1. Prepare corn bread batter according to package directions. Spread into a greased 11-in. x 7-in. baking dish.
2. In a large skillet, cook beef over medium heat until meat is no longer pink; drain. Add the tomatoes, vegetables, tomato paste and seasoning. Bring to a boil. Reduce heat; simmer, uncovered, for 5 minutes. Pour over top. Sprinkle with cheese.
3. Bake, uncovered, at 350° for 25-30 minutes or until golden brown. Sprinkle with onions.

Balsamic Chicken Fettuccine

Skip the marinara and serve noodles an elegant new way! Not only is our easy balsamic-infused entree a meal in itself, it's a different twist on an Italian classic.

—TASTE OF HOME TEST KITCHEN

PREP/TOTAL TIME: 25 MIN.
MAKES: 5 SERVINGS

- **8 ounces uncooked fettuccine**
- **1½ pounds boneless skinless chicken breasts, cut into strips**
- **2 tablespoons plus ½ cup balsamic vinaigrette, divided**
- **½ pound sliced fresh mushrooms**
- **1 medium red onion, chopped**
- **2 cans (14½ ounces each) diced tomatoes, undrained**
- **2 cups frozen broccoli florets**
- **½ teaspoon Italian seasoning**

1. Cook fettuccine according to package directions. Meanwhile, in a large skillet, saute the chicken in 1 tablespoon vinaigrette until no longer pink. Remove and keep warm.
2. In the same skillet, saute mushrooms and onion in 1 tablespoon vinaigrette until tender. Add the tomatoes, broccoli, Italian seasoning and remaining vinaigrette; cook 5-6 minutes longer or until heated through.
3. Drain fettuccine. Add fettuccine and chicken to skillet and toss to coat.

WEEK #2 Pantry List

Choose recipes from pp. 100-103, then check to see which staples you already have. Shop for what you'll need with this list. Visit *tasteofhome.com/simple* to print (February/March 2012).

REFRIGERATED

- ☐ bacon strips ____ (amount you need)
- ☐ butter ____
- ☐ Dijon mustard ____
- ☐ eggs ____
- ☐ fresh parsley ____
- ☐ ground beef ____
- ☐ mayonnaise ____
- ☐ medium carrots ____
- ☐ medium green pepper ____
- ☐ ready-to-serve roasted chicken breast strips ____
- ☐ shredded cheddar cheese ____
- ☐ shredded Swiss cheese ____
- ☐ sliced fresh mushrooms ____
- ☐ sour cream ____
- ☐ 2% milk ____

FROZEN

- ☐ frozen peas ____
- ☐ frozen puff pastry ____

Pantry Staples

BOTTLES, CANS AND JARS

- ☐ canned black beans ____
- ☐ canned chili starter ____
- ☐ canned chopped green chilies ____
- ☐ canned condensed cream of celery soup, undiluted ____
- ☐ canned light water-packed tuna ____
- ☐ canned sliced ripe olives ____
- ☐ jarred jalapeno jelly ____
- ☐ jarred marinated quartered artichoke hearts ____
- ☐ jarred roasted garlic Parmesan spaghetti sauce ____
- ☐ olive oil ____

BAGS, BOXES AND PACKAGES

- ☐ all-purpose flour ____
- ☐ linguine ____
- ☐ medium apples ____
- ☐ medium onions ____
- ☐ medium potatoes ____
- ☐ medium tomatoes ____
- ☐ medium Yukon Gold potatoes ____
- ☐ seasoned bread crumbs ____

SPICES/SEASONINGS

- ☐ dried oregano ____
- ☐ dried thyme ____
- ☐ garlic powder ____
- ☐ pepper ____
- ☐ salt ____
- ☐ seafood seasoning ____

Chili Hash

A little prep time, a dash in the pan and you'll have a satisfying home-cooked meal for those you love on a where-did-the-time-go weeknight.

—TASTE OF HOME TEST KITCHEN

PREP/TOTAL TIME: 30 MIN. **MAKES:** 4 SERVINGS

- **1 pound medium potatoes, cubed**
- **½ cup water**
- **1 pound ground beef**
- **1 medium onion, chopped**
- **1 can (15½ ounces) chili starter**
- **1 cup frozen peas**
- **2 tablespoons minced fresh parsley**
- **¼ teaspoon salt**
- **Sour cream, optional**

1. Place potatoes and water in a microwave-safe dish. Cover and microwave on high for 7 minutes or until tender.

2. Meanwhile, in a large skillet, cook beef and onion over medium heat until meat is no longer pink; drain. Drain potatoes and add to the skillet. Stir in the chili starter, peas, parsley and salt. Bring to a boil. Reduced heat; simmer, uncovered, for 5 minutes. Serve with sour cream if desired.

Shhh! SIMPLE SECRET

This dish gets much of its flavor from the chili starter. There are several brands on the market. We used Tabasco Homestyle Chili Starter, so our hash was a bit spicy.

Chicken & Bacon Tart

If you're one of those folks who think bacon is a food group, you'll love this weeknight-friendly twist with a sweet and spicy kick from jalapeno jelly. Crisp puff pastry and store-bought chicken strips make prep work goof-proof!

—TASTE OF HOME TEST KITCHEN

PREP: 25 MIN. **BAKE:** 15 MIN. **MAKES:** 4 SERVINGS

- **¼ pound bacon strips, cut into thirds**
- **2 medium onions, halved and thinly sliced**
- **2 medium apples, peeled and thinly sliced**
- **1 package (9 ounces) ready-to-serve roasted chicken breast strips**
- **¼ cup jalapeno pepper jelly**
- **½ teaspoon dried thyme**
- **¼ teaspoon salt**
- **1 sheet frozen puff pastry, thawed**
- **¾ cup shredded cheddar cheese**
- **¼ teaspoon pepper**
- **1 tablespoon minced fresh parsley**

1. In a large skillet, cook bacon over medium heat until crisp. Remove to paper towels with a slotted spoon. Saute onions and apples in drippings until tender. Stir in the chicken, jelly, thyme and salt.

2. On a lightly floured surface, unfold puff pastry. Roll into a 10-in. x 9-in. rectangle. Transfer to a 15-in. x 10-in. x 1-in. parchment paper-lined baking sheet. Prick with a fork.

3. Spread chicken mixture over pastry to within 1 in. of edges. Sprinkle with cheese and pepper. Press edges with a fork, forming a decorative border.

4. Bake at 425° for 10 minutes. Sprinkle with bacon; bake 5-10 minutes longer or until golden brown. Sprinkle with parsley.

Mediterranean Tuna Linguine

This will remind you of a fancier tuna noodle casserole without the hassle. The creamy dish comes together quickly in a skillet. Serve it with a simple spinach salad and store-bought breadsticks for weekday elegance in no time.

—TASTE OF HOME TEST KITCHEN

PREP/TOTAL TIME: 20 MIN.
MAKES: 5 SERVINGS

- **8 ounces uncooked linguine**
- **2 cans (10¾ ounces each) condensed cream of celery soup, undiluted**
- **1 cup 2% milk**
- **1 teaspoon garlic powder**
- **½ teaspoon seafood seasoning**
- **3 cans (5 ounces each) light water-packed tuna, drained and flaked**
- **1 jar (7½ ounces) marinated quartered artichoke hearts, drained**
- **2 medium tomatoes, chopped**
- **1 cup sliced ripe olives, drained**

1. Cook linguine according to package directions.

2. Meanwhile, in a large saucepan, combine the soup, milk, garlic powder and seafood seasoning. Stir in the tuna, artichoke hearts, tomatoes and olives. Bring to a boil. Reduce heat; drain linguine and stir into soup mixture.

Jazzy Spaghetti Sauce

Artichoke hearts and bacon give a simple meat sauce new dimensions. It's quick to fix, but if you're short on time, cook the beef mixture ahead. Reheat with sauce and artichokes.

—TASTE OF HOME TEST KITCHEN

PREP/TOTAL TIME: 25 MIN.
MAKES: 4 SERVINGS

- **1 pound ground beef**
- **½ pound sliced fresh mushrooms**
- **1 medium onion, chopped**
- **1 jar (24 ounces) roasted garlic Parmesan spaghetti sauce**
- **1 jar (7½ ounces) marinated quartered artichoke hearts, drained**
- **¼ pound bacon strips, cooked and crumbled**
- **Hot cooked linguine**

1. In a Dutch oven, cook the beef, mushrooms and onion over medium heat until meat is no longer pink; drain. Stir in spaghetti sauce and artichoke hearts. Heat through. Sprinkle with bacon and serve with linguine.

PERFECT PAIR

Consider adding fresh vegetables like green pepper or zucchini to the sauce. They'll enrich it even more and amp up the flavor.

Southwest Chicken Pockets

Black beans, convenient chicken strips and chilies star in these feisty and filling loaded pockets. Eat 'em out of hand (or with a fork if you feel civilized)! Serve a little salsa on the side for an extra burst of flavor.

—TASTE OF HOME TEST KITCHEN

PREP: 15 MIN. **BAKE:** 20 MIN. **MAKES:** 4 SERVINGS

- **1 medium onion, chopped**
- **2 teaspoons olive oil**
- **1 package (9 ounces) ready-to-serve roasted chicken breast strips**
- **1 can (15 ounces) black beans, rinsed and drained**
- **1 medium tomato, seeded and chopped**
- **1 can (4 ounces) chopped green chilies, divided**
- **1 sheet frozen puff pastry, thawed**
- **¼ cup shredded cheddar cheese**
- **1 egg, beaten**
- **½ cup sour cream**

1. In a large skillet, saute onion in oil until tender. Remove from the heat; stir in the chicken, beans, tomato and 1/4 cup chilies.

2. On a lightly floured surface, roll puff pastry into a 14-in. square. Cut into four squares. Spoon chicken mixture into the center of each square; sprinkle with cheese.

3. Brush egg over edges. Fold dough over filling, forming a triangle; pinch seams to seal. Transfer to a greased baking sheet and brush with remaining egg. Bake at 400° for 18-22 minutes or until golden brown.

4. Meanwhile, in a small bowl, combine sour cream and remaining chilies. Serve with pockets.

Shhh! SIMPLE SECRET

To make your pastry pockets uniform, break up the larger pieces of chicken into bite-size pieces as you add them to the skillet. Also, pinch seams well so the filling doesn't ooze out as they bake.

Vegetarian Potato au Gratin

Fill up on veggies and load up on great taste with this creamy, hearty casserole. You'll appreciate the homey bread-crumb topping and hands-free bake time at the end of a long day. The Yukon Gold potatoes add a nutty, buttery flavor to the entree.

—TASTE OF HOME TEST KITCHEN

PREP: 15 MIN. **BAKE:** 50 MIN. + STANDING **MAKES:** 6 SERVINGS

- **3 medium carrots, thinly sliced**
- **1 medium green pepper, chopped**
- **4 tablespoons butter, divided**
- **3 tablespoons all-purpose flour**
- **1 teaspoon dried oregano**
- **½ teaspoon salt**
- **2½ cups 2% milk**
- **1 can (15 ounces) black beans, rinsed and drained**
- **3 cups (12 ounces) shredded Swiss cheese, divided**
- **4 medium Yukon Gold potatoes, thinly sliced**
- **½ cup seasoned bread crumbs**

1. In a large saucepan, saute carrots and pepper in 3 tablespoons butter until tender. Stir in the flour, oregano and salt until blended; gradually add milk. Bring to a boil; cook and stir for 2 minutes or until thickened. Stir in beans and 2 cups cheese until cheese is melted.

2. Layer half of the potatoes and sauce in a greased 13-in. x 9-in. baking dish; repeat layers. Sprinkle with remaining cheese. In a microwave, melt the remaining butter. Stir in bread crumbs. Sprinkle over top.

3. Cover and bake at 400° for 50-55 minutes. Let stand for 10 minutes before serving.

123 MAKE IT SIMPLE

To make perfectly uniform vegetable slices quickly, use a mandoline for the Vegetarian Potato au Gratin.

Tuna Cakes With Mustard Mayo

These patties take the cake! Canned tuna is the surprise ingredient in these veggie-packed rounds. If you'd like, add more zip to the creamy mustard-mayo sauce with prepared horseradish.

—TASTE OF HOME TEST KITCHEN

PREP/TOTAL TIME: 30 MIN.
MAKES: 4 SERVINGS

- **2 eggs**
- **3 tablespoons minced fresh parsley, divided**
- **½ teaspoon seafood seasoning**
- **2 cans (5 ounces each) light water-packed tuna, drained and flaked**
- **½ cup seasoned bread crumbs**
- **½ cup shredded carrots**
- **2 tablespoons butter, divided**
- **1 package (12 ounces) frozen peas**
- **¼ teaspoon pepper**
- **⅓ cup mayonnaise**
- **1 tablespoon Dijon mustard**
- **1 teaspoon 2% milk**

1. In a large bowl, combine the eggs, 2 tablespoons parsley and seafood seasoning. Stir in tuna, bread crumbs and carrot. Shape into eight patties.

2. In a large skillet, brown patties in 1 tablespoon butter for 3-4 minutes on each side or until golden brown.

3. Meanwhile, microwave peas according to package directions. Stir in the pepper and remaining butter and parsley. Combine the mayonnaise, mustard and milk. Serve with tuna cakes and peas.

WEEK #3 Pantry List

Choose recipes from pp. 104-107, then check to see which staples you already have. Shop for what you'll need with this list. Visit *tasteofhome.com/simple* to print (June/July 2012).

PRODUCE

- ☐ broccoli coleslaw mix _____ (amount you need)
- ☐ fresh baby spinach _____
- ☐ fresh basil leaves _____
- ☐ garlic cloves _____
- ☐ lemon _____
- ☐ lemon juice _____
- ☐ medium tomatoes _____
- ☐ medium yellow summer squash _____
- ☐ medium zucchini _____
- ☐ red onions _____
- ☐ sweet orange pepper _____

MEAT

- ☐ boneless skinless chicken breast halves _____
- ☐ ground beef _____

DAIRY AND REFRIGERATED

- ☐ butter _____
- ☐ eggs _____
- ☐ feta cheese _____
- ☐ orange juice _____
- ☐ refrigerated cheese ravioli _____
- ☐ ricotta cheese _____
- ☐ shredded Parmesan cheese _____

FROZEN

- ☐ frozen lemon butter grilled fish filets _____

PACKAGED

- ☐ cornstarch _____
- ☐ Greek vinaigrette _____
- ☐ linguine _____
- ☐ marinara or spaghetti sauce _____
- ☐ mayonnaise _____
- ☐ olive oil _____
- ☐ pitted Greek olives _____
- ☐ ready-to-serve rice pilaf with orzo pasta _____
- ☐ salsa _____
- ☐ seasoned bread crumbs _____
- ☐ sugar _____
- ☐ teriyaki sauce _____
- ☐ whole pita breads _____

SPICES/SEASONINGS

- ☐ Cajun seasoning _____
- ☐ garlic salt _____
- ☐ pepper _____
- ☐ salt _____

Hearty Pita Spinach Salad

Greek flavors combine in perfect harmony for a main dish you won't be able to stop munching. Serve this with a tall glass of lemonade or iced tea and enjoy it alfresco some warm summer night.

—TASTE OF HOME TEST KITCHEN

PREP/TOTAL TIME: 25 MIN. **MAKES:** 4 SERVINGS

- **2 whole pita breads**
- **2 tablespoons olive oil**
- **¼ teaspoon salt**
- **¼ teaspoon pepper**
- **¾ pound ground beef**
- **¾ cup Greek vinaigrette, divided**
- **1 package (6 ounces) fresh baby spinach**
- **2 medium tomatoes, cut into wedges**
- **4 ounces feta cheese, cubed**
- **1 cup pitted Greek olives**
- **1 small red onion, thinly sliced**

1. Cut pita breads into strips; arrange in a single layer on an ungreased baking sheet. In a small bowl, combine the oil, salt and pepper; brush over pita strips. Bake at 400° for 8-10 minutes or until crisp, turning once.

2. Meanwhile, in a large skillet, cook beef over medium heat until no longer pink; drain. Add ¼ cup vinaigrette. Arrange spinach on a serving platter; top with tomatoes, cheese, olives, onion and beef mixture. Drizzle remaining vinaigrette over salad. Serve immediately with toasted pita strips.

SIMPLE SWAP

Save a little time and use feta crumbles instead of a block. Block feta is packaged in brine to keep it in optimal condition. Though slightly drier, the crumbles still have feta's characteristic tang.

Spinach Stuffed Chicken with Linguine

Worthy of an anniversary or an unexpected promotion, this elegant stuffed and rolled chicken looks gorgeous and tastes simply delicious!

—TASTE OF HOME TEST KITCHEN

PREP: 20 MIN. **BAKE:** 25 MIN. **MAKES:** 4 SERVINGS

- **3 garlic cloves, minced**
- **⅓ cup butter, divided**
- **1 package (6 ounces) fresh baby spinach**
- **¼ cup shredded Parmesan cheese**
- **¼ teaspoon salt**
- **4 boneless skinless chicken breast halves (6 ounces each)**
- **½ cup ricotta cheese**
- **1 egg, beaten**
- **¾ cup seasoned bread crumbs**
- **8 ounces uncooked linguine**
- **½ cup salsa**

1. In a large skillet, saute garlic in 1 tablespoon butter until tender. Add spinach and cook just until wilted. Remove from the heat; stir in Parmesan cheese and salt.

2. Flatten chicken to 1/4-in. thickness. Spread ricotta cheese and spinach mixture over the center of each chicken breast. Roll up and secure with toothpicks.

3. Place egg in a shallow bowl. Place bread crumbs in a separate shallow bowl. Dip chicken in egg, then coat with crumbs. In a large skillet, brown chicken in 2 tablespoons butter. Place chicken, seam side down, in a greased 11-in. x 7-in. baking dish.

4. Bake, uncovered, at 375° for 25-30 minutes or until a thermometer reads 170°.

5. Meanwhile, cook linguine according to package directions. Drain linguine; toss with remaining butter and salsa. Discard toothpicks from chicken. Serve with linguine.

Cajun Fish Tacos

Classic fish tacos often feature deep-fried fish, a corn tortilla, cabbage and a thin mayo-based sauce. But we found that fish + pita bread = total yumminess in this streamlined version using lemon-flavored fish with a Cajun twist.

—TASTE OF HOME TEST KITCHEN

PREP/TOTAL TIME: 25 MIN.
MAKES: 4 SERVINGS

- **2 packages (7.6 ounces each) frozen lemon butter grilled fish fillets**
- **3 cups broccoli coleslaw mix**
- **½ cup thinly sliced sweet orange pepper**
- **½ cup mayonnaise**
- **1 tablespoon lemon juice**
- **1 teaspoon sugar**
- **1¾ teaspoons Cajun seasoning, divided**
- **4 whole pita breads, warmed**
- **Lemon wedges, optional**

1. Cook fish according to package directions. Meanwhile, in a small bowl, combine the coleslaw mix, pepper, mayonnaise, lemon juice, sugar and 1½ teaspoons Cajun seasoning.

2. Slice fillets. Spoon coleslaw mixture onto pita breads, top with fish. Sprinkle with remaining Cajun seasoning. Serve with lemon wedges if desired.

Greek Ravioli Skillet

Looking to please picky little palates? One tester loved this simple skillet entree so much, she made it at home for her 2-year-old daughter, who said "Mmmmm!" after every bite.

—TASTE OF HOME TEST KITCHEN

PREP/TOTAL TIME: 30 MIN.
MAKES: 6 SERVINGS

- **1 package (20 ounces) refrigerated cheese ravioli**
- **1 pound ground beef**
- **1 medium zucchini, sliced**
- **1 small red onion, chopped**
- **3 cups marinara or spaghetti sauce**
- **½ cup water**
- **¼ teaspoon pepper**
- **2 medium tomatoes, chopped**
- **½ cup cubed feta cheese**
- **½ cup pitted Greek olives, halved**
- **2 tablespoons minced fresh basil, divided**

1. Cook ravioli according to package directions. Meanwhile, in a large skillet, cook the beef, zucchini and onion over medium heat until meat is no longer pink; drain.

2. Drain ravioli; add to skillet. Stir in the marinara sauce, water and pepper. Bring to a boil. Reduce heat; simmer, uncovered, for 5 minutes. Add the tomatoes, cheese, olives and 1 tablespoon basil. Sprinkle with remaining basil.

Teriyaki Chicken and Vegetables

Smart ingredients, including packaged coleslaw and pasta mixes, make it easy to serve up a colorful combo in just 30 minutes. A refreshing orange teriyaki sauce gives this chicken a lively Asian flavor and such a pretty glisten!

—TASTE OF HOME TEST KITCHEN

PREP/TOTAL TIME: 30 MIN. **MAKES:** 4 SERVINGS

- **1 tablespoon plus ⅓ cup cornstarch, divided**
- **1 cup orange juice**
- **6 tablespoons teriyaki sauce**
- **4 boneless skinless chicken breast halves (6 ounces each)**
- **¼ teaspoon salt**
- **3 tablespoons olive oil, divided**
- **2 medium yellow summer squash, halved and thinly sliced**
- **1 small red onion, halved and thinly sliced**
- **1 package (12 ounces) broccoli coleslaw mix**
- **2 packages (8.8 ounces each) ready-to-serve rice pilaf with orzo pasta**

1. In a small bowl, combine 1 tablespoon cornstarch, orange juice and teriyaki sauce; set aside.

2. Flatten chicken slightly. Place salt and remaining cornstarch in a large resealable plastic bag. Add chicken, one piece at a time, and shake to coat. In a large skillet over medium heat, cook chicken in batches in 2 tablespoons oil for 5-6 minutes on each side or until chicken juices run clear. Remove and keep warm.

3. In the same skillet, saute squash and onion in remaining oil for 2 minutes. Add coleslaw mix; saute 1 minute longer or until vegetables are crisp-tender. Stir juice mixture and add to pan. Bring to a boil; cook and stir for 2 minutes or until thickened.

4. Add chicken to skillet; heat through. Meanwhile, prepare rice pilaf according to package directions. Serve with chicken mixture.

Shhh! SIMPLE SECRET

For the above recipe, cook the sliced vegetables with the broccoli slaw about 1 minute; they will continue cooking as the sauce thickens. This way, the veggies will be tender, not overcooked, when you serve them.

Stacked Vegetables and Ravioli

Fresh squash, zucchini and basil meet ricotta cheese and ravioli in this crowd-pleasing casserole with delicious summer flavors. One bite and you'll know: This is what easy livin' is all about.

—TASTE OF HOME TEST KITCHEN

PREP: 20 MIN. **BAKE:** 30 MIN. + STANDING **MAKES:** 6 SERVINGS

- **2 yellow summer squash**
- **2 medium zucchini**
- **1 package (9 ounces) refrigerated cheese ravioli**
- **1 cup ricotta cheese**
- **1 egg**
- **½ teaspoon garlic salt**
- **1 jar (24 ounces) marinara or spaghetti sauce**
- **10 fresh basil leaves, divided**
- **¾ cup shredded Parmesan cheese**

1. Using a vegetable peeler, cut squash and zucchini into very thin lengthwise strips. In a Dutch oven, cook ravioli according to package directions, adding the vegetable strips during the last 3 minutes of cooking.

2. Meanwhile, in a small bowl, combine the ricotta cheese, egg and garlic salt; set aside. Drain ravioli and vegetables.

3. Spread ½ cup marinara sauce into a greased 11-in. x 7-in. baking dish. Layer with half of the ravioli and vegetables, half of the ricotta mixture, seven basil leaves and 1 cup marinara sauce. Layer with remaining ravioli and vegetables and marinara sauce. Dollop remaining ricotta mixture over the top; sprinkle with Parmesan cheese.

4. Cover and bake at 350° for 25 minutes. Uncover and bake 5-10 minutes longer or until cheese is melted. Let stand for 10 minutes before cutting. Thinly slice remaining basil; sprinkle over top.

Summer Fish Skillet

On busy nights when you have other fish to fry, this fresh-tasting combo with cubed feta cheese and convenient fish fillets will offer just the dinner-hour help you need!

—TASTE OF HOME TEST KITCHEN

PREP/TOTAL TIME: 30 MIN.
MAKES: 4 SERVINGS

- **2 packages (7.6 ounces each) frozen lemon butter grilled fish fillets**
- **1 tablespoon olive oil**
- **2 medium yellow summer squash, halved and sliced**
- **2 medium sweet orange peppers, chopped**
- **½ cup chopped red onion**
- **2 cups fresh salsa, drained**
- **4 ounces feta cheese, cubed**
- **2 packages (8.8 ounces each) ready-to-serve rice pilaf with orzo pasta**

1. In a large skillet, cook fish fillets in oil over medium heat, for 15-20 minutes, turning once or until fish flakes easily with a fork; remove and keep warm.

2. In the same skillet, saute the squash, peppers and onion until tender. Add salsa; cook 2 minutes longer. Return fish to skillet. Add cheese and heat through.

3. Prepare rice pilaf according to package directions. Serve with fish and vegetables.

WEEK #4 Pantry List

Choose recipes from pp. 108-111, then check to see which staples you already have. Shop for what you'll need with this list. Visit *tasteofhome.com/simple* to print (October/November 2012).

PRODUCE
- ☐ fresh baby carrots _____ (amount you need)
- ☐ fresh baby spinach _____
- ☐ medium eggplant _____
- ☐ medium onions _____
- ☐ medium zucchini _____
- ☐ sliced fresh mushrooms _____
- ☐ small tart apples _____

MEAT
- ☐ bacon strips _____
- ☐ boneless pork loin chops _____
- ☐ boneless skinless chicken breasts _____
- ☐ cooked medium shrimp _____
- ☐ Italian sausage links _____

DAIRY AND REFRIGERATED
- ☐ butter _____
- ☐ eggs _____
- ☐ grated Parmesan cheese _____
- ☐ heavy whipping cream _____
- ☐ provolone cheese _____
- ☐ sharp shredded cheddar cheese _____

FROZEN
- ☐ frozen Brussels sprouts _____
- ☐ frozen garlic bread _____

PACKAGED
- ☐ all-purpose flour _____
- ☐ brown sugar _____
- ☐ chicken broth _____
- ☐ chopped walnuts _____
- ☐ condensed cream of celery soup, undiluted _____
- ☐ diced tomatoes with garlic and onion _____
- ☐ Dijon mustard _____
- ☐ fettuccine _____
- ☐ flaked coconut _____
- ☐ golden raisins _____
- ☐ hoisin sauce _____
- ☐ instant rice _____
- ☐ maple syrup _____
- ☐ olive oil _____
- ☐ panko (Japanese) bread crumbs _____
- ☐ roasted garlic and olive oil couscous _____
- ☐ spaghetti sauce _____
- ☐ whole-berry cranberry sauce _____

SPICES/SEASONINGS
- ☐ curry powder _____
- ☐ dried marjoram _____
- ☐ dried oregano _____
- ☐ dried sage leaves _____
- ☐ ground cinnamon _____
- ☐ ground ginger _____
- ☐ Italian seasoning _____
- ☐ pepper _____
- ☐ salt _____

Pan-Fried Chicken with Hoisin Cranberry Sauce

No need for sides—this recipe makes a complete meal in just 30 minutes. The sweet, tangy cranberry sauce is perfect with the chicken and couscous.

—TASTE OF HOME TEST KITCHEN

PREP/TOTAL TIME: 30 MIN. **MAKES:** 4 SERVINGS

- **4 boneless skinless chicken breast halves (6 ounces each)**
- **¼ teaspoon salt**
- **¼ teaspoon ground ginger**
- **¼ teaspoon pepper**
- **½ cup all-purpose flour**
- **2 eggs, beaten**
- **1 cup panko (Japanese) bread crumbs**
- **2 tablespoons olive oil**

SAUCE
- **1 can (14 ounces) whole-berry cranberry sauce**
- **¼ cup hoisin sauce**
- **1 teaspoon brown sugar**
- **¼ teaspoon salt**
- **¼ teaspoon ground ginger**

COUSCOUS
- **1 medium zucchini, chopped**
- **2 teaspoons olive oil**
- **1¼ cups water**
- **2 teaspoons hoisin sauce**
- **1 package (5.8 ounces) roasted garlic and olive oil couscous**

1. Flatten chicken slightly; sprinkle with salt, ginger and pepper. Place the flour, eggs and bread crumbs in separate shallow bowls. Coat chicken with flour, dip in eggs, then coat with crumbs.

2. Cook chicken in oil in a large skillet over medium heat for 4-6 minutes on each side or until no longer pink.

3. Combine the cranberry sauce, hoisin sauce, brown sugar, salt and ginger in a small saucepan; heat through.

4. Saute zucchini in oil in a large saucepan until crisp-tender; add water and hoisin sauce. Bring to a boil. Stir in couscous. Remove from the heat; cover and let stand for 5-10 minutes or until water is absorbed. Fluff with a fork. Serve with chicken and cranberry sauce.

Chicken & Shrimp Fettuccine

Saucy and special, this hearty pasta works as well for Wednesday night as it does for a Saturday dinner with company. You'll love the rich combination of bacon, chicken, shrimp and fresh baby spinach.

—TASTE OF HOME TEST KITCHEN

PREP/TOTAL TIME: 30 MIN. **MAKES:** 5 SERVINGS

- **8 ounces uncooked fettuccine**
- **4 bacon strips, chopped**
- **¾ pound boneless skinless chicken breasts, cubed**
- **1 can (14½ ounces) diced tomatoes with garlic and onion, drained**
- **2 cups fresh baby spinach, coarsely chopped**
- **¾ cup heavy whipping cream**
- **½ teaspoon dried sage leaves**
- **½ cup grated Parmesan cheese, divided**
- **¾ pound peeled and deveined cooked medium shrimp**

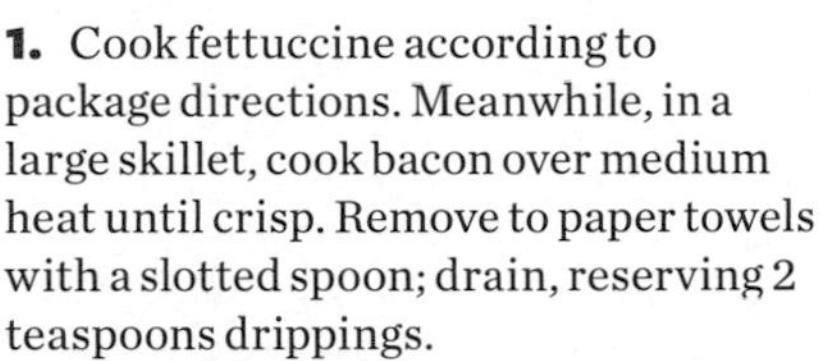

1. Cook fettuccine according to package directions. Meanwhile, in a large skillet, cook bacon over medium heat until crisp. Remove to paper towels with a slotted spoon; drain, reserving 2 teaspoons drippings.

2. In the same skillet, saute chicken in reserved drippings until chicken juices run clear. Remove and keep warm.

3. Add the tomatoes, spinach, cream, sage and 1/4 cup cheese to the skillet; cook and stir over medium heat until slightly thickened and spinach is wilted. Drain fettuccine and add to skillet. Stir in the chicken and shrimp; heat through. Remove from the heat. Sprinkle with bacon and remaining cheese.

BETTER FOR YOU

For a healthier version of Chicken & Shrimp Fettuccine, replace cream with half-and-half and the bacon with turkey bacon, using just two strips instead of four. Cook the chicken in 2 tsp. olive oil instead of the drippings.

Toasted Sausage Cacciatore Sammies

A hot sandwich will warm your family down to their toes. This one's packed with Italian sausage, eggplant and fresh mushrooms, and so tasty you'll want to prepare it again and again!

—TASTE OF HOME TEST KITCHEN

PREP/TOTAL TIME: 30 MIN.
MAKES: 4 SERVINGS

- **1 loaf frozen garlic bread**
- **3 Italian sausage links, chopped**
- **1 medium eggplant, cubed**
- **½ pound sliced fresh mushrooms**
- **1 medium onion, halved and thinly sliced**
- **1 jar (14 ounces) spaghetti sauce**
- **½ teaspoon Italian seasoning**
- **6 slices provolone cheese**

1. Bake garlic bread according to package directions. Meanwhile, cook the sausage, eggplant, mushrooms and onion in a large skillet over medium heat until meat is no longer pink.

2. Stir in spaghetti sauce and Italian seasoning; heat through. Spoon over cut sides of garlic bread and top with cheese. Cut into slices.

Maple-Dijon Sausage & Sprouts

Dijon mustard and maple syrup tickle the taste buds in this yummy skillet supper with sausage and plenty of veggies. Add a convenient package of couscous, and you've got dinner on the table in just 30 minutes!

—TASTE OF HOME TEST KITCHEN

PREP/TOTAL TIME: 30 MIN.
MAKES: 4 SERVINGS

- **4 Italian sausage links, casings removed**
- **1 package (16 ounces) frozen Brussels sprouts**
- **½ pound sliced fresh mushrooms**
- **1 cup fresh baby carrots, halved**
- **1 medium onion, chopped**
- **2 tablespoons maple syrup**
- **2 tablespoons Dijon mustard**
- **½ teaspoon dried sage leaves**
- **½ teaspoon pepper**
- **1 package (5.8 ounces) roasted garlic and olive oil couscous**
- **¼ cup grated Parmesan cheese**

1. Cook sausage in a large skillet until no longer pink; drain. Add Brussels sprouts, mushrooms, carrots and onion; cook until vegetables are crisp-tender. Add the syrup, mustard, sage and pepper; cover and cook 4-6 minutes longer or until Brussels sprouts are tender.

2. Meanwhile, prepare couscous according to package directions. Serve with sausage mixture and sprinkle with cheese.

Bombay Rice with Shrimp

A co-worker whose family is from India shared this delicious recipe with me. I've served it many times at family get-togethers, and the mild curry flavor and pleasant sweetness are always well received.

—SHERRY FLAQUEL CUTLER BAY, FLORIDA

PREP: 25 MIN. **BAKE:** 20 MIN. **MAKES:** 6 SERVINGS

- **1½ cups uncooked instant rice**
- **1 can (10¾ ounces) condensed cream of celery soup, undiluted**
- **½ cup water**
- **2 teaspoons curry powder**
- **1 teaspoon salt**
- **1 pound peeled and deveined cooked medium shrimp**
- **1 medium onion, chopped**
- **½ cup chopped walnuts**
- **½ cup flaked coconut**
- **½ cup golden raisins**
- **1 small tart apple, chopped**

1. Cook rice according to package directions.

2. Meanwhile, combine the soup, water, curry and salt in a large bowl. Stir in the shrimp, onion, walnuts, coconut, raisins, apple and rice. Transfer to a greased 11-in. x 7-in. baking dish.

3. Bake, uncovered, at 350° for 20-25 minutes or until heated through.

123 MAKE IT SIMPLE

"When you need to coat a baking dish with nonstick spray for recipes like Bombay Rice with Shrimp, hold the dish over your open dishwasher door. The door catches any mess and will be cleaned the next time you run the dishwasher," says reader Cynthia Lesko of Leander, Texas.

Caramel-Apple Pork Chops

With bacon, walnuts, pork chops and a scrumptious caramelized apple and onion mixture—how could anyone resist this fall family-pleaser? Best of all, the main dish cooks in one skillet, so cleanup is easy!

—TASTE OF HOME TEST KITCHEN

PREP: 15 MIN. **COOK:** 20 MIN. **MAKES:** 4 SERVINGS

- **4 bacon strips, chopped**
- **4 boneless pork loin chops (6 ounces each)**
- **3 small tart apples, peeled and thinly sliced**
- **1 medium onion, chopped**
- **4 teaspoons brown sugar**
- **1 tablespoon butter**
- **¼ teaspoon salt**
- **¼ teaspoon ground cinnamon**
- **¼ teaspoon pepper**
- **½ cup chicken broth**
- **2 packages (6 ounces each) fresh baby spinach**
- **3 tablespoons chopped walnuts, toasted**

1. Cook bacon in a large skillet over medium heat until crisp. Remove to paper towels; drain, reserving 3 teaspoons drippings. In the same skillet, cook pork chops in 2 teaspoons reserved drippings over medium heat for 2-3 minutes on each side or until lightly browned. Remove and keep warm.

2. Saute apples and onion in 1 teaspoon reserved drippings in the same skillet until apples are crisp-tender. Stir in the brown sugar, butter, salt, cinnamon and pepper. Add broth; bring to a boil. Add pork chops. Reduce heat; cover and simmer for 4-5 minutes or until a thermometer reads 145°.

3. Remove chops to serving platter; let stand for 5 minutes. Add spinach to skillet and cook until wilted. Serve with chops. Sprinkle with bacon and walnuts.

Pork & Vegetable Skillet

Some handy store-bought items and a few dried herbs make this vibrant stovetop dish with a creamy sauce so simple to whip up.

—TASTE OF HOME TEST KITCHEN

PREP/TOTAL TIME: 30 MIN.
MAKES: 6 SERVINGS

- **1½ pounds boneless pork loin chops, cubed**
- **2 tablespoons olive oil, divided**
- **3 cups cubed eggplant**
- **1 medium zucchini, chopped**
- **1 medium onion, chopped**
- **1 cup fresh baby carrots, cut in half lengthwise**
- **1 can (14½ ounces) diced tomatoes with garlic and onion, undrained**
- **1 can (10¾ ounces) condensed cream of celery soup, undiluted**
- **1 cup (4 ounces) sharp shredded cheddar cheese**
- **¼ cup water**
- **½ teaspoon salt**
- **½ teaspoon dried oregano**
- **½ teaspoon dried marjoram**
- **Hot cooked fettuccine**

1. Cook pork in a large skillet over medium heat in 1 tablespoon oil until browned; remove and keep warm.

2. In the same skillet, saute the eggplant, zucchini, onion and carrots in remaining oil until tender. Stir in the tomatoes, soup, cheese, water, salt and seasonings; add pork. Bring to a boil. Reduce heat; simmer, uncovered, for 5 minutes. Serve with fettuccine.

Breakfast & Brunch Favorites

"You can't go wrong with peanut butter and Nutella, but the secret here is using really juicy strawberries. Never tried Nutella? Look for the hazelnut-flavored spread near the peanut butter at your grocery store."

FRANCES PIETSCH FLOWER MOUND, TEXAS
Nutty Waffle Sandwiches, page 116

Asparagus Mushroom Quiche

Nothing says Mother's Day like a quiche. The buttery crust and fresh fillings—in this case, spring favorites asparagus, mushrooms and onion—show Mom how much you care. But don't be intimidated: A super-easy refrigerated pastry makes this recipe an absolute cinch to put together.

—**TRISHA KRUSE** EAGLE, IDAHO

PREP: 20 MIN. **BAKE:** 30 MIN. + STANDING **MAKES:** 8 SERVINGS

- **1 sheet refrigerated pie pastry**
- **1 pound fresh asparagus, cut into 1-inch pieces**
- **1 medium onion, chopped**
- **1 cup sliced fresh mushrooms**
- **2 tablespoons butter**
- **3 eggs**
- **1⅓ cups heavy whipping cream**
- **2 teaspoons minced fresh basil**
- **½ teaspoon salt**
- **½ teaspoon pepper**

1. Unroll pastry into a 9-in. deep-dish pie plate; flute edges.
2. Place asparagus in a steamer basket; place in a large saucepan over 1 in. of water. Bring to a boil; cover and steam for 3-5 minutes or until crisp-tender.
3. In a large skillet, saute onion and mushrooms in butter until tender. Stir in asparagus. Transfer to crust. In a small bowl, whisk the eggs, cream, basil, salt and pepper; pour over top.
4. Bake at 375° for 30-35 minutes or until a knife inserted near the center comes out clean. Let stand for 10 minutes before cutting.

Best Scrambled Eggs

They don't call them the best for nothing. Some people are skeptical about trying these eggs, but once they do, they're hooked for life.

—**LAURIE TIETZE** LONGVIEW, TEXAS

PREP/TOTAL TIME: 20 MIN.
MAKES: 4 SERVINGS

- **8 eggs**
- **5 slices process American cheese, chopped**
- **¼ cup cubed fully cooked ham**
- **¼ cup 2% milk**
- **1 tablespoon spicy brown mustard**
- **⅛ teaspoon salt**
- **⅛ teaspoon pepper**

1. Heat a nonstick skillet coated with cooking spray over medium heat. Whisk all the ingredients; add to skillet. Cook and stir until set.

Mini Caramel Rolls

Here's the perfect warm treat for pajama-clad family mornings. These ooey-gooey baked rolls come together in moments—thanks to a tube of refrigerated crescent rolls—and disappear just as quickly!

—**KAYLA WIEGAND** CONGERVILLE, ILLINOIS

PREP: 20 MIN. **BAKE:** 15 MIN.
MAKES: 12 SERVINGS

- **⅓ cup packed brown sugar**
- **⅓ cup butter, cubed**
- **2 tablespoons light corn syrup**
- **1½ teaspoons 2% milk**
- **1 tube (8 ounces) refrigerated crescent rolls**
- **2 teaspoons sugar**
- **½ teaspoon ground cinnamon**

1. In a small saucepan, combine the brown sugar, butter, corn syrup and milk. Cook and stir over medium heat until butter is melted and sugar is dissolved. Pour into a greased 9-in. pie plate; set aside.
2. Separate crescent dough into four rectangles; gently press perforations to seal. In a small bowl, combine sugar and cinnamon; sprinkle evenly over rectangles. Roll up jelly-roll style, starting with a long side; pinch seams to seal.
3. Cut each into nine slices; place cut side down in prepared pie plate. Bake at 375° for 15-18 minutes or until golden brown. Cool in pie plate for 1 minute before inverting onto a serving plate.

Nutty Waffle Sandwiches

PREP/TOTAL TIME: 15 MIN.
MAKES: 4 SERVINGS

- **8 frozen multigrain waffles**
- **½ cup Nutella**
- **2 medium bananas, sliced**
- **1 cup sliced fresh strawberries**
- **½ cup peanut butter**

1. Toast waffles according to package directions. Spread four waffles with Nutella. Layer with bananas and strawberries. Spread remaining waffles with peanut butter; place over top.

You can't go wrong with peanut butter and Nutella, but the secret here is using really juicy strawberries. Never tried Nutella? Look for the hazelnut-flavored spread near the peanut butter at your grocery store.
—**FRANCES PIETSCH** FLOWER MOUND, TEXAS

Easy Cinnamon Rolls

Cute as a button and melt-in-your-mouth fabulous when warm, these carefree rolls are the perfect sweet treat to help you welcome the day.

—**JOANN FRAZIER HENSLEY**
MCGAHEYSVILLE, VIRGINIA

PREP: 25 MIN. + RISING
BAKE: 15 MIN. **MAKES:** 1 DOZEN

- **¼ cup sugar**
- **1 teaspoon ground cinnamon**
- **1 package (16 ounces) frozen bread dough dinner rolls, thawed but still cold**
- **2 tablespoons butter, melted**
- **½ cup confectioners' sugar**
- **1 tablespoon 2% milk**
- **6 red candied cherries, halved**

1. In a shallow bowl, combine sugar and cinnamon; set aside. Shape each roll into a 12-in. rope. Coil each rope. Dip in butter, then roll in sugar mixture.
2. Place coil on a greased 13-in. x 9-in. baking pan. Sprinkle with remaining cinnamon-sugar. Cover and let rise in a warm place until doubled, about 1 hour.
3. Bake at 350° for 15-20 minutes or until golden brown. In a small bowl, combine confectioners' sugar and milk until smooth. Drizzle over warm rolls. Top each with a cherry half.

Shhh! SIMPLE SECRET

If you have ripe bananas that aren't ready to be used, put them in a tightly sealed plastic bag and refrigerate for longer storage. The peel will become brown but the flesh will remain unchanged.

Cream Cheese & Chive Omelet

The first bite of creamy filling lets you know this isn't any old omelet. Make it once, and we suspect you'll be fixing it often.

—ANNE TROISE MANALAPAN, NEW JERSEY

PREP/TOTAL TIME: 15 MIN. **MAKES:** 2 SERVINGS

- **1 tablespoon olive oil**
- **4 eggs**
- **2 tablespoons minced chives**
- **2 tablespoons water**
- **⅛ teaspoon salt**
- **⅛ teaspoon pepper**
- **2 ounces cream cheese, cubed**
- **Salsa**

1. In a large nonstick skillet, heat oil over medium-high heat. Whisk the eggs, chives, water, salt and pepper. Add egg mixture to skillet (mixture should set immediately at edges).

2. As eggs set, push cooked edges toward the center, letting uncooked portion flow underneath. When the eggs are set, sprinkle cream cheese on one side; fold other side over filling. Slide omelet onto a plate; cut in half. Serve with salsa.

Blueberry-Oat Smoothies

Here's a "Wow, this is different!" smoothie. I never thought to put oatmeal in a smoothie before, but after soaking, there is no stiffness to the oats at all! If using fresh blueberries, two or three ice cubes may be added to the blender to make a chillier treat.

—KIM FORNI CLAREMONT NEW HAMPSHIRE

PREP/TOTAL TIME: 10 MIN. **MAKES:** 3 SERVINGS

- **1 cup unsweetened apple juice**
- **1 cup vanilla yogurt**
- **1 cup frozen unsweetened blueberries**
- **½ cup quick-cooking oats**
- **2 tablespoons maple syrup**

1. In a blender, combine all ingredients; cover and process for 30 seconds or until smooth. Pour into chilled glasses and serve immediately.

Apricot Cream Biscuits

Melt-in-your-mouth good when warm, these shortcut biscuits with a hint of orange prove that the right mix really can offer homemade taste.

—BETTY SAINT TURNER ATTALLA, ALABAMA

PREP/TOTAL TIME: 30 MIN. **MAKES:** 1 DOZEN

- **3 cups biscuit/baking mix**
- **2 teaspoons grated orange peel**
- **1 cup heavy whipping cream**
- **¼ cup apricot preserves**
- **2 tablespoons cream cheese, softened**
- **2 teaspoons sugar**

1. In a large bowl, combine baking mix and orange peel. Stir in cream just until moistened. Turn onto a lightly floured surface; knead 8-10 times. Roll out to ½-in. thickness; cut with a floured 2½-in. biscuit cutter.

2. Place 2 in. apart on an ungreased baking sheet. Using the end of a wooden spoon handle, make a 1¼-in.-wide and ¼-in.-deep indentation in the center of each biscuit.

3. In a small bowl, beat apricot preserves and cream cheese until blended. Drop by teaspoonfuls into the center of each biscuit. Sprinkle with sugar.

4. Bake at 400° for 10-15 minutes or until golden brown. Serve warm.

Coconut-Pecan Coffee Cake

I've learned to keep copies of the recipe on hand when I serve my moist and satisfying coffee cake. It has a nice level of coconut flavor from the pudding mix.

—**BETH TROPEANO** CHARLOTTE, NORTH CAROLINA

PREP: 15 MIN. **BAKE:** 35 MIN. **MAKES:** 15 SERVINGS

- **1 package (18¼ ounces) yellow cake mix**
- **1 package (3.4 ounces) instant coconut cream pudding mix**
- **1 teaspoon vanilla extract**

FILLING

- **½ cup chopped pecans**
- **⅓ cup sugar**
- **½ teaspoon ground cinnamon**

GLAZE

- **1 cup confectioners' sugar**
- **1 to 2 tablespoons 2% milk**
- **½ teaspoon vanilla extract**

1. Prepare cake mix batter according to package directions, adding pudding mix and vanilla; set aside. In a small bowl, combine the pecans, sugar and cinnamon.
2. Spread half of the cake batter into a greased 13-in. x 9-in. baking pan. Sprinkle with half of filling. Top with remaining batter and filling.
3. Bake at 350° for 34-38 minutes or until a toothpick inserted near the center comes out clean. Cool on a wire rack. In a small bowl, combine the glaze ingredients until smooth. Drizzle over warm coffee cake.

Slow-Cooked Fruited Oatmeal with Nuts

The beauty of this breakfast is that you can set the slow cooker overnight and, with nothing more than a ladle, spoons and bowls, feed a hungry crowd in the morning.

—**TRISHA KRUSE** EAGLE, IDAHO

PREP: 15 MIN. **COOK:** 6 HOURS **MAKES:** 6 SERVINGS

- **3 cups water**
- **2 cups old-fashioned oats**
- **2 cups chopped apples**
- **1 cup dried cranberries**
- **1 cup fat-free milk**
- **2 teaspoons butter, melted**
- **1 teaspoon pumpkin pie spice**
- **1 teaspoon ground cinnamon**
- **6 tablespoons chopped almonds, toasted**
- **6 tablespoons chopped pecans, toasted**
- **Additional fat-free milk**

1. In a 3-qt. slow cooker coated with cooking spray, combine the first eight ingredients. Cover and cook on low for 6-8 hours or until liquid is absorbed.
2. Spoon oatmeal into bowls. Sprinkle with almonds and pecans; drizzle with additional milk if desired.

Toasting Nuts

To toast nuts, spread them in a 15-in. x 10-in. x 1-in. baking pan. Bake at 350° for 5-10 minutes or until lightly browned, stirring occasionally. Or, spread in a dry nonstick skillet and heat over low heat until lightly browned, stirring occasionally. Be sure to watch the nuts closely, because they can burn very quickly.

Blue Cheese Quiche with Caramelized Pears

Pop the quiche in the oven, and you'll have just enough time to whip up a fruit salad and refresh guests' drinks before it's done.

—MAGGIE CARRICK
GAITHERSBURG, MARYLAND

PREP: 25 MIN. **BAKE:** 30 MIN.
MAKES: 8 SERVINGS

- **1 sheet frozen puff pastry, thawed**
- **8 turkey bacon strips, diced**
- **1 cup (4 ounces) crumbled blue cheese**
- **8 eggs**
- **1 cup heavy whipping cream**
- **½ cup shredded Parmesan cheese**
- **¾ teaspoon salt**
- **½ teaspoon ground nutmeg**
- **½ teaspoon pepper**

TOPPING

- **1 medium onion, thinly sliced**
- **2 teaspoons olive oil**
- **3 medium pears, thinly sliced**
- **1 tablespoon brown sugar**

1. Unfold puff pastry; press into a greased 9-in. fluted tart pan with removable bottom. In a large skillet, cook bacon over medium heat until crisp. Spoon bacon into crust and sprinkle with blue cheese. In a large bowl, whisk the eggs, cream, Parmesan cheese, salt, nutmeg and pepper; pour over top.

2. Bake at 350° for 30-35 minutes or until a knife inserted near the center comes out clean. Meanwhile, in a large skillet, saute onion in oil until tender. Add pears and brown sugar; cook 4 minutes longer. Serve with quiche.

"Sweet sauteed onions and pears match the bold flavor of blue cheese in this decadent version of a brunch classic."

—MAGGIE CARRICK
GAITHERSBURG, MARYLAND

Loaded Breakfast Potatoes

My kids love loaded potatoes in restaurants, so I modified them to make at home. Using the microwave for the potatoes will save you about 10 minutes. I also use thin-skinned red potatoes instead of russets to save on peeling time.

—**TENA KROPP** AURORA, ILLINOIS

PREP/TOTAL TIME: 30 MIN.
MAKES: 6 SERVINGS

- **1½ pounds red potatoes, cubed**
- **¼ pound bacon strips, chopped**
- **¾ cup cubed fully cooked ham**
- **1 cup (4 ounces) shredded cheddar cheese**
- **½ teaspoon salt**
- **¼ teaspoon pepper**
- **Sour cream**

1. Place potatoes in a microwave-safe dish and cover with water. Cover and microwave on high for 4-5 minutes or until tender.
2. Meanwhile, in a large skillet, cook bacon over medium heat until crisp. Remove to paper towels with a slotted spoon. Drain potatoes; saute in drippings until lightly browned. Add the ham, cheese, salt, pepper and bacon. Cook and stir over medium heat until cheese is melted. Serve with sour cream.

Green Breakfast Smoothie

You'll be surprised at the creaminess of this smoothie. It's packed with healthy pears, avocado and spinach!

—**TASTE OF HOME TEST KITCHEN**

PREP/TOTAL TIME: 10 MIN.
MAKES: 2 SERVINGS

- **¾ cup unsweetened apple juice**
- **1 cup crushed ice**
- **2 cups fresh baby spinach**
- **1 medium pear, coarsely chopped**
- **1 medium ripe avocado, peeled and cubed**
- **3 tablespoons honey**

1. In a blender, combine all ingredients; cover and process for 1 minute or until smooth. Pour into chilled glasses and serve immediately.

Chocolate Challah French Toast

This decadent breakfast treat is one I often serve—with pleasure—from the kitchen of our family-run bed and breakfast.

—**MARIE PARKER** MILWAUKEE, WISCONSIN

PREP: 15 MIN. + SOAKING **COOK:** 10 MIN. **MAKES:** 2 SERVINGS

- **4 slices challah or egg bread (¾ inch thick)**
- **⅔ cup sugar**
- **⅓ cup baking cocoa**
- **¼ teaspoon salt**
- **⅛ teaspoon baking powder**
- **4 eggs**
- **1 cup 2% milk**
- **1 teaspoon vanilla extract**
- **2 tablespoons butter**
- **Optional toppings: confectioners' sugar, fresh raspberries, sliced fresh strawberries, sliced ripe banana and maple syrup**

1. Arrange bread slices in a 13-in. x 9-in. dish. In a small bowl, combine the sugar, cocoa, salt and baking powder. In another bowl, whisk the eggs, milk and vanilla. Gradually whisk into dry ingredients until smooth. Pour over bread. Let stand 10 minutes, turning the bread once.
2. In a large skillet, melt butter over medium heat. Cook bread for 3-4 minutes each side or until toasted. Serve with toppings of your choice.

Ham & Cheese Bagels

I came up with this recipe one day when I needed something quick and healthy for lunch but didn't want to go to a lot of trouble.

—NITA GRAFFIS DOVE CREEK, COLORADO

PREP/TOTAL TIME: 30 MIN. **MAKES:** 6 SERVINGS

- **4 teaspoons butter, softened**
- **6 plain bagels, split**
- **6 slices deli ham**
- **6 slices cheddar cheese**
- **2 ounces cream cheese, softened**
- **⅛ teaspoon salt**
- **⅛ teaspoon pepper**
- **1 large tomato, sliced**
- **1 medium ripe avocado, peeled and sliced**

1. Spread butter over cut sides of bagels. Place buttered sides up on an ungreased baking sheet. Broil 4-6 in. from the heat for 3-4 minutes or until lightly browned. Set aside bagel tops.
2. On the bottom of each bagel, place a slice of ham and cheddar cheese. Broil 3-4 minutes longer or until cheese is melted.
3. Meanwhile, spread bagel tops with cream cheese; sprinkle with salt and pepper. Layer bottom halves with tomato and avocado. Replace tops.

Yogurt & Honey Fruit Cups

Fresh winter fruit gets dressed up in a sweet and creamy sauce that will disappear as fast as it comes together.

—TASTE OF HOME TEST KITCHEN

PREP/TOTAL TIME: 10 MIN. **MAKES:** 6 SERVINGS

- **4-½ cups cut-up fresh fruit (pears, apples, bananas, grapes, etc.)**
- **¾ cup (6 ounces) mandarin orange, vanilla or lemon yogurt**
- **1 tablespoon honey**
- **½ teaspoon grated orange peel**
- **¼ teaspoon almond extract**

1. Divide fruit among six individual serving bowls. Combine the yogurt, honey, orange peel and extract; spoon over the fruit.

Cranberry Pancakes

PREP/TOTAL TIME: 30 MIN. **MAKES:** 3 SERVINGS

- **1 cup fresh or frozen cranberries**
- **⅔ cup cranberry juice**
- **½ cup packed brown sugar**
- **2 tablespoons honey**
- **½ teaspoon lemon juice**

PANCAKES

- **2 cups biscuit/baking mix**
- **2 tablespoons brown sugar**
- **2 teaspoons baking powder**
- **½ teaspoon ground cinnamon**
- **2 eggs**
- **1¼ cups 2% milk**
- **½ teaspoon grated lemon peel**
- **½ cup chopped fresh or frozen cranberries**
- **Lemon peel strips, optional**

1. In a small saucepan, bring the cranberries, cranberry juice and brown sugar to a boil. Reduce heat; simmer, uncovered, for 5 minutes. Cool slightly. With a slotted spoon, remove 1/4 cup cranberries and set aside.
2. In a blender, process the remaining cranberry mixture until smooth. Stir in the honey, lemon juice and reserved cranberries; keep warm.
3. In a large bowl, combine the biscuit mix, brown sugar, baking powder and cinnamon. In another bowl, whisk the eggs, milk and lemon peel. Stir into dry ingredients just until moistened. Stir in cranberries.
4. Drop batter by 1/4 cupfuls onto a greased hot griddle; turn when bubbles form on top. Cook until second side is golden brown. Serve with syrup and garnish servings with lemon peel strips if desired.

Maple & Chipotle Sausages

We blend sweet and smoky flavors with a touch of spiciness in these breakfast sausages that will be ready in moments.

—TASTE OF HOME TEST KITCHEN

PREP/TOTAL TIME: 15 MIN. **MAKES:** 4 SERVINGS

- **1 package (7 ounces) brown-and-serve sausage links**
- **¼ cup maple syrup**
- **1 teaspoon chipotle peppers in adobo sauce**
- **½ teaspoon garlic powder**
- **¼ teaspoon ground ginger**
- **¼ teaspoon onion powder**

1. In a large skillet, cook sausage links according to package directions. Combine the remaining ingredients; stir into skillet. Bring to a boil; cook and stir until sausages are glazed.

123 MAKE IT SIMPLE

Ease rushed mornings by getting a head start on this meal the night before. For pancakes, combine the wet ingredients and refrigerate overnight. You can also combine the dry ingredients, cover and store on the counter.

“Adding a touch of baking powder to the biscuit/baking mix takes your morning meal to new heights. Flip these towering pancakes onto the plate and watch the family run to the table.”

—TASTE OF HOME TEST KITCHEN

Appetizers & Beverages

"The meat falls off the bones of these succulent wings! The 'spice' in the recipe title comes from a generous sprinkling of red pepper flakes."

SUE BAYLESS PRIOR LAKE, MINNESOTA
Sweet & Spicy Chicken Wings, page 129

Family-Favorite Turkey Egg Rolls

Finger foods give an ordinary weekday menu extra flair! This recipe is so easy, kids can help prepare it. Serve with sweet-and-sour or hot mustard dipping sauce.

—**VIRGINIA REHM** WAYNESVILLE, MISSOURI

PREP: 25 MIN. **COOK:** 5 MIN./BATCH **MAKES:** 1 DOZEN

- **½ pound ground turkey**
- **4½ cups coleslaw mix**
- **3 tablespoons sesame seeds**
- **1 tablespoon reduced-sodium soy sauce**
- **2 teaspoons Worcestershire sauce**
- **¾ teaspoon ground ginger**
- **½ teaspoon seasoned salt**
- **12 egg roll wrappers**
- **Oil for deep-fat frying**
- **Sweet-and-sour sauce**

1. In a large skillet, cook turkey over medium heat until no longer pink; drain. Stir in the coleslaw mix, sesame seeds, soy sauce, Worcestershire sauce, ginger and seasoned salt. Cook for 3-4 minutes or until cabbage is crisp-tender.
2. Place 1/4 cup of turkey mixture in the center of one egg roll wrapper. (Keep remaining wrappers covered with a damp paper towel until ready to use.) Fold bottom corner over filling. Fold sides toward center over filling. Moisten remaining corner with water; roll up tightly to seal. Repeat.
3. In an electric skillet or deep-fat fryer, heat oil to 375°. Fry egg rolls, a few at a time, for 3-4 minutes or until golden brown, turning often. Drain on paper towels. Serve with sweet-and-sour sauce.

Cheese-Trio Artichoke & Spinach Dip

No appetizer spread is complete without at least one amazing dip, and this one is it! Creamy, cheesy and chock-full of veggies, it will quickly become your new go-to appetizer.

—**DIANE SPEARE** KISSIMMEE, FLORIDA

PREP: 20 MIN. **COOK:** 2 HOURS **MAKES:** 4 CUPS

- **1 cup chopped fresh mushrooms**
- **1 tablespoon butter**
- **2 garlic cloves, minced**
- **1½ cups mayonnaise**
- **1 package (8 ounces) cream cheese, softened**
- **1 cup plus 2 tablespoons grated Parmesan cheese, divided**
- **1 cup (4 ounces) shredded part-skim mozzarella cheese, divided**
- **1 can (14 ounces) water-packed artichoke hearts, rinsed, drained and chopped**
- **1 package (10 ounces) frozen chopped spinach, thawed and squeezed dry**
- **¼ cup chopped sweet red pepper**
- **Toasted French bread baguette slices**

1. In a large skillet, saute mushrooms in butter until tender. Add garlic; cook 1 minute longer.
2. In a large bowl, combine the mayonnaise, cream cheese, 1 cup Parmesan cheese and 3/4 cup mozzarella cheese. Add the mushroom mixture, artichokes, spinach and red pepper.
3. Transfer to a 3-qt slow cooker. Sprinkle with remaining cheeses. Cover and cook on low for 2-3 hours or until heated through. Serve with baguette slices.

Peanut Chicken Wings

Creamy peanut butter and chili powder prove they're an ideal match for any wing. Round out the menu with cut-up veggies, ranch or blue cheese salad dressing, and store-bought sweet potato fries.

—JANET VAUPEL ROCKWELL
HOLLIS, NEW HAMPSHIRE

PREP: 15 MIN. + MARINATING
BAKE: 35 MIN. **MAKES:** 9 SERVINGS

- **2 pounds chicken wings**
- **2 tablespoons creamy peanut butter**
- **1 tablespoon lemon juice**
- **1 tablespoon canola oil**
- **1 tablespoon reduced-sodium soy sauce**
- **½ teaspoon salt**
- **½ teaspoon chili powder**
- **½ teaspoon browning sauce, optional**
- **Dash garlic powder**

1. Cut chicken wings into three sections; discard wing tip sections. In a large resealable plastic bag, combine the peanut butter, lemon juice, oil, soy sauce, salt, chili powder, browning sauce if desired and garlic powder. Add wings; seal bag and turn to coat. Refrigerate overnight.
2. Drain and discard marinade. Transfer wings to a greased 13-in. x 9-in. baking dish. Bake, uncovered, at 375° for 35-40 minutes or until chicken juices run clear, turning every 10 minutes.

Editor's Note: *Uncooked chicken wing sections (wingettes) may be substituted for whole chicken wings.*

Berry Delicious Smoothies

My son and I love this summery smoothie. It's fun to make and healthy, too!

—ELIZABETH STEWART
CRAB ORCHARD, WEST VIRGINIA

PREP/TOTAL TIME: 10 MIN.
MAKES: 4 SERVINGS

- **1½ cups fat-free strawberry Greek yogurt**
- **¾ cup acai mixed berry V8 juice blend**
- **1 cup frozen unsweetened strawberries**
- **1 cup frozen unsweetened blueberries**
- **½ cup frozen unsweetened raspberries**
- **½ cup frozen unsweetened blackberries**
- **½ cup frozen pitted dark sweet cherries**
- **¼ cup wheat bran**
- **1 teaspoon ground flaxseed**

1. In a blender, combine all ingredients; cover and process for 30 seconds or until smooth. Pour into chilled glasses and serve immediately.

"The meat falls off the bones of these succulent wings! The 'spice' in the recipe title comes from a generous sprinkling of red pepper flakes."

—**SUE BAYLESS** PRIOR LAKE, MINNESOTA

Sweet & Spicy Chicken Wings

PREP: 25 MIN. **COOK:** 5 HOURS
MAKES: ABOUT 1 DOZEN

- **3 pounds chicken wings**
- **1½ cups ketchup**
- **1 cup packed brown sugar**
- **1 small onion, finely chopped**
- **¼ cup finely chopped sweet red pepper**
- **2 tablespoons chili powder**
- **2 tablespoons Worcestershire sauce**
- **1½ teaspoons crushed red pepper flakes**
- **1 teaspoon ground mustard**
- **1 teaspoon dried basil**
- **1 teaspoon dried thyme**
- **1 teaspoon pepper**

1. Cut wings into three sections; discard wing tip sections. Place chicken in a 4-qt. slow cooker. In a small bowl, combine the remaining ingredients. Pour over chicken; stir until coated. Cover and cook on low for 5-6 hours or until chicken juices run clear.

Editor's Note: *Uncooked chicken wing sections (wingettes) may be substituted for whole chicken wings.*

Creamy Cranberry Meatballs

Extras from tonight's rich and juicy appetizers can become tomorrow's entree. Simply serve them over a bed of fluffy noodles or rice—if there are any left!

—AMY WARREN MAINEVILLE, OHIO

PREP: 10 MIN. **COOK:** 3 HOURS
MAKES: ABOUT 5 DOZEN

- **2 envelopes (0.87 ounce each) brown gravy mix**
- **1 package (32 ounces) frozen fully cooked Swedish meatballs**
- **⅔ cup jellied cranberry sauce**
- **2 teaspoons Dijon mustard**
- **¼ cup heavy whipping cream**

1. Prepare gravy mix according to package directions. In a 4-qt. slow cooker, combine the meatballs, cranberry sauce, mustard and gravy. Cover and cook on low for 3-4 hours or until heated through, adding cream during the last 30 minutes of cooking.

Lemon Mint Spritzer

Looking for a refreshing beverage that's wonderful for those outdoor grilling parties during hot weather? Try a splash of this cooling combo of lemon and mint.

—LAURA NIX ELLIJAY, GEORGIA

PREP/TOTAL TIME: 10 MIN. **MAKES:** 12 SERVINGS (1 CUP EACH)

- **2 medium lemons**
- **2 cans (12 ounces each) frozen lemonade concentrate, thawed**
- **¼ cup confectioners' sugar**
- **¼ cup fresh mint leaves, chopped**
- **2 bottles (1 liter each) carbonated water, chilled**
- **Ice cubes**

1. Cut lemons into wedges and squeeze the juice into a large pitcher. Stir in the lemonade concentrate, confectioners' sugar and mint; add lemon wedges. Chill until serving.
2. Just before serving, stir in carbonated water. Serve over ice.

Super Mango Smoothies

This packs a nutritional punch, first thing in the morning, to keep you healthy and going strong all day. It also tastes great!

—KAREN CLAUSEN WAUBAY, SOUTH DAKOTA

PREP/TOTAL TIME: 10 MIN. **MAKES:** 2 SERVINGS

- **1½ cups peach mango juice blend**
- **1 cup frozen pineapple chunks**
- **1 cup frozen mango chunks**
- **2 tablespoons 2% cottage cheese**
- **2 tablespoons ground flaxseed**
- **1 tablespoon toasted wheat germ**

1. In a blender, combine all ingredients; cover and process for 1 minute or until smooth. Pour into chilled glasses; serve immediately.

Savory Corn Bread Pops

Not all pops were created sweet, but they're all delicious in our book. These handheld treats make festive appetizers, too.
—TASTE OF HOME FOOD STYLING TEAM

PREP: 1 HOUR **BAKE:** 25 MIN. + FREEZING **MAKES:** 2½ DOZEN

- **1 package (8½ ounces) corn bread/muffin mix**
- **2 packages (3 ounces each) cream cheese, softened**
- **2 tablespoons Louisiana-style hot sauce**
- **1 to 3 tablespoons finely chopped pickled jalapeno slices**
- **30 lollipop sticks**
- **¼ cup butter, melted**
- **Crushed corn chips**

1. Prepare and bake corn bread according to package directions, using a greased 8-in. baking pan. Cool completely on a wire rack.
2. In a small bowl, beat the cream cheese, hot sauce and pickled jalapenos until blended. Crumble corn bread over cream cheese mixture and mix well. Shape into 1-in. balls. Place on baking sheets; insert sticks. Freeze for at least 2 hours or until firm.
3. Dip in melted butter and roll in corn chips. Refrigerate until serving.

Mocha Cappuccino Punch

Coffee, meet ice cream! An inventive way to indulge a crowd, this luscious java punch will quench the urgent chocolate cravings for you and 12 of your favorite friends.
—FANCHEON RESLER BLUFFTON, INDIANA

PREP: 15 MIN. + CHILLING **MAKES:** 13 SERVINGS (¾ CUP EACH)

- **1 cup hot water**
- **2 tablespoons instant coffee granules**
- **¼ teaspoon ground cinnamon**
- **1 can (14 ounces) fat-free sweetened condensed milk**
- **½ cup chocolate syrup**
- **1 quart half-and-half cream**
- **1 quart chocolate ice cream**
- **2 cups club soda, chilled**
- **Baking cocoa**

1. In a small bowl, whisk the water, coffee granules and cinnamon until coffee granules are dissolved. Stir in milk and chocolate syrup. Cover and refrigerate until chilled.
2. Transfer milk mixture to a punch bowl; stir in half-and-half cream. Add scoops of ice cream; gradually pour in club soda. Dust top with cocoa. Serve immediately.

Apple Spiced Tea

When was the last time you stopped for afternoon tea? After you try this sweetly spiced drink, you'll want to make it a regular event.
—SUSAN WESTERFIELD ALBUQUERQUE, NEW MEXICO

PREP/TOTAL TIME: 10 MIN. **MAKES:** 1 SERVING

- **½ cup apple cider or juice**
- **¼ teaspoon minced fresh gingerroot**
- **2 whole allspice**
- **2 whole cloves**
- **1 black tea bag**
- **½ cup boiling water**
- **1 tablespoon brown sugar**

1. In a small bowl, combine the first five ingredients. Add boiling water. Cover and steep for 5 minutes. Strain, discarding tea bag and spices. Stir in sugar. Serve immediately.

Sun-Dried Tomato and Parmesan Spread

Garlic lovers will literally eat this up! Fresh basil gives it a lovely aroma; crushed red peppers offer a hint of heat; and sun-dried tomatoes make the creamy sandwich spread bright. Terrific on crackers, too.
—ANNDREA BAILEY HUNTINGTON BEACH, CALIFORNIA

PREP/TOTAL TIME: 25 MIN. **MAKES:** 2 CUPS

- **1 package (8 ounces) cream cheese, softened**
- **½ cup sour cream**
- **¼ cup grated Parmesan cheese**
- **¼ cup oil-packed sun-dried tomatoes, patted dry and chopped**
- **¼ cup mayonnaise**
- **2 tablespoons minced fresh basil or 2 teaspoons dried basil**
- **2 garlic cloves, minced**
- **¼ teaspoon salt**
- **¼ teaspoon crushed red pepper flakes**
- **¼ teaspoon pepper**

1. Place all ingredients in a food processor; cover and process until blended. Chill until serving.

Tartlets are like cake pops—tiny and tasty and a tempting way to experiment with different fillings. But this prize-winning combo is too good to toy with. —**JENNIFER LARISON** TUCSON, ARIZONA

Chocolate Butterscotch Tartlets

PREP: 40 MIN. + CHILLING
MAKES: 3¾ DOZEN

- **1 cup (6 ounces) semisweet chocolate chips**
- **½ cup butterscotch chips**
- **1½ cups heavy whipping cream, divided**
- **1½ teaspoons apricot brandy**
- **4½ teaspoons confectioners' sugar**
- **¼ teaspoon vanilla extract**
- **3 packages (1.9 ounces each) frozen miniature phyllo tart shells**
- **Grated orange peel**

1. Place chocolate and butterscotch chips in a small bowl. In a small saucepan, bring 1 cup cream just to a boil. Pour over chips; whisk until smooth. Stir in brandy. Cool to room temperature, stirring occasionally. Refrigerate until chilled.
2. In a large bowl, beat remaining cream until it begins to thicken. Add confectioners' sugar and vanilla; beat until stiff peaks form. Spoon chocolate mixture into tart shells; top with whipped cream and garnish with orange peel. Refrigerate until serving.

Chili con Queso El Dorado

Used as a dip or a sauce on burgers, chicken or pork, this creamy cheese dip is spiced with chilies, chipotle peppers and hot pepper sauce.

—**CAROLYN KUMPE** EL DORADO, CALIFORNIA

PREP/TOTAL TIME: 25 MIN.
MAKES: 4 CUPS

- **1 cup chopped green onions**
- **1 tablespoon olive oil**
- **1 garlic clove, minced**
- **4 cans (4 ounces each) chopped green chilies**
- **2 chipotle peppers in adobo sauce, finely chopped**
- **2 cans (5 ounces each) evaporated milk**
- **2 cups (8 ounces) shredded Monterey Jack cheese**
- **¼ cup minced fresh cilantro**
- **⅛ teaspoon salt**
- **2 to 4 drops hot pepper sauce**
- **Tortilla chips**

1. In a large saucepan, saute onions in oil until tender. Add garlic; cook 1 minute longer. Add chilies and chipotle peppers; cook 2 minutes longer. Gradually stir in milk; heat through.
2. Remove from heat; stir in cheese until melted. Stir in cilantro, salt and pepper sauce. Serve warm with tortilla chips.

Bella Basil Raspberry Tea

Beautiful basil and fresh raspberries lend bright color and refreshing flavor to this grown-up iced tea. You'll love the fun fizz and make-ahead convenience for parties.

—**LAURIE BOCK** LYNDEN, WASHINGTON

PREP: 45 MIN. + CHILLING **MAKES:** 6 SERVINGS

- **3 cups fresh raspberries**
- **1 cup sugar**
- **1 cup packed fresh basil leaves, coarsely chopped**
- **¼ cup lime juice**
- **2 individual black tea bags**
- **1 bottle (1 liter) carbonated water or 1 bottle (750 milliliters) sparkling rose wine**
- **Ice cubes**
- **Fresh basil sprigs, optional**

1. In a large saucepan, combine the raspberries, sugar, basil and lime juice. Mash berries. Cook over medium heat for 7 minutes or until juices are released from berries.
2. Remove from the heat; add tea bags. Cover and steep for 20 minutes. Strain, discarding tea bags and raspberry seeds. Transfer tea to a 2-qt. pitcher. Cover and refrigerate until serving.
3. Just before serving, slowly add carbonated water to tea. Serve over ice and garnish with basil sprigs if desired.

Crispy Mexican Truffles

These no-bake chocolate indulgences scream cinnamon, cayenne and crunch! "I can't wait to make these at home," said one taste tester. The cayenne pepper isn't overwhelming, but adds an unexpected hint of heat.

—**SHELLY BEVINGTON-FISHER** HERMISTON, OREGON

PREP: 30 MIN. + CHILLING **MAKES:** 2½ DOZEN

- **6 ounces cream cheese, softened**
- **2 cups confectioners' sugar**
- **8 ounces bittersweet chocolate, melted and cooled**
- **2 teaspoons vanilla extract**
- **1 cup crushed cornflakes**
- **2 teaspoons ground cinnamon**
- **½ teaspoon cayenne pepper**

1. In a large bowl, beat cream cheese until smooth. Beat in the confectioners' sugar, chocolate and vanilla. Cover and refrigerate for at least 1 hour or until easy to handle.
2. In a small bowl, combine the cornflakes, cinnamon and cayenne. Shape chocolate mixture into 1-in. balls; roll in cornflake mixture. Store in an airtight container in the refrigerator.

Pineapple Colada Shake

With refreshing coconut and pineapple flavors, this frothy shake is sinfully delicious! With its hint of cinnamon and creamy texture, it just begs to be your poolside companion.

—MELISSA JELINEK MENOMONEE FALLS, WISCONSIN

PREP/TOTAL TIME: 5 MIN. **MAKES:** 1 SERVING

¼ cup coconut-flavored rum
½ cup vanilla ice cream
½ cup canned crushed pineapple
Ground cinnamon
Fresh pineapple wedge and maraschino cherry

1. Place the rum, ice cream and pineapple in a blender. Cover and process for 30 seconds or until blended. Transfer to a chilled glass. Sprinkle with cinnamon. Garnish with pineapple and a cherry.

Shhh! SIMPLE SECRET

A quick and easy way to clean a blender is to fill it halfway with hot water, add a drop of dishwashing liquid, cover it and blend on high for 10-15 seconds. Rinse it well with hot water and allow to air dry until the next time you need to use it!

Maple Jalapenos

Craving something sweet with just a little jolt of heat? Try these creamy, sweet, hot and savory treats. After one bite, I'm betting you'll be back for more!

—NICOLE LARSON AMERICAN FORK, UTAH

PREP: 45 MIN. **BAKE:** 20 MIN. **MAKES:** 50 APPETIZERS

25 jalapeno peppers
1 package (8 ounces) cream cheese, softened
1 cup (4 ounces) crumbled feta cheese
½ cup maple syrup
½ pound bacon strips, cooked and crumbled
¼ cup packed brown sugar

1. Cut jalapenos in half lengthwise and remove seeds. Set aside. In a small bowl, beat the cream cheese, feta cheese and syrup until smooth. Spoon into pepper halves.
2. Place in two greased 15-in. x 10-in. x 1-in. baking pans. Top with bacon and sprinkle with brown sugar. Bake at 350° for 20 minutes for spicy flavor, 30 minutes for medium and 40 minutes for mild.

Editor's Note: *Wear disposable gloves when cutting hot peppers; the oils can burn skin. Avoid touching your face.*

Chicken Nachos for One

You will so look forward to "me time" when you have the ingredients for these nachos on hand! I've had nachos many different ways, and these are among the best.

—**REGINA MORALES** ORLANDO, FLORIDA

PREP/TOTAL TIME: 10 MIN.
MAKES: 1 SERVING

- **¾ cup coarsely chopped ready-to-use grilled chicken breast strips**
- **2 tablespoons water**
- **¼ teaspoon taco seasoning**
- **¼ cup shredded Mexican cheese blend**
- **2 cups tortilla chips**
- **½ cup refried black beans, warmed**
- **1 tablespoon salsa**

1. In a small skillet, combine the chicken, water and taco seasoning. Bring to a boil. Reduce heat; simmer, uncovered, for 2 minutes, stirring occasionally. Remove from the heat. Sprinkle with cheese; cover and let stand for 1 minute or until melted.
2. Arrange chips on a serving plate, top with beans, chicken mixture and salsa. Serve immediately.

Cinnamon Apple Shakes

Is there such a thing as Milkshake Monday? If not, it's time to shake things up and put these on the menu.

—**NATALIE CARTER** AUSTIN, TEXAS

PREP/TOTAL TIME: 10 MIN.
MAKES: 4 SERVINGS

- **3 cups vanilla ice cream**
- **¾ cup 2% milk**
- **½ cup cinnamon applesauce**
- **¼ cup caramel ice cream topping**
- **½ teaspoon rum extract**

1. In a blender, combine all ingredients; cover and process until smooth. Pour into chilled glasses. Serve immediately.

Panko

Panko is a Japanese-style bread crumb made from crustless bread that is coarsely ground into large, airy flakes. When used as a coating for food, the crumbs offer a light, crunchy texture. Panko bread crumbs also tend to absorb less grease than standard bread crumbs.

Panko Chicken with Fresh Marinara

Here's a crowd-pleasing appetizer that makes for a great weeknight entree, too! We're giving your hometown restaurant a run for its money with these crispy, crunchy tenders served with a chunky homemade sauce.

—**ALLISON PATON** SCARBOROUGH, MAINE

PREP: 25 MIN. **COOK:** 5 MIN./BATCH **MAKES:** 4 SERVINGS

- **1 egg**
- **1 cup panko (Japanese) bread crumbs**
- **1 tablespoon all-purpose flour**
- **1 tablespoon minced fresh parsley**
- **½ teaspoon garlic powder**
- **Dash salt and pepper**
- **1 pound chicken tenderloins**
- **¼ cup olive oil**

MARINARA

- **6 medium tomatoes, seeded and finely chopped**
- **1 medium onion, finely chopped**
- **8 medium fresh mushrooms, finely chopped**
- **2 garlic cloves, minced**
- **1 teaspoon Italian seasoning**
- **¼ teaspoon salt**

1. In a shallow bowl, beat the egg. In another shallow bowl, combine the bread crumbs, flour, parsley, garlic powder, salt and pepper. Dip chicken in egg, then roll in crumb mixture.
2. In a large skillet over medium heat, cook chicken in oil in batches for 2-3 minutes on each side or until juices run clear. Drain on paper towels.
3. Meanwhile, in a small saucepan, combine the marinara ingredients; heat through. Serve with chicken.

Speedy Sides & Salads

"Everyone loves a good pasta salad, and this one will make 'em feel like you fussed. Convenient store-bought dressing, artichoke hearts, olives, pepperoni and mozzarella cubes give it extra flavor and flair."

CLARA COULSON MINNEY WASHINGTON COURTHOUSE, OHIO
Pepperoni-Artichoke Pasta Salad, page 143

Country Corn

I cook church dinners for 120 people, so I'm always looking for fast, inexpensive menu items. After watching a chef prepare this side dish, I made it at church several times. There were never leftovers.
—KATHLEEN MANCUSO NISKAYUNA, NEW YORK

PREP/TOTAL TIME: 20 MIN. **MAKES:** 6 SERVINGS

- **6 green onions, chopped**
- **3 tablespoons butter**
- **1 package (16 ounces) frozen corn, thawed**
- **2 teaspoons cornstarch**
- **½ cup half-and-half cream**
- **¼ cup water**
- **½ teaspoon salt**
- **¼ to ½ teaspoon pepper**
- **1 cup grape tomatoes, halved**

1. In a large skillet, saute onions in butter for 2-3 minutes or until tender. Stir in the corn; cover and cook for 4-5 minutes or until heated through.
2. Meanwhile, in a small bowl, combine the cornstarch, cream, water, salt and pepper until smooth. Gradually stir into corn mixture. Bring to a boil. Cook, uncovered, for 2 minutes or until thickened. Stir in tomatoes.

Broccoli Salad with Cucumber

Cucumber adds freshness and texture to this easy broccoli salad. The shredded cheddar and bacon bits ratchet up the flavor.
—LISA CARTER WARREN, INDIANA

PREP/TOTAL TIME: 10 MIN. **MAKES:** 4 SERVINGS

- **2 cups fresh broccoli florets**
- **⅔ cup chopped cucumber**
- **½ cup shredded cheddar cheese**
- **½ cup mayonnaise**
- **3 tablespoons chopped onion**
- **3 tablespoons bacon bits**

1. Place all ingredients in a large bowl and toss to coat. Cover and refrigerate until serving.

Honey Mustard Coleslaw

I tinkered around with a family cole slaw recipe until I arrived at this sweet and tangy combination. The packaged shredded cabbage is a real time-saver, and the honey helps the dressing come together faster. An added bonus is there is no mess to clean up!
—REBECCA ANDERSON MELISSA, TEXAS

PREP/TOTAL TIME: 10 MIN. **MAKES:** 5 SERVINGS

- **1 package (14 ounces) coleslaw mix**
- **½ cup mayonnaise**
- **2 tablespoons honey**
- **1 tablespoon cider vinegar**
- **1 tablespoon spicy brown mustard**
- **½ teaspoon lemon-pepper seasoning**
- **⅛ teaspoon celery seed**

1. Place coleslaw mix in a large bowl. Combine the remaining ingredients. Pour over coleslaw mix and toss to coat. Chill until serving.

Shhh! SIMPLE SECRET

Cider vinegar, made from apples, has a faint fruity flavor and is used in recipes where a slightly milder vinegar flavor is preferred. As a general rule, if more sharpness is desired, use white vinegar. If a milder flavor is desired, use cider vinegar.

I was inspired by my grandmother to cook and loved going to her house for Sunday dinner. She passed her cooking skills down, and today my mom and I still make this potato salad. —**SALLY MINER** EL MIRAGE, ARIZONA

Deli-Style Potato Salad

PREP: 25 MIN. **COOK:** 20 MIN. + CHILLING
MAKES: 8 SERVINGS

- **1 pound potatoes, peeled and cubed**
- **6 hard-cooked eggs**
- **8 whole baby dill pickles, sliced**
- **1 small onion, chopped**
- **4 radishes, sliced**

DRESSING

- **1 cup Miracle Whip**
- **1 tablespoon 2% milk**
- **1 teaspoon prepared mustard**
- **½ teaspoon dill pickle juice**
- **¼ teaspoon sugar**
- **¼ teaspoon salt**
- **¼ teaspoon pepper**
- **Paprika, optional**

1. Place potatoes in a large saucepan and cover with water. Bring to a boil. Reduce heat; cover and cook for 10-15 minutes or until tender. Drain and set aside to cool.

2. Coarsely chop four eggs. In a large bowl, combine the chopped eggs, pickles, onion and radishes; add potatoes. In a small bowl, combine the Miracle Whip, milk, mustard, pickle juice, sugar, salt and pepper. Pour over potato mixture; stir to combine.

3. Slice remaining eggs and arrange over salad; sprinkle with paprika if desired. Cover and refrigerate for 4 hours before serving.

How to Boil Eggs

To hard-cook eggs, place a single layer of eggs in a saucepan and add enough water to cover by 1 inch. Put a lid on the pan and bring to a boil. Remove from the heat and let stand for 15 minutes. Immediately rinse with cold water and cover with ice water until completely cool.

Snappy Green Beans

PREP/TOTAL TIME: 15 MIN.
MAKES: 6 SERVINGS

- **2 pounds fresh green beans, trimmed**
- **2 teaspoons butter, melted**
- **2 tablespoons minced fresh parsley**
- **2 teaspoons lemon juice**
- **½ teaspoon salt**
- **⅛ teaspoon pepper**

1. Place beans in a large saucepan and cover with water; bring to a boil. Cook, uncovered, for 8-10 minutes or until crisp-tender. Drain well.
2. Remove from the heat. Add the butter, parsley, lemon juice, salt and pepper; toss to coat.

This streamlined side dish is a great way to serve fresh green beans. It's simple yet looks elegant, and the buttery citrus flavors and mild seasonings can accompany just about any entree. **—TAMMY NEUBAUER** IDA GROVE, IOWA

Zucchini Corn Medley

One day when I was a girl, a neighbor brought over a dish similar to this one. Years later, I decided to re-create it. My family likes the recipe today as much as I did back then.

—MARIAN QUAID-MALTAGLIATI
NIPOMO, CALIFORNIA

PREP/TOTAL TIME: 20 MIN.
MAKES: 6 SERVINGS

- **2 medium zucchini, cut into ½-inch slices**
- **¼ cup water**
- **1 can (15½ ounces) hominy, drained**
- **1 can (15¼ ounces) whole kernel corn, drained**
- **1 jalapeno pepper, seeded and chopped**
- **½ teaspoon salt**
- **1 cup (4 ounces) shredded pepper jack cheese**

1. In a 1½-qt. microwave-safe dish, combine zucchini and water. Cover and microwave on high for 1½ minutes; drain. Stir in the hominy, corn, jalapeno and salt. Cover and microwave on high for 2-3 minutes.
2. Sprinkle with cheese. Cook, uncovered, on high for 1-2 minutes until cheese is melted and vegetables are tender. Let stand for 2 minutes before serving.

Editor's Note: *We recommend wearing disposable gloves when cutting hot peppers. Avoid touching your face. This recipe was tested in a 1,100-watt microwave.*

Roasted Russet & Sweet Potato Wedges

Fried fish wouldn't be complete without chips. A cool sour cream sauce tames the heat in these taters, but if you're looking for more spice, add chili powder to the seasonings.

—THERESA EISCHENS HUTCHINSON, MINNESOTA

PREP: 20 MIN. **BAKE:** 25 MIN. **MAKES:** 8 SERVINGS

- **2 medium russet potatoes, peeled**
- **2 medium sweet potatoes, peeled**
- **2 tablespoons olive oil**
- **2 teaspoons garlic powder**
- **2 teaspoons ground cumin**
- **2 teaspoons paprika**
- **1 teaspoon seasoned salt**
- **¼ to ½ teaspoon crushed red pepper flakes**
- **⅛ teaspoon pepper**

DIP

- **½ cup sour cream**
- **½ teaspoon seasoned salt**
- **½ teaspoon garlic powder**

1. Cut each russet and sweet potato lengthwise into eight wedges; place in two greased 15-in. x 10-in. x 1-in. baking pans. Drizzle with oil. Combine the seasonings; sprinkle over potatoes and toss to coat.

2. Bake at 400° for 25-30 minutes or until tender, turning once.

3. Combine the dip ingredients. Serve with potatoes.

Two varieties of sweet potatoes are readily available. One has a pale skin with a light yellow flesh and a dry mealy texture. The other has dark skin with a dark orange flesh that cooks to a moist texture. This variety is commonly known as a yam. True yams, though not readily available, are interchangeable with sweet potatoes in most recipes.

Italian Linguini Salad

This recipe tastes great with any meaty entree. Create a main dish out of this salad by simply adding grilled shrimp or chicken.

—TAMMY KELLER BRADENTON, FLORIDA

PREP/TOTAL TIME: 20 MIN. **MAKES:** 8 SERVINGS

- **8 ounces uncooked linguine**
- **1 medium cucumber, quartered and sliced**
- **2 medium tomatoes, seeded and chopped**
- **½ cup thinly sliced green onions**
- **¾ cup Italian salad dressing**

1. Cook linguine according to package directions. Meanwhile, in a large bowl, combine the cucumber, tomatoes and onions. Drain linguine; rinse under cold water. Add linguine to vegetable mixture. Drizzle with dressing; toss to coat. Refrigerate until serving.

The-Best-of-Both-Worlds Dressing

For a creamy, pleasant-tasting blue cheese dressing that is delicious over a variety of greens, try this easy-to-make recipe.

—NAOMI GIDDIS TWO BUTTES, COLORADO

PREP/TOTAL TIME: 10 MIN. **MAKES:** 2 CUPS

- **1 cup mayonnaise**
- **½ cup half-and-half cream**
- **¼ cup 2% milk**
- **2 tablespoons French salad dressing**
- **½ cup crumbled blue cheese**

1. In a small bowl, whisk the mayonnaise, cream, milk and salad dressing. Stir in cheese. Cover and refrigerate until serving.

Summer Salads with Mandarin Oranges

Fresh and pretty, this arranged salad is a terrific way to get fruit and veggies into your day. Sweet oranges and a tangy dressing make a delightful match.

—FRANCIS GARLAND ANNISTON, ALABAMA

PREP/TOTAL TIME: 25 MIN. **MAKES:** 6 SERVINGS

- **3 tablespoons red wine vinegar**
- **1 tablespoon lemon juice**
- **1 garlic clove, minced**
- **¾ teaspoon minced chives**
- **¾ teaspoon minced fresh parsley**
- **⅛ teaspoon salt**
- **⅛ teaspoon coarsely ground pepper**
- **½ cup olive oil**
- **4 cups torn Boston lettuce**
- **2 plum tomatoes, chopped**
- **1 medium ripe avocado, peeled and cubed**
- **½ small cucumber, halved and sliced**
- **1 can (11 ounces) mandarin oranges, drained**
- **¼ cup sliced ripe olives**

1. In a small bowl, whisk the first seven ingredients. Gradually whisk in oil. Set aside.

2. Divide lettuce among six serving plates. Top with tomatoes, avocado, cucumber, oranges and olives. Drizzle with dressing.

White Bean and Spinach Salads

This is one of my favorite summertime salads. Fresh parsley, tarragon and chives give the homemade dressing special flavor. Packaged pre-cut matchstick carrots make it a snap to fix!

—ELISABETH LARSEN PLEASANT GROVE, UTAH

PREP/TOTAL TIME: 20 MIN. **MAKES:** 4 SERVINGS

- **¼ cup olive oil**
- **2 tablespoons white wine vinegar**
- **2 teaspoons minced fresh parsley**
- **2 teaspoons minced fresh tarragon**
- **2 teaspoons lemon juice**
- **1 teaspoon minced chives**
- **1 teaspoon Dijon mustard**
- **½ teaspoon sugar**
- **½ teaspoon salt**
- **⅛ teaspoon pepper**
- **1 can (15 ounces) cannellini or white kidney beans, rinsed and drained**
- **½ cup julienned carrot**
- **¼ cup roasted sweet red peppers, chopped**
- **2 tablespoons chopped red onion**
- **4 cups fresh baby spinach**

1. In a small bowl, whisk the first 10 ingredients. In another bowl, combine the beans, carrot, red peppers and onion. Add dressing and toss to coat.

2. Divide spinach among four serving plates. Top with bean mixture.

Pepperoni-Artichoke Pasta Salad

Everyone loves a good pasta salad, and this one will make 'em feel like you fussed. Convenient store-bought dressing, artichoke hearts, olives, pepperoni and mozzarella cubes give it extra flavor and flair.

—CLARA COULSON MINNEY WASHINGTON COURT HOUSE, OHIO

PREP/TOTAL TIME: 30 MIN. **MAKES:** 6 SERVINGS

- **1 cup uncooked bow tie pasta**
- **1 cup cubed part-skim mozzarella cheese**
- **¾ cup water-packed artichoke hearts, rinsed, drained and chopped**
- **1 can (2¼ ounces) sliced ripe olives, drained**
- **2 ounces sliced pepperoni**
- **1 small red onion, halved and sliced**
- **¼ cup shredded Parmesan cheese**
- **¼ cup chopped green pepper**
- **½ cup Italian salad dressing**

1. Cook pasta according to package directions. Meanwhile, in a large bowl, combine the mozzarella cheese, artichokes, olives, pepperoni, onion, Parmesan cheese and green pepper.
2. Drain pasta and rinse in cold water. Add to salad. Drizzle with salad dressing and toss to coat. Chill until serving.

Herby Potatoes with Sour Cream

Colorful potatoes, a fun farmers market find, are flecked with home-grown herbs and have a peppery bite tamed by cool sour cream. Red potatoes will work in this recipe you won't be able to stop eating!

—EMILY FALKE SANTA BARBARA, CALIFORNIA

PREP: 15 MIN. **BAKE:** 35 MIN. **MAKES:** 4 SERVINGS

- **2 tablespoons butter, melted**
- **2 tablespoons olive oil**
- **2 tablespoons minced fresh basil**
- **2 tablespoons minced fresh parsley**
- **1 tablespoon minced fresh rosemary**
- **1 tablespoon minced fresh thyme**
- **1 teaspoon paprika**
- **½ teaspoon kosher salt**
- **¼ teaspoon cayenne pepper**
- **1½ pounds small red, purple and yellow potatoes, halved**
- **¾ cup sour cream**
- **2 tablespoons minced fresh chives**

1. In a large bowl, combine the first nine ingredients. Add potatoes; toss to coat. Transfer to a greased 15-in. x 10-in. x 1-in. baking pan. Bake at 375° for 35-40 minutes or until tender, stirring occasionally.
2. In a small bowl, combine sour cream and chives; serve with potatoes.

Scalloped Potatoes & Ham

This creamy oven favorite slow cooks in the kitchen while I'm away. It's ready to serve when I get home, making it a real winner in my book!

—**JONI HILTON** ROCKLIN, CALIFORNIA

PREP: 15 MIN. **COOK:** 8 HOURS
MAKES: 16 SERVINGS

- **1 can (10¾ ounces) condensed cheddar cheese soup, undiluted**
- **1 can (10¾ ounces) condensed cream of mushroom soup, undiluted**
- **1 cup 2% milk**
- **10 medium potatoes, peeled and thinly sliced**
- **3 cups cubed fully cooked ham**
- **2 medium onions, chopped**
- **1 teaspoon paprika**
- **1 teaspoon pepper**

1. In a small bowl, combine the soups and milk. In a greased 5-qt. slow cooker, layer half of the potatoes, ham, onions and soup mixture. Repeat layers. Sprinkle with paprika and pepper.
2. Cover and cook on low for 8-10 hours or until potatoes are tender.

Shrimp & Spinach Salad

A store-bought salad dressing gives cooked shrimp a fast flavor boost and tops this refreshing salad. It's a recipe you'll turn to again and again.

—**TASTE OF HOME TEST KITCHEN**

PREP/TOTAL TIME: 15 MIN.
MAKES: 4 SERVINGS

- **1 pound peeled and deveined cooked medium shrimp**
- **4 green onions, thinly sliced**
- **¾ cup tangy tomato bacon salad dressing**
- **1 package (6 ounces) fresh baby spinach**
- **1 cup shredded carrots**
- **2 hard-cooked eggs, sliced**
- **2 plum tomatoes, cut into wedges**

1. In a large skillet, cook shrimp and onions in salad dressing over medium heat for 5-6 minutes or until heated through.
2. Divide spinach among four plates. Top with shrimp mixture, carrots, eggs and tomatoes. Serve immediately.

Tossed Salad

When you're trying to clean out the fridge and use up produce, it doesn't get any simpler than making an oil-and-vinegar dressing to toss with fresh veggies.

—**LAURA ODELL** EDEN, NORTH CAROLINA

PREP/TOTAL TIME: 15 MIN. **MAKES:** 6 SERVINGS

- **5 cups torn mixed greens**
- **1 medium tomato, diced**
- **1 cup sliced radishes**
- **1 cup sliced red onion**
- **¼ cup bacon bits**
- **⅔ cup canola oil**
- **⅓ cup cider vinegar**
- **1¼ teaspoons salt**
- **½ teaspoon pepper**

1. In a salad bowl, toss the first five ingredients. In a small bowl, whisk the remaining ingredients. Pour over salad and toss to coat.

Fiesta Corn Chip Salad

Whenever I share this corn salad with friends and family, the recipe is always requested! It's quick, easy and great alongside just about any main course.

—**MANDY MCKINNON** NORTH CANTON, OHIO

PREP/TOTAL TIME: 10 MIN. **MAKES:** 10 SERVINGS

- **2 cans (15¼ ounces each) whole kernel corn, drained**
- **2 cups (8 ounces) shredded Mexican cheese blend**
- **1 medium sweet red pepper, chopped**
- **1 cup mayonnaise**
- **⅛ teaspoon salt**
- **⅛ teaspoon pepper**
- **1 package (9¼ ounces) chili cheese-flavored corn chips, crushed**

1. In a large bowl, combine the corn, cheese, red pepper, mayonnaise, salt and pepper. Chill until serving. Just before serving, stir in corn chips.

Summer's Best Spinach Salad

When we're hosting parties or milestone events, such as a graduation, we rely on buffets with lots of make-ahead treats. This salad is one of our go-to recipes.

—**PAT STEVENS** GRANBURY, TEXAS

PREP/TOTAL TIME: 10 MIN. **MAKES:** 4 SERVINGS

- **3 cups fresh baby spinach**
- **5 canned apricot halves, drained and quartered**
- **1 medium ripe avocado, peeled and sliced**
- **½ cup ranch salad dressing**
- **1½ teaspoons minced fresh cilantro**
- **½ to ¾ teaspoon grated lime peel**

1. In a large serving bowl, combine the spinach, apricots and avocado. In a small bowl, combine the remaining ingredients; drizzle over salad.

Shhh! SIMPLE SECRET

To quickly ripen an avocado, place the avocado in a paper bag with an apple. Poke the bag with a toothpick in several spots and leave at room temperature. The avocado should be ripe in 1 to 3 days.

Zesty Broccoli

I've been a vegetarian for more than 20 years and often experiment to find flavors compatible with the many vegetables I prepare. This dish is not only beautiful to serve, it's delicious and nutritious, too!

—LOUISA KEMYAN PALM SPRINGS, CALIFORNIA

PREP/TOTAL TIME: 15 MIN. **MAKES:** 4 SERVINGS

- **4 cups fresh broccoli florets**
- **¼ cup water**
- **2 teaspoons olive oil**
- **1 to 2 garlic cloves, minced**
- **½ teaspoon salt**
- **Dash crushed red pepper flakes**

1. In a large saucepan, combine the first five ingredients. Bring to a boil. Reduce heat; cover and simmer for 5 minutes or until broccoli is crisp-tender. Drain. Add pepper flakes; toss to combine.

Coconut Fruit Salad

This refreshing fruit salad will taste equally delicious at breakfast, lunch or dinner!

—MILDRED SHERRER FORT WORTH, TEXAS

PREP/TOTAL TIME: 10 MIN. **MAKES:** 4 SERVINGS

- **1 can (11 ounces) mandarin oranges, drained**
- **1 can (8 ounces) pineapple chunks, drained**
- **1 large banana, sliced**
- **1 large apple, chopped**
- **⅓ cup golden raisins**
- **¼ cup flaked coconut, toasted**

1. In a large bowl, combine the first five ingredients. Sprinkle with coconut just before serving.

Black Bean & Corn Salsa

Who knew it was so simple to jazz up store-bought salsa or that a few everyday ingredients could give it so much flavor? This one's perfect as a chip dipper or on top of tacos, burritos, eggs...stop us before we go on!

—PATRICIA SWART GALLOWAY, NEW JERSEY

PREP/TOTAL TIME: 5 MIN. **MAKES:** 4 SERVINGS

- **1 cup chunky salsa**
- **½ cup canned black beans, rinsed and drained**
- **½ cup canned whole kernel corn, drained**
- **Tortilla chips**

1. In a small bowl, combine the salsa, beans and corn. Refrigerate until serving. Serve with tortilla chips.

PERFECT PAIR

The Black Bean & Corn Salsa pairs wonderfully with the Mexican Fiesta Steak Stir-Fry on page 173. Add refreshing glasses of lemonade or cold cerveza to bring a bit of summer sunshine to the table on any chilly winter's night.

Chicken & Brie Salad

Think you don't have time to eat? Think again! This elegant salad puts a few hardworking ingredients to delicious use, and it's ready in just moments.

—TASTE OF HOME TEST KITCHEN

PREP/TOTAL TIME: 10 MIN. **MAKES:** 7 SERVINGS

- **1 package (10 ounces) hearts of romaine salad mix**
- **3 cups cubed rotisserie chicken**
- **2 cups honey-roasted cashews**
- **2 cups seedless red grapes**
- **4 ounces Brie cheese, cubed**
- **1 cup red wine vinaigrette**

1. In a large bowl, combine the first five ingredients. Drizzle with vinaigrette and toss to coat.

Lemon Date Couscous

Couscous is a great carrier for bold flavors and cooks so quickly. It makes a wonderful accompaniment to many main dishes.

—ROXANNE CHAN ALBANY, CALIFORNIA

PREP/TOTAL TIME: 10 MIN. **MAKES:** 4 SERVINGS

- **¾ cup uncooked couscous**
- **½ cup fresh baby spinach**
- **½ cup shredded carrots**
- **¼ cup chopped dates**
- **2 tablespoons sliced almonds**
- **1 teaspoon lemon juice**
- **¼ teaspoon grated lemon peel**
- **⅛ teaspoon salt**
- **⅛ teaspoon lemon-pepper seasoning**
- **Thinly sliced green onions**

1. Cook couscous according to package directions.
2. Meanwhile, in a small bowl, combine the spinach, carrots, dates, almonds, lemon juice, peel, salt and lemon-pepper. Stir in couscous. Garnish with green onions.

BBQ Pork Salad

I needed a dinner for those too-hot-to-cook nights during summer. This is hearty enough for my meat-and-potatoes husband, not to mention delicious! It looks beautiful served in a glass bowl.

—VICTORIA SKREDSVIG SNOHOMISH, WASHINGTON

PREP/TOTAL TIME: 10 MIN. **MAKES:** 4 SERVINGS

- **1 package (10 ounces) ready-to-serve salad greens**
- **1 can (11 ounces) mandarin oranges, drained**
- **1 cup refrigerated fully cooked barbecued shredded pork, warmed**
- **1 cup smoked almonds**
- **1 medium apple, chopped**
- **½ cup fresh snow or sugar snap peas**
- **¼ cup reduced-fat balsamic vinaigrette**

1. In a large bowl combine the first six ingredients. Drizzle with vinaigrette; serve immediately.

Keeping Veggies Green

Blanching and shocking fresh snow or sugar snap peas makes them more tender and locks in their green color. To blanch, fill a medium saucepan 3/4 full of water and bring to a boil. Boil the snow or sugar snap peas for 15-30 seconds, depending on their size. Drain and submerge in ice water. Drain and pat dry.

Mandarin Watermelon Salad

Fruit tossed with feta? You betcha! There's nothin' better. Fresh mint, cilantro and parsley add the perfect pop. I'm always looking for something different to serve my mom, who's a vegetarian—and she loved this!

—JADE BAUSELL MIAMI, FLORIDA

PREP/TOTAL TIME: 20 MIN. **MAKES:** 8 SERVINGS

- **4½ cups cubed seedless watermelon**
- **1 can (11 ounces) mandarin oranges, drained**
- **½ small red onion, sliced**
- **¼ cup crumbled feta cheese**
- **2 tablespoons minced fresh mint**
- **2 tablespoons minced fresh cilantro**
- **2 tablespoons lime juice**
- **1 tablespoon minced fresh parsley**

1. Place all ingredients in a large bowl; gently toss to combine. Serve immediately.

Tortellini Tossed Salad

Fast, satisfying and delicious, this hearty salad with cheese tortellini will surprise and delight the whole family. For a change of pace, serve it with your favorite salad dressing.

—TASTE OF HOME TEST KITCHEN

PREP/TOTAL TIME: 25 MIN. **MAKES:** 6 SERVINGS

- **1 package (9 ounces) refrigerated cheese tortellini**
- **4 ounces sliced pancetta, chopped**
- **1 package (10 ounces) ready-to-serve Italian blend salad greens**
- **1 cup (4 ounces) shredded cheddar cheese**
- **1 medium red onion, halved and thinly sliced**
- **¾ cup poppy seed salad dressing**

1. Cook tortellini according to package directions. Meanwhile, in a large skillet, cook pancetta over medium heat until crisp. Remove to paper towels to drain. Drain tortellini and rinse in cold water.
2. In a large bowl, combine the salad greens, cheese, onion, tortellini and pancetta. Drizzle with salad dressing; toss to coat. Serve immediately.

Seasoned Oven Fries

With fewer than five ingredients and less than 30 minutes, you can whip up these tasty homemade fries for an anytime side!

—PAT FREDERICKS OAK CREEK, WISCONSIN

PREP/TOTAL TIME: 25 MIN. **MAKES:** 6 SERVINGS

- **6 medium baking potatoes**
- **2 tablespoons butter, melted**
- **2 tablespoons canola oil**
- **1 teaspoon seasoned salt**

1. Cut each potato lengthwise into thirds; cut each portion into thirds. In a large resealable plastic bag, combine the butter, oil and seasoned salt. Add potatoes; shake to coat.
2. Place in a single layer on a greased baking sheet. Bake, uncovered, at 450° for 10-12 minutes on each side or until tender.

Fiesta Rice and Bean Salad

My entire family loves this salad—especially when I fix it with fresh-picked sweet corn. The summery ingredients and fragrant cilantro make it a good match for a barbecued main course.

—DIANE LYNCH SUGAR GROVE, ILLINOIS

PREP: 40 MIN. + CHILLING **MAKES:** 10 SERVINGS

- **1 package (6.2 ounces) fast-cooking long grain and wild rice mix**
- **2 cups fresh or frozen corn**
- **1 can (15 ounces) black beans, rinsed and drained**
- **1 bunch green onions, chopped**
- **1 small sweet red pepper, chopped**
- **1 small sweet orange pepper, chopped**
- **½ cup minced fresh cilantro**
- **1 can (2¼ ounces) sliced ripe olives, drained**
- **½ cup reduced-fat Italian salad dressing**
- **1 tablespoon lime juice**
- **¼ teaspoon pepper**

1. Prepare rice mix according to package directions; cool. Meanwhile, in a large saucepan, bring 4 cups water to a boil. Add corn; cover and cook for 5-6 minutes or until tender. Drain corn and rinse in cold water.
2. In a large bowl, combine the rice, corn, black beans, green onions, red and orange peppers, cilantro and olives. Combine the salad dressing, lime juice and pepper; drizzle over salad and toss to coat. Cover and refrigerate for at least 2 hours before serving.

Quick Soups & Sandwiches

“After enjoying coconut soup at a Thai restaurant, I added coconut milk to my fish chowder recipe. The simple ingredients allow the seafood to shine.”

MICHALENE BASKETT DECATUR, GEORGIA
Coconut Shrimp Chowder, page 157

Herbed Potato Soup

Rosemary and thyme add just the right amount of seasoning to this creamy, satisfying soup.

—**JO CROUCH** EAST ALTON, ILLINOIS

PREP/TOTAL TIME: 30 MIN.
MAKES: 5 SERVINGS

- **3 medium potatoes, peeled and diced**
- **2 cups water**
- **1 large onion, chopped**
- **¼ cup butter, cubed**
- **¼ cup all-purpose flour**
- **1 teaspoon salt**
- **½ teaspoon dried thyme**
- **¼ teaspoon dried rosemary, crushed**
- **¼ teaspoon pepper**
- **1½ cups 2% milk**

1. Place potatoes and water in a large saucepan. Bring to a boil. Reduce heat; cover and simmer for 15-20 minutes or until tender.

2. Meanwhile, in another large saucepan, saute onion in butter until tender. Stir in the flour, salt, thyme, rosemary and pepper until blended. Gradually add milk. Bring to a boil; cook and stir for 2 minutes or until thickened. Add potatoes with cooking liquid; heat through.

Vegetarian Reubens

Portobello mushrooms and baby spinach take the place of corned beef in this fresh take on a lunchtime staple.

—**TASTE OF HOME TEST KITCHEN**

PREP/TOTAL TIME: 20 MIN. **MAKES:** 4 SERVINGS

- **1 package (6 ounces) sliced baby portobello mushrooms**
- **2 tablespoons olive oil, divided**
- **1 package (6 ounces) fresh baby spinach**
- **8 slices marble rye bread**
- **¼ cup prepared Thousand Island salad dressing**
- **8 slices process Swiss cheese**
- **1 cup sauerkraut, rinsed and well drained**
- **2 tablespoons butter, softened**

1. In a large skillet, saute mushrooms in 1 tablespoon oil until lightly browned; remove with a slotted spoon and set aside. In the same skillet, saute spinach in remaining oil until wilted. Remove from the heat.

2. Spread bread slices with salad dressing and top with a cheese slice. Layer four slices with mushrooms, spinach and sauerkraut. Top with remaining bread. Butter outsides of sandwiches.

3. In a small skillet over medium heat, toast sandwiches for 2-3 minutes on each side or until cheese is melted.

Shhh! SIMPLE SECRET

Baby portobello mushrooms are also labeled as cremini mushrooms. They have a meaty flavor that suits vegetarian dishes, but if you can't find them, it's fine to use white mushrooms instead.

Chunky Chicken Noodle Soup

PREP/TOTAL TIME: 25 MIN.
MAKES: 6 SERVINGS

- **½ cup finely chopped carrot**
- **¼ cup finely chopped celery**
- **¼ cup finely chopped onion**
- **1 teaspoon butter**
- **6 cups chicken broth**
- **1½ cups cubed cooked chicken**
- **1 teaspoon salt**
- **½ teaspoon dried marjoram**
- **½ teaspoon dried thyme**
- **⅛ teaspoon pepper**
- **1¼ cups uncooked medium egg noodles**
- **1 tablespoon minced fresh parsley**

1. Saute the carrot, celery and onion in butter in a Dutch oven until tender. Stir in the broth, chicken and seasonings. Bring to a boil. Reduce heat. Add noodles; cook for 10 minutes or until noodles are tender. Sprinkle with parsley.

“Marjoram and thyme come through nicely in this old-fashioned soup that tastes just like Grandma used to make. You can modify the recipe to include vegetables your family enjoys. My kids love carrots, so I always toss in extra.”

—**COLEEN MARTIN** BROOKFIELD, WISCONSIN

Autumn Pumpkin Chili

I've prepared this chili often, and everyone loves it, even the most finicky grandchildren. It's also earned thumbs up with family and friends who have tried it. It's a definite "keeper" in my book!

—KIMBERLY NAGY
PORT HADLOCK, WASHINGTON

PREP: 20 MIN. **COOK:** 7 HOURS
MAKES: 4 SERVINGS

- **1 medium onion, chopped**
- **1 small green pepper, chopped**
- **1 small sweet yellow pepper, chopped**
- **1 tablespoon canola oil**
- **1 garlic clove, minced**
- **1 pound ground turkey**
- **1 can (15 ounces) solid-pack pumpkin**
- **1 can (14½ ounces) diced tomatoes, undrained**
- **4½ teaspoons chili powder**
- **¼ teaspoon pepper**
- **¼ teaspoon salt**
- **Optional toppings: shredded cheddar cheese, sour cream and sliced green onions**

1. Saute the onion and green and yellow peppers in oil in a large skillet until tender. Add garlic; cook 1 minute longer. Crumble turkey into skillet. Cook over medium heat until meat is no longer pink.
2. Transfer to a 3-qt. slow cooker. Stir in the pumpkin, tomatoes, chili powder, pepper and salt. Cover and cook on low for 7-9 hours. Serve with toppings of your choice.

Egg Drop Soup

Planning an Asian-inspired meal? Start it off with this traditional Chinese soup that uses just five ingredients.

—MARY KELLEY MINNEAPOLIS, MINNESOTA

PREP/TOTAL TIME: 10 MIN.
MAKES: 4 SERVINGS

- **5 cups chicken broth**
- **½ teaspoon sugar**
- **1 egg, lightly beaten**
- **⅓ cup sliced fresh spinach**
- **2 green onions, sliced**

1. In a large saucepan, bring broth and sugar to a boil over medium heat.
2. Reduce heat to low. Drizzle beaten egg into hot broth. Remove from the heat; stir in spinach and onions.

Asian Turkey Lettuce Wraps

Chopped frozen vegetables make these wraps a snap to prepare. Add some Asian chili sauce if you want to spice it up a bit.

—SUSAN RILEY ALLEN, TEXAS

PREP/TOTAL TIME: 20 MIN. **MAKES:** 5 SERVINGS

- **1¼ pounds extra-lean ground turkey**
- **1 package (16 ounces) frozen stir-fry vegetable blend, thawed**
- **⅓ cup reduced-sodium teriyaki sauce**
- **¼ cup hoisin sauce**
- **3 tablespoons reduced-fat creamy peanut butter**
- **2 tablespoons minced fresh gingerroot**
- **1 tablespoon rice vinegar**
- **1 tablespoon sesame oil**
- **3 garlic cloves, minced**
- **4 green onions, chopped**
- **10 Boston lettuce leaves**
- **Additional hoisin sauce, optional**

1. In a large nonstick skillet coated with cooking spray, cook turkey over medium heat until no longer pink.
2. Coarsely chop stir-fry vegetables; add to the pan. Stir in the teriyaki sauce, hoisin sauce, peanut butter, ginger, vinegar and oil. Stir-fry over medium-high heat for 5 minutes. Add garlic; cook 1 minute longer.
3. Remove from the heat; stir in onions. Place a scant ½ cup turkey mixture on each lettuce leaf; fold lettuce over filling. Serve with additional hoisin sauce if desired.

Spicy Cajun Salsa Burgers

A few on-hand seasonings and jarred salsa create these flavorful and juicy burgers for the grill.

—DAVID DALTON ORLEANS, INDIANA

PREP/TOTAL TIME: 20 MIN. **MAKES:** 4 SERVINGS

- **½ cup salsa**
- **1 teaspoon Creole seasoning**
- **½ teaspoon garlic powder**
- **½ teaspoon crushed red pepper flakes**
- **½ teaspoon pepper**
- **1 pound ground beef**
- **4 kaiser rolls, split and toasted**

1. In a small bowl, combine the salsa, Creole seasoning, garlic powder, pepper flakes and pepper. Crumble beef over mixture and mix well. Shape into four patties.

2. Grill, covered, over medium heat for 4-5 minutes on each side or until a thermometer reads 160°. Serve on buns.

Editor's Note: *The following spices may be substituted for 1 teaspoon Creole seasoning: ¼ teaspoon each salt, garlic powder and paprika; and a pinch each of dried thyme, ground cumin and cayenne pepper.*

Deli Sandwich Spread

Creamy, chivy and tangy, this sandwich spread would also be delicious as a dip. Just 10 minutes to whip up, and it chills as you finish preparing the rest of the meal. To lighten up the calories, use light sour cream and/or mayonnaise.

—CATHY TANG REDMOND, WASHINGTON

PREP: 10 MIN. + CHILLING **MAKES:** 1 CUP

- **⅔ cup mayonnaise**
- **¼ cup sour cream**
- **3 tablespoons honey Dijon mustard**
- **1 tablespoon minced chives**
- **1 teaspoon dried minced onion**
- **1 teaspoon Italian seasoning**

1. In a small bowl, combine all the ingredients. Cover and refrigerate for at least 1 hour before serving.

When assembling sandwiches ahead of time, one way to keep moisture (via meat or cheese fillings) from turning the bread soggy is to spread butter or margarine on the inner side of the bread.

BLT Catfish Sandwiches

A classic gets a rockin' new twist with lemon-grilled catfish and tangy chili sauce instead of mayo. I love to serve these sandwiches with sweet red pepper strips and grilled potato wedges. They're always a huge hit!

—MARY ANN DELL PHOENIXVILLE, PENNSYLVANIA

PREP/TOTAL TIME: 30 MIN. **MAKES:** 4 SERVINGS

- **2 tablespoons chili sauce**
- **2 tablespoons ketchup**
- **¼ teaspoon hot pepper sauce**
- **4 tablespoons lemon juice, divided**
- **4 catfish fillets (6 ounces each)**
- **½ teaspoon lemon-pepper seasoning**
- **¼ teaspoon salt**
- **8 slices whole wheat bread, toasted**
- **8 cooked bacon strips**
- **4 lettuce leaves**
- **4 thin slices tomato**
- **4 slices red onion**

1. In a small bowl, combine the chili sauce, ketchup, pepper sauce and 2 tablespoons lemon juice; set aside.
2. Drizzle remaining lemon juice over fillets; sprinkle with lemon-pepper and salt. Using long-handled tongs, moisten a paper towel with cooking oil and lightly coat the grill rack.
3. Grill catfish, covered, over medium-hot heat or broil 4 in. from the heat for 3-5 minutes on each side or until fish flakes easily with a fork.
4. Layer four slices of toast with catfish, bacon, lettuce, tomato and onion. Spread sauce mixture over remaining toast slices; place on top.

Coconut Shrimp Chowder

After enjoying coconut soup at a Thai restaurant, I added coconut milk to my fish chowder recipe. The simple ingredients allow the seafood to shine.

—MICHALENE BASKETT DECATUR, GEORGIA

PREP/TOTAL TIME: 30 MIN. **MAKES:** 5 SERVINGS

- **1 medium onion, chopped**
- **2 teaspoons canola oil**
- **¼ teaspoon cayenne pepper**
- **2 cups chicken broth**
- **1 package (10 ounces) frozen corn**
- **¼ teaspoon salt**
- **¼ teaspoon pepper**
- **1 can (13.66 ounces) coconut milk**
- **1 pound uncooked medium shrimp, peeled and deveined**
- **¼ cup lime juice**
- **2 tablespoons minced fresh cilantro**
- **1 medium ripe avocado, peeled and cubed**

1. In a large saucepan, saute onion in oil until tender. Add pepper. Stir in the broth, corn, salt and pepper. Bring to a boil. Reduce heat; simmer, uncovered, for 5 minutes. Remove from the heat and stir in coconut milk. Cool slightly.
2. In a food processor, process soup in batches until blended. Return all to pan. Add shrimp; cook and stir over medium heat for 5-6 minutes or until shrimp turn pink. Stir in lime juice and cilantro. Garnish servings with avocado.

Cream of Potato & Cheddar Soup

My daughter shares Yukon Gold potatoes from her garden so I can make this comforting soup. It's the simple ingredients that make it taste so incredible; with sharp cheese and croutons, it's heavenly!
—**CINDI BAUER** MARSHFIELD, WISCONSIN

PREP: 25 MIN. **COOK:** 7½ HOURS
MAKES: 11 SERVINGS (2¾ QUARTS)

- **8 medium Yukon Gold potatoes, peeled and cubed**
- **1 large red onion, chopped**
- **1 celery rib, chopped**
- **2 cans (14½ ounces each) reduced-sodium chicken broth**
- **1 can (10¾ ounces) condensed cream of celery soup, undiluted**
- **1 teaspoon garlic powder**
- **½ teaspoon white pepper**
- **1½ cups (6 ounces) shredded sharp cheddar cheese**
- **1 cup half-and-half cream**
- **Optional toppings: salad croutons, crumbled cooked bacon and additional shredded sharp cheddar cheese**

1. Combine the first seven ingredients in a 4- or 5-qt. slow cooker. Cover and cook on low for 7-9 hours or until potatoes are tender.
2. Stir in cheese and cream. Cover and cook 30 minutes longer or until cheese is melted. Garnish servings with toppings of your choice.

Yukon Gold potatoes are usually smaller than russets and have a thin golden skin and a light yellow flesh. Their buttery, nutty flavor adds yumminess to any potato dish.

"There's plenty of sweet and a little heat from the chipotle pepper in this family-friendly shredded beef."

—**DAVID KLEIMAN** NEW BEDFORD, MASSACHUSETTS

Sweet & Savory Slow-Cooked Beef

Add your favorite barbecue sauce or try a different flavor each time you make it to see which you like it best.

—**DAVID KLEIMAN**
NEW BEDFORD, MASSACHUSETTS

PREP: 20 MIN. **COOK:** 8 HOURS
MAKES: 16 SERVINGS

- **1 beef top round roast (4 pounds)**
- **1 bottle (18 ounces) barbecue sauce**
- **½ cup water**
- **¼ cup packed brown sugar**
- **1 chipotle pepper in adobo sauce, chopped**
- **2 tablespoons Worcestershire sauce**
- **2 tablespoons steak sauce**
- **1½ teaspoons reduced-sodium soy sauce**
- **1 teaspoon celery salt**
- **1 teaspoon garlic salt**
- **1 teaspoon seasoned salt**
- **1 teaspoon pepper**
- **16 onion rolls, split**

1. Cut roast in half; place in a 6-qt. slow cooker. Combine the barbecue sauce, water, brown sugar, chipotle pepper, Worcestershire sauce, steak sauce, soy sauce and seasonings. Pour over meat.
2. Cover and cook on low for 8-10 hours or until meat is tender. Remove roast and cool slightly. Skim fat from cooking juices. Shred meat with two forks and return to slow cooker; heat through. Serve on rolls.

Editor's Note: *Wear disposable gloves when cutting hot peppers; the oils can burn skin. Avoid touching your face.*

Shhh! SIMPLE SECRET

Whether you're buying large or small cuts of meat, ordering from a butcher ensures you'll get the right weight and cut for your recipe. If you find that the meat your recipe calls for is too expensive, ask the butcher if there's a cheaper cut that would work.

Sesame Chicken Wraps

Wrap up lunch-hour prep work in no time with these refreshing handhelds. A simple Asian dressing gives these sandwiches so much flavor!

—**ANDRE HOUSEKNECHT** FEASTERVILLE, PENNSYLVANIA

PREP/TOTAL TIME: 10 MIN. **MAKES:** 2 SERVINGS

- **1 package (6 ounces) ready-to-use grilled chicken breast strips**
- **¼ cup plus 2 tablespoons sesame ginger salad dressing, divided**
- **2 whole wheat tortillas (8 inches)**
- **½ cup bean sprouts**
- **½ cup julienned carrot**
- **¼ cup chopped sweet red pepper**
- **2 tablespoons chopped red onion**

1. In a small bowl, combine chicken and 1/4 cup salad dressing. Spoon over tortillas. Top with bean sprouts, carrot, pepper and onion. Drizzle with remaining dressing; roll up and secure with toothpicks.

PERFECT PAIR

Jazz up your midday meal by serving these sandwiches in a cool bento lunch box. Simply cut the wraps in smaller pieces and fill the other compartments with fruits and veggies.

Southwest Pulled Pork

I made this on a whim one Sunday morning when friends called and said they planned to drop by in the afternoon. It makes a lot, and I was able to serve our friends and neighbors a casual supper. The seasonings and green chilies give the meat a spicy kick and taste fantastic with cool sour cream and fresh salsa.

—**DEB LEBLANC** PHILLIPSBURG, KANSAS

PREP: 20 MIN. **COOK:** 8 HOURS **MAKES:** 14 SERVINGS

- **1 boneless pork shoulder butt roast (4 pounds)**
- **2 tablespoons chili powder**
- **1 tablespoon brown sugar**
- **1½ teaspoons ground cumin**
- **1 teaspoon salt**
- **½ teaspoon pepper**
- **½ teaspoon cayenne pepper**
- **1 large sweet onion, coarsely chopped**
- **2 cans (4 ounces each) chopped green chilies**
- **1 cup chicken broth**
- **14 kaiser rolls, split**

1. Cut roast in half. In a small bowl, combine the chili powder, brown sugar, cumin, salt, pepper and cayenne; rub over meat. Transfer to a 5-qt. slow cooker. Top with onion and chilies. Pour broth around meat.

2. Cover and cook on low for 8-10 hours or until tender. Remove roast; cool slightly. Skim fat from cooking juices. Shred pork with two forks and return to slow cooker; heat through. Serve on rolls.

Philadelphia Beef Sandwich

This is the ideal family-pleasing sandwich to wrap, pack and take to a deck or tailgating party. Green peppers, onions and melted cheese with beef make a great flavor combination.

—TASTE OF HOME TEST KITCHEN

PREP/TOTAL TIME: 20 MIN. **MAKES:** 6 SERVINGS

- **1 round loaf (1 pound) unsliced Italian bread**
- **1 large sweet onion, thinly sliced**
- **1 large green pepper, thinly sliced**
- **1 tablespoon olive oil**
- **1½ cups water**
- **½ cup concentrated au jus sauce**
- **1 pound thinly sliced deli roast beef**
- **3 tablespoons horseradish sauce**
- **7 slices mozzarella cheese**

1. Cut bread in half. Carefully hollow out bottom and top of loaf, leaving a ¾-in. shell (discard removed bread or save for another use).

2. In a large skillet, saute onion and green pepper in oil for 5 minutes or until tender. Meanwhile, in a small saucepan, combine water and au jus sauce; bring to a boil. Add beef. Reduce heat to medium; cook for 3 minutes or until meat is heated through. Remove beef with a slotted spoon; reserving ¼ cup au jus.

3. Spoon the onion and green pepper onto the bread bottom. Top with beef; drizzle with reserved au jus. Spread top with horseradish sauce and top with cheese.

4. Transfer to a baking sheet. Broil 3-4 in. from the heat for 1-2 minutes or until cheese is melted. Replace bread top. Cut into six wedges with a serrated knife.

Sausage Pineapple Lettuce Wraps

These wraps are a delicious mix of sweet, spicy, tangy and crunchy. Pineapple is the tasty surprise inside each wrap.

—AYSHA SCHURMAN AMMON, IDAHO

PREP/TOTAL TIME: 30 MIN. **MAKES:** 2½ DOZEN

- **1 can (8 ounces) crushed pineapple**
- **¼ cup soy sauce**
- **1 tablespoon rice vinegar**
- **1 teaspoon cornstarch**
- **1 garlic clove, minced**
- **½ teaspoon ground ginger**
- **½ teaspoon pepper**
- **1 pound bulk spicy pork sausage**
- **1 can (8 ounces) sliced water chestnuts, drained and finely chopped**
- **30 Bibb or Boston lettuce leaves**
- **30 pineapple chunks (about 2 cups)**
- **1 tablespoon sesame seeds, toasted**
- **Teriyaki sauce, optional**

1. Drain pineapple, reserving 3 tablespoons juice. In a small bowl, combine the soy sauce, vinegar, cornstarch, garlic, ginger, pepper and reserved pineapple juice; set aside.

2. In a large skillet, cook sausage over medium heat until no longer pink; drain. Stir in water chestnuts and crushed pineapple. Gradually stir in soy sauce mixture. Bring to a boil; cook and stir for 2 minutes or until thickened.

3. Place about 2 tablespoons sausage mixture on each lettuce leaf; fold lettuce over filling. Top with a pineapple chunk; secure with a toothpick. Sprinkle with sesame seeds and serve with teriyaki sauce if desired.

Portobello Burger with Muffuletta Topping

A tasty tomato-olive mixture, melty cheese and smoky grilled mushroom add so much flavor to this recipe, one of my tasters called it "one of the best grilled mushroom burgers I've had." For a change, switch another cheese or spinach for the provolone and lettuce.
—TAMRA DUNCAN LINCOLN, ARKANSAS

PREP/TOTAL TIME: 25 MIN. **MAKES:** 1 SERVING

- **1 large portobello mushroom, stem removed**
- **1 teaspoon olive oil**
- **⅛ teaspoon dried oregano**
- **Salt and pepper, to taste**
- **1 plum tomato, chopped**
- **2 pitted green olives, chopped**
- **1 tablespoon mayonnaise**
- **1 multigrain hamburger bun, split and toasted**
- **1 lettuce leaf**
- **1 slice provolone cheese**

1. Brush mushroom with oil and sprinkle with oregano. Season with salt and pepper. Using long-handled tongs, moisten a paper towel with cooking oil and lightly coat the grill rack. Grill mushroom, covered, over medium heat or broil 4 in. from the heat for 6-8 minutes on each side or until tender.
2. Combine tomato and olives; season with salt and pepper. Spread mayonnaise over bun bottom. Top with lettuce, mushroom, cheese and tomato mixture; replace bun top.

Cajun Popcorn Shrimp Sandwiches

These seafood sammies are great if you like some heat in your food. Adjust the seasoning and hot sauce to your liking.
—KENT WHITAKER ROSSVILLE, GEORGIA

PREP/TOTAL TIME: 30 MIN.
MAKES: 4 SERVINGS

- **2 tablespoons butter, melted**
- **1 teaspoon garlic powder**
- **¼ to ½ teaspoon Cajun seasoning**
- **3½ cups frozen breaded popcorn shrimp**
- **½ cup mayonnaise**
- **1 tablespoon hot pepper sauce**
- **1 teaspoon sweet pickle relish**
- **½ teaspoon prepared mustard**
- **8 pita pocket halves, warmed**
- **1 cup shredded lettuce**
- **8 thin slices tomato**

1. In a large resealable plastic bag, combine the butter, garlic powder and Cajun seasoning; add shrimp. Seal bag and toss to coat. Prepare shrimp according to package directions for baking.
2. In a small bowl, combine the mayonnaise, pepper sauce, relish and mustard. Spread into warmed pitas. Fill each pita half with shrimp, lettuce and tomato slices.

Italian Shredded Beef Sandwiches

Everyone loves these easy sandwiches! For extra pizzazz, top with provolone cheese and banana pepper rings.
—MARGIE WILLIAMS MT. JULIET, TENNESSEE

PREP: 15 MIN. **COOK:** 9 HOURS
MAKES: 12 SERVINGS

- **1 beef rump roast or bottom round roast (3 pounds)**
- **2 cups water**
- **1 envelope zesty Italian salad dressing mix**
- **1 envelope au jus gravy mix**
- **1 medium onion, thinly sliced**
- **1 can (4 ounces) chopped green chilies**
- **12 Italian rolls, split**

1. Cut roast in half. Place in a 4-qt. slow cooker. Combine the water and salad dressing and au jus mixes; pour over meat. Top with onion and chilies.
2. Cover and cook on low for 9-11 hours or until meat is tender. Remove meat. When cool enough to handle, shred meat. Skim fat from cooking juices. Return meat to slow cooker; heat through. Serve on rolls.

Vegetable Meatball Soup

This is a delicious soup recipe that takes less than 30 minutes to prepare and is a great way to use up leftover meatballs. The broth is so light and flavorful, everyone wants the recipe!
—SUSAN WESTERFIELD ALBUQUERQUE, NEW MEXICO

PREP/TOTAL TIME: 25 MIN. **MAKES:** 6 SERVINGS (2 QUARTS)

- **1 package (12 ounces) frozen fully cooked Italian meatballs**
- **2 cans (14½ ounces each) beef broth**
- **2 cups frozen Italian vegetable blend**
- **1 can (14½ ounces) Italian diced tomatoes, undrained**
- **1½ cups water**
- **⅓ cup small pasta shells**
- **Shredded Parmesan cheese, optional**

1. In a Dutch oven, combine the meatballs, broth, vegetable blend, tomatoes, water and pasta. Bring to a boil. Reduce heat; simmer, uncovered, for 10-12 minutes or until pasta is tender. Garnish servings with cheese if desired.

Most soups freeze nicely. The exceptions are soups made with cream and potatoes. Those are better when eaten fresh. Pasta in soup can get mushy in the freezer. It's best to add the pasta when ready to eat, not before freezing.

Hearty Chicken & Wild Rice Soup

Garlic and herb cream cheese adds subtle notes of flavor to this creamy, hearty soup. On a chilly day, it's like having a bowl full of warming comfort!
—SHELISA TERRY HENDERSON, NEVADA

PREP/TOTAL TIME: 25 MIN. **MAKES:** 6 SERVINGS (2¼ QUARTS)

- **1 package (6.2 ounces) fast-cooking long grain and wild rice mix**
- **2 cans (10¾ ounces each) condensed cream of chicken and mushroom soup, undiluted**
- **3 cups 2% milk**
- **2 packages (6 ounces each) ready-to-use grilled chicken breast strips**
- **2 cups frozen California-blend vegetables, thawed and coarsely chopped**
- **¾ cup spreadable garlic and herb cream cheese**

1. Prepare rice mix according to package directions using a Dutch oven. Stir in the remaining ingredients; heat through.

Beef Gyros

Going out to restaurants for gyros can be expensive, so I came up with this homemade version. Usually, I set out the fixings so everyone can assemble their own.

—SHERI SCHEERHORN HILLS, MINNESOTA

PREP/TOTAL TIME: 30 MIN. **MAKES:** 5 SERVINGS

- **1 cup ranch salad dressing**
- **½ cup chopped seeded peeled cucumber**
- **1 pound beef top sirloin steak, cut into thin strips**
- **2 tablespoons olive oil**
- **5 whole pita breads, warmed**
- **1 medium tomato, chopped**
- **1 can (2¼ ounces) sliced ripe olives, drained**
- **½ small onion, thinly sliced**
- **1 cup (4 ounces) crumbled feta cheese**
- **2½ cups shredded lettuce**

1. In a small bowl, combine salad dressing and cucumber; set aside. In a large skillet, cook beef in oil over medium heat until no longer pink.

2. Layer half of each pita with steak, tomato, olives, onion, cheese, lettuce and dressing mixture. Fold each pita over filling; secure with toothpicks.

Kielbasa Spinach Soup

This is one of my favorite meal-in-a-bowl soups because it's very tasty with little preparation. Collard greens or chopped kale can be used instead of spinach. The hot pepper sauce adds real kick, but it's fine to leave it out and let each person flavor their own serving.

—ANTOINETTE PISICCHIO EASTON, PENNSYLVANIA

PREP/TOTAL TIME: 20 MIN. **MAKES:** 4 SERVINGS

- **1 carton (32 ounces) chicken broth**
- **1 package (10 ounces) frozen chopped spinach**
- **½ pound smoked kielbasa or Polish sausage, halved and sliced**
- **1 can (15 ounces) white kidney or cannellini beans, rinsed and drained**
- **⅔ cup uncooked elbow macaroni**
- **8 to 10 drops hot pepper sauce**

1. Combine the broth, spinach and kielbasa in a large saucepan. Bring to a boil. Add beans and macaroni. Reduce heat; simmer, uncovered, for 7-9 minutes or until macaroni is tender. Stir in pepper sauce.

Adding a garnish to soup before serving gives color and adds to the flavor and texture. Easy ideas include: a sprinkle of nuts, chopped fresh herbs, sliced green onions, slivers of fresh vegetables, croutons, shredded cheese or crumbled bacon.

Stovetop Dinners

"Although I enjoy this dish throughout the year, it's even more special when I use my garden to supply most of the vegetables in it. A splash of white wine adds an impressive touch, as well as the addition of fresh basil. I have also roasted the vegetables and added chicken breasts with delicious results."

CARLY CURTIN ELLICOTT CITY, MARYLAND
Garden Vegetable Primavera, page 172

Country Chuck Roast with Mushroom Gravy

Here's a tender, savory roast that practically melts in your mouth. It may look a little complicated, but the hands-free oven time makes it my go-to company recipe on cold days.
—**MARY KAY LABRIE** CLERMONT, FLORIDA

PREP: 30 MIN. **COOK:** 1¾ HOURS **MAKES:** 8 SERVINGS

- **1 boneless beef chuck roast (2½ to 3 pounds)**
- **3 garlic cloves, halved**
- **1 tablespoon brown sugar**
- **1½ teaspoons kosher salt**
- **½ teaspoon pepper**
- **2 tablespoons olive oil**
- **1 large sweet onion, quartered**
- **1 can (10½ ounces) condensed beef consomme, undiluted**
- **2 tablespoons Worcestershire sauce**
- **1 tablespoon stone-ground mustard**
- **1 bay leaf**
- **3 to 4 drops browning sauce, optional**
- **½ pound sliced fresh mushrooms**
- **1 bottle (12 ounces) light beer or nonalcoholic beer**
- **1 teaspoon dried thyme**
- **3 tablespoons cornstarch**
- **3 tablespoons cold water**

1. With a sharp knife, cut six 1-in.-long slits in meat; insert a garlic clove half into each slit. Combine the brown sugar, salt and pepper; rub over roast.
2. In an ovenproof Dutch oven, brown roast in oil on all sides. Add the onion, beef consomme, Worcestershire sauce, mustard, bay leaf and browning sauce if desired.
3. Cover and bake at 350° for 1¾ to 2¼ hours or until meat is tender. Remove roast to a serving platter; keep warm.
4. Discard bay leaf. Add the mushrooms, beer and thyme to the pan. Bring to a boil. Cook until liquid is reduced by half. Combine cornstarch and water until smooth; gradually stir into pan. Bring to a boil; cook and stir for 2 minutes or until thickened. Serve with roast.

Skillet Cassoulet

This dish is chock-full of flavor, and the touch of spice from the kielbasa makes a nice hearty combo for a tasty meal.
—**BARBARA BRITTAIN** SANTEE, CALIFORNIA

PREP/TOTAL TIME: 25 MIN.
MAKES: 3 SERVINGS

- **¼ pound smoked turkey kielbasa, cut into ½-inch slices**
- **¼ pound fully cooked boneless ham, cubed**
- **2 medium carrots, sliced**
- **1 celery rib, sliced**
- **½ medium red onion, sliced**
- **2 teaspoons canola oil**
- **2 garlic cloves, minced**
- **1 can (15 ounces) cannellini or white kidney beans, rinsed and drained**
- **1 can (14½ ounces) no-salt-added diced tomatoes, drained**
- **¾ teaspoon dried thyme**
- **⅛ teaspoon pepper**

1. In a large skillet, saute the kielbasa, ham, carrots, celery and onion in oil until sausage is browned and vegetables are tender. Add garlic; cook 1 minute longer.
2. Stir in the remaining ingredients. Bring to a boil. Reduce heat; simmer, uncovered, for 4-5 minutes or until heated through.

Pasta with Garlic Oil

My family is Italian, and this is one of our old faves with plenty of garlic, mushrooms and herbs. To help the sauce adhere, don't rinse the pasta in water after you drain it.
—**PAM VITTORI** CHICAGO HEIGHTS, ILLINOIS

PREP/TOTAL TIME: 20 MIN.
MAKES: 5 SERVINGS

- **8 ounces uncooked spaghetti**
- **2 garlic cloves, minced**
- **⅓ cup olive oil**
- **½ cup jarred sliced mushrooms**
- **¼ cup sliced ripe olives**
- **2 to 3 teaspoons minced fresh basil**
- **2 to 3 teaspoons minced fresh parsley**
- **⅛ teaspoon garlic salt**
- **⅛ to ¼ teaspoon pepper**
- **Shredded Parmesan cheese, optional**

1. Cook spaghetti according to package directions.
2. Meanwhile, in a large skillet, saute garlic in oil. Stir in the mushrooms, olives, basil, parsley, garlic salt and pepper. Cook for 5 minutes. Drain spaghetti; place in a serving bowl. Pour sauce over pasta; toss to coat. Sprinkle with Parmesan cheese if desired.

Sliced deli ham and Swiss cheese come together in a restaurant-quality entree that cooks in moments. It's wonderful for company or a special weeknight meal.

—**ANGELA SPENGLER** CLOVIS, NEW MEXICO

Stacked Chicken Cordon Bleu

PREP: 25 MIN. **COOK:** 15 MIN.
MAKES: 4 SERVINGS

- **4 boneless skinless chicken breast halves (5 ounces each)**
- **¼ cup all-purpose flour**
- **¼ teaspoon salt**
- **¼ teaspoon pepper**
- **1 egg**
- **1 tablespoon water**
- **½ cup dry bread crumbs**
- **½ cup ground almonds**
- **¼ cup olive oil**
- **4 thin slices deli ham**
- **2 slices Swiss cheese, halved**

SAUCE

- **⅔ cup condensed cream of chicken and mushroom soup, undiluted**
- **2 tablespoons sour cream**
- **2 tablespoons 2% milk**
- **¼ teaspoon pepper**
- **⅛ teaspoon salt**
- **Minced fresh parsley**

1. Flatten chicken to ½-in. thickness; set aside. In a shallow bowl, combine the flour, salt and pepper. In another shallow bowl, whisk egg and water. In a third bowl, combine bread crumbs and almonds. Coat chicken with flour mixture, then dip in egg mixture and coat with bread crumb mixture.

2. In a large skillet, cook chicken in oil over medium heat for 5-6 minutes on each side or until a thermometer reads 170°. Top with ham and cheese; cover and cook 1-2 minutes longer or until cheese is melted.

3. Meanwhile, in a small saucepan, combine the soup, sour cream, milk, pepper and salt. Cook and stir over medium heat until heated through. Serve with chicken; sprinkle with parsley.

123 MAKE IT SIMPLE

When flattening chicken breasts, place them inside a heavy-duty resealable plastic bag or between two sheets of heavy plastic wrap to prevent messy splatters. Pound with the flat side of a meat mallet. The spiky side will tear the meat.

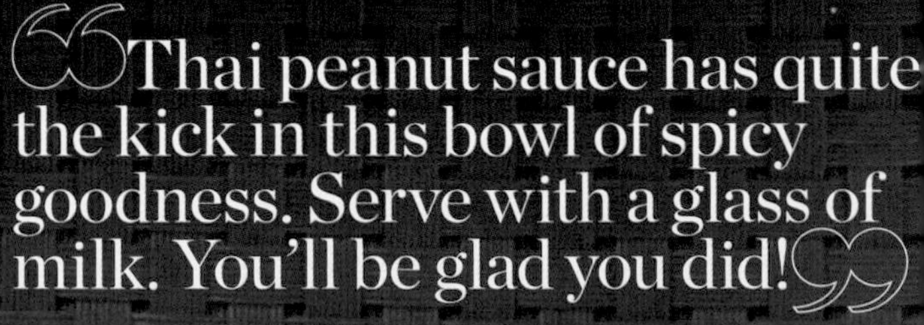

"Thai peanut sauce has quite the kick in this bowl of spicy goodness. Serve with a glass of milk. You'll be glad you did!"

—ALICIA VILBAUM FLAGSTAFF, ARIZONA

Spicy Asian Noodle Bowls

PREP/TOTAL TIME: 25 MIN.
MAKES: 4 SERVINGS

- **8 ounces thick rice noodles**
- **1 pound boneless skinless chicken breasts, cut into 1-inch cubes**
- **1 tablespoon sesame oil**
- **1 can (8 ounces) sliced water chestnuts, drained**
- **1 can (8 ounces) whole baby corn, drained**
- **1 cup frozen peas**
- **⅛ teaspoon salt**
- **⅛ teaspoon dried basil**
- **⅛ teaspoon pepper**
- **1 cup Thai peanut sauce, divided**

1. Cook noodles according to package directions.
2. Meanwhile, in a large skillet, cook chicken in oil over medium heat for 10-15 minutes or until juices run clear. Add the water chestnuts, corn, peas, salt, basil and pepper; heat through. Stir in ¼ cup peanut sauce. Remove from the heat and keep warm.
3. Drain noodles; divide among four soup bowls. Drizzle each with 2 tablespoons peanut sauce and toss to coat. Top with chicken mixture. Drizzle with remaining peanut sauce.

Ham & Pea Fettuccine

This fast and easy weeknight dinner makes smart use of items you can pick up quickly at the deli. What's more, it's delish!
—WILLIE DEWAARD CORALVILLE, IOWA

PREP/TOTAL TIME: 20 MIN.
MAKES: 3 SERVINGS

- **4 ounces uncooked fettuccine**
- **1 cup cubed fully cooked ham**
- **¾ cup frozen peas, thawed**
- **¼ cup chopped walnuts**
- **1 green onion, chopped**
- **¼ teaspoon dried thyme**
- **¼ teaspoon pepper**
- **2 tablespoons olive oil**
- **⅓ cup shredded cheddar cheese**

1. Cook the fettuccine according to package directions.
2. Meanwhile, in a large skillet, saute the ham, peas, walnuts, onion, thyme and pepper in oil until heated through. Drain fettuccine. Add to ham mixture and toss to coat. Sprinkle with cheese; cover for 1 minute or until cheese is melted.

Speedy Stovetop Spaghetti

Here's a take on a favorite you'll make over and over again. This dish tastes like it's cooked all day, but it's ready to eat in 40 minutes. The pasta cooks right in the skillet, and the 20-minute simmer gives me plenty of time to fix the rest of the meal.
—KRISTIN NANNEY MARBLE HILL, MISSOURI

PREP: 10 MIN. **COOK:** 30 MIN. **MAKES:** 4 SERVINGS

- **1 pound bulk Italian sausage**
- **½ cup finely chopped onion**
- **1 garlic clove, minced**
- **3 ounces uncooked spaghetti, broken into 1-inch pieces**
- **1 tablespoon minced fresh parsley or 1 teaspoon dried parsley flakes**
- **1 teaspoon dried basil**
- **1 can (28 ounces) diced tomatoes, undrained**
- **1 can (15 ounces) tomato sauce**
- **3 tablespoons dry red wine or beef broth**
- **½ teaspoon sugar**
- **3 tablespoons shredded Parmesan cheese**

1. Saute the sausage, onion and garlic in a large skillet for 5-7 minutes or until sausage is no longer pink; drain. Stir in the spaghetti, parsley, basil, tomatoes, tomato sauce, wine and sugar.
2. Bring to a boil. Reduce heat; cover and simmer for 20 minutes or until spaghetti is tender. Sprinkle with cheese. Cover and cook 2-3 minutes longer or until cheese is melted.

Garden Vegetable Primavera

Although I enjoy this dish throughout the year, it's even more special when I use my garden to supply most of the vegetables in it. A splash of white wine adds an impressive touch, as well as the addition of fresh basil. I have also roasted the vegetables and added chicken breasts with delicious results.

—**CARLY CURTIN** ELLICOTT CITY, MARYLAND

PREP/TOTAL TIME: 30 MIN. **MAKES:** 4 SERVINGS

- **8 ounces uncooked fettuccine**
- **2 medium zucchini, coarsely chopped**
- **1 medium carrot, sliced**
- **1 teaspoon Italian seasoning**
- **¼ teaspoon salt**
- **1 tablespoon olive oil**
- **1 cup grape tomatoes**
- **2 garlic cloves, minced**
- **½ cup reduced-sodium chicken broth**
- **⅓ cup white wine**
- **½ cup grated Parmesan cheese**
- **¼ cup minced fresh basil**

1. Cook fettuccine according to package directions.
2. Meanwhile, in a large skillet, saute the zucchini, carrot, Italian seasoning and salt in oil until vegetables are crisp-tender. Add tomatoes and garlic; cook 1 minute longer. Add broth and wine, stirring to loosen browned bits from pan. Bring to a boil; cook until liquid is reduced by half.
3. Drain fettuccine. Add the fettuccine, cheese and basil to the skillet and toss to coat.

Desert Oasis Chicken

Boneless, skinless chicken breasts cook quickly and pair nicely with sweet and spicy ingredients like these.

—**ROXANNE CHAN** ALBANY, CALIFORNIA

PREP/TOTAL TIME: 20 MIN. **MAKES:** 4 SERVINGS

- **4 boneless skinless chicken breast halves (5 ounces each)**
- **1 tablespoon olive oil**
- **¼ teaspoon salt**
- **¼ teaspoon crushed red pepper flakes**
- **¼ teaspoon ground cumin**
- **¼ teaspoon ground cinnamon**
- **1 cup canned apricot halves, sliced**
- **⅓ cup dried tropical fruit**
- **¼ cup water**
- **1 tablespoon honey**
- **Minced fresh parsley**

1. Flatten chicken slightly; rub with oil. Combine the salt, pepper flakes, cumin and cinnamon. Sprinkle over chicken.
2. In a large skillet, brown chicken on both sides. Add the apricots, tropical fruit, water and honey; bring to a boil. Reduce heat; cover and simmer for 5-6 minutes or until a thermometer reads 170°. Garnish with parsley.

Bistro Herb-Rubbed Pork Tenderloin

A mouthwatering rub featuring fresh tarragon, thyme and rosemary releases rich, bold flavor as this pork entree sizzles. Served with a delectable thickened sauce, it's crazy good!

—**NAYLET LAROCHELLE** MIAMI, FLORIDA

PREP: 20 MIN. + MARINATING **COOK:** 20 MIN. **MAKES:** 4 SERVINGS

- **3 tablespoons minced fresh tarragon**
- **2 tablespoons minced fresh thyme**
- **1 tablespoon minced fresh rosemary**
- **2 garlic cloves**
- **2 teaspoons smoked paprika**
- **1 teaspoon kosher salt**
- **¼ teaspoon coarsely ground pepper**

- 6 **tablespoons olive oil, divided**
- 1 **pork tenderloin (1 pound), cut into 12 slices**
- 1 **tablespoon all-purpose flour**
- ½ **cup beef broth**
- 2 **tablespoons minced fresh chives**

1. In a small bowl, combine the tarragon, thyme, rosemary, garlic, paprika, salt, pepper and 4 tablespoons oil. Flatten pork slices to ¼-in. thickness. Rub slices with herb mixture; cover and refrigerate for 15 minutes.
2. In a large skillet, cook pork in remaining oil in batches over medium-high heat for 1-2 minutes on each side or until browned. Remove and keep warm.
3. Stir flour into pan until blended; gradually add broth. Bring to a boil; cook and stir for 2 minutes or until thickened. Serve with pork and sprinkle with chives.

Mexican Fiesta Steak Stir-Fry

The best part of throwing a weeknight party is being able to enjoy time with family. With this flavorful stir-fry on the menu, you'll be out of the kitchen with time to spare!

—**PATRICIA SWART** GALLOWAY, NEW JERSEY

PREP/TOTAL TIME: 30 MIN. **MAKES:** 4 SERVINGS

- 1 **pound boneless beef top loin steak, trimmed and cut into thin strips**
- 3 **garlic cloves, minced**
- 1 **to 2 tablespoons canola oil**
- 1 **package (14 ounces) frozen pepper strips, thawed**
- 1⅓ **cups chopped sweet onion**
- 2 **plum tomatoes, chopped**
- 1 **can (4 ounces) chopped green chilies**
- ½ **teaspoon salt**
- ½ **teaspoon dried oregano**
- ¼ **teaspoon pepper**
- **Hot cooked rice**

1. In a large skillet or wok, stir-fry beef and garlic in oil until meat is no longer pink. Remove and keep warm.
2. Add peppers and onion to pan; stir-fry until tender. Stir in the tomatoes, chilies, salt, oregano, pepper and beef; heat through. Serve with rice.

Gnocchi Chicken Skillet

These cute dumplings are usually boiled or baked, but can also be sauteed. What a fun alternative to a traditional pasta dinner!

—**TASTE OF HOME TEST KITCHEN**

PREP/TOTAL TIME: 20 MIN. **MAKES:** 4 SERVINGS

- 1 **package (16 ounces) potato gnocchi**
- 1 **pound ground chicken**
- ½ **cup chopped onion**
- 2 **tablespoons olive oil**
- 1 **jar (26 ounces) spaghetti sauce**
- ¼ **teaspoon salt**
- ¼ **to ½ teaspoon dried oregano**
- **Shredded Parmesan cheese, optional**

1. Cook gnocchi according to package directions. Meanwhile, in a large skillet, cook chicken and onion in oil over medium heat until chicken is no longer pink; drain if necessary. Stir in the spaghetti sauce, salt and oregano; cook for 5-10 minutes or until heated through.
2. Drain gnocchi; gently stir into skillet. Garnish servings with cheese if desired.

Editor's Note: *Look for potato gnocchi in the pasta or frozen foods section.*

Gnocchi are Italian dumplings traditionally made with potatoes and flour or farina. Eggs and seasonings are added before the dough is shaped into long ropes, cut into small pieces and rolled into balls. The balls are usually rolled over the tines of a fork, cheese grater or a special gnocchi board to make small ridges in the dough.

Creole Shrimp Pasta

Having grown up in Louisiana, we love the fresh Gulf shrimp season. Tossed with a spicy Creole sauce, this pasta dish pays homage to the bounty of the bayou.
—**MELISSA COX** BOSSIER CITY, LOUISIANA

PREP: 25 MIN. **COOK:** 15 MIN. **MAKES:** 6 SERVINGS

- **1 package (16 ounces) penne pasta**
- **1 large red onion, finely chopped**
- **3 tablespoons butter**
- **3 tablespoons olive oil**
- **3 garlic cloves, minced**
- **1 pound uncooked large shrimp, peeled and deveined**
- **2 tablespoons seafood seasoning**
- **¼ cup heavy whipping cream**
- **2 tablespoons lemon juice**
- **2 tablespoons Worcestershire sauce**
- **1 tablespoon Cajun seasoning**
- **1 tablespoon Louisiana-style hot sauce**
- **¼ teaspoon pepper**

1. Cook pasta according to package directions. Meanwhile, in a Dutch oven, saute onion in butter and oil until tender. Add garlic; cook 1 minute longer. Sprinkle shrimp with seafood seasoning; add to pan.
2. Stir in the cream, lemon juice, Worcestershire sauce, Cajun seasoning, hot sauce and pepper. Drain pasta, reserving ¾ cup cooking liquid. Stir reserved cooking liquid into pan. Cook and stir for 6-8 minutes or until shrimp turn pink. Add pasta and toss to coat.

Chicken Rellenos with Cilantro-Lime Cream Sauce

PREP: 25 MIN. **BAKE:** 15 MIN.
MAKES: 4 SERVINGS (1½ CUPS SAUCE)

- **4 boneless skinless chicken breast halves (6 ounces each)**
- **1 can (4 ounces) chopped green chilies**
- **½ cup cubed pepper jack cheese**
- **2 tablespoons olive oil**
- **3 garlic cloves, minced**
- **6 ounces reduced-fat cream cheese, cubed**
- **½ cup chicken broth**
- **2 tablespoons lime juice**
- **¼ cup minced fresh cilantro**
- **1 teaspoon grated lime peel**

1. Cut a pocket in the thickest part of each chicken breast. Combine chilies and pepper jack cheese; spoon into each pocket. Secure with toothpicks.
2. In a large ovenproof skillet, brown chicken on both sides in oil. Bake, uncovered, at 350° for 15-20 minutes or until a thermometer reads 170°. Remove chicken from skillet; keep warm.
3. Add garlic to skillet; cook for 1 minute. Stir in the cream cheese, broth and lime juice until blended. Bring to a boil. Stir in cilantro and lime peel.
4. Remove toothpicks from chicken. Serve with cream sauce.

"There's a lot of mouthwatering flavor in this simple dinner recipe. The creamy cilantro and lime sauce would taste terrific with rice or egg noodles."

—**JULIE DE MATTEO**
CLEMENTON, NEW JERSEY

Baja Fish Tacos

Crisp mahi mahi pans out beautifully when dressed up with fresh lime, cilantro and smoky adobo. One bite and you'll be hooked!

—**BROOKE KELLER** LEXINGTON, KENTUCKY

PREP: 30 MIN. **COOK:** 5 MIN./BATCH **MAKES:** 8 SERVINGS

- **1 cup reduced-fat ranch salad dressing**
- **3 tablespoons adobo sauce**
- **2 tablespoons minced fresh cilantro**
- **2 tablespoons lime juice**
- **2 pounds mahi mahi, cut into 1-inch strips**
- **¼ teaspoon salt**
- **¼ teaspoon pepper**
- **⅔ cup all-purpose flour**
- **3 eggs, beaten**
- **2 cups panko (Japanese) bread crumbs**
- **1 cup canola oil**
- **16 corn tortillas (6 inches), warmed**
- **3 cups shredded cabbage**
- **Additional minced fresh cilantro and lime wedges**

1. In a small bowl, combine the salad dressing, adobo sauce, cilantro and lime juice. Chill until serving.

2. Sprinkle mahi mahi with salt and pepper. Place the flour, eggs and bread crumbs in separate shallow bowls. Coat mahi mahi with flour, then dip in eggs and coat with bread crumbs. In a large skillet, heat oil over medium heat; cook fish in batches for 2-3 minutes on each side or until golden brown. Drain on paper towels.

3. Place fish in tortillas; top with cabbage, sauce mixture and additional cilantro. Serve with lime wedges.

Herb-Crusted Perch Fillets with Pea Puree

Become a culinary Picasso when you decorate plates with a creamy pea puree. Flecked with a crisp herb coating, this perch is the perfect subject for your canvas.

—**GREGORY ROYSTER** NORTH LAUDERDALE, FLORIDA

PREP: 35 MIN. **COOK:** 10 MIN./BATCH **MAKES:** 2 SERVINGS

- **1 cup frozen peas**
- **½ cup chicken broth**
- **1 garlic clove, halved**
- **1 tablespoon heavy whipping cream**
- **2 tablespoons plus ⅓ cup olive oil, divided**
- **¼ cup all-purpose flour**
- **1 egg, beaten**
- **½ cup panko (Japanese) bread crumbs**
- **1 tablespoon dried basil**
- **1 tablespoon snipped fresh dill**
- **1 tablespoon minced fresh thyme**
- **8 perch fillets (about ¾ pound)**
- **¼ teaspoon salt**
- **⅛ teaspoon white pepper**
- **Lemon wedges**

1. In a small saucepan, combine the peas, broth and garlic. Bring to a boil. Reduce heat; simmer, uncovered, for 4-5 minutes or until peas are tender; cool slightly. Drain peas and garlic; transfer to a food processor. Add cream and 2 tablespoons oil. Cover and process until pureed; set aside.

2. Place flour and egg in separate shallow bowls. In another shallow bowl, combine the bread crumbs, basil, dill and thyme. Sprinkle fillets with salt and pepper. Dip perch, skin side up, in the flour, egg, then bread crumb mixture.

3. In a large skillet, cook fillets in remaining oil in batches over medium heat for 3-4 minutes on each side or until fish flakes easily with a fork. Serve with pea puree and lemon wedges.

Pasta Primavera

Chock-full of veggies, this simple, colorful pasta makes a filling dinner. In smaller servings, it works equally well as a side dish.
—STEPHANIE MARCHESE WHITEFISH BAY, WISCONSIN

PREP/TOTAL TIME: 25 MIN. **MAKES:** 4 SERVINGS

- **8 ounces uncooked linguine**
- **1 cup thinly sliced fresh broccoli**
- **1 medium carrot, thinly sliced**
- **½ cup sliced green onions**
- **¼ cup butter, cubed**
- **1½ cups sliced fresh mushrooms**
- **1 garlic clove, minced**
- **1 teaspoon dried basil**
- **½ teaspoon salt**
- **¼ teaspoon pepper**
- **6 ounces fresh or frozen snow peas (about 2 cups), thawed**
- **¼ cup dry white wine or chicken broth**
- **¼ cup shredded Parmesan cheese**

1. Cook linguine according to package directions.
2. Meanwhile, in a large skillet, cook the broccoli, carrot and onions in butter for 3 minutes. Add the mushrooms, garlic, basil, salt and pepper; cook 1 minute longer. Add the snow peas and wine. Cover and cook for 2 minutes or until the peas are crisp-tender.
3. Drain the linguine; add to skillet and toss to coat. Sprinkle with cheese.

Beef Tostadas

Chipotle sauce gives these beefy open-faced tostadas just the right amount of heat. They're sure to fire up a fiesta at supper!
—TASTE OF HOME TEST KITCHEN

PREP/TOTAL TIME: 15 MIN. **MAKES:** 6 SERVINGS

- **1 pound lean ground beef (90% lean)**
- **1 cup chopped sweet red pepper**
- **½ cup chili sauce**
- **1 teaspoon taco seasoning**
- **¼ teaspoon salt**
- **¼ teaspoon pepper**
- **½ cup sour cream**
- **3 teaspoons chipotle sauce**
- **6 tostada shells**
- **3 cups shredded lettuce**
- **1½ cups guacamole**
- **1½ cups shredded Mexican cheese blend**

1. In a large skillet, cook beef and red pepper over medium heat until meat is no longer pink; drain. Stir in the chili sauce, taco seasoning, salt and pepper; heat through.
2. In a small bowl, combine sour cream and chipotle sauce. Layer each tostada with lettuce, meat mixture, guacamole, cheese and chipotle cream.

Cranberry Sweet-and-Sour Pork

This fresh take on a beloved Asian-style dish is sure to cause a stir at the dinner table.

—**GERT SNYDER** WEST MONTROSE, ONTARIO

PREP/TOTAL TIME: 20 MIN. **MAKES:** 6 SERVINGS

- **1 tablespoon cornstarch**
- **½ cup unsweetened pineapple juice**
- **1 cup whole-berry cranberry sauce**
- **½ cup barbecue sauce**
- **1½ pounds pork tenderloin, cut into ½-inch cubes**
- **1 tablespoon canola oil**
- **½ teaspoon salt**
- **¼ teaspoon pepper**
- **1 medium green pepper, cut into strips**
- **¾ cup pineapple tidbits**
- **Hot cooked rice or chow mein noodles**

1. In a small bowl, combine cornstarch and pineapple juice until smooth. Stir in cranberry and barbecue sauces; set aside.

2. In a large skillet, stir-fry pork in oil for 3 minutes or until meat is no longer pink. Sprinkle with salt and pepper. Remove from the pan and keep warm.

3. Add green pepper and pineapple to pan; stir-fry for 2 minutes. Stir cornstarch mixture and add to skillet. Bring to a boil. Cook and stir for 2 minutes or until thickened. Add pork; heat through. Serve with rice or noodles.

Sirloin Stir-Fry with Ramen Noodles

I created this recipe when I was craving good Chinese food. The leftovers taste just as yummy when reheated the next day.

—**ANNETTE HEMSATH** SUTHERLIN, OREGON

PREP/TOTAL TIME: 30 MIN. **MAKES:** 4 SERVINGS

- **2 packages (3 ounces each) beef ramen noodles**
- **2 tablespoons cornstarch**
- **2 cups beef broth, divided**
- **1 pound beef top sirloin steak, cut into thin strips**
- **2 tablespoons canola oil**
- **2 tablespoons reduced-sodium soy sauce**
- **2 cans (14 ounces each) whole baby corn, rinsed and drained**
- **2 cups fresh broccoli florets**
- **1 cup diced sweet red pepper**
- **1 cup shredded carrots**
- **4 green onions, cut into 1-inch pieces**
- **½ cup unsalted peanuts**

1. Set aside seasoning packets from noodles. Cook noodles according to package directions.

2. Meanwhile, in a small bowl, combine cornstarch and ¼ cup broth until smooth; set aside. In a large skillet or wok, stir-fry beef in oil until no longer pink. Add soy sauce; cook for 3-4 minutes or until liquid has evaporated. Remove beef and keep warm.

3. Add the corn, broccoli, red pepper, carrots, onions and remaining broth to the pan. Sprinkle with contents of seasoning packets. Stir-fry for 5-7 minutes or until vegetables are crisp-tender.

4. Stir the cornstarch mixture and add to skillet. Bring to a boil; cook and stir for 2 minutes or until thickened. Drain noodles. Add beef and noodles to pan; heat through. Garnish with peanuts.

top tip
No wok? No worries. A 12-inch nonstick skillet with high sides works great for stir-fries.

Sweet and Sour Shrimp in a Hurry

Quick, easy and convenient, this family-friendly recipe is proof you can whip up a delicious and satisfying dinner in just minutes.
—**TASTE OF HOME TEST KITCHEN**

PREP/TOTAL TIME: 20 MIN. **MAKES:** 4 SERVINGS

- **1 small onion, cut into thin wedges**
- **⅔ cup sweet-and-sour sauce**
- **1 package (14 ounces) frozen sugar snap peas**
- **1 pound peeled and deveined cooked medium shrimp**
- **1 can (8¾ ounces) whole baby corn, drained**
- **4 teaspoons reduced-sodium soy sauce**
- **Hot cooked rice**

1. In a large nonstick skillet, cook onion in 2 tablespoons sweet-and-sour sauce over medium heat for 3 minutes. Stir in the peas; cook and stir for 3-5 minutes or until crisp-tender. Add the shrimp, corn, soy sauce and remaining sweet-and-sour sauce; heat through. Serve with rice.

Balsamic Pork Stir-Fry

The solution to expensive Chinese take-out is right here, but I think this pork stir-fry is even tastier.
—**SUSAN JONES** APPLETON, WISCONSIN

PREP/TOTAL TIME: 30 MIN. **MAKES:** 5 SERVINGS

- **1 pork tenderloin (1 pound), cut into thin strips**
- **⅔ cup balsamic vinaigrette, divided**
- **1½ cups sliced fresh carrots**
- **1 cup sliced fresh mushrooms**
- **1 can (8 ounces) sliced water chestnuts, drained**
- **2 tablespoons hoisin sauce**
- **Hot cooked rice**

1. In a large skillet or wok, stir-fry pork in 2 tablespoons vinaigrette for 3-4 minutes or until browned. Remove and keep warm.
2. Stir-fry carrots in 2 tablespoons vinaigrette for 2 minutes. Add mushrooms; stir-fry 2 minutes longer. Add water chestnuts and stir-fry 2-3 minutes longer or until vegetables are crisp-tender. Add hoisin sauce and remaining vinaigrette. Bring to a boil; cook for 1 minute. Add pork and heat through. Serve with rice.

Sizzling Chicken Lo Mein

All the high school students at the school where I work love this scrumptious chicken dish. It is the most requested recipe I have.
—**KRIS CAMPION** MARSHALL, MINNESOTA

PREP/TOTAL TIME: 30 MIN. **MAKES:** 4 SERVINGS

- **8 ounces uncooked linguine**
- **¾ pound boneless skinless chicken breasts, cubed**
- **2 tablespoons olive oil**
- **5 tablespoons stir-fry sauce, divided**
- **4 tablespoons teriyaki sauce, divided**
- **1 package (12 ounces) frozen stir-fry vegetable blend**

1. Cook linguine according to package directions. Meanwhile, in a large skillet or wok, stir-fry chicken in oil until no longer pink. Add 2 tablespoons each stir fry sauce and teriyaki sauce. Remove chicken from pan.
2. Stir-fry vegetables and 1 tablespoon each stir-fry sauce and teriyaki sauce in the same pan for 4-6 minutes or until vegetables are crisp-tender. Drain linguine. Add the linguine, chicken and remaining sauces to the pan; stir-fry for 2-3 minutes or until heated through.

Pepperoni Penne Carbonara

Sun-dried tomatoes and turkey pepperoni lend fantastic flavor to this creamy, hearty pasta dish, which makes a nice change of pace from everyday spaghetti.
—**TASTE OF HOME TEST KITCHEN**

PREP/TOTAL TIME: 30 MIN. **MAKES:** 6 SERVINGS

- **3 cups uncooked penne pasta**
- **2 cups chopped sun-dried tomatoes (not packed in oil)**
- **3 cups boiling water**
- **¼ cup butter, cubed**
- **½ teaspoon minced garlic**
- **1 cup sliced turkey pepperoni**
- **1 cup shredded Parmesan cheese**
- **1 cup heavy whipping cream**
- **3 tablespoons minced fresh basil**
- **½ teaspoon salt**
- **¼ teaspoon pepper**

1. Cook pasta according to package directions. Meanwhile, in a large bowl, soak tomatoes in boiling water for 10 minutes; drain well.
2. In a large skillet, saute tomatoes in butter for 3 minutes. Add garlic; cook 1 minute longer.
3. Stir in the pepperoni, cheese, cream, basil, salt and pepper. Cook over low heat for 3 minutes or until heated through. Drain penne; toss with sauce.

Chicken Fajita Alfredo

Would you like a to-go box for those fajitas? Yes—especially when you know you can fix a hearty recipe like this with the leftovers! Other homemade or restaurant fajitas would work equally well in this dish.
—TASTE OF HOME TEST KITCHEN

PREP/TOTAL TIME: 30 MIN.
MAKES: 5 SERVINGS

- **8 ounces cellentani or spiral pasta**
- **½ pound sliced fresh mushrooms**
- **1 yellow summer squash, sliced**
- **2 teaspoons olive oil**
- **2 garlic cloves, minced**
- **1 serving leftover Chili's chicken fajitas, coarsely chopped**
- **2 cans (14½ ounces each) diced tomatoes with basil, oregano and garlic, undrained**
- **¾ cup Alfredo sauce**
- **¾ teaspoon dried oregano**

1. Cook pasta according to package directions.
2. Meanwhile, in a Dutch oven, saute mushrooms and squash in oil until tender. Add garlic; saute 1 minute longer. Stir in the fajitas, tomatoes, Alfredo sauce and oregano. Bring to a boil. Reduce heat; simmer, uncovered, for 5-10 minutes, stirring occasionally. Drain pasta; add to fajita mixture and toss to coat.

Pasta & Broccoli Sausage Simmer

I created this meal when trying to use up a large head of broccoli. My family requests it at least once a week, which is handy because we always have the ingredients.
—LISA MONTGOMERY ELMIRA, ONTARIO

PREP/TOTAL TIME: 30 MIN.
MAKES: 8 SERVINGS

- **3 cups uncooked spiral pasta**
- **2 pounds smoked kielbasa or Polish sausage, cut into ¼-inch slices**
- **2 medium bunches broccoli, cut into florets**
- **1 cup sliced red onion**
- **2 cans (14½ ounces each) diced tomatoes, undrained**
- **2 tablespoons minced fresh basil or 2 teaspoons dried basil**
- **2 tablespoons minced fresh parsley or 2 teaspoons dried parsley flakes**
- **2 teaspoons sugar**

1. Cook pasta according to directions.
2. Meanwhile, in a Dutch oven, saute the sausage, broccoli and onion for 5-6 minutes or until broccoli is crisp-tender.
3. Add the tomatoes, basil, parsley and sugar. Cover and simmer for 10 minutes. Drain pasta; stir into the sausage mixture.

Chicken Taco Rice

This flavorful and versatile recipe is so easy to vary. It was given to me by a friend, and whenever I prepare it, I think of the amazing friendships that have helped to shape my life.

—**HEATHER RAY** MILWAUKEE, WISCONSIN

PREP: 15 MIN. **COOK:** 20 MIN. **MAKES:** 4 SERVINGS

- **1 pound boneless skinless chicken breasts, cut into 1-inch strips**
- **1 medium green pepper, chopped**
- **⅓ cup chopped onion**
- **2 tablespoons olive oil**
- **1 can (14½ ounces) reduced-sodium chicken broth**
- **1 can (8 ounces) tomato sauce**
- **3 tablespoons taco seasoning**
- **2 cups instant brown rice**
- **1 can (15¼ ounces) whole kernel corn, drained**

Optional Toppings: reduced-fat sour cream and shredded cheddar cheese

1. In a large skillet, saute the chicken, pepper and onion in oil until chicken is no longer pink. Add the broth, tomato sauce and taco seasoning. Bring to a boil. Stir in rice and corn.

2. Reduce heat; cover and simmer for 5 minutes or until liquid is absorbed. Remove from the heat. Let stand for 5 minutes. Serve with toppings of your choice.

Pork Medallions with Brandy Cream Sauce

I adapted this easy, elegant main dish from a recipe my mother-in-law cooked for our family. Cayenne lends a bit of heat to its rich, creamy sauce.

—**JUDY ARMSTRONG** PRAIRIEVILLE, LOUISIANA

PREP: 25 MIN. **COOK:** 25 MIN. **MAKES:** 4 SERVINGS

- **12 ounces uncooked linguine**
- **1 pork tenderloin (1 pound), cut into 1-inch slices**
- **¼ cup all-purpose flour**
- **2 tablespoons olive oil**
- **3 tablespoons butter, divided**
- **1¾ cups sliced baby portobello mushrooms**
- **5 green onions, thinly sliced**
- **2 garlic cloves, minced**
- **1½ cups heavy whipping cream**
- **¼ cup brandy**
- **2 tablespoons minced fresh thyme**
- **1 tablespoon Dijon mustard**
- **½ teaspoon salt**
- **½ teaspoon pepper**
- **¼ teaspoon cayenne pepper**
- **2 plum tomatoes, seeded and chopped**
- **2 tablespoons shredded Parmesan cheese**

1. Cook linguine according to package directions. Meanwhile, flatten pork slices to ¼-in. thickness. Place flour in a large resealable plastic bag. Add pork, a few pieces at a time, and shake to coat.

2. In a large skillet over medium-high heat, cook pork in oil and 2 tablespoons butter in batches for 3-4 minutes on each side or until juices run clear. Set aside and keep warm.

3. In the same skillet, saute mushrooms and onions in remaining butter until tender. Add garlic; cook 1 minute longer. Add the cream, brandy, thyme, mustard, salt, pepper and cayenne. Bring to a boil; cook until liquid is reduced by half, about 8 minutes.

4. Drain linguine. Stir tomatoes into sauce mixture; add pork and heat through. Serve with linguine and sprinkle with cheese.

Gravy

Casseroles & Oven Suppers

“Guests will fall in love at first sight of this impressive citrus and savory herb-roasted chicken—a big hit when my best friend’s mom came for a visit.”

SARA VASQUES MILFORD, NEW HAMPSHIRE
Rosemary-Orange Roasted Chicken, page 190

Easy Cheddar Chicken Potpie

My kids love chicken potpie, and I really like that this is so quick and easy to put together with frozen veggies and store-bought gravy. To make it even simpler, my friend and I decided to top it with a biscuit crust instead of homemade pastry. It's delicious!

—LINDA DREES PALESTINE, TEXAS

PREP: 20 MIN. **BAKE:** 25 MIN. **MAKES:** 6 SERVINGS

- **1 package (16 ounces) frozen vegetables for stew, thawed and coarsely chopped**
- **1 jar (12 ounces) chicken gravy**
- **2 cups (8 ounces) shredded cheddar cheese**
- **2 cups cubed cooked chicken**
- **1 cup biscuit/baking mix**
- **¼ teaspoon dried thyme**
- **2 eggs**
- **¼ cup 2% milk**

1. Combine vegetables and gravy in a large saucepan. Bring to a boil. Reduce heat; stir in the cheese and chicken. Cook and stir until cheese is melted. Pour into a greased 11-in. x 7-in. baking dish.

2. Combine biscuit mix and thyme in a small bowl. In another bowl, whisk eggs and milk; stir into dry ingredients just until moistened. Drop by tablespoonfuls over chicken mixture; spread gently.

3. Bake, uncovered, at 375° for 23-27 minutes or until golden brown. Let stand for 5 minutes before serving.

Nutty Oven-Fried Chicken

PREP: 10 MIN. **BAKE:** 1 HOUR **MAKES:** 6 SERVINGS

- **½ cup evaporated milk**
- **1 cup biscuit/baking mix**
- **⅓ cup finely chopped pecans**
- **2 teaspoons paprika**
- **½ teaspoon salt**
- **½ teaspoon poultry seasoning**
- **½ teaspoon rubbed sage**
- **1 broiler/fryer chicken (3 to 4 pounds), cut up**
- **⅓ cup butter, melted**

1. Place milk in a shallow bowl. In another shallow bowl, combine the baking mix, pecans and seasonings. Dip chicken pieces in milk, then coat generously with pecan mixture.

2. Place in a lightly greased 13-in. x 9-in. baking dish. Drizzle with butter. Bake, uncovered, at 350° for 1 hour or until chicken is golden brown and crispy and juices run clear.

"The pecans that give this dish its unique nutty flavor are plentiful in the South. I love to prepare and serve this easy dish because the chicken comes out moist, tasty and crispy." —DIANE HIXON NICEVILLE, FLORIDA

Buffalo Chicken Pasta Bake

Sure, 10-cent wing night at your local pub is a blast, but a night at home with a clever casserole can't be beat. Not fond of blue cheese? Use ranch salad dressing instead.

—**LINDSAY SPRUNK** NOBLESVILLE, INDIANA

PREP: 30 MIN. **BAKE:** 25 MIN. **MAKES:** 8 SERVINGS

- **1 package (16 ounces) penne pasta**
- **1 pound boneless skinless chicken breasts, cubed**
- **⅛ teaspoon salt**
- **⅛ teaspoon pepper**
- **2 tablespoons olive oil, divided**
- **2 medium carrots, finely chopped**
- **2 celery ribs, finely chopped**
- **¾ cup finely chopped red onion**
- **4 garlic cloves, minced**
- **¾ cup blue cheese salad dressing**
- **¾ cup mayonnaise**
- **½ cup Louisiana-style hot sauce**
- **1½ cups (6 ounces) shredded Swiss cheese**
- **½ cup dry bread crumbs**
- **3 tablespoons butter, melted**

1. Cook pasta according to package directions. Meanwhile, sprinkle chicken with salt and pepper. In a large skillet, saute chicken in 1 tablespoon oil until no longer pink. Remove from the skillet. In the same skillet, saute the carrots, celery and onion in remaining oil until tender. Add garlic; cook 1 minute longer. Remove from the heat.

2. Stir in the salad dressing, mayonnaise and hot sauce. Drain pasta. Add pasta and chicken to skillet; toss to coat. Transfer to a greased 13-in. x 9-in. baking dish. Sprinkle with cheese and bread crumbs. Drizzle with butter.

3. Bake, uncovered, at 350° for 25-30 minutes or until heated through and cheese is melted.

Sweet & Tender Beef Ribs

Wondering if they taste as good as they look? The answer is yes! These satisfying ribs live up to every delicious bit of their name.

—**HEATHER BATES** ATHENS, MAINE

PREP: 1½ HOURS **BROIL:** 5 MIN. **MAKES:** 5 SERVINGS

- **5 pounds beef back ribs**
- **1½ cups maple syrup**
- **⅓ cup molasses**
- **3 tablespoons orange marmalade**
- **2 tablespoons ketchup**
- **1½ teaspoons dried minced onion**
- **1 teaspoon prepared mustard**
- **1 garlic clove, minced**
- **¼ teaspoon salt**
- **¼ teaspoon onion powder**
- **¼ teaspoon pepper**

1. Cut ribs into serving size portions. Place in a greased 15-in. x 10-in. x 1-in. baking pan. Cover and bake at 350° for 1¼ hours or until tender.

2. In a small saucepan, combine the remaining ingredients. Bring to a boil; cook and stir for 10-15 minutes or until thickened. Drain ribs; place on a broiler pan. Brush with some of the barbecue sauce. Broil 4-5 in. from the heat for 5-10 minutes or until sauce is bubbly. Serve with remaining sauce.

Crab Imperial Casserole

PREP: 20 MIN. **BAKE:** 25 MIN. **MAKES:** 8 SERVINGS

- **3 cups uncooked spiral pasta**
- **1¾ cups sliced fresh mushrooms**
- **5 tablespoons butter, cubed**
- **2 tablespoons all-purpose flour**
- **¾ teaspoon pepper**
- **½ teaspoon salt**
- **1½ cups 2% milk**
- **4 cans (6 ounces each) lump crabmeat, drained**
- **1 can (10¾ ounces) condensed cream of mushroom soup, undiluted**
- **¼ cup crushed butter-flavored crackers**

1. Cook pasta according to package directions. Meanwhile, in a large skillet, saute mushrooms in butter until tender. Stir in the flour, pepper and salt until blended; gradually add milk. Bring to a boil. Cook and stir for 2 minutes or until thickened. Stir in crab and soup until blended.
2. Drain pasta and transfer to a large bowl. Add crab mixture; toss to coat. Transfer to a greased 13-in. x 9-in. baking dish; sprinkle with cracker crumbs. Bake, uncovered, at 350° for 25-30 minutes or until bubbly.

“This recipe serves eight, but plan to double it. Fresh mushrooms and lump crabmeat make it hard to turn down seconds of a casserole this rich!”

—**BARBARA CARLUCCI** ORANGE PARK, FLORIDA

Indian Baked Chicken

Cumin and turmeric give this hearty entree just the right amount of Indian flavor while maintaining mass appeal for picky eaters in the bunch.

—**STEPHANIE KURIN** MUNCIE, INDIANA

PREP: 15 MIN. **BAKE:** 1 HOUR
MAKES: 6 SERVINGS

- **1 pound small red potatoes, quartered**
- **4 medium carrots, cut into 1-inch pieces**
- **1 large onion, cut into 1-inch pieces**
- **6 boneless skinless chicken thighs (about 1½ pounds)**
- **1 can (14½ ounces) chicken broth**
- **1 can (6 ounces) tomato paste**
- **2 tablespoons olive oil**
- **1 tablespoon ground turmeric**
- **1 teaspoon chili powder**
- **1 teaspoon ground cumin**
- **½ teaspoon salt**
- **½ teaspoon garlic powder**
- **½ teaspoon pepper**

1. Place the potatoes, carrots and onion in a greased 13-in. x 9-in. baking dish; add chicken. In a small bowl, combine the remaining ingredients and pour over the top.
2. Cover and bake at 400° for 1 to 1¼ hours or until a thermometer inserted into chicken reads 180° and the vegetables are tender.

Chili-Spiced Pork Chops

I like my food spicy, and my husband likes his mild. This pleasantly seasoned dish makes us both happy, and our son enjoys it, too! It's a cinch to whip up, so I always keep all the ingredients on hand.

—**ANDREA KEITH** KENTWOOD, MICHIGAN

PREP/TOTAL TIME: 30 MIN.
MAKES: 6 SERVINGS

- **¾ cup seasoned bread crumbs**
- **3 tablespoons chili powder**
- **½ teaspoon seasoned salt**
- **1 egg**
- **¼ cup fat-free milk**
- **6 bone-in pork rib chops (7 ounces each, ¾ inch thick)**

1. In a shallow bowl, combine the bread crumbs, chili powder and seasoned salt. In another shallow bowl, combine the egg and milk. Dip chops in egg mixture, then coat with crumbs.
2. Transfer to a 15-in. x 10-in. x 1-in. baking pan coated with cooking spray. Bake at 350° for 20-25 minutes or until thermometer reads 160°.

Creamy Chicken Lasagna Roll-Ups

I love to experiment with new pasta dishes. Ingredients I had on hand and frozen sauce led to these tasty lasagna-flavored roll-ups.
—**CYNDY GERKEN** NAPLES, FLORIDA

PREP: 35 MIN. **BAKE:** 45 MIN. **MAKES:** 10 SERVINGS

- **10 lasagna noodles**
- **¾ pound boneless skinless chicken breasts, cubed**
- **1½ teaspoons herbes de Provence**
- **½ teaspoon salt, divided**
- **½ teaspoon pepper, divided**
- **1 tablespoon olive oil**
- **2 cups ricotta cheese**
- **½ cup grated Parmesan cheese, divided**
- **¼ cup 2% milk**
- **2 tablespoons minced fresh parsley**
- **4 cups spaghetti sauce**
- **8 ounces fresh mozzarella cheese, thinly sliced**

1. Cook lasagna noodles according to package directions.
2. Meanwhile, sprinkle chicken with herbes de Provence, 1/4 teaspoon salt and 1/4 teaspoon pepper. In a large skillet, cook chicken in oil over medium heat for 5-7 minutes or until no longer pink; set aside.
3. In a large bowl, combine ricotta, 1/4 cup Parmesan cheese, milk, parsley and remaining salt and pepper. Add chicken.
4. Drain noodles. Spread 1 cup spaghetti sauce into a greased 13-in. x 9-in. baking dish. Spread 1/3 cup chicken mixture over each noodle; carefully roll up. Place seam side down over sauce. Top with remaining sauce and Parmesan cheese.
5. Cover and bake at 375° for 30 minutes. Uncover; top with mozzarella cheese. Bake 15-20 minutes longer or until bubbly and cheese is melted.
Editor's Note: *Look for herbes de Provence in the spice aisle.*

Moist & Savory Meat Loaf

Serve this deliciously moist entree with extra sauce for those who love to have their meat loaf smothered!
—**TASTE OF HOME TEST KITCHEN**

PREP: 20 MIN. **BAKE:** 1¼ HOURS + STANDING
MAKES: 8 SERVINGS

- **1 medium onion, chopped**
- **2 teaspoons canola oil**
- **2 eggs, lightly beaten**
- **⅓ cup 2% milk**
- **2 teaspoons Worcestershire sauce**
- **2 teaspoons Dijon mustard**
- **⅔ cup finely crushed cheese crackers**
- **1 teaspoon salt**
- **½ teaspoon pepper**
- **½ teaspoon dried thyme**
- **1½ pounds ground beef**
- **½ pound ground pork**
- **¾ cup ketchup**
- **¼ cup packed brown sugar**

1. Saute onion in oil in a small skillet until tender. Cool to room temperature.
2. Combine the eggs, milk, Worcestershire sauce, mustard, crackers, salt, pepper, thyme and onion in a large bowl. Crumble beef and pork over mixture and mix well. Shape into a loaf; place in a greased 11-in. x 7-in. baking dish.
3. Bake, uncovered, at 350° for 1 hour. Combine ketchup and brown sugar; spread half of sauce over meat loaf. Bake 15-20 minutes longer or until no pink remains and a thermometer reads 160°. Let stand for 10 minutes before slicing. Serve with remaining sauce.

Philly Cheesesteak Pizza

Try this fun take on the traditional sandwich. Deli roast beef and crescent roll dough make this easy recipe hard to resist.
—**MARIA REGAKIS** SOMERVILLE, MASSACHUSETTS

PREP/TOTAL TIME: 30 MIN. **MAKES:** 6 SERVINGS

- **1 tube (8 ounces) refrigerated crescent rolls**
- **1 medium green pepper, chopped**
- **1 medium onion, chopped**

2 tablespoons olive oil
¼ teaspoon beef bouillon granules
½ pound thinly sliced deli roast beef
1 tablespoon prepared Italian salad dressing
1½ cups (6 ounces) shredded part-skim mozzarella cheese

1. Unroll crescent roll dough into one long rectangle; seal perforations. Press onto the bottom and up the sides of an ungreased 13-in. x 9-in. baking pan. Bake at 375° for 7-10 minutes or until lightly browned.
2. Meanwhile, in a large skillet, saute the green pepper and onion in oil and bouillon until vegetables are tender; set aside.
3. Arrange beef over crust. Brush with salad dressing; sprinkle with cheese. Bake 4-5 minutes longer or until cheese is melted. Top with green pepper mixture. Cut into 12 pieces.

Sloppy Joe Veggie Casserole

Sloppy joe flavor combines with the nutrition of veggie lasagna in this dynamic duo. My family loves this easy-to-prepare hot dish.
—SUE SCHMIDTKE ORO VALLEY, ARIZONA

PREP: 25 MIN. **BAKE:** 30 MIN. **MAKES:** 8 SERVINGS

2½ cups uncooked penne pasta
1 pound ground beef
1 small onion, chopped
1 package (16 ounces) frozen mixed vegetables
1½ cups water
1 can (15 ounces) tomato sauce
1 can (6 ounces) tomato paste
1 envelope sloppy joe mix
1 tablespoon dried parsley flakes
½ teaspoon dried oregano
2 cups (16 ounces) 2% cottage cheese
1½ cups (6 ounces) shredded Colby-Monterey Jack cheese

1. Cook pasta according to package directions.
2. Meanwhile, cook beef and onion in a large skillet over medium heat until meat is no longer pink; drain. Add the vegetables, water, tomato sauce, tomato paste, sloppy joe mix, parsley and oregano. Bring to a boil. Reduce heat; simmer, uncovered, for 7-9 minutes or until vegetables are crisp-tender. Drain pasta; stir into beef mixture.
3. Spoon half of the mixture into a greased 13-in. x 9-in. baking dish. Top with cottage cheese, ¾ cup Colby-Monterey Jack and the remaining pasta mixture.
4. Cover and bake at 350° for 25 minutes. Uncover; sprinkle with remaining Colby-Monterey Jack cheese. Bake 5-10 minutes longer or until bubbly and cheese is melted.

Italian Pesto Pizzas

These individual pizzas, ready in 30 minutes or less, give you good reason not to call out for dinner. The pesto base fills the kitchen with a wonderful aroma while they're baking.
—KELLY EVANS KALAMAZOO, MICHIGAN

PREP/TOTAL TIME: 30 MIN. **MAKES:** 4 SERVINGS

4 whole wheat pitas or flat breads
¼ cup prepared pesto
2 cups shredded part-skim mozzarella cheese
2 cups fresh baby spinach
½ cup sliced fresh mushrooms
½ cup chopped sweet yellow pepper
1 plum tomato, halved and sliced
¼ cup chopped red onion
¼ cup grated Parmesan cheese
2 tablespoons sliced ripe olives, optional
¼ teaspoon crushed red pepper flakes
2 fresh basil leaves, thinly sliced

1. Place pita breads on an ungreased baking sheet; spread with pesto. Layer with mozzarella cheese, spinach, mushrooms, yellow pepper, tomato, onion, Parmesan cheese, olives if desired and pepper flakes.
2. Bake at 425° for 10-12 minutes or until cheese is melted. Top pizzas with basil.

Rosemary-Orange Roasted Chicken

PREP: 30 MIN.
BAKE: 2½ HOURS + STANDING
MAKES: 4 SERVINGS

- ¼ cup butter, softened
- 1 tablespoon minced fresh rosemary or 1 teaspoon dried rosemary, crushed
- 2 teaspoons grated orange peel
- ½ teaspoon pepper, divided
- 1 broiler/fryer chicken (3 to 4 pounds)
- ⅓ cup orange juice
- ½ teaspoon salt
- 2 medium onions, quartered
- 1 medium apple, quartered
- 1 large carrot, chopped
- 1 celery rib, chopped
- 4 fresh thyme sprigs
- 4 sprigs fresh parsley
- 2 bay leaves
- 1 fresh rosemary sprig
- 2 cups white wine or chicken broth

GRAVY

- Chicken broth
- 3 tablespoons butter
- 2 tablespoons all-purpose flour
- ⅛ teaspoon ground nutmeg, optional

1. In a small bowl, combine the butter, minced rosemary, orange peel and 1/8 teaspoon pepper. With fingers, carefully loosen skin from the chicken; rub butter mixture under the skin. Brush chicken with orange juice. Sprinkle salt and remaining pepper over chicken and inside cavity.

2. Place one onion and half of the apple inside the cavity. Tuck wings under chicken; tie drumsticks together. Place breast side up on a rack in a roasting pan. Arrange the carrot, celery, thyme, parsley, bay leaves, rosemary sprig and remaining onion and apple around chicken. Pour wine into pan.

3. Bake, uncovered, at 350° for 2½ to 3 hours or until a thermometer reads 180°, basting occasionally with drippings. Cover loosely with foil if chicken browns too quickly. Cover and let stand for 15 minutes before slicing.

4. For gravy, pour drippings and loosened browned bits into a measuring cup. Skim fat. Add enough broth to the drippings to measure 1 cup. In a small saucepan, melt butter. Stir in flour until smooth; gradually add broth mixture and nutmeg if desired. Bring to a boil; cook and stir for 2 minutes or until thickened. Serve with chicken.

Guests will fall in love at first sight of this impressive citrus and savory herb-roasted chicken—a big hit when my best friend's mom came for a visit.
—**SARA VASQUES** MILFORD, NEW HAMPSHIRE

Mediterranean Rack of Lamb

It's elegant. It's special. And it will have your guests thinking you went all out. They don't have to know how simple the lamb is!

—SUSAN NILSSON STERLING, VIRGINIA

PREP: 10 MIN. **BAKE:** 30 MIN. **MAKES:** 4 SERVINGS

- **2 racks of lamb (1½ pounds each)**
- **¼ cup grated lemon peel**
- **¼ cup minced fresh oregano or 4 teaspoons dried oregano**
- **6 garlic cloves, minced**
- **1 tablespoon olive oil**
- **¼ teaspoon salt**
- **¼ teaspoon pepper**

1. Place lamb in a shallow roasting pan. In small bowl, combine the lemon peel, oregano, garlic, oil, salt and pepper. Rub over lamb.
2. Bake at 375° for 30-40 minutes or until meat reaches desired doneness (for medium-rare, a thermometer should read 145°; medium, 160°; well-done, 170°). Let stand for 5 minutes before cutting.

Philly-Style Mac and Cheese

My son loves macaroni and cheese, and I'm always looking for ways to sneak in some veggies. This version is a huge hit with us both!

—JENNIFER BERRY LEXINGTON, OHIO

PREP: 30 MIN. **BAKE:** 25 MIN. **MAKES:** 6 SERVINGS

- **2 cups uncooked elbow macaroni**
- **½ pound sliced fresh mushrooms**
- **1 medium onion, chopped**
- **1 medium green pepper, chopped**
- **¼ cup butter, cubed**
- **¼ cup all-purpose flour**
- **1 cup 2% milk**
- **1 cup beef broth**
- **2 cups (8 ounces) shredded provolone cheese**
- **2 cups (8 ounces) shredded part-skim mozzarella cheese**
- **1 teaspoon garlic powder**
- **1 teaspoon Montreal steak seasoning**
- **½ teaspoon onion powder**
- **1 package (10½ ounces) frozen Steak-umm sliced steaks, browned**
- **½ cup French-fried onions**

1. Cook macaroni according to package directions.
2. Meanwhile, in a large skillet, saute the mushrooms, onion and green pepper in butter until tender. Stir in flour until blended; gradually add milk and broth. Bring to a boil; cook and stir for 2 minutes or until thickened. Reduce heat. Stir in the cheeses, garlic powder, steak seasoning and onion powder.
3. Drain macaroni; add to sauce mixture. Stir in steak. Transfer to an ungreased 13-in. x 9-in. baking dish; sprinkle fried onions over top. Bake, uncovered, at 350° for 25-30 minutes or until bubbly.

Bourbon-Glazed Ham

Smoky and sweet flavors come through in every bite of this Kentucky-style ham. This recipe is the only ham I ever make.

—SUE SCHILLER TOMAHAWK, WISCONSIN

PREP: 15 MIN. **BAKE:** 2½ HOURS + STANDING
MAKES: 16 SERVINGS

- **1 fully cooked bone-in ham (8 to 10 pounds)**
- **¾ cup bourbon, divided**
- **2 cups packed brown sugar**
- **1 tablespoon ground mustard**
- **1 tablespoon orange marmalade**
- **⅛ teaspoon ground coriander**

1. Place ham on a rack in a shallow roasting pan. Score surface of the ham, making diamond shapes ½ in. deep. Brush with 2 tablespoons bourbon. Bake, uncovered, at 325° for 2 hours.
2. In a small bowl, combine the brown sugar, mustard, marmalade, coriander and remaining bourbon; spoon over ham. Bake 30 minutes longer or until a thermometer reads 140°. Let stand for 15 minutes before slicing.

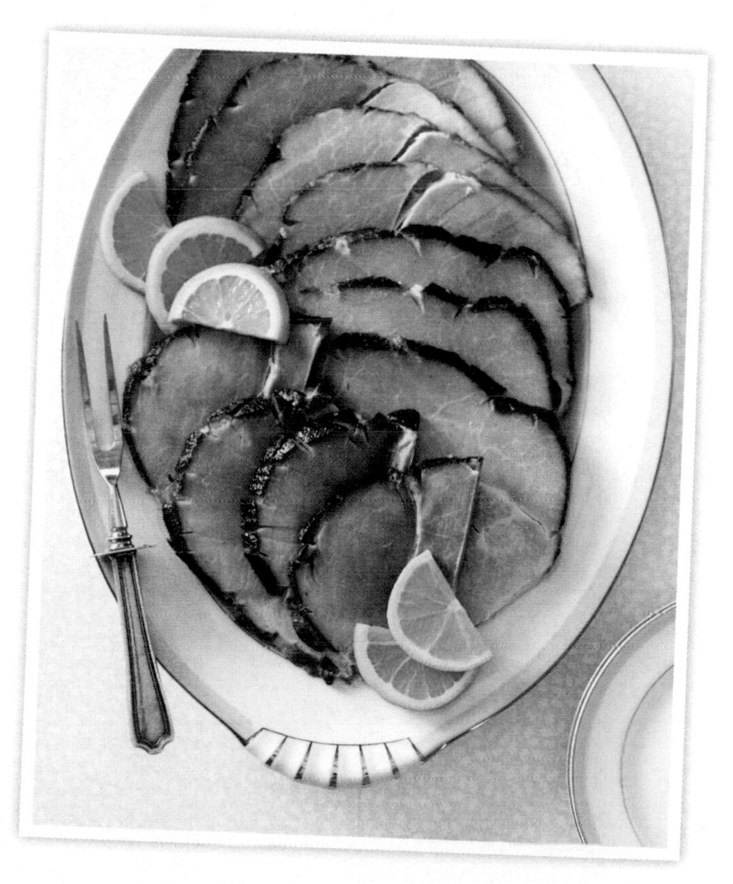

Mom's Turkey Tetrazzini

Filled with family-friendly flavors, a pleasant peppery kick and a creamy from-scratch sauce, this hearty dish is just the kind of stick-to-your-ribs comfort food you've been looking for!

—**JUDY BATSON** TAMPA, FLORIDA

PREP: 25 MIN. **BAKE:** 25 MIN. + STANDING **MAKES:** 6 SERVINGS

- **1 package (12 ounces) fettuccine**
- **½ pound sliced fresh mushrooms**
- **1 medium onion, chopped**
- **¼ cup butter, cubed**
- **3 tablespoons all-purpose flour**
- **3 cups 2% milk**
- **1 cup white wine or chicken broth**
- **3 cups cubed cooked turkey**
- **¾ teaspoon salt**
- **½ teaspoon pepper**
- **½ teaspoon hot pepper sauce**
- **½ cup shredded Parmesan cheese**
- **Paprika, optional**

1. Cook fettuccine according to package directions.
2. Meanwhile, in a large skillet, saute mushrooms and onion in butter until tender. Stir in flour until blended; gradually add milk and wine. Bring to a boil; cook and stir for 2 minutes or until thickened. Stir in the turkey, salt, pepper and pepper sauce.
3. Drain fettuccine. Layer half of the fettuccine, turkey mixture and cheese in a greased 13-in. x 9-in. baking dish. Repeat layers. Sprinkle with paprika if desired.
4. Cover and bake at 375° for 25-30 minutes or until heated through. Let stand for 10 minutes before serving.

Golombki

Tender cabbage rolls are stuffed with a delicious mixture of ground beef and onion. Instant rice and canned tomato soup speed along the prep work, and the long oven time gives you a chance to whip up a side dish and pour the wine.

—**VALERIE LIPINSKI** BUFFALO, NEW YORK

PREP: 25 MIN. **BAKE:** 55 MIN. **MAKES:** 5 SERVINGS

- **1 medium head cabbage**
- **½ cup uncooked instant rice**
- **1 pound ground beef**
- **1 small onion, chopped**
- **½ teaspoon salt**
- **¼ teaspoon pepper**
- **2 cans (10¾ ounces each) condensed tomato soup, undiluted**
- **1¼ cups water**

1. Cook cabbage in boiling water just until outer leaves pull away easily from head. Set aside 10 large leaves for rolls. Refrigerate remaining cabbage for another use. Cut out the thick vein from the bottom of each leaf, making a V-shaped cut.
2. Cook rice according to package directions. Meanwhile, in a large skillet, cook beef and onion over medium heat until meat is no longer pink; drain. Stir in the cooked rice, salt and pepper.
3. Place ⅓ cup beef mixture on a cabbage leaf; overlap cut ends of leaf. Fold in sides. Beginning from the cut end, roll up. Repeat. Place seam side down in a greased 13-in. x 9-in. baking dish. Combine soup and water; pour over top.
4. Cover and bake at 350° for 55-65 minutes or until cabbage is tender.

Chicken Madeira Pastry

It's easy to fold restaurant leftovers into puff pastry for a beautiful supper that feeds the whole family. Any homemade leftover chicken you have on hand would also work well in this recipe.

—**TASTE OF HOME TEST KITCHEN**

PREP: 20 MIN. **BAKE:** 20 MIN. **MAKES:** 4 SERVINGS

- 1 **package (6½ ounces) garlic-herb spreadable cheese**
- 3 **tablespoons 2% milk**
- 1 **tablespoon Dijon mustard**
- 1½ **cups frozen peas and pearl onions**
- 1¼ **cups cubed leftover chicken from Cheesecake Factory's Chicken Madeira**
- 1 **sheet frozen puff pastry, thawed**
- 1½ **cups refrigerated mashed potatoes**
- 1 **egg, beaten**

1. Combine the spreadable cheese, milk and mustard in a small saucepan. Cook and stir over low heat for 2-3 minutes or until smooth. Set aside 1/4 cup for serving. Add the peas and pearl onions and chicken to the saucepan; heat through.
2. Roll out pastry on a lightly floured surface into a 15-in. x 10-in. rectangle; transfer to an ungreased baking sheet. Spread potatoes lengthwise down the center third of rectangle to within 1-inch of the ends; top with chicken mixture.
3. Cut eight strips on each long side about 3 inches into the center. Bring one strip from each side over filling and pinch ends to seal; repeat. Brush with egg.
4. Bake at 400° for 20-25 minutes or until golden brown. Serve with reserved sauce.

Cajun Chicken Pasta Bake

Here's a recipe that's quick, simple and tastes so good, my family alaways wants seconds. So I make two and freeze one!
—**KIM WEISHUHN** PENSACOLA, FLORIDA

PREP: 30 MIN. **BAKE:** 20 MIN.
MAKES: 2 CASSEROLES (6 SERVINGS EACH)

- 2 **packages (12 ounces each) bow tie pasta**
- 2 **pounds boneless skinless chicken breasts, cut into 1-inch strips**
- 2 **tablespoons olive oil, divided**
- 2 **bunches green onions, chopped**
- 2 **medium green peppers, chopped**
- 2 **medium sweet red peppers, chopped**
- 1 **can (14½ ounces) reduced-sodium chicken broth**
- 2 **cans (10¾ ounces each) condensed cream of chicken soup, undiluted**
- 1 **can (10¾ ounces) condensed cream of mushroom soup, undiluted**
- ¾ **cup 2% milk**
- 2½ **teaspoons Cajun seasoning**
- 1½ **teaspoons garlic powder**
- 2 **cups (8 ounces) shredded Colby-Monterey Jack cheese**

1. Cook pasta according to package directions to al dente.
2. Meanwhile, in a Dutch oven, saute chicken in 1 tablespoon oil until juices run clear. Remove with a slotted spoon and set aside. In the same pan, saute onions and peppers in remaining oil until tender. Add the broth, soups, milk, Cajun seasoning and garlic powder. Bring to a boil and remove from the heat.
3. Drain pasta. Add pasta and chicken to soup mixture; toss to coat. Divide between two greased 13-in. x 9-in. baking dishes. Sprinkle with cheese. Cover and freeze one casserole for up to 3 months. Cover and bake the remaining casserole at 350° for 20-25 minutes or until bubbly.
To use frozen casserole: *Thaw in the refrigerator overnight. Remove from the refrigerator 30 minutes before baking. Cover and bake at 350° for 55-60 minutes or until bubbly.*

Sesame Salmon with Wasabi Mayo

I love salmon and created this recipe to mimic the bold flavors of sushi. It's remarkably easy and turns out well every time. Be sure to watch the salmon as it bakes to avoid overcooking.
—**CAROLYN KETCHUM** WAKEFIELD, MASSACHUSETTS

PREP: 15 MIN. **BAKE:** 20 MIN. **MAKES:** 6 SERVINGS

- 2 **tablespoons butter, melted**
- 3 **tablespoons sesame oil, divided**
- 1 **salmon fillet (2 pounds)**
- ¼ **teaspoon salt**
- ¼ **teaspoon pepper**
- ⅓ **cup mayonnaise**
- 1½ **teaspoons lemon juice**
- 1 **teaspoon prepared wasabi**
- 4 **green onions, chopped**
- 2 **tablespoons sesame seeds, toasted**

1. Drizzle butter and 2 tablespoons oil into a 13-in. x 9-in. baking dish; tilt to coat bottom. Place salmon in dish; brush with remaining oil and sprinkle with salt and pepper.
2. Bake, uncovered, at 425° for 18-22 minutes or until fish flakes easily with a fork. Meanwhile, combine the mayonnaise, lemon juice and wasabi. Sprinkle salmon with onions and sesame seeds. Serve with sauce.

Wasabi, also called Japanese horseradish, is a pale-green condiment with a sharp, fiery flavor. It's available in both paste and powder form in most grocery stores' ethnic aisles, and can also be found in specialty and Asian markets.

Loaded Mexican Pizza

My husband, Steve, is a picky eater, but this healthy pizza has lots of flavor and he actually looks forward to it. Leftovers are no problem because this is one of those rare meals that tastes even better the next day.

—**MARY BARKER** KNOXVILLE, TENNESSEE

PREP/TOTAL TIME: 30 MIN. **MAKES:** 6 SLICES

- **1 can (15 ounces) black beans, rinsed and drained**
- **1 medium red onion, chopped**
- **1 small sweet yellow pepper, chopped**
- **3 teaspoons chili powder**
- **¾ teaspoon ground cumin**
- **3 medium tomatoes, chopped**
- **1 jalapeno pepper, seeded and finely chopped**
- **1 garlic clove, minced**
- **1 prebaked 12-inch thin pizza crust**
- **2 cups chopped fresh spinach**
- **2 tablespoons minced fresh cilantro**
- **Hot pepper sauce to taste**
- **½ cup shredded reduced-fat cheddar cheese**
- **½ cup shredded pepper jack cheese**

1. In a small bowl, mash black beans. Stir in the onion, yellow pepper, chili powder and cumin. In another bowl, combine the tomatoes, jalapeno and garlic.
2. Place crust on an ungreased 12-in. pizza pan; spread with bean mixture. Top with tomato mixture and spinach. Sprinkle with cilantro, pepper sauce and cheeses.
3. Bake at 400° for 12-15 minutes or until cheese is melted.

Editor's Note: *Wear disposable gloves when cutting hot peppers; the oils can burn skin. Avoid touching your face.*

Baked Spaghetti

You'll get requests for this yummy spaghetti casserole again and again. It's especially popular with my grandchildren, who just love all the cheese.

—**LOUISE MILLER** WESTMINSTER, MARYLAND

PREP: 25 MIN. **BAKE:** 1 HOUR
MAKES: 10 SERVINGS

- **1 package (16 ounces) spaghetti**
- **1 pound ground beef**
- **1 medium onion, chopped**
- **1 jar (24 ounces) meatless spaghetti sauce**
- **½ teaspoon seasoned salt**
- **2 eggs**
- **⅓ cup grated Parmesan cheese**
- **5 tablespoons butter, melted**
- **2 cups (16 ounces) 4% cottage cheese**
- **4 cups (16 ounces) part-skim shredded mozzarella cheese**

1. Cook spaghetti according to package directions. Meanwhile, in a large skillet, cook beef and onion over medium heat until meat is no longer pink; drain. Stir in spaghetti sauce and seasoned salt; set aside.
2. In a large bowl, whisk the eggs, Parmesan cheese and butter. Drain spaghetti; add to egg mixture and toss to coat.
3. Place half of the spaghetti mixture in a greased 13-in. x 9-in. baking dish. Top with half of the cottage cheese, meat sauce and mozzarella cheese. Repeat layers.
4. Cover and bake at 350° for 40 minutes. Uncover; bake 20-25 minutes longer or until cheese is melted.

To prevent spaghetti from sticking together when cooking, use a large pot and 3 quarts of water for every 8 ounces of pasta. Add 1 tablespoon olive oil. (This will also prevent water from boiling over.) Allow the water to come to a full boil before stirring the pasta. Stir to keep the strands separate.

Baked
(16 oz) spaghetti
ground beef
chopped
1 jar (24 oz) meatless
spaghetti sauce
1/2 teaspoon seasoned salt
2 eggs

Lighted-Up Delights

"Whole wheat flour and two kinds of berries add an extra helping of nutrition to these hearty pancakes. It's a breakfast I feel good about serving."

SARAH HAENGEL BOWIE, MARYLAND
Almond Berry Pancakes, page 201

Cardamom Sour Cream Waffles

Sweet, with just the right amount of spice, these easy waffles make it nearly impossible to skip your morning meal.

—BARBIE MILLER OAKDALE, MINNESOTA

PREP: 15 MIN. **COOK:** 5 MIN./BATCH **MAKES:** 14 WAFFLES

- **¾ cup all-purpose flour**
- **¾ cup whole wheat flour**
- **1½ teaspoons baking powder**
- **1 teaspoon ground cardamom**
- **¾ teaspoon baking soda**
- **½ teaspoon ground cinnamon**
- **¼ teaspoon salt**
- **2 eggs**
- **1 cup fat-free milk**
- **¾ cup reduced-fat sour cream**
- **½ cup packed brown sugar**
- **1 tablespoon butter, melted**
- **1 teaspoon vanilla extract**

1. In a large bowl, combine the first seven ingredients. In another bowl, whisk the eggs, milk, sour cream, brown sugar, butter and vanilla. Stir into dry ingredients just until combined.
2. Bake in a preheated waffle iron according to manufacturer's directions until golden brown. Top with fruit if desired.

Nutrition Facts: *2 waffles equals 235 calories, 6 g fat (3 g saturated fat), 74 mg cholesterol, 375 mg sodium, 39 g carbohydrate, 2 g fiber, 8 g protein.* **Diabetic Exchanges:** *2½ starch, 1 fat.*

Mediterranean Shrimp Linguine

This picture-perfect linguine is a feast for the eyes and, with just a hint of heat, a treat for the palate!

—MEGAN HIDALGO QUARRYVILLE, PENNSYLVANIA

PREP: 20 MIN. **COOK:** 20 MIN. **MAKES:** 8 SERVINGS

- **1 package (16 ounces) linguine**
- **2 pounds uncooked medium shrimp, peeled and deveined**
- **1 medium onion, chopped**
- **6 tablespoons olive oil**
- **4 garlic cloves, minced**
- **1 cup chopped roasted sweet red peppers**
- **2 cans (2¼ ounces each) sliced ripe olives, drained**
- **½ cup minced fresh parsley**
- **½ cup white wine or chicken broth**
- **½ teaspoon crushed red pepper flakes**
- **½ teaspoon kosher salt**
- **½ teaspoon dried oregano**
- **½ teaspoon pepper**
- **¾ cup crumbled feta cheese**
- **2 tablespoons lemon juice**

1. Cook linguine according to package directions.
2. Meanwhile, in a large skillet, saute shrimp and onion in oil until shrimp turn pink. Add garlic; cook 1 minute longer. Stir in the red peppers, olives, parsley, wine, pepper flakes, salt, oregano and pepper. Reduce heat.
3. Drain linguine, reserving ½ cup cooking water. Add linguine and reserved water to the skillet. Stir in cheese and lemon juice; cook and stir until cheese is melted.

Nutrition Facts: *1⅓ cups equals 462 calories, 16 g fat (3 g saturated fat), 144 mg cholesterol, 610 mg sodium, 48 g carbohydrate, 3 g fiber, 28 g protein.*

Pork Medallions with Raspberry-Balsamic Sauce

PREP/TOTAL TIME: 30 MIN. **MAKES:** 4 SERVINGS

- **1 pork tenderloin (1 pound), cut into 1-inch slices**
- **1 teaspoon garlic powder**
- **1 tablespoon olive oil**
- **½ cup seedless raspberry jam**
- **2 tablespoons balsamic vinegar**
- **2 teaspoons Dijon mustard**

1. Flatten pork to ½-in. thickness; sprinkle with garlic powder.
2. In a large skillet over medium heat, cook pork in oil for 3-5 minutes on each side or until no longer pink. Remove and keep warm. Add the jam, vinegar and mustard to the pan. Cook and stir for 2-3 minutes or until thickened. Serve with pork.

Nutrition Facts: *3 ounces cooked pork with about 2 tablespoons sauce equals 271 calories, 7 g fat (2 g saturated fat), 63 mg cholesterol, 107 mg sodium, 28 g carbohydrate, trace fiber, 23 g protein.* **Diabetic Exchanges:** *3 lean meat, 1½ starch, ½ fat.*

> "When I entertain, I prefer spending time with company to being holed up in the kitchen. This fast entree lets me serve a spectacular dinner with almost no hassle."
>
> **—LISA VARNER** EL PASO, TEXAS

Sausage & Salsa Breakfast Burritos

The best of breakfast gets wrapped up snugly in a hand-held feast for a guilt-free meal on the go.

—MICHELLE BURNETT EDEN, UTAH

PREP/TOTAL TIME: 20 MIN. **MAKES:** 6 SERVINGS

- **5 breakfast turkey sausage links**
- **2 cartons (8 ounces each) egg substitute**
- **½ cup salsa**
- **¼ teaspoon pepper**
- **6 whole wheat tortilla (8 inches), warmed**
- **½ cup shredded reduced-fat cheddar cheese**

1. Cook sausage links according to package directions. Meanwhile, in a large bowl, whisk the egg substitute, salsa and pepper. Pour into a large nonstick skillet coated with cooking spray. Cook and stir over medium heat until eggs are nearly set. Chop the sausage links. Add to egg mixture; cook and stir until completely set.
2. Spoon ⅓ cup egg mixture off center on each tortilla and sprinkle with 4 teaspoons cheese. Fold sides and ends over filling and roll up.

Nutrition Facts: *1 burrito equals 265 calories, 10 g fat (3 g saturated fat), 25 mg cholesterol, 602 mg sodium, 25 g carbohydrate, 2 g fiber, 18 g protein.* **Diabetic Exchanges:** *2 lean meat, 1½ starch, 1 fat.*

BETTER FOR YOU

A standard three-egg omelet prepared with cooking spray (without cheese or butter) has 635 mg cholesterol and 15 g fat. Instead, substitute four egg whites for two whole eggs to save 10 g fat and a whopping 423 mg cholesterol.

Parsley-Crusted Cod

Struggling to increase your family's fish servings? You'll appreciate this easy cod with staple ingredients. The flavors are mild and delicious, so even picky eaters will enjoy this recipe.
—**JUDY GREBETZ** RACINE, WISCONSIN

PREP/TOTAL TIME: 30 MIN.
MAKES: 4 SERVINGS

- **¾ cup dry bread crumbs**
- **1 tablespoon minced fresh parsley**
- **2 teaspoons grated lemon peel**
- **1 garlic clove, minced**
- **¼ teaspoon kosher salt**
- **¼ teaspoon pepper**
- **2 tablespoons olive oil**
- **4 cod fillets (6 ounces each)**

1. In a shallow bowl, combine the first six ingredients. Brush oil over one side of fillets; gently press into crumb mixture.
2. Place crumb side up in a 13-in. x 9-in. baking dish coated with cooking spray. Bake at 400° for 15-20 minutes or until fish flakes easily with a fork.

Nutrition Facts: *1 fillet equals 215 calories, 8 g fat (1 g saturated fat), 65 mg cholesterol, 194 mg sodium, 6 g carbohydrate, trace fiber, 28 g protein.* **Diabetic Exchanges:** *5 lean meat, 1½ fat, ½ starch.*

Asian Spaghetti

Give the cod an Asian twist with a quick side that has a touch of heat. We love this recipe with its bright, crisp-tender snow peas and carrots, but you could easily substitute any veggies you have on hand.
—**ANNE SMITHSON** CARY, NORTH CAROLINA

PREP/TOTAL TIME: 20 MIN.
MAKES: 5 SERVINGS

- **8 ounces uncooked angel hair pasta**
- **1 cup sliced fresh mushrooms**
- **1 cup fresh snow peas**
- **¾ cup shredded carrots**
- **4 green onions, cut into 1-inch pieces**
- **2 tablespoons canola oil**
- **1 garlic clove, minced**
- **¼ cup reduced-sodium soy sauce**
- **1 teaspoon sugar**
- **¼ teaspoon cayenne pepper**
- **2 tablespoons sesame seeds, toasted**

1. Cook pasta according to package directions. Meanwhile, in a large skillet, saute the mushrooms, snow peas, carrots and onions in oil until crisp-tender. Add garlic; cook 1 minute longer.
2. In a small bowl, combine the soy sauce, sugar and cayenne. Drain pasta. Add pasta and soy sauce mixture to skillet and toss to coat. Heat through. Sprinkle with sesame seeds.

Nutrition Facts: *¾ cup equals 274 calories, 8 g fat (1 g saturated fat), 0 cholesterol, 521 mg sodium, 42 g carbohydrate, 4 g fiber, 9 g protein.*

Almond Berry Pancakes

PREP: 15 MIN. **COOK:** 5 MIN./BATCH **MAKES:** 10 PANCAKES

- **¾ cup all-purpose flour**
- **½ cup whole wheat flour**
- **¼ cup sugar**
- **2 teaspoons baking powder**
- **Dash salt**
- **1 egg, lightly beaten**
- **1¼ cups fat-free milk**
- **2 tablespoons butter, melted**
- **½ teaspoon almond extract**
- **½ cup fresh raspberries**
- **½ cup fresh blueberries**

1. In a large bowl, combine the flours, sugar, baking powder and salt. In a small bowl, combine the egg, milk, butter and extract; stir into dry ingredients just until moistened.
2. Pour batter by 1/4 cupfuls onto a greased hot griddle; sprinkle with berries. Turn when bubbles form on top. Cook until the second side is golden brown.

Nutrition Facts: *2 pancakes equals 239 calories, 6 g fat (3 g saturated fat), 56 mg cholesterol, 262 mg sodium, 40 g carbohydrate, 3 g fiber, 7 g protein.* **Diabetic Exchanges:** *2½ starch, 1 fat.*

> "Whole wheat flour and two kinds of berries add an extra helping of nutrition to these hearty pancakes. It's a breakfast I feel good about serving."
>
> —**SARAH HAENGEL** BOWIE, MARYLAND

Herb Breakfast Frittata

I came up with this recipe on a snowy day by using what I had in the refrigerator. Yukon Gold potatoes give my frittata a comforting bottom crust.

—**KATHERINE HANSEN** BRUNSWICK, MAINE

PREP/TOTAL TIME: 30 MIN. **MAKES:** 4 SERVINGS

- **¼ cup thinly sliced red onion**
- **1 tablespoon olive oil**
- **1 large Yukon Gold potato, peeled and thinly sliced**
- **6 eggs**
- **1 teaspoon minced fresh rosemary or ¼ teaspoon dried rosemary, crushed**
- **1 teaspoon minced fresh thyme or ¼ teaspoon dried thyme**
- **¼ teaspoon salt**
- **⅛ teaspoon crushed red pepper flakes**
- **⅛ teaspoon pepper**
- **2 tablespoons shredded cheddar cheese**

1. In an 8-in. ovenproof skillet, saute onion in oil until tender. Using a slotted spoon, remove onion and keep warm. Arrange potato in a single layer over bottom of pan.
2. In a small bowl, whisk the eggs, seasonings and onion; pour over potatoes. Cover and cook for 4-6 minutes or until nearly set.
3. Uncover skillet. Broil 3-4 in. from the heat for 2-3 minutes or until eggs are completely set. Sprinkle with cheese. Let stand for 5 minutes. Cut into wedges.

Nutrition Facts: *1 wedge equals 204 calories, 12 g fat (4 g saturated fat), 321 mg cholesterol, 277 mg sodium, 13 g carbohydrate, 1 g fiber, 11 g protein.* **Diabetic Exchanges:** *1 starch, 1 medium-fat meat, 1 fat.*

Mustard Turkey Cutlets

Loaded with protein, turkey cutlets are low in fat and fast to the table. Fragrant rosemary perks up the apple juice as the Dijon cuts the sweetness in the glaze, offering a delightful blend of flavors.

—DEB WILLIAMS PEORIA, ARIZONA

PREP/TOTAL TIME: 25 MIN. **MAKES:** 4 SERVINGS

- **2 teaspoons cornstarch**
- **½ teaspoon salt, divided**
- **⅛ teaspoon plus ¼ teaspoon pepper, divided**
- **½ cup thawed apple juice concentrate**
- **¼ cup Dijon mustard**
- **1½ tablespoons minced fresh rosemary or 1½ teaspoons dried rosemary, crushed**
- **1 package (17.6 ounces) turkey breast cutlets**
- **1 teaspoon olive oil**

1. In a small saucepan, combine the cornstarch, 1/4 teaspoon salt and 1/8 teaspoon pepper. Gradually whisk in the juice concentrate, mustard and rosemary until blended. Cook and stir over medium-high heat until thickened and bubbly. Reduce the heat; cook and stir 2 minutes longer. Set aside 1/4 cup sauce.
2. Brush turkey with oil; sprinkle with remaining salt and pepper. Using long-handled tongs, moisten a paper towel with cooking oil and lightly coat the grill rack.
3. Grill, covered, over medium heat or broil 4 in. from the heat for 2-3 minutes on each side or until no longer pink, basting occasionally with remaining sauce. Brush with reserved sauce before serving.

Nutrition Facts: *4 ounces cooked turkey equals 230 calories, 2 g fat (trace saturated fat), 77 mg cholesterol, 725 mg sodium, 19 g carbohydrate, trace fiber, 31 g protein.* **Diabetic Exchanges:** *4 lean meat, 1 starch.*

Orzo with Peppers & Spinach

Sweet bell peppers are a good source of vitamin C, which helps the body fight infection and absorb folate and iron. And what bright flavor and color!

—TAMMI KETTENBACH JERSEYVILLE, ILLINOIS

PREP/TOTAL TIME: 30 MIN. **MAKES:** 5 SERVINGS

- **1 cup uncooked orzo pasta**
- **1 each medium sweet orange, red and yellow pepper, chopped**
- **1 cup sliced fresh mushrooms**
- **1 tablespoon olive oil**
- **3 garlic cloves, minced**
- **2 cups fresh baby spinach**
- **½ teaspoon Italian seasoning**
- **¼ teaspoon salt**
- **¼ teaspoon pepper**
- **½ cup grated Parmesan cheese**

1. Cook pasta according to package directions. Meanwhile, in large skillet cook the peppers and mushrooms in oil over medium heat until tender. Add garlic; cook 1 minute longer. Add the spinach, Italian seasoning, salt and pepper; cook and stir 1-2 minutes longer or just until spinach is wilted.
2. Drain pasta. Add pasta and cheese to skillet; heat through.

Nutrition Facts: *1 cup equals 234 calories, 6 g fat (2 g saturated fat), 7 mg cholesterol, 256 mg sodium, 36 g carbohydrate, 3 g fiber, 10 g protein.*

Lemon Beans with Prosciutto

For a change of pace, pair fish with a refreshing and tangy partner. Prosciutto and white wine turn green beans and fish into a feast.

—LORI WIESE HUMBOLDT, MINNESOTA

PREP/TOTAL TIME: 25 MIN. **MAKES:** 6 SERVINGS

- **8 thin slices prosciutto or deli ham, julienned**
- **2 teaspoons olive oil**
- **½ cup white wine or reduced-sodium chicken broth**
- **¼ cup lemon juice**
- **2 tablespoons butter**
- **1½ pounds fresh green beans, trimmed**

1. In a large nonstick skillet coated with cooking spray, cook prosciutto in oil over medium heat until crisp. Remove to paper towels with a slotted spoon; drain.
2. In the same skillet, combine the wine, lemon juice and butter. Bring to a boil. Reduce heat; simmer, uncovered, for 5-6 minutes or until sauce is reduced by half.
3. Meanwhile, place beans in a large saucepan and cover with water. Bring to a boil. Cover and cook for 4-7 minutes or until crisp-tender; drain. Add beans to skillet; toss to coat. Sprinkle with prosciutto just before serving.

Nutrition Facts: *3/4 cup equals 127 calories, 8 g fat (3 g saturated fat), 27 mg cholesterol, 397 mg sodium, 8 g carbohydrate, 3 g fiber, 7 g protein.* **Diabetic Exchanges:** *1 lean meat, 1 vegetable, 1 fat.*

Sweet Onion & Carrot Medley

Carrots, onion and peas, oh my! Tender veggies are tossed in a tasty honey-garlic mixture. Keep in mind that olive oil pours quickly, so it's a good idea to measure it—even an extra teaspoon adds 40 calories and 4.5 g fat.

—**FRAN SCOTT** BIRMINGHAM, MICHIGAN

PREP/TOTAL TIME: 30 MIN. **MAKES:** 6 SERVINGS

- **2 cups fresh baby carrots**
- **½ pound fresh sugar snap peas, trimmed**
- **1 large sweet onion, halved and thinly sliced**
- **4 teaspoons olive oil**
- **2 garlic cloves, minced**
- **1 tablespoon minced chives**
- **2 teaspoons honey**
- **½ teaspoon salt**
- **¼ teaspoon pepper**

1. Place 1 in. of water in a large skillet; add carrots. Bring to a boil. Reduce heat; cover and simmer for 5 minutes. Stir in peas; cover and cook 3 minutes longer. Drain; remove from pan and set aside.
2. In the same skillet, saute onion in oil until tender. Add garlic; cook 1 minute longer. Stir in the chives, honey, salt, pepper and vegetables; heat through.

Nutrition Facts: *¾ cup equals 86 calories, 3 g fat (trace saturated fat), 0 cholesterol, 240 mg sodium, 13 g carbohydrate, 2 g fiber, 2 g protein.* **Diabetic Exchanges:** *1 starch, ½ fat.*

Peking Shrimp

In the summer, we spend as much time as possible at our vacation home on the beach. I prepare lots of seafood because it's fresh and readily available there, but this main dish is a year-round favorite.

—**JANET EDWARDS** BEAVERTON, OREGON

PREP/TOTAL TIME: 25 MIN. **MAKES:** 4 SERVINGS

- **1 tablespoon cornstarch**
- **¼ cup cold water**
- **¼ cup corn syrup**
- **2 tablespoons reduced-sodium soy sauce**
- **2 tablespoons sherry or chicken broth**
- **1 garlic clove, minced**
- **¼ teaspoon ground ginger**
- **1 small green pepper, cut into 1-inch pieces**
- **2 tablespoons canola oil**
- **1 pound uncooked medium shrimp, peeled and deveined**
- **1 medium tomato, cut into wedges**
- **Hot cooked rice, optional**

1. In a small bowl, combine cornstarch and water until smooth. Stir in the corn syrup, soy sauce, sherry, garlic and ginger; set aside.
2. In a nonstick skillet or wok, stir-fry green pepper in oil for 3 minutes. Add shrimp; stir-fry 3 minutes longer or until shrimp turn pink.
3. Stir cornstarch mixture and add to the pan. Bring to a boil; cook and stir for 2 minutes or until thickened. Add tomato; heat through. Serve with rice if desired.

Nutrition Facts: *¾ cup (calculated without rice) equals 237 calories, 8 g fat (1 g saturated fat), 168 mg cholesterol, 532 mg sodium, 21 g carbohydrate, 1 g fiber, 19 g protein.* **Diabetic Exchanges:** *2 lean meat, 1½ fat, 1 starch, 1 vegetable.*

Corn Syrup Substitute

For each cup of light corn syrup in a recipe, substitute 1 cup of sugar and ¼ cup water. For each cup of dark corn syrup, substitute 1 cup of packed brown sugar and ¼ cup water.

Garden Orzo Risotto

No one will believe this rich, creamy dish was prepared in less than 30 minutes! I developed the recipe when my garden tomatoes, zucchini and basil were coming on strong. Using orzo instead of arborio rice makes the risotto so much easier to prepare.

—**CINDY BEBERMAN** ORLAND PARK, ILLINOIS

PREP/TOTAL TIME: 30 MIN. **MAKES:** 6 SERVINGS

- **1 small zucchini, chopped**
- **1 shallot, chopped**
- **2 tablespoons olive oil**
- **2 garlic cloves, minced**
- **1 cup uncooked whole wheat orzo pasta**
- **2 cups vegetable broth**
- **1 cup 2% milk**
- **1 package (6 ounces) fresh baby spinach**
- **2 medium tomatoes, seeded and chopped**
- **¼ cup minced fresh basil**
- **⅓ cup grated Parmesan cheese**
- **Salt and pepper to taste**

1. In a large saucepan, saute zucchini and shallot in oil until almost tender. Add garlic; cook 1 minute longer. Add the orzo, broth and milk. Bring to a boil. Reduce heat to medium-low; cook and stir for 10-15 minutes or until liquid is almost absorbed.
2. Stir in the spinach, tomatoes and basil; cook and stir until spinach is wilted. Remove from the heat; stir in the cheese, salt and pepper.

Nutrition Facts: *⅔ cup equals 202 calories, 7 g fat (2 g saturated fat), 7 mg cholesterol, 429 mg sodium, 27 g carbohydrate, 6 g fiber, 8 g protein.* **Diabetic Exchanges:** *1 starch, 1 vegetable, 1 fat.*

Asparagus Salad with Grilled Salmon

This salad's a little sweet, a little savory and very refreshing. Healthy asparagus boasts anti-inflammatory nutrients and vitamins A, B and C. It's fabulous grilled; you'll want to fix this again!

—**JENNE DELKUS** DES PERES, MISSOURI

PREP/TOTAL TIME: 30 MIN.
MAKES: 4 SERVINGS

- **⅓ cup maple syrup**
- **2 tablespoons Dijon mustard**
- **1 tablespoon olive oil**
- **1 teaspoon snipped fresh dill**
- **4 salmon fillets (4 ounces each)**
- **1 pound fresh asparagus, trimmed**
- **4 cups spring mix salad greens**
- **1 cup shredded carrots**
- **1 hard-cooked egg, cut into eight wedges**
- **Coarsely ground pepper**

1. In a small bowl, whisk the syrup, mustard, oil and dill; set aside.
2. Place salmon skin side down on grill rack. Grill, covered, over medium heat for 5 minutes. Meanwhile, in a shallow bowl, drizzle asparagus with 1 tablespoon dressing; toss to coat. Arrange asparagus on a grilling grid; place on the grill rack with salmon. Spoon 1 tablespoon dressing over salmon.
3. Grill salmon and asparagus, covered, for 4-6 minutes or until salmon flakes easily with a fork and asparagus is crisp-tender, turning asparagus once.
4. Divide salad greens among four plates and sprinkle with carrots. Remove skin from salmon. Arrange the egg wedges, asparagus and salmon over salads. Drizzle with remaining dressing; sprinkle with pepper.

Editor's Note: *If you do not have a grilling grid, use a disposable foil pan. Poke holes in the bottom of the pan with a meat fork to allow liquid to drain.*

Nutrition Facts: *1 serving equals 336 calories, 16 g fat (3 g saturated fat), 110 mg cholesterol, 294 mg sodium, 26 g carbohydrate, 3 g fiber, 23 g protein.*
Diabetic Exchanges: *3 lean meat, 2 fat, 1 starch, 1 vegetable.*

top tip
Salmon is rich in beneficial omega-3 fatty acids DHA and EPA. For convenience, grill it with the skin on to help it stay moist and intact.

Tuna with Tuscan White Bean Salad

PREP/TOTAL TIME: 30 MIN.
MAKES: 4 SERVINGS

- **1 can (15 ounces) white kidney or cannellini beans, rinsed and drained**
- **3 celery ribs, finely chopped**
- **1 medium sweet red pepper, finely chopped**
- **1 plum tomato, seeded and finely chopped**
- **½ cup fresh basil leaves, thinly sliced**
- **¼ cup finely chopped red onion**
- **3 tablespoons olive oil**
- **2 tablespoons red wine vinegar**
- **1 tablespoon lemon juice**
- **¼ teaspoon salt**
- **¼ teaspoon pepper**

TUNA

- **4 tuna steaks (6 ounces each)**
- **1 tablespoon olive oil**
- **¼ teaspoon salt**
- **¼ teaspoon pepper**

1. In a large bowl, combine the first six ingredients. In a small bowl, whisk the oil, vinegar, lemon juice, salt and pepper. Pour over bean mixture; toss to coat. Refrigerate until serving.
2. Brush tuna with oil. Sprinkle with salt and pepper. Using long-handled tongs, moisten a paper towel with cooking oil and lightly coat the grill rack. Grill tuna, covered, over high heat or broil 3-4 in. from the heat for 3-4 minutes on each side for medium-rare or until slightly pink in the center. Serve with salad.

Nutrition Facts: *1 tuna steak with 1 cup salad equals 409 calories, 16 g fat (2 g saturated fat), 77 mg cholesterol, 517 mg sodium, 20 g carbohydrate, 6 g fiber, 45 g protein.* **Diabetic Exchanges:** *5 lean meat, 3 fat, 1 starch, 1 vegetable.*

Once the tuna hits the grill, do not move it around or it may tear. This recipe is for tuna that is still pink in the middle (medium rare). Increase the cooking time for tuna that's well done. I often enjoy this dish with Sauvignon Blanc.
—VANCE WERNER JR. FRANKLIN, WISCONSIN

BETTER FOR YOU

Fresh tuna is considered an oily fish and has a fat content of more than 6 percent. Due to a higher fat content, oily fish has a firm, meaty texture and a rich flavor. Fresh tuna stays moist during cooking and is suitable for baking, grilling and broiling.

Zucchini Pesto with Shrimp and Farfalle

Wonderful zucchini-basil pesto takes advantage of summer's best produce and adds fantastic flavor to this simple pasta toss. You'll feel like you're dining in a fine restaurant, but the seasonal ingredients make it easy on your pocketbook.

—AMBER MASSEY FORT WORTH, TEXAS

PREP: 25 MIN. **COOK:** 15 MIN. **MAKES:** 6 SERVINGS

- **8 ounces uncooked multigrain bow tie pasta**
- **1 pound zucchini, sliced**
- **2 tablespoons olive oil, divided**
- **1 cup loosely packed basil leaves**
- **½ cup shredded Parmigiano-Reggiano or Parmesan cheese, divided**
- **3 tablespoons pine nuts, toasted**
- **4 garlic cloves, peeled and halved**
- **1 large sweet onion, chopped**
- **1 pound peeled and deveined cooked medium shrimp**
- **½ cup reduced-fat evaporated milk**
- **1 teaspoon lemon juice**
- **1¾ teaspoons kosher salt**
- **½ teaspoon grated lemon peel**
- **½ teaspoon coarsely ground pepper**

1. Cook pasta according to package directions. Meanwhile, in a Dutch oven, saute zucchini in 1 tablespoon oil until tender. Remove from the pan and cool slightly.

2. Drain pasta, reserving ⅓ cup cooking liquid. In a food processor, combine the basil, ¼ cup cheese, pine nuts, garlic, reserved cooking liquid and ⅔ cup cooked zucchini. Cover and process until pureed.

3. In the same Dutch oven, cook onion in remaining oil until tender. Stir in the shrimp, pasta and remaining zucchini. Add the pureed mixture, milk, lemon juice, salt, lemon peel and pepper; toss to coat. Heat through. Sprinkle with remaining cheese.

Nutrition Facts: *1½ cup equals 368 calories, 12 g fat (3 g saturated fat), 121 mg cholesterol, 827 mg sodium, 37 g carbohydrate, 5 g fiber, 29 g protein.* **Diabetic Exchanges:** *2 lean meat, 1½ fat, 2 starch, 1 vegetable.*

Chicken & Fruit Spinach Salads

Here's a smart choice for busy nights! It takes 10 minutes to prepare and stops hungry tummies from growling in moments. Serve with whole grain rolls to round out the meal.

—JESSE KLAUSMEIER BURBANK, CALIFORNIA

PREP/TOTAL TIME: 10 MIN. **MAKES:** 4 SERVINGS

- **1 package (6 ounces) fresh baby spinach**
- **1 package (10 ounces) ready-to-use grilled chicken breast strips**
- **1 can (11 ounces) mandarin oranges, drained**
- **1 cup sliced fresh strawberries**
- **2 slices red onion, separated into rings**
- **½ cup reduced-fat raspberry vinaigrette**
- **¼ cup honey-roasted sliced almonds**

1. Divide spinach among four serving plates. Top with chicken, oranges, strawberries and onion. Drizzle with vinaigrette and sprinkle with almonds.

Nutrition Facts: *1 serving equals 223 calories, 10 g fat (1 g saturated fat), 42 mg cholesterol, 835 mg sodium, 17 g carbohydrate, 2 g fiber, 21 g protein.* **Diabetic Exchanges:** *2 lean meat, 2 fat, 1 starch.*

Basil Crab Cakes

I love crabmeat any way it's served, especially in these crab cakes. If you don't have time to dash to the store, substitute 2 teaspoons of dried basil for the fresh.

—MRS. PRISCILLA GILBERT INDIAN HARBOUR BEACH, FLORIDA

PREP: 15 MIN. + CHILLING **COOK:** 10 MIN./BATCH
MAKES: 4 SERVINGS

- **1 egg white**
- **¼ cup mayonnaise**
- **2 tablespoons minced fresh basil**
- **2 teaspoons Dijon mustard**
- **2 teaspoons Worcestershire sauce**
- **¼ teaspoon salt**
- **¼ teaspoon pepper**
- **2 drops hot pepper sauce**
- **½ pound lump crabmeat, drained**
- **6 saltines, finely crushed**
- **1 tablespoon canola oil**
- **Seafood cocktail sauce, optional**

1. In a small bowl, combine the first eight ingredients. Stir in crab and cracker crumbs. Refrigerate for at least 30 minutes.
2. Shape mixture into four patties. In a large skillet, cook crab cakes in oil in batches for 3-4 minutes on each side or until golden brown. Serve with cocktail sauce if desired.

Nutrition Facts: *1 crab cake (calculated without cocktail sauce) equals 214 calories, 16 g fat (2 g saturated fat), 55 mg cholesterol, 568 mg sodium, 4 g carbohydrate, trace fiber, 13 g protein.* **Diabetic Exchanges:** *2½ fat, 2 lean meat.*

Blackened Halibut

Try serving these spicy fillets with garlic mashed potatoes, hot, crusty bread and a crisp salad to lure in your crew. This is what my family eats when we want to celebrate.

—BRENDA WILLIAMS SANTA MARIA, CALIFORNIA

PREP/TOTAL TIME: 25 MIN. **MAKES:** 4 SERVINGS

- **2 tablespoons garlic powder**
- **1 tablespoon salt**
- **1 tablespoon onion powder**
- **1 tablespoon dried oregano**
- **1 tablespoon dried thyme**
- **1 tablespoon cayenne pepper**
- **1 tablespoon pepper**
- **2½ teaspoons paprika**
- **4 halibut fillets (4 ounces each)**
- **2 tablespoons butter**

1. In a large resealable plastic bag, combine the first eight ingredients. Add fillets, two at a time, and shake to coat.
2. In a large cast-iron skillet, cook fillets in butter over medium heat for 3-4 minutes on each side or until fish flakes easily with a fork.

Nutrition Facts: *1 fillet equals 189 calories, 8 g fat (4 g saturated fat), 51 mg cholesterol, 758 mg sodium, 3 g carbohydrate, 1 g fiber, 24 g protein.* **Diabetic Exchanges:** *3 lean meat, 1 fat.*

Salmon with Tangy Raspberry Sauce

We love salmon at our house and are always finding new ways to make it. This recipe turned out really well; the raspberry sauce adds a nice sweetness. My son calls it salmon candy!

—ANNA-MARIE WILLIAMS LEAGUE CITY, TEXAS

PREP/TOTAL TIME: 25 MIN. **MAKES:** 4 SERVINGS

- **1 teaspoon smoked paprika**
- **¼ teaspoon salt**
- **¼ teaspoon pepper**
- **4 salmon fillets (6 ounces each)**
- **2 tablespoons olive oil**
- **2 tablespoons red raspberry preserves**
- **1 tablespoon white vinegar**
- **1 tablespoon honey**

1. Combine the paprika, salt and pepper; sprinkle over salmon. Drizzle with oil. Moisten a paper towel with cooking oil; using long-handled tongs, lightly coat the grill rack. Place salmon skin side down on grill rack.
2. Grill, covered, over medium heat or broil 4 in. from the heat for 10-12 minutes or until fish flakes easily with a fork. In a small bowl, whisk the preserves, vinegar and honey; spoon over fillets.

Nutrition Facts: *1 fillet with 1 tablespoon sauce equals 367 calories, 23 g fat (4 g saturated fat), 85 mg cholesterol, 233 mg sodium, 11 g carbohydrate, trace fiber, 29 g protein.* **Diabetic Exchanges:** *5 lean meat, 1½ fat, 1 starch.*

Tropical Tilapia

Take a walk on the wild side and venture into the tropics with this one-skillet dish. Cool mint balances the sweet heat from the jelly.

—ROXANNE CHAN ALBANY, CALIFORNIA

PREP/TOTAL TIME: 25 MIN. **MAKES:** 4 SERVINGS

- **4 tilapia fillets (4 ounces each)**
- **1 teaspoon Caribbean jerk seasoning**
- **1 can (15 ounces) mixed tropical fruit, undrained**
- **¼ cup dried tropical fruit**
- **2 green onions, chopped**
- **¼ cup red jalapeno pepper jelly**
- **2 tablespoons sliced almonds**
- **2 tablespoons minced fresh mint**
- **1 tablespoon lime juice**
- **Hot cooked rice**

1. Season fillets with jerk seasoning. In a large nonstick skillet coated with cooking spray, cook fillets over medium-high heat for 3-5 minutes or until fish flakes easily with a fork, turning once. Transfer to a serving platter and keep warm.
2. In the same skillet, combine the fruit, onions, jelly and almonds; heat through. Stir in mint and lime juice. Serve with fish and rice.

Nutrition Facts: *1 fillet with ½ cup salsa (calculated without rice) equals 283 calories, 3 g fat (1 g saturated fat), 55 mg cholesterol, 128 mg sodium, 45 g carbohydrate, 3 g fiber, 22 g protein.*

Hot Shrimp Salad

Wok this way to try an Asian stir-fry shrimp combo with thinly sliced romaine wilted at the end of cooking. "I could eat this all day, every day," said a good friend.

—ANGELA LEINENBACH
MECHANICSVILLE, VIRGINIA

PREP/TOTAL TIME: 25 MIN.
MAKES: 4 SERVINGS

- **1 medium onion, halved and sliced**
- **2 celery ribs, sliced**
- **1 small green pepper, thinly sliced**
- **1 small sweet red pepper, thinly sliced**
- **2 tablespoons peanut oil**
- **1 pound uncooked medium shrimp, peeled and deveined**
- **1 cup bean sprouts**
- **1 garlic clove, minced**
- **1 teaspoon minced fresh gingerroot**
- **2 tablespoons reduced-sodium soy sauce**
- **1 tablespoon lemon juice**
- **1 teaspoon sugar**
- **1 teaspoon sesame oil**
- **½ teaspoon salt**
- **6 romaine leaves, thinly sliced**

1. In a large skillet or wok, stir-fry the sliced onion, celery and peppers in peanut oil for 2 minutes. Add the shrimp, bean sprouts, garlic and ginger; stir fry 2-3 minutes longer or until the shrimp turn pink.
2. In a small bowl, combine the soy sauce, lemon juice, sugar, sesame oil and salt; add to the pan. Bring to a boil. Stir in romaine. Remove from the heat. Serve immediately.

Nutrition Facts: *1¼ cups equals 217 calories, 10 g fat (2 g saturated fat), 138 mg cholesterol, 752 mg sodium, 11 g carbohydrate, 3 g fiber, 21 g protein.*
Diabetic Exchanges: *3 lean meat, 2 vegetable, 1½ fat.*

Shhh! SIMPLE SECRET

Shrimp are available in the shell, come fresh or frozen and are available in different varieties, sizes (medium, large, extra large, jumbo) and colors (gray, brown, pink, red). Fresh shrimp should have a firm texture and smell fresh, like the ocean.

Makeover Beef Stroganoff

Our pros lightened up this classic dish, slashing calories, saturated fat, sodium and cholesterol, but they kept every bit of its satisfying taste.

—**CANDACE CLARK** CONNELL, WASHINGTON

PREP/TOTAL TIME: 30 MIN. **MAKES:** 6 SERVINGS

- **½ cup plus 1 tablespoon all-purpose flour, divided**
- **½ teaspoon pepper, divided**
- **1 beef top round steak (1½ pounds), cut into thin strips**
- **2 tablespoons canola oil**
- **1 cup sliced fresh mushrooms**
- **1 small onion, chopped**
- **1 garlic clove, minced**
- **1 can (14½ ounces) reduced-sodium beef broth**
- **½ teaspoon salt**
- **1 cup (8 ounces) reduced-fat sour cream**
- **3 cups cooked yolk-free noodles**

1. Combine 1/2 cup flour and 1/4 teaspoon pepper in a large resealable plastic bag. Add beef, a few pieces at a time, and shake to coat.
2. In a large nonstick skillet over medium-high heat, cook beef in oil in batches until no longer pink. Remove and keep warm. In the same skillet, saute mushrooms and onion in drippings until tender. Add garlic; cook 1 minute longer.
3. Whisk remaining flour and broth until smooth; stir into skillet. Bring to a boil; cook and stir for 2 minutes or until thickened. Add the beef, salt and remaining pepper; heat through. Add sour cream; heat through (do not boil). Serve with noodles.

Nutrition Facts: *1 cup beef Stroganoff with 1/2 cup noodles equals 351 calories, 12 g fat (4 g saturated fat), 78 mg cholesterol, 393 mg sodium, 25 g carbohydrate, 2 g fiber, 33 g protein.* **Diabetic Exchanges:** *3 lean meat, 2 fat, 1½ starch.*

Makeover Macaroni and Cheese

Creamy and cheesy with comfort in every bite, this lightened-up classic is sure to become a family favorite at your house, too!

—**NANCY LANGROCK** SOUTHBURY, CONNECTICUT

PREP/TOTAL TIME: 30 MIN. **MAKES:** 8 SERVINGS

- **1 package (16 ounces) elbow macaroni**
- **2 tablespoons all-purpose flour**
- **2 cups fat-free milk**
- **1 package (16 ounces) reduced-fat process cheese (Velveeta), cubed**
- **1 cup (4 ounces) shredded sharp cheddar cheese, divided**

1. Cook macaroni according to package directions. Meanwhile, in a large saucepan, combine flour and milk until smooth. Bring to a boil; cook and stir for 2 minutes or until thickened. Stir in process cheese and 1/2 cup cheddar cheese until smooth. Drain macaroni; stir into cheese sauce.
2. Remove from the heat; sprinkle with remaining cheese. Cover and let stand for 5 minutes or until cheese is melted.

Nutrition Facts: *1 cup equals 403 calories, 11 g fat (6 g saturated fat), 36 mg cholesterol, 944 mg sodium, 54 g carbohydrate, 2 g fiber, 23 g protein.*

Delectable Desserts

"This foolproof recipe makes a picture-perfect pie that tastes as delicious as it looks. What a wonderful way to use fresh summer raspberries and practice a little baking skill at the same time!"

JEAN BOELSMA BETHEL, MAINE
Raspberry Peach Pie, on page 217

Chocolate Cake in a Mug

Why is this the most dangerous cake recipe in the world? Because you're now only minutes away from chocolate cake any time of the day or night!

—**RUTH CHANEY** DELTA JUNCTION, ALASKA

PREP/TOTAL TIME: 10 MIN. **MAKES:** 1 SERVING

- **¼ cup sugar**
- **¼ cup all-purpose flour**
- **2 tablespoons baking cocoa**
- **⅛ teaspoon salt**
- **1 egg**
- **3 tablespoons canola oil**
- **3 tablespoons 2% milk**
- **⅛ teaspoon vanilla extract**
- **3 tablespoons semisweet chocolate chips**
- **Optional toppings: coffee ice cream and caramel ice cream topping**

1. In a small bowl, combine the sugar, flour, cocoa and salt. In another bowl, whisk the egg, oil, milk and vanilla. Stir into dry ingredients just until moistened. Stir in chocolate chips.
2. Transfer to a 14-oz. microwave-safe mug coated with cooking spray. Microwave, uncovered, on high for 1¼ to 1½ minutes or until top appears dry. Cool for 1 minute. Serve with toppings of your choice.
Editor's Note: *This recipe was tested in a 1,100-watt microwave.*

For even baking, it's important to make cookies the same size. For drop cookies, fill a teaspoon or tablespoon (from your flatware set) with dough; use another spoon or spatula to push the mound of dough off the spoon and onto a cool baking sheet. Or drop the dough with a small ice cream scoop.

Gingerbread Fruitcake Cookies

Two of my favorite things, gingerbread and fruitcake, meet in a truly great cookie. You'd never know this recipe starts with a mix. It bursts with fruit, nuts and gingerbread flavor, topped with a delightful orange glaze.

—**JAMIE JONES** MADISON, GEORGIA

PREP: 20 MIN. **BAKE:** 10 MIN./BATCH + COOLING
MAKES: 3 DOZEN

- **1 package (14½ ounces) gingerbread cake/cookie mix**
- **¼ cup water**
- **¼ cup butter, melted**
- **1 container (8 ounces) chopped mixed candied fruit**
- **½ cup chopped pecans**
- **½ cup raisins**
- **1¼ cups confectioners' sugar**
- **1 to 2 tablespoons orange juice**

1. Place the cookie mix, water and butter in a large bowl; beat until well blended. Stir in the candied fruit, pecans and raisins. Drop by tablespoonfuls 2 in. apart onto ungreased baking sheets.
2. Bake at 350° for 8-10 minutes or until set. Cool for 1 minute before removing from pans to wire racks to cool completely.
3. Combine confectioners' sugar and enough orange juice to achieve desired consistency; stir until smooth. Spread over cookies. Let stand until set.

Fresh peaches and berries shine in this pretty, refreshing sauce. It's terrific on ice cream, but also adds a sweet and tangy touch to pancakes, waffles or French toast at brunch. —**SANDRA GOULD** VERNDALE, MINNESOTA

Berry-Cherry Peach Sauce

PREP/TOTAL TIME: 20 MIN.
MAKES: 2 CUPS

- **2 cups fresh or frozen sliced peeled peaches**
- **½ cup fresh or frozen blueberries**
- **6 fresh or frozen pitted dark sweet cherries, halved**
- **1 cup plus 1 tablespoon orange juice, divided**
- **⅓ cup sugar**
- **1 tablespoon cornstarch**
- **Vanilla ice cream**

1. In a large saucepan, combine the peaches, blueberries, cherries, 1 cup orange juice and sugar; cook and stir over low heat until sugar is dissolved. Bring to a boil. Reduce heat; simmer, uncovered, for 7 minutes or until peaches are tender.
2. Combine cornstarch and remaining orange juice until smooth; stir into hot fruit mixture. Bring to a boil; cook and stir for 2 minutes or until thickened. Remove from the heat. Serve with ice cream.

Triple Chip Cookies

Sweet and salty, just the way we like them! A tube of refrigerated peanut butter cookie dough is the base for these delightful cookies made with potato chips.
—**TASTE OF HOME TEST KITCHEN**

PREP/TOTAL TIME: 30 MIN.
MAKES: ABOUT 2½ DOZEN

- **1 tube (16½ ounces) refrigerated peanut butter cookie dough**
- **1 cup coarsely crushed potato chips**
- **½ cup butterscotch chips**
- **½ cup swirled milk chocolate and peanut butter chips**

1. Let cookie dough stand at room temperature for 5-10 minutes to soften. In a large bowl, combine the cookie dough and chips.
2. Drop by tablespoonfuls 2 in. apart onto ungreased baking sheets. Bake at 350° for 10-12 minutes or until lightly browned. Remove to wire racks. Store in an airtight container.

“This foolproof recipe makes a picture-perfect pie that tastes as delicious as it looks. What a wonderful way to use fresh summer raspberries—and practice a little baking skill at the same time!”

—**JEAN BOELSMA** BETHEL, MAINE

Raspberry Peach Pie

PREP: 20 MIN. + CHILLING
BAKE: 15 MIN. + COOLING
MAKES: 8 SERVINGS

- **1¼ cups all-purpose flour**
- **½ teaspoon salt**
- **⅓ cup shortening**
- **¼ cup cold water**

FILLING

- **4 medium peaches, peeled and sliced**
- **1⅓ cups sugar**
- **5 teaspoons lemon juice**
- **¼ cup cornstarch**
- **⅓ cup water**
- **3 cups fresh raspberries**

1. In a large bowl, combine flour and salt. Cut in shortening until mixture resembles coarse crumbs. Stir in water until mixture forms a ball. Roll out pastry to fit in a 9-in. pie plate.
2. Transfer to pie plate; trim and flute edges. Line unpricked pastry with a double thickness of heavy-duty foil. Fill with dried beans, uncooked rice or pie weights.
3. Bake at 450° for 8 minutes. Remove the foil and weights; bake 5-7 minutes longer or until golden brown. Cool on a wire rack.
4. In a large saucepan, combine the peaches, sugar and juice. Combine cornstarch and water until smooth. Stir into peach mixture. Bring to a boil; cook and stir for 1 minute or until thickened. Remove from the heat; cool to room temperature. Fold in raspberries. Spoon into crust.
5. Refrigerate for at least 4 hours or overnight. Refrigerate leftovers.

Editor's Note: *Let pie weights cool before storing. Beans and rice may be reused for pie weights, but not for cooking.*

For a flaky crust, don't overmix when adding water to the flour and shortening mixture. It causes the flour's gluten (the protein that gives baked goods their structure) to develop and makes pastry tough. Also, keep dough cold to roll it with ease. To transfer the rolled dough to a pie plate, fold it in quarters, rolling it over a rolling pin or using a flat-edged baking sheet.

Mango Sorbet Dessert

Here's an all-around wonderful dessert recipe that's easy to whip up with store-bought angel food cake. It's packed with fruity flavor.
—KATIE ROSE PEWAUKEE, WISCONSIN

PREP/TOTAL TIME: 10 MIN. **MAKES:** 4 SERVINGS

- **½ cup seedless raspberry preserves**
- **1 tablespoon orange juice**
- **¼ teaspoon almond extract**
- **4 slices angel food cake**
- **4 scoops mango sorbet**
- **1 cup fresh raspberries**
- **¼ cup sliced almonds**

1. In a small microwave-safe bowl, combine preserves and orange juice. Microwave, uncovered, on high for 30 seconds or until heated through. Stir in extract.
2. Divide cake slices among four dessert plates. Top each with sorbet, preserve mixture, raspberries and almonds.

Cherry Cordial Cookies

One of my dad's favorite candies is chocolate-covered cherry cordials. I decided to re-create that flavor in these cookies. They were a hit with my taste testers! For extra ease, you could prepare the dough ahead and freeze up to 3 months.

—**NOELLE MYERS** GRAND FORKS, NORTH DAKOTA

PREP: 20 MIN. **BAKE:** 10 MIN. + STANDING **MAKES:** ABOUT 3½ DOZEN

- **1 package (17½ ounces) sugar cookie mix**
- **¾ cup chopped dried cherries**
- **½ cup butter, softened**
- **1 egg**
- **¾ cup cherry preserves**
- **1½ cups semisweet chocolate chips**
- **⅔ cup white baking chips**

1. Place the cookie mix, cherries, butter and egg in a large bowl; beat until well mixed. Shape into 1-in. balls; place 2 in. apart on ungreased baking sheets. Bake at 350° for 10-12 minutes or until edges are browned.
2. Meanwhile, place cherry preserves in a small microwave-safe bowl. Microwave on high for 1 minute. Stir in chocolate chips until melted. If necessary, microwave in 10- to 20-second intervals until chips are melted; stir until blended.
3. Using the back of a tablespoon, make an indentation in the center of each warm cookie. Fill indentations with cherry mixture. Remove to wire racks to cool completely.
4. Microwave the white baking chips until melted. Drizzle over cookies. Let stand until set.

Almond Macaroons

PREP: 10 MIN.
BAKE: 20 MIN./BATCH + COOLING
MAKES: 3 DOZEN

- **1 package (14 ounces) flaked coconut**
- **1 can (14 ounces) sweetened condensed milk**
- **¼ cup sliced almonds, finely chopped**
- **1 teaspoon vanilla extract**
- **1 teaspoon almond extract**
- **1 cup milk chocolate chips**

1. Mix the first five ingredients in a large bowl. Drop by tablespoonfuls 2 in. apart onto parchment paper-lined baking sheets; gently shape into mounds.
2. Bake at 325° for 16-20 minutes or until lightly browned. Remove to wire racks to cool completely. In a microwave, melt chips; stir until smooth. Drizzle over cooled cookies. Let stand until set. Store in an airtight container.

Chocolate Mint Parfaits

You just can't go wrong with the popular combination of chocolate and mint. Instant pudding mix gets this crowd-pleasing dessert on the table in a flash.

—**KARALEE REINKE** OMAHA, NEBRASKA

PREP/TOTAL TIME: 15 MIN.
MAKES: 4 SERVINGS

- **2 cups plus 1 tablespoon cold 2% milk, divided**
- **1 package (3.9 ounces) instant chocolate pudding mix**
- **4 ounces cream cheese, softened**
- **1 tablespoon sugar**
- **¼ teaspoon peppermint extract**
- **1 cup whipped topping**
- **Mint Andes candies, optional**

1. In a large bowl, whisk 2 cups milk and pudding mix for 2 minutes; set aside. In a small bowl, beat the cream cheese, sugar, extract and remaining milk. Fold in whipped topping.
2. Spoon half of the pudding into four parfait glasses. Top with half of cream cheese mixture. Repeat layers. Garnish with candies if desired.

“These cookies have a wonderful texture that is chewy on the inside and crispy outside. The milk chocolate drizzle dresses them up—everyone loves them! And they're so easy. With six ingredients, you can whip them up at the last minute.”

—**DEENA DILLION** OSSIAN, INDIANA

Million Dollar Pecan Bars

Who wants to eat like a millionaire? Invest 15 minutes of your time, and enjoy a big payoff when you pull these rich bars of golden layered delight from the oven.

—LAURA DAVIS RUSK, TEXAS

PREP: 15 MIN. **BAKE:** 20 MIN.
MAKES: 2 DOZEN

- **¾ cup butter, softened**
- **¾ cup packed brown sugar**
- **2 eggs**
- **2 teaspoons vanilla extract**
- **1 package (18¼ ounces) butter pecan cake mix**
- **2½ cups quick-cooking oats**

FILLING

- **1 can (14 ounces) sweetened condensed milk**
- **2 cups milk chocolate chips**
- **1 cup butterscotch chips**
- **1 tablespoon butter**
- **1 teaspoon vanilla extract**
- **1½ cups chopped pecans**

1. In a large bowl, cream butter and brown sugar until light and fluffy. Add eggs, one at a time, beating well after each addition. Beat in vanilla. Add cake mix just until blended. Stir in oats. Press 3 cups onto the bottom of a greased 13-in. x 9-in. baking pan.

2. In a large microwave-safe bowl, combine milk and chips. Microwave, uncovered, on high for 2 minutes; stir. Cook 1 to 2½ minutes longer or until chips are melted, stirring every 30 seconds. Stir in butter and vanilla until melted. Stir in pecans. Spread over crust.

3. Crumble the remaining oat mixture and sprinkle over the top. Bake at 350° for 20-25 minutes or until the topping is golden brown. Cool on a wire rack. Cut into bars.

Store chocolate tightly wrapped in a cool, dry place. When chocolate is stored in a spot that's too warm, it develops grayish-white streaks or spots called a fat bloom. In damp storage, it develops a rough feel called a sugar bloom. You can still melt chocolate with blooms and incorporate it into batter or dough for baked goods.

Triple-Layer Pretzel Brownies

Think of a brownie pie with a pretzel crust and peanut butter-chocolate topping. Now stop thinking about it and make it happen!

—CATHIE AYERS HILTON, NEW YORK

PREP: 30 MIN. **BAKE:** 35 MIN. + COOLING **MAKES:** 2 DOZEN

- **3 cups crushed pretzels**
- **¾ cup butter, melted**
- **3 tablespoons sugar**
- **1 package fudge brownie mix (13-inch x 9-inch pan size)**
- **¾ cup semisweet chocolate chips**
- **½ cup creamy peanut butter**

1. In a small bowl, combine the pretzels, butter and sugar. Press into an ungreased 13-in. x 9-in. baking dish. Bake at 400° for 8 minutes. Cool on a wire rack.

2. Reduce heat to 350°. Prepare the brownie mix batter according to package directions. Pour over prepared crust. Bake for 35-40 minutes or until a toothpick inserted near the center comes out with moist crumbs (do not overbake). Cool completely on a wire rack.

3. In a microwave, melt chocolate chips and peanut butter; stir until smooth. Spread over top. Refrigerate for 30 minutes or until firm. Cut into bars. Store in an airtight container.

Blueberry-Rhubarb Crisp

PREP/TOTAL TIME: 25 MIN. **MAKES:** 6 SERVINGS

- **2½ cups diced fresh or frozen rhubarb, thawed**
- **⅓ cup sugar**
- **2 tablespoons all-purpose flour**
- **1 can (21 ounces) blueberry pie filling**

TOPPING

- **¾ cup all-purpose flour**
- **¾ cup old-fashioned oats**
- **⅓ cup packed brown sugar**
- **¾ teaspoon ground cinnamon**
- **½ cup cold butter, cubed**

1. In a 2-qt. microwave-safe dish, combine the rhubarb, sugar and flour. Cover and microwave on high for 3 minutes; stir. Add pie filling.
2. In a small bowl, combine the flour, oats, brown sugar and cinnamon. Cut in butter until mixture is crumbly; sprinkle over fruit. Cover and cook 4-5 minutes longer or until bubbly and rhubarb is tender. Serve warm.
Editor's Notes: *If using frozen rhubarb, measure rhubarb while still frozen, then thaw completely. Drain in a colander, but do not press liquid out. This recipe was tested in a 1,100-watt microwave.*

"This comforting microwave recipe is unbeatable when served warm with a scoop of vanilla ice cream!"

—LORRI CAMPBELL MANKATO, MINNESOTA

Apricot Crisp

One of the most delicious ways to use canned fruit, these tropical cobbler cups with flaky coconut and a buttery crumb topping are an easy, fancy treat any time of year.

—TASTE OF HOME TEST KITCHEN

PREP/TOTAL TIME: 25 MIN. **MAKES:** 4 SERVINGS

- **3 cans (15 ounces each) reduced-sugar apricot halves, drained**
- **2 tablespoons brown sugar**
- **½ teaspoon ground ginger**

TOPPING

- **¼ cup all-purpose flour**
- **3 tablespoons brown sugar**
- **3 tablespoons quick-cooking oats**
- **2 tablespoons flaked coconut**
- **¼ cup cold butter, cubed**

1. In a large bowl, combine the apricots, brown sugar and ginger. Divide among four greased 8-oz. baking dishes.
2. In a small bowl, combine the flour, brown sugar, oats and coconut. Cut in butter until mixture resembles coarse crumbs. Sprinkle over apricots.
3. Bake at 400° for 15 minutes or until filling is bubbly and top is golden brown.
Editor's Note: *Crisp may be baked in a greased 8-in. square baking dish for 23-25 minutes.*

White Chocolate Berry Parfaits

Just 15 minutes and a few ingredients are all you need to create these family-friendly parfaits built for weeknight fun!

—JULIE PUDERBAUGH BERWICK, PENNSYLVANIA

PREP/TOTAL TIME: 15 MIN. **MAKES:** 4 SERVINGS

- **1 package (3.3 ounces) instant white chocolate pudding mix**
- **1 cup sliced fresh strawberries**
- **½ cup Oreo cookie crumbs**
- **½ cup whipped topping**

1. Prepare pudding according to package directions.
2. Spoon 1/4 cup pudding into each of four parfait glasses. Top with half of the strawberries and cookie crumbs. Repeat layers. Garnish with whipped topping. Chill until serving.

What's not to love about peanut butter, chocolate, ice cream and Oreo cookies? This fancy frozen dessert is a cinch to put together. What a great dessert to have on hand for unexpected guests this summer!
—**DANA SOUTHWICK** MANTON, CALIFORNIA

Peanut Butter-Chocolate Ice Cream Torte

PREP: 30 MIN. + FREEZING
MAKES: 12 SERVINGS

- **24 Oreo cookies**
- **⅓ cup butter, melted**

FILLING

- **1 quart chocolate ice cream, softened**
- **1½ cups creamy peanut butter**
- **1 quart peanut butter ice cream with peanut butter cup pieces, softened**

TOPPING

- **2 cups (12 ounces) semisweet chocolate chips**
- **1 cup heavy whipping cream**
- **1½ cups coarsely chopped miniature peanut butter cups**

1. Place cookies in a food processor. Cover and pulse until fine crumbs form. Transfer to a large bowl and stir in butter. Press onto the bottom and 1-in. up the sides of a greased 10-in. springform pan; cover and freeze for at least 15 minutes.

2. Spread chocolate ice cream into crust; cover and freeze until firm. Spread peanut butter over chocolate layer and top with peanut butter ice cream. Cover and freeze until firm.

3. Place chocolate chips in a large bowl. In a small saucepan, bring cream just to a boil. Pour over chocolate; whisk until smooth. Cool to room temperature, stirring occasionally. Spread over top of dessert. Immediately sprinkle with peanut butter cups. Cover and freeze for 1 hour before serving.

Cake Cutting

To cut the torte with ease, place the cake on your counter. It's okay if it hasn't thawed from the freezer. Dip a long straight-edged knife in hot water before and between cutting the slices. The knife will simply glide through the cake. Repeat dipping the knife in hot water as needed.

Sweet & Savory Ice Cream Sandwiches

PREP: 25 MIN. + FREEZING **MAKES:** 4 SERVINGS

- **4 ounces bittersweet chocolate, chopped**
- **¼ cup chopped walnuts, toasted**
- **4 dried figs, finely chopped**
- **¼ teaspoon minced fresh thyme**
- **4 heaping scoops vanilla ice cream**
- **8 pizzelle cookies**
- **½ cup Mascarpone cheese**
- **½ teaspoon balsamic vinegar**

1. In a microwave, melt chocolate; stir until smooth. Set aside to cool. In a small bowl, combine the walnuts, figs and thyme.
2. Top four cookies with a scoop of ice cream. Sprinkle with half of the walnut mixture and drizzle with melted chocolate. Combine cheese and vinegar. Spread over remaining cookies; place over tops of sandwiches.
3. Press remaining walnut mixture into sides. Wrap in plastic wrap. Freeze for at least 1 hour.

"When you're craving a dessert with grown-up flavors that brings out the little kid in you, this extraordinary ice cream sandwich will do the trick!"

—TASTE OF HOME TEST KITCHEN

Sicilian Ice Cream Sandwiches

Chocolate, Nutella, pistachios and cherries come together to create this Sicily-inspired ice cream dessert.
—TASTE OF HOME TEST KITCHEN

PREP: 20 MIN. + FREEZING **MAKES:** 4 SERVINGS

- **1 teaspoon shortening**
- **⅔ cup miniature semisweet chocolate chips, divided**
- **4 miniature croissants, split**
- **¼ cup Nutella**
- **4 scoops pistachio gelato**
- **12 maraschino cherries, divided**
- **⅓ cup pistachios, coarsely chopped**

1. In a microwave, melt shortening and ⅓ cup chocolate chips; stir until smooth. Set aside.
2. Toast croissants. Spread cut sides of croissants with Nutella. Place a scoop of gelato on croissant bottoms. Slice eight cherries; arrange over gelato. Replace croissant tops.
3. In a shallow bowl, combine pistachios and remaining chocolate chips. Press into sides of sandwiches. Drizzle with melted chocolate. Top each with a cherry. Place on a baking sheet; freeze for at least 1 hour.

Cool & Creamy Ice Cream Sandwiches

The unlikely combination of ingredients (including jalapeno peppers and strawberry ice cream) in this cool dessert creates a wonderfully grown-up version of the classic ice cream sandwich.
—TASTE OF HOME TEST KITCHEN

PREP: 20 MIN. + FREEZING **MAKES:** 4 SERVINGS

- **6 tablespoons chopped seeded jalapeno peppers**
- **4 teaspoons butter**
- **¼ cup jalapeno pepper jelly**
- **8 soft snickerdoodle cookies**
- **4 scoops strawberry ice cream**
- **4 fresh strawberries, hulled and sliced**

1. In a small skillet, saute peppers in butter until tender. Add jelly; set aside to cool.
2. Place a scoop of ice cream on the bottom of half of the cookies. Top with strawberries, jalapeno mixture and remaining cookies. Wrap in plastic wrap. Freeze for at least 1 hour.
Editor's Note: *Wear disposable gloves when cutting hot peppers; the oils can burn skin. Avoid touching your face.*

The Elvis Ice Cream Sandwich

Bring back memories of the King of Rock and Roll with this creamy concoction that combines peanut butter, bananas and bacon.
—TASTE OF HOME TEST KITCHEN

PREP: 20 MIN. + FREEZING **MAKES:** 4 SERVINGS

- **½ cup peanut butter chips**
- **2 teaspoons shortening**
- **2 cups peanut butter ice cream with peanut butter cup pieces, softened**
- **8 slices banana bread**
- **4 strips ready-to-serve fully cooked bacon, halved**
- **1 tablespoon honey**

1. In a microwave, melt chips and shortening; stir until smooth. Cool slightly.
2. Spread ice cream over half of the bread slices. Top with bacon; drizzle with melted chips and honey. Top with remaining bread. Wrap in plastic wrap. Freeze for at least 1 hour.

After Hours Ice Cream Sandwiches

Try these frosty ice cream treats tailored to adults.
—TASTE OF HOME TEST KITCHEN

PREP: 10 MIN. + FREEZING **MAKES:** 4 SERVINGS

- **8 teaspoons RumChata liqueur**
- **4 ladyfingers, split**
- **½ cup coffee ice cream, softened**
- **Baking cocoa**

1. Brush liqueur over bottoms of the ladyfinger halves. Spread two tablespoons ice cream over the bottom of half of the ladyfingers. Top with remaining ladyfinger halves.
2. Wrap in plastic wrap. Freeze for at least 1 hour. Just before serving, dust with cocoa.

Caramel-Pecan Ice Cream Sandwiches

Cool, creamy, salty, sweet, crunchy and nutty...what's there not to like? Bet you can't eat just one of these.
—TASTE OF HOME TEST KITCHEN

PREP: 15 MIN. + FREEZING **MAKES:** 4 SERVINGS

- **8 pretzel crisps**
- **2 ounces milk chocolate candy coating, melted**
- **8 teaspoons marshmallow creme**
- **½ cup chocolate ice cream, softened**
- **2 teaspoons hot caramel ice cream topping, warmed**
- **4 teaspoons chopped pecans**

1. Dip pretzel crisps into melted chocolate, allowing excess to drip off. Place on waxed paper; let stand until set.
2. Spread marshmallow creme over the bottom of each pretzel crisp. Spread 2 tablespoons ice cream over half of the pretzel crisps. Drizzle with ice cream topping and top with remaining pretzel crisps. Press pecans into sides. Wrap in plastic wrap. Freeze for at least 1 hour.

Shhh! SIMPLE SECRET

To soften in the refrigerator, transfer ice cream from the freezer to the refrigerator 20-30 minutes before using. Or let it stand at room temperature for 10-15 minutes. Hard ice cream can also be softened in the microwave at 30% power for about 30 seconds.

Cake with Lemon Sauce

PREP/TOTAL TIME: 10 MIN. **MAKES:** 4 SERVINGS

- **1 package (3 ounces) cream cheese, softened**
- **1¾ cups cold milk**
- **1 package (3.4 ounces) instant lemon pudding mix**
- **4 slices pound cake or angel food cake**
- **Fresh raspberries, optional**

1. In a small bowl, beat the cream cheese until smooth. Add milk and pudding mix; beat for 2 minutes or until smooth and thickened. Serve with cake. Garnish with raspberries if desired.

> "Lovely lemon flavors bring a touch of springtime to the table in just 10 minutes! Top it with your favorite fresh fruit for the perfect mealtime finale."
>
> —**CLAIRE DION** CANTERBURY, CONNECTICUT

Chocolate Lover's Cream Pie

You had us at Nutella, a sweet hazelnut-cocoa spread. Finding true love in a pie has never been simpler.

—**JENN STEWART** LAVERGNE, TENNESSEE

PREP: 20 MIN. + CHILLING
MAKES: 8 SERVINGS

- **2 cups heavy whipping cream**
- **3 tablespoons sugar**
- **½ teaspoon vanilla extract**
- **1 package (8 ounces) cream cheese, softened**
- **¾ cup confectioners' sugar**
- **⅔ cup Nutella**
- **1 chocolate crumb crust (9 inches)**
- **Grated chocolate**

1. In a large bowl, beat cream until it begins to thicken. Add sugar and vanilla; beat until stiff peaks form.

2. In another bowl, beat the cream cheese, confectioners' sugar and Nutella until smooth. Fold in half of the whipped cream. Spoon into crust. Spread remaining whipped cream over top. Garnish with chocolate. Refrigerate for at least 1 hour. Store leftovers in the refrigerator.

Pineapple Orange Cheesecake

Fresh pineapple and orange marmalade lend sunny sweetness to a store-bought cheesecake for an easy after-dinner dessert fix.

—**TASTE OF HOME TEST KITCHEN**

PREP/TOTAL TIME: 15 MIN.
MAKES: 6 SERVINGS

- **2 cups cubed fresh pineapple**
- **2 tablespoons brown sugar**
- **2 tablespoons butter**
- **⅓ cup orange marmalade**
- **1 package (30 ounces) frozen New York-style cheesecake, thawed**
- **Whipped topping, optional**

1. In a large skillet, saute pineapple and brown sugar in butter for 8 minutes. Spread orange marmalade over cheesecake; top with pineapple mixture. Garnish with whipped topping if desired.

For better volume, freeze the bowl and beaters for about 30 minutes before whipping heavy cream.

Sacher Bars

Is your mouth watering yet? This rich take on a Viennese classic using apricot preserves and chocolate leaves guests speechless. Unless you count "mmm."

—**LORRAINE CALAND** SHUNIAH, ONTARIO

PREP: 30 MIN. **BAKE:** 20 MIN. + COOLING **MAKES:** 6¼ DOZEN

- **¾ cup butter, cubed**
- **3 ounces unsweetened chocolate, chopped**
- **3 eggs**
- **1½ cups sugar**
- **1½ teaspoons vanilla extract**
- **1¼ cups all-purpose flour**
- **¾ cup apricot preserves**
- **2 ounces semisweet chocolate, chopped**

1. Line a greased 15-in. x 10-in. x 1-in. baking pan with waxed paper. Grease and flour the paper; set aside. In a microwave, melt butter and unsweetened chocolate; stir until smooth. In a large bowl, beat eggs and sugar. Stir in vanilla and chocolate mixture. Gradually add flour.

2. Transfer to prepared pan. Bake at 325° for 15-20 minutes or until a toothpick inserted near the center comes out clean (do not overbake). Cool for 10 minutes before removing from pan to a wire rack to cool completely.

3. In a microwave, heat jam until melted. Cut cake into four 7½-in. x 5-in. rectangles. Spread half of the preserves over two rectangles. Top each with remaining cake and spread with remaining preserves. Cut into bars.

4. In a microwave, melt semisweet chocolate; stir until smooth. Drizzle over bars. Let stand until set. Store in an airtight container in the refrigerator.

Crunchy Amaretto Peach Cobbler

If you're looking for a fast dessert so comforting and delicious that your guests won't want to leave, then this is the dish for you! The ingredients aren't complicated, and there's only five of them!

—**DEBRA KEIL** OWASSO, OKLAHOMA

PREP: 10 MIN. **BAKE:** 30 MIN. **MAKES:** 12 SERVINGS

- **2 cans (21 ounces each) peach pie filling**
- **½ cup Amaretto**
- **1 package (17½ ounces) sugar cookie mix**
- **1 cup sliced almonds**
- **½ cup butter, cubed**

1. Spread the peach pie filling into an ungreased 13-in. x 9-in. baking dish and drizzle with the Amaretto. Sprinkle the sugar cookie mix and sliced almonds over the filling; dot with the cubed butter.

2. Bake at 350° for 30-35 minutes or until the filling is bubbly and topping is golden brown. Serve warm.

123 MAKE IT SIMPLE

If you make the Crunchy Amaretto Peach Cobbler ahead of time, this five-ingredient dessert can be reheated upon guests' arrival and served with ice cream or whipped cream. Offer coffee and tea in your favorite mugs.

Outrageous Chocolate Mint Cookies

Similar to a brownie in texture, this pleasantly chewy cookie mimics the flavors of the Girl Scouts' beloved Thin Mints. (Maybe you'll want to rename these delicious morsels Thick Mints!)

—TINA COWAN CHANDLER, ARIZONA

PREP: 20 MIN. **BAKE:** 10 MIN./BATCH **MAKES:** 3 DOZEN

- **1 cup 60% cacao bittersweet chocolate baking chips**
- **¼ cup butter, cubed**
- **2 eggs**
- **¾ cup packed brown sugar**
- **1 teaspoon vanilla extract**
- **⅔ cup all-purpose flour**
- **½ teaspoon baking powder**
- **½ teaspoon salt**
- **1 cup (6 ounces) semisweet chocolate chips**
- **36 mint Andes candies, chopped**

1. In a microwave, melt bittersweet chocolate chips and butter; stir until smooth. Cool slightly. In a large bowl, beat eggs and brown sugar. Stir in vanilla and chocolate mixture. Combine the flour, baking powder and salt; gradually add to chocolate mixture. Stir in semisweet chocolate chips and candies.

2. Drop by teaspoonfuls 3 in. apart on greased baking sheets. Bake at 350° for 8-10 minutes or until edges are set. Cool for 2 minutes before removing from pans to wire racks. Store in an airtight container.

Peanut Butter-Hazelnut Brownies

Over the years I'd been adding this and that to my basic brownie recipe and then I came up with this one!

—DENISE WHEELER NEWAYGO, MICHIGAN

PREP: 20 MIN. **BAKE:** 35 MIN. + COOLING **MAKES:** 2 DOZEN

- **1 cup butter, softened**
- **2 cups sugar**
- **4 eggs**
- **2 teaspoons vanilla extract**
- **1 cup all-purpose flour**
- **¾ cup baking cocoa**
- **½ teaspoon baking powder**
- **Dash salt**
- **1½ cups coarsely crushed malted milk balls**
- **½ cup creamy peanut butter**
- **½ cup Nutella**

1. In a large bowl, cream butter and sugar until light and fluffy. Add eggs, one at a time, beating well after each addition. Beat in vanilla. Combine the flour, cocoa, baking powder and salt; gradually add to creamed mixture. Fold in malted milk balls.

2. Spread into a greased 13-in. x 9-in. baking pan. In a small microwave-safe bowl, combine peanut butter and Nutella; cover and microwave at 50% power for 1-2 minutes or until smooth, stirring twice. Drizzle over batter; cut through batter with a knife to swirl.

3. Bake at 350° for 35-40 minutes or until a toothpick inserted near the center comes out clean (do not overbake). Cool on a wire rack.

Frozen desserts are ideal for party hosts, but guests who don't have far to travel will also appreciate this make-ahead favorite. I've prepared it with chocolate, vanilla and white chocolate instant pudding, too.

—**TAMMY CAMPBELL** CHESAPEAKE, VIRGINIA

Toffee Cream Pie

PREP: 15 MIN. + FREEZING
MAKES: 8 SERVINGS

- **1½ cups half-and-half cream**
- **1 package (3.4 ounces) instant vanilla pudding mix**
- **6 Heath candy bars (1.4 ounces each), chopped**
- **1 carton (8 ounces) frozen whipped topping, thawed, divided**
- **1 chocolate crumb crust (9 inches)**

1. In a large bowl, whisk cream and pudding mix for 2 minutes. Let stand for 2 minutes or until soft-set. Stir in 1 cup chopped candy. Fold in 2 cups whipped topping. Transfer to crust.
2. Spread remaining whipped topping over top and sprinkle with remaining candy. Cover and freeze for at least 4 hours or until firm.

Chocolate-Peanut Butter Cup Cookies

If you want to enjoy one of these soft, fully loaded treats the day after you make them, you'd better find a good hiding spot!
—JENNIFER KREY CLARENCE, NEW YORK

PREP: 25 MIN. **BAKE:** 10 MIN.
MAKES: 4 DOZEN

- **1 cup butter, softened**
- **¾ cup creamy peanut butter**
- **1 cup packed brown sugar**
- **½ cup sugar**
- **2 egg yolks**
- **¼ cup 2% milk**
- **2 teaspoons vanilla extract**
- **2⅔ cups all-purpose flour**
- **⅓ cup baking cocoa**
- **1 teaspoon baking soda**
- **1 cup milk chocolate chips**
- **1 cup peanut butter chips**
- **6 packages (1½ ounces each) peanut butter cups, chopped**

1. In a large bowl, cream the butter, peanut butter and sugars until light and fluffy. Beat in the egg yolks, milk and vanilla. Combine the flour, cocoa and baking soda; gradually add to creamed mixture and mix well. Stir in chips and peanut butter cups.
2. Drop heaping tablespoonfuls 2 in. apart onto ungreased baking sheets. Bake at 350° for 8-10 minutes or until set (do not overbake). Cool for 2 minutes before removing from pans to wire racks. Store in an airtight container.

Dark Chocolate Carrot Cake

Carrot cake has a dark side—and it's divine! Cream cheese and shredded carrots in the batter keep this cake moist, while toasted nuts and cinnamon boost the flavor.
—DARLENE BRENDEN SALEM, OREGON

PREP: 20 MIN. **BAKE:** 25 MIN. + COOLING **MAKES:** 16 SERVINGS

- **1 package (18¼ ounces) dark chocolate cake mix**
- **4 ounces cream cheese, softened**
- **1 package (3.9 ounces) instant chocolate pudding mix**
- **1 cup 2% milk**
- **3 eggs**
- **1 teaspoon ground cinnamon**
- **3 cups shredded carrots**
- **1 cup chopped walnuts, toasted, divided**
- **2 cans (16 ounces each) cream cheese frosting**

1. In a large bowl, combine the cake mix, cream cheese, pudding mix, milk, eggs and cinnamon; beat on low speed for 30 seconds. Beat on medium for 2 minutes. Stir in carrots and ½ cup walnuts. Pour into three greased and floured 8-in. round baking pans.
2. Bake at 350° for 25-30 minutes or until a toothpick inserted near the center comes out clean. Cool for 10 minutes before removing from pans to wire racks to cool completely.
3. Spread frosting between layers and over top and sides of cake. Sprinkle top with remaining walnuts. Store in the refrigerator.

Strawberry Tarragon Crumble

I created this special berry dessert with fresh tarragon from my garden. The pretty layers are laced with the tarragon's mild anise flavor and a balance of sweet and salty ingredients. Yum!
—**TAMARA HURON** NEW MARKET, ALABAMA

PREP/TOTAL TIME: 20 MIN. **MAKES:** 4 SERVINGS

- **2 cups chopped fresh strawberries**
- **3 tablespoons sugar**
- **2 tablespoons minced fresh tarragon**
- **1 tablespoon orange juice**

TOPPING

- **1 cup coarsely crushed graham crackers**
- **8 chocolate-covered miniature pretzels, crushed**
- **3 tablespoons butter, melted**
- **1 tablespoon honey**
- **1 teaspoon vanilla extract**
- **1 cup reduced-fat whipped topping**
- **Additional minced fresh tarragon**

1. In a small bowl, combine the strawberries, sugar, tarragon and orange juice. In another bowl, combine the graham crackers, pretzels, butter, honey and vanilla.
2. In each of four parfait glasses, layer 3 tablespoons graham cracker mixture, 1/4 cup strawberries and 2 tablespoons whipped topping. Repeat layers. Garnish with additional tarragon.

Brown Butter Spice Cookies

PREP: 20 MIN. + CHILLING **BAKE:** 10 MIN./BATCH
MAKES: ABOUT 2 DOZEN

- **½ cup unsalted butter, cubed**
- **1 cup packed brown sugar**
- **1 egg**
- **1 tablespoon spiced rum**
- **1¼ cups all-purpose flour**
- **1½ teaspoons ground cinnamon**
- **½ teaspoon baking soda**
- **¼ teaspoon salt**
- **¼ teaspoon ground ginger**
- **¼ teaspoon ground nutmeg**
- **½ cup dark chocolate chips**

1. Place butter in a small heavy saucepan. Cook over medium heat for 5-7 minutes or until golden brown; cool slightly.
2. Beat brown sugar and browned butter in a large bowl until blended. Beat in egg, then rum. Combine the flour, cinnamon, baking soda, salt, ginger and nutmeg; gradually add to brown sugar mixture and mix well. Stir in chips. Cover and refrigerate for at least 30 minutes.
3. Drop by rounded tablespoonfuls 2 in. apart onto greased baking sheets. Bake at 350° for 10-12 minutes or until bottoms are lightly browned. Remove to wire racks to cool.

> “If you like spice cake, you'll love this recipe! Browned butter, dark chocolate and a splash of rum produce an unconventional spice cookie that's guaranteed to please.”
> —**KRISTIN KENNEY** NEWPORT BEACH, CALIFORNIA

Candy-Licious Fudge

A no-fuss fudge prepared in the microwave that tastes like a candy bar? It sounds too good to be true, but this recipe turned out to be good and true!

—DEE LANCASTER OZARK, MISSOURI

PREP: 15 MIN. + CHILLING
MAKES: 2¼ POUNDS

- **1 teaspoon butter**
- **1 can (14 ounces) sweetened condensed milk**
- **1 package (11 ounces) peanut butter and milk chocolate chips**
- **1 cup milk chocolate chips**
- **⅔ cup milk chocolate English toffee bits**
- **1 cup chopped pecans**
- **2 teaspoons vanilla extract**

1. Line a 9-in. square baking pan with foil and grease the foil with butter; set aside. In a large microwave-safe bowl combine the milk, chips and toffee bits. Microwave, uncovered, on high for 1 minute; stir. Cook 1-2 minutes longer, stirring every minute, or until chips are melted. Stir in pecans and vanilla. Transfer to prepared pan. Cover and refrigerate for at least 1 hour. Using foil, lift fudge out of pan. Gently peel off foil; cut into 1-in. squares. Store in an airtight container.

Editor's Note: *This recipe was tested in a 1,100-watt microwave.*

Rhubarb Sundaes

Here's a simple dessert sauce with so much flavor! It's terrific over ice cream, but it's also guaranteed to inspire you to try it on pancakes or waffles, pound cake and more!

—TASTE OF HOME TEST KITCHEN

PREP/TOTAL TIME: 15 MIN.
MAKES: 1 CUP

- **2 cups chopped fresh or frozen rhubarb**
- **⅓ cup sugar**
- **¼ cup water**
- **¼ teaspoon ground cinnamon**
- **½ teaspoon honey**
- **Vanilla ice cream**
- **Chopped walnuts, optional**

1. In a small saucepan, bring the rhubarb, sugar, water and cinnamon to a boil. Reduce heat; simmer, uncovered, for 8-10 minutes or until rhubarb is tender and the sauce has reached desired consistency. Remove from the heat; stir in honey. Serve warm over ice cream. Sprinkle with walnuts if desired.

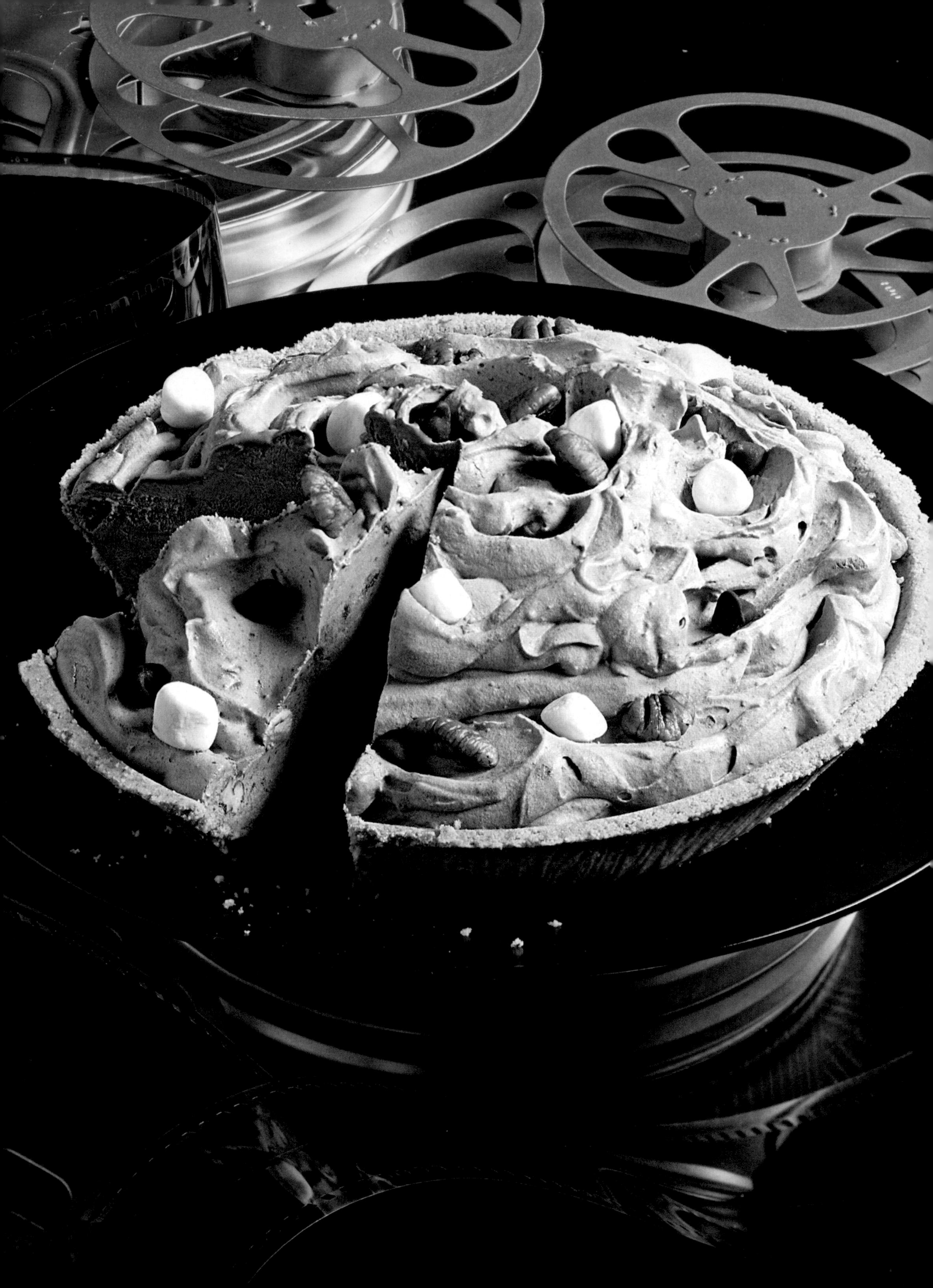

Effortless Entertaining

“Whip up this easy chocolaty pie the night before, and you’ll feel like a champ when you serve it on party day.”

ADDRENNE ROTH DONNA, TEXAS
Rocky Road Freezer Pie, page 249

HOST AN ELEGANT **SUMMER SHOWER**

PLAN A SIMPLE BUT SOPHISTICATED EVENT FOR YOUR FAVORITE COUPLE THAT LOVES TO COOK

Once a way to shower the bride-to-be with gifts before the big day, wedding showers are increasingly becoming a couples' affair. The next time you're hosting, make the day memorable as you set the happy couple up with some fun gifts that'll help them to cook up a blissful future in the kitchen! Our lovely hors d'oeuvres and chic sweets will appeal to all. And everyone will love taking the adorable homemade truffles (which cost practically pennies to whip up) home with them at the end! Ask guests to share a favorite recipe with the bride and groom, and you'll get them started on the right foot (or feet) for years to come!

Champagne Fruit Punch

Toast the happy couple at your next bridal shower with a fun and fruity drink! It's the perfect refreshment on a hot day.
—KELLY TRAN SALEM, OREGON

PREP/TOTAL TIME: 10 MIN. **MAKES:** 16 SERVINGS (¾ CUP EACH)

- **2 cups fresh or frozen raspberries**
- **1 can (12 ounces) frozen orange juice concentrate, thawed**
- **1 can (12 ounces) frozen cherry pomegranate juice concentrate, thawed**
- **1 can (6 ounces) unsweetened pineapple juice, chilled**
- **1 medium lemon, thinly sliced**
- **1 bottle (1 liter) club soda, chilled**
- **1 bottle (750 milliliters) Champagne or white sparkling grape juice, chilled**

1. In a punch bowl, combine the first five ingredients. Slowly stir in club soda and Champagne. Serve immediately.

CUPCAKE GARNISHES

FOR THE GROOM'S TOP HAT Form hat and brim by placing a chocolate-dipped marshmallow in the circle's center. Let stand until the chocolate is set.

FOR THE BRIDE'S BOUQUET Pipe the bouquet stems onto waxed paper. Immediately attach sprinkles to the stems. Let the bouquets stand until set.

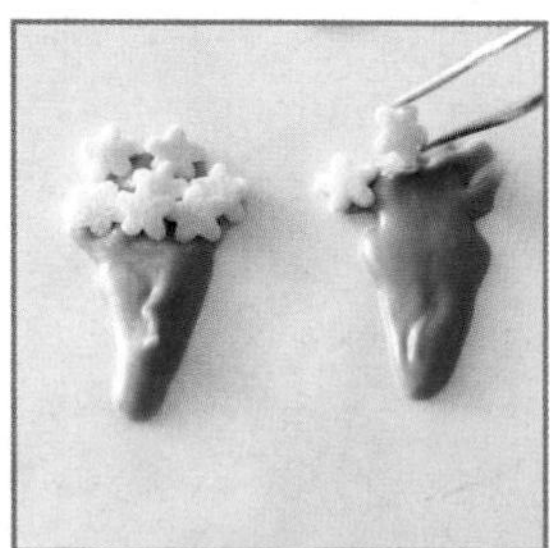

Bride and Groom Cupcakes

Who doesn't love a bitty bite of cake? For party day ease, make the cupcakes 1 month before and freeze. Prep the accessories 2 days ahead and store at room temp in an airtight container. Whip up the frosting and assemble all in no time on the big day!
—TASTE OF HOME TEST KITCHEN

PREP: 1½ HOURS **BAKE:** 20 MIN. + COOLING **MAKES:** 2 DOZEN

- **1 package (18¼ ounces) strawberry cake mix**

FROSTING

- **1 cup shortening**
- **1 cup butter, softened**
- **8 cups confectioners' sugar**
- **7 to 8 tablespoons 2% milk, divided**
- **2 teaspoons clear vanilla extract**
- **½ cup baking cocoa**
- **2 teaspoons grated lemon peel**
- **½ teaspoon lemon extract**

DECORATIONS

- **1 cup dark chocolate candy coating disks, melted**
- **½ cup vanilla candy coating disks, melted**
- **1 large marshmallow**
- **½ cup green candy coating disks, melted**
- **White pearl dragees, flower sprinkles, white edible glitter and colored sugar**
- **Small piece of tulle**

1. Prepare and bake cake batter according to package directions for cupcakes. Cool completely.

2. In a large bowl, beat shortening and butter until light and fluffy. Add the confectioners' sugar, 6 tablespoons milk and vanilla; beat until smooth.

3. Transfer half of the frosting to another bowl. Add baking cocoa and 1-2 tablespoons remaining milk to achieve desired consistency. Add lemon peel and extract to remaining frosting.

4. Using melted chocolate, pipe 12 bow ties onto waxed paper. For bride's crown, pipe a 1¼-in. ring with melted vanilla coating. Immediately arrange dragees onto ring.

5. For groom's hat, spoon a ½-teaspoon round of melted chocolate onto waxed paper into a 1¾ inch circle. Cut a ¼-in. slice from the top of marshmallow. Dip marshmallow in chocolate coating and place in the center of chocolate round.

6. For bride's bouquet, using melted green coating, pipe 12 bouquet stems onto waxed paper. Immediately attach with flower sprinkles. Let decorations stand until set.

7. Pipe frosting onto cupcakes. For bride, add crown to the top of a lemon cupcake and attach a piece of tulle for veil; add a bouquet and sprinkle with glitter.

8. For groom, add the top hat to the top of a chocolate cupcake. Attach a bow tie and pearl dragees for buttons.

9. Decorate remaining cupcakes with bouquets, bow ties, dragees, glitter and colored sugar as desired.

Nutter Butter Truffles

Send guests home with sweet memories of the day! Prepare these truffles 5 to 7 days in advance and store in the fridge for ease.
—**KATHY CARLAN** CANTON, GEORGIA

PREP: 1 HOUR + CHILLING **MAKES:** 4 DOZEN

- **1 package (1 pound) Nutter Butter sandwich cookies**
- **1 package (8 ounces) cream cheese, softened**
- **8 ounces milk chocolate candy coating, melted**
- **8 ounces white candy coating, melted**
- **3 ounces bittersweet chocolate, melted**

1. Place cookies in a food processor; cover and process until finely crushed. Add cream cheese; process until blended. Roll into 1-in. balls.
2. Dip half of the balls in milk chocolate, allowing excess to drip off. Place on waxed paper. Repeat with remaining balls and white coating. Drizzle bittersweet chocolate over truffles. Let stand until set. Store in an airtight container in the refrigerator.

Rustic Antipasto Tart

Ready-made ingredients keep this gorgeous tart a hassle-free treat.
—**CHERYL LAMA** ROYAL OAK, MICHIGAN

PREP: 15 MIN. **BAKE:** 25 MIN. **MAKES:** 12 SERVINGS

- **1 sheet refrigerated pie pastry**
- **2 tablespoons prepared pesto**
- **1 cup shredded part-skim mozzarella cheese, divided**
- **4 ounces sliced turkey pepperoni**
- **1 jar (7 ounces) roasted sweet red peppers, drained and thinly sliced**
- **1 jar (7½ ounces) marinated quartered artichoke hearts, drained**
- **1 tablespoon water**

1. Unroll pastry onto a parchment paper-lined baking sheet. Spread pesto to within 2 in. of edges; sprinkle with ½ cup cheese. Layer with pepperoni and ¼ cup cheese. Top with red peppers and artichokes; sprinkle with remaining cheese.
2. Fold up edges of pastry over filling, leaving center uncovered. Brush folded pastry with water. Bake at 425° for 25-30 minutes or until crust is golden and cheese is melted. Serve warm.

Roast Beef Aioli Bundles

Don't let these dainty bundles fool you. They're hearty but handy to hold, and everyone will gobble them up!
—**TASTE OF HOME TEST KITCHEN**

PREP/TOTAL TIME: 30 MIN. **MAKES:** 16 APPETIZERS

- **16 fresh asparagus spears, trimmed**
- **⅓ cup mayonnaise**
- **1 garlic clove, minced**
- **1 teaspoon Dijon mustard**
- **1 teaspoon lemon juice**
- **⅛ teaspoon ground cumin**
- **8 thin slices deli roast beef, cut in half lengthwise**
- **1 medium sweet yellow pepper, thinly sliced**
- **1 medium sweet orange pepper, thinly sliced**
- **1 medium sweet red pepper, thinly sliced**
- **16 whole chives**

1. In a large skillet, bring 1 in. of water to a boil. Add asparagus; cover and cook for 3 minutes. Drain and immediately place in ice water. Drain and pat dry.
2. In a small bowl, combine the mayonnaise, garlic, mustard, lemon juice and cumin. Place roast beef slices on a work surface; spread each slice with 1 teaspoon aioli. Top each with an asparagus spear and pepper strips. Roll up tightly; tie bundles with chives. Serve immediately.

Tortellini & Shrimp Skewers with Sun-Dried Tomato Sauce

These fresh skewers and tasty sauce will keep guests reaching for more!

—**CACIE BIDDLE** BRIDGEPORT, WEST VIRGINIA

PREP: 30 MIN. **COOK:** 15 MIN.
MAKES: 32 APPETIZERS (2 CUPS SAUCE)

- **1 package (9 ounces) refrigerated spinach tortellini**
- **1 package (8 ounces) cream cheese, softened**
- **½ cup sour cream**
- **¼ cup fresh basil leaves**
- **¼ cup oil-packed sun-dried tomatoes**
- **¼ cup 2% milk**
- **¼ cup reduced-fat mayonnaise**
- **2 garlic cloves**
- **½ teaspoon Louisiana-style hot sauce**
- **¼ teaspoon salt**
- **¼ teaspoon pepper**
- **2 tablespoons olive oil**
- **1 pound peeled and deveined cooked medium shrimp**
- **32 frilled toothpicks**

1. Cook tortellini according to package directions.

2. Meanwhile, in a food processor, combine the cream cheese, sour cream, basil, tomatoes, milk, mayonnaise, garlic, hot sauce, salt and pepper; cover and process until blended. Transfer to a small bowl. Chill until serving.

3. Drain the tortellini and transfer to a large bowl. Drizzle with olive oil; toss to coat. Thread the cooked tortellini and shrimp onto toothpicks. Serve with the sauce.

Simple Menu Planning

Round out this wedding shower menu with a nice cheese and sausage platter or cut-up veggies and store-bought dip. Served in pretty bowls or on platters, they'll look tempting and minimize prep work and cleanup.

FRESH TAKE ON **LOADED POTATOES**

SKIP THE PLAIN OLD POTATOES AND TOPPINGS! THESE BAKED TATERS **TAKE MEALS FROM BLAND AND BORING TO SATISFYING AND FUN!**

The Bistro Baked Potato

Bistro fare meets baked potatoes in this continental take on a stuffed potato.

—TASTE OF HOME TEST KITCHEN

PREP: 25 MIN. **GRILL:** 20 MIN.
MAKES: 4 SERVINGS

- **4 large baking potatoes**
- **1 beef top sirloin steak (1 pound)**
- **1 teaspoon coarsely ground pepper**
- **2 cups cherry tomatoes**
- **2 jars (7½ ounces each) marinated quartered artichoke hearts, drained**
- **2 garlic cloves, minced**
- **1 cup reduced-fat mayonnaise**
- **¾ cup shredded Asiago cheese, divided**
- **3 cups fresh baby spinach, coarsely chopped**

1. Scrub and pierce potatoes; place on a microwave-safe plate. Microwave, uncovered, on high for 15 minutes or until tender, turning once.

2. Sprinkle steak with pepper. Grill, covered, over medium heat or broil 4 in. from the heat for 7-10 minutes on each side or until meat reaches desired doneness (for medium-rare, a thermometer should read 145°; medium, 160°; well-done, 170°). Let stand for 5 minutes.

3. Place tomatoes in a grill wok or basket. Grill, uncovered, over medium heat for 2-4 minutes or until tomatoes begin to soften. Keep warm.

4. In a large saucepan, heat artichokes and garlic over medium heat for 2 minutes. Add mayonnaise and ½ cup cheese; stir until cheese is melted. Stir in spinach and heat through.

5. With a sharp knife, cut an "X" in each potato; fluff pulp with a fork. Slice steak into thin strips. Top potatoes with steak, artichoke sauce and tomatoes. Sprinkle with remaining cheese.

Editor's Note: *If you do not have a grill wok or basket, use a disposable foil pan. Poke holes in the bottom of the pan with a meat fork to allow liquid to drain.*

Buenos Dias Baked Potatoes

Convenience products take the heavy labor out of this Tex-Mex baked potato entree.

—TASTE OF HOME TEST KITCHEN

PREP/TOTAL TIME: 30 MIN. **MAKES:** 4 SERVINGS

- **4 large baking potatoes**
- **1½ cups frozen pepper strips**
- **1 medium onion, halved and thinly sliced**
- **1 tablespoon butter**
- **2 packages (6 ounces each) ready-to-use Southwestern chicken strips**
- **1 cup salsa con queso dip**
- **2 tablespoons canned chopped green chilies**
- **1 chipotle pepper in adobo sauce, minced**
- **Optional toppings: salsa, sliced avocado and French-fried onions**

1. Scrub and pierce potatoes; place on a microwave-safe plate. Microwave, uncovered, on high for 15 minutes or until tender, turning once.
2. In a large skillet, saute pepper strips and onion in butter until crisp tender. Stir in the chicken strips, salsa dip, chilies, and chipotle pepper. Heat through.
3. With a sharp knife, cut an "X" in each potato; fluff pulp with a fork. Spoon chicken mixture over potatoes and serve with toppings of your choice.

That's Amore Baked Potatoes

We add a touch of Italy to these baked potatoes with beefed up spaghetti sauce, pepperoni and more. Now, that's amore!

—TASTE OF HOME TEST KITCHEN

PREP: 20 MIN. **COOK:** 15 MIN. **MAKES:** 4 SERVINGS

- **4 large baking potatoes**
- **½ pound ground beef**
- **1 medium green pepper, chopped**
- **1 medium carrot, shredded**
- **1 small onion, chopped**
- **2 garlic cloves, minced**
- **1 jar (24 ounces) spaghetti sauce with mushrooms**
- **5 ounces pepperoni, chopped**
- **¼ cup dry red wine or reduced-sodium beef broth**
- **2 teaspoons minced fresh oregano**
- **½ teaspoon salt**
- **1 cup (4 ounces) shredded reduced-fat Colby-Monterey Jack cheese**

1. Scrub and pierce potatoes; place on a microwave-safe plate. Microwave, uncovered, on high for 15 minutes or until tender, turning once.
2. In a Dutch oven, cook the ground beef, green pepper, carrot, onion and garlic over medium heat until meat is no longer pink; drain. Add the spaghetti sauce, pepperoni, wine, oregano and salt. Bring to a boil. Reduce heat; simmer, uncovered, for 10 minutes.
3. With a sharp knife, cut an "X" in each potato; fluff pulp with a fork. Spoon sauce over potatoes and sprinkle with cheese. Microwave until cheese is melted.

Very Veggie Baked Potatoes

Take a break from heavy meat dishes with these chock-full-of-vegetables baked potatoes.

—TASTE OF HOME TEST KITCHEN

PREP: 25 MIN. **GRILL:** 10 MIN. **MAKES:** 4 SERVINGS

- **4 large baking potatoes**
- **2 medium yellow summer squash, sliced**
- **2 small zucchini, sliced**
- **1 small eggplant, sliced**
- **2 medium leeks (white portion only), sliced lengthwise into quarters**
- **2 tablespoons reduced-fat Italian salad dressing**
- **⅛ teaspoon salt**
- **1 package (6½ ounces) garlic-herb spreadable cheese**
- **¼ cup reduced-fat sour cream**
- **¼ cup fresh basil leaves, thinly sliced**

1. Scrub and pierce potatoes; place on a microwave-safe plate. Microwave, uncovered, on high for 15 minutes or until tender, turning once.
2. In a large bowl, combine the squash, zucchini, eggplant and leeks. Add salad dressing and toss to coat. Transfer vegetables to a grill wok or basket. Grill, uncovered, over medium heat for 8-12 minutes or until tender, stirring frequently. Sprinkle with salt and keep warm.
3. Combine spreadable cheese and sour cream. With a sharp knife, cut an "X" in each potato. Fluff pulp with a fork. Spoon grilled vegetables over potatoes; dollop with cheese mixture. Garnish with basil.

Editor's Note: *If you do not have a grill wok or basket, use a disposable foil pan. Poke holes in the bottom of the pan with a meat fork to allow liquid to drain.*

Hungry Man's Baked Potatoes

Sweet potatoes are topped with bacon, veggies, pulled pork and goat cheese for a unique take on a baked potato dinner.

—TASTE OF HOME TEST KITCHEN

PREP/TOTAL TIME: 30 MIN. **MAKES:** 4 SERVINGS

- **4 large sweet potatoes**
- **3 thick-sliced bacon strips, cut into quarters**
- **1 cup fresh or frozen corn**
- **1 medium red onion, halved and thinly sliced**
- **2 cups refrigerated fully cooked barbecued shredded pork**
- **¼ cup crumbled goat cheese**
- **¼ cup minced fresh cilantro**

1. Scrub and pierce potatoes; place on a microwave-safe plate. Microwave, uncovered, on high for 12-15 minutes or until tender, turning once.
2. In a large skillet, cook bacon over medium heat until crisp. Remove to paper towels with a slotted spoon; drain, reserving 1 tablespoon drippings. Saute corn and onion in drippings until tender.
3. With a sharp knife, cut an "X" in each potato; fluff pulp with a fork. Place pork in a microwave-safe bowl. Microwave, uncovered, for 1-2 minutes or until heated through. Top potatoes with pork, corn mixture, bacon, goat cheese and cilantro.

DEVILED EGGS ON PARADE!

YOU'LL WANT TO GIVE THESE TASTY NEW TWISTS FROM THE TASTE OF HOME TEST KITCHEN A TRY

At Easter, deviled eggs are all the rage. Sure, the classic version is tasty. But why make plain old eggs when you can easily give them an upgrade? We're sharing a dozen new egg-ceptional variations. Time to get crackin' and find a new favorite!

Dill-icious Deviled Eggs

A cute carrot garnish tops these dill-ectable deviled eggs that come together in a snap!

PREP/TOTAL TIME: 20 MIN. **MAKES:** 1 DOZEN

- **6 hard-cooked eggs**
- **¼ cup mayonnaise**
- **2 teaspoons snipped fresh dill**
- **½ teaspoon Dijon mustard**
- **Dash each salt and pepper**
- **1 small carrot**
- **12 small fresh dill sprigs**

1. Cut eggs in half lengthwise. Remove yolks; set whites aside. In a small bowl, mash yolks. Add mayonnaise, dill, mustard, salt and pepper; mix well. Stuff or pipe into egg whites.
2. For garnish, cut 12 small pieces from carrot so they resemble carrots; set aside remaining carrot for another use. Place a carrot piece on top of each egg; add a dill sprig. Refrigerate until serving.

Hop-To-It Deviled Eggs

Make sweet Easter baskets filled with fantastic flavor! These adorable eggs would be a wonderful project for the kids, while moms and dads finish up preparations for an Easter feast.

PREP/TOTAL TIME: 20 MIN. **MAKES:** 1 DOZEN

- **6 hard-cooked eggs**
- **¼ cup mayonnaise**
- **1 tablespoon sweet pickle relish**
- **½ teaspoon honey mustard**
- **Dash salt**
- **Dash pepper**
- **¼ cup alfalfa sprouts**
- **12 chives**
- **¼ cup candy-coated sunflower kernels**

1. Cut eggs in half widthwise. Cut a thin slice from the bottom of each half so they sit flat. Remove yolks; set whites aside. In a small bowl, mash yolks. Add the mayonnaise, relish, mustard, salt and pepper; mix well. Stuff or pipe into egg whites.
2. Top with sprouts. Tuck the ends of a chive into each egg, forming a handle. Refrigerate until serving. Just before serving, garnish with sunflower kernels.

Chicks-on-the-Ranch Deviled Eggs

A hint of Dijon mustard, Parmesan cheese and ranch salad dressing take the flavor of these adorable deviled eggs to new heights!

PREP/TOTAL TIME: 25 MIN. **MAKES:** ½ DOZEN

- **6 hard-cooked eggs**
- **¼ cup shredded Parmesan cheese**
- **¼ cup prepared ranch salad dressing**
- **1 teaspoon Dijon mustard**
- **Dash pepper**
- **5 carrot chips**
- **12 capers**
- **Fresh dill sprigs**

1. Cut a thin slice from the bottom of each egg so it sits flat. Cut the top third from each egg. Carefully remove yolks and place in a small bowl; mash with a fork. Add the cheese, salad dressing, mustard and pepper; stir until well blended. Spoon into the egg white bottoms; replace tops.
2. Cut 12 feet and 12 small triangles for beaks from carrot chips.Gently press the capers into the filling for eyes; add beaks. Insert a dill sprig in top of eggs for tuft of feathers. Place feet in front of chicks. Chill until serving.

Little Italy Deviled Eggs

We're in love with these simple deviled eggs with sun-dried tomatoes and fresh basil. One taste, and we guarantee you'll declare your affection, too!

PREP/TOTAL TIME: 20 MIN. **MAKES:** 1 DOZEN

- **6 hard-cooked eggs**
- **⅓ cup mayonnaise**
- **2 tablespoons chopped walnuts, toasted and finely chopped**
- **2 tablespoons oil-packed sun-dried tomatoes, finely chopped**
- **2 teaspoons grated Parmesan cheese**
- **⅛ teaspoon garlic powder**
- **Dash each salt and pepper**
- **Fresh basil leaves**

1. Cut eggs in half lengthwise. Remove yolks; set whites aside. In a small bowl, mash yolks. Add the mayonnaise, walnuts, tomatoes, cheese, garlic powder, salt and pepper; mix well. Stuff into egg whites. Refrigerate until serving.
2. Just before serving, garnish with basil.

Tater Salad Deviled Eggs

Potato salad and deviled eggs—two of our favorite things come together in one mouthwatering appetizer.

PREP: 30 MIN. + COOLING **MAKES:** 1 DOZEN

- **¾ cup cubed small red potatoes**
- **6 hard-cooked eggs**
- **¼ cup mayonnaise**
- **2 teaspoons dill pickle relish**
- **1 teaspoon Dijon mustard**
- **Dash each salt and pepper**
- **2 teaspoons minced fresh parsley**

1. Place potatoes in a small saucepan and cover with water. Bring to a boil. Reduce heat; cover and simmer for 10-15 minutes or until tender. Drain and cool.

2. Cut eggs in half lengthwise. Remove yolks; set whites aside. In a small bowl, mash yolks. Add the potatoes, mayonnaise, relish, mustard, salt and pepper; mix well. Stuff into egg whites. Sprinkle with parsley. Refrigerate until serving.

Lil' Devil Eggs

Look out! Hot stuff coming through! These fun and spicy eggs will be the talk of any buffet table.

PREP/TOTAL TIME: 20 MIN. **MAKES:** 1 DOZEN

- **1 small sweet red pepper**
- **6 hard-cooked eggs**
- **¼ cup reduced-fat chipotle mayonnaise**
- **2 tablespoons finely chopped pickled jalapeno slices**
- **½ to ¾ teaspoon hot pepper sauce**
- **Dash salt**
- **Smoked paprika**

1. Cut pepper in half, finely chop one half and set aside. Cut eggs in half widthwise. Cut a thin slice from the bottom of each half so they sit flat. Remove yolks. In a small bowl, mash yolks. Add the chopped pepper, mayonnaise, jalapeno, pepper sauce and salt; mix well. Stuff into egg whites. Sprinkle with paprika.
2. Cut horns from remaining pepper half and press into filling. Refrigerate until serving.

Salsa Dipper Deviled Eggs

Like a fiesta for your mouth, these fun salsa-topped eggs make any gathering feel like a party!

PREP/TOTAL TIME: 20 MIN. **MAKES:** 1 DOZEN

- **6 hard-cooked eggs**
- **⅓ cup salsa, divided**
- **2 tablespoons mayonnaise**
- **1 green onion, finely chopped**
- **Dash each salt and pepper**
- **6 blue tortilla chips**

1. Cut eggs in half lengthwise. Remove yolks; set whites aside. In a small bowl, mash yolks. Add 1/4 cup salsa, mayonnaise, onion, salt and pepper; mix well. Stuff or pipe into egg whites. Refrigerate until serving.
2. Just before serving, break tortilla chips in half. Garnish eggs with chips and remaining salsa.

Lone Star Deviled Eggs

No, these weren't created deep in the heart of Texas, but the barbecue flavor will make you think you're visiting the Lone Star State!

PREP/TOTAL TIME: 20 MIN. **MAKES:** 1 DOZEN

- **6 hard-cooked eggs**
- **3 tablespoons mayonnaise**
- **4 tablespoons barbecue sauce, divided**
- **½ teaspoon Dijon mustard**
- **Dash each salt and pepper**
- **¾ cup refrigerated fully cooked barbecued shredded beef**

1. Cut eggs in half lengthwise. Remove yolks; set whites aside. In a small bowl, mash yolks. Add the mayonnaise, 2 tablespoons barbecue sauce, mustard, salt and pepper; mix well. Stuff or pipe into egg whites.
2. Cut beef into 1-inch pieces. Garnish eggs with beef and remaining barbecue sauce. Refrigerate until serving.

Dazzling Dirty Martini Deviled Eggs

Blue cheese-stuffed olives and a splash of vodka flavor these tasty deviled eggs. They're perfect for an evening of drinks, appetizers and great conversation with friends.

PREP/TOTAL TIME: 20 MIN. **MAKES:** 1 DOZEN

- **14 blue cheese-stuffed olives, divided**
- **6 hard-cooked eggs**
- **3 tablespoons mayonnaise**
- **1½ teaspoons minced fresh parsley**
- **1½ teaspoons vodka**
- **½ teaspoon olive juice**
- **⅛ teaspoon cayenne pepper**
- **¼ teaspoon kosher salt**
- **¼ teaspoon coarsely ground pepper**

1. Finely chop eight olives and set aside. Cut eggs in half lengthwise. Remove yolks. In a small bowl, mash yolks. Add the chopped olives, mayonnaise, parsley, vodka, olive juice and cayenne; mix well. Stuff or pipe into egg whites.
2. Cut remaining olives in half. Garnish eggs with olive halves and sprinkle with salt and pepper. Refrigerate until serving.

Hoisin-It-Nice Deviled Eggs

Add an Asian twist to deviled eggs! Shrimp, hoisin and soy sauce boost flavor and amp up the fun.

PREP/TOTAL TIME: 25 MIN. **MAKES:** 1 DOZEN

- **12 uncooked small shrimp, peeled and deveined**
- **3 teaspoons hoisin sauce, divided**
- **1 garlic clove, minced**
- **1½ teaspoons reduced-sodium soy sauce, divided**
- **2 teaspoons canola oil**
- **6 hard-cooked eggs**
- **¼ cup mayonnaise**
- **Dash ground ginger**
- **Minced chives**

1. In a small skillet, saute the shrimp, 2 teaspoons hoisin sauce, garlic and 1 teaspoon soy sauce in oil until shrimp turn pink. Remove from the heat; set aside.
2. Cut eggs in half lengthwise. Remove yolks; set whites aside. In a small bowl, mash yolks. Add mayonnaise, ginger and remaining hoisin and soy sauce; mix well. Stuff or pipe into egg whites. Garnish with shrimp and chives. Refrigerate until serving.

Curry On Deviled Eggs

Hummus and curry powder in deviled eggs? You bet! One bite of these, and you'll never go back to plain deviled eggs again!

PREP/TOTAL TIME: 20 MIN. **MAKES:** 1 DOZEN

- **6 hard-cooked eggs**
- **⅓ cup hummus**
- **2 tablespoons olive oil**
- **2 tablespoons minced roasted sweet red peppers**
- **1½ teaspoons lemon juice**
- **¼ teaspoon salt**
- **¼ teaspoon curry powder**
- **Dash pepper**
- **Chives and additional roasted sweet red peppers**

1. Cut eggs in half lengthwise. Remove yolks; set whites aside. In a small bowl, mash yolks. Add the hummus, oil, minced red peppers, lemon juice, salt, curry powder and pepper; mix well. Stuff or pipe into egg whites.
2. Garnish eggs with chives and additional red peppers. Refrigerate until serving.

West Coaster Deviled Eggs

Fresh flavors shine in these simple eggs with a hint of heat and a bacon-y finish. Yum!

PREP/TOTAL TIME: 20 MIN. **MAKES:** 1 DOZEN

- **3 thick-sliced bacon strips**
- **6 hard-cooked eggs**
- **2 tablespoons mayonnaise**
- **2 tablespoons guacamole**
- **1 teaspoon minced fresh cilantro**
- **⅛ teaspoon garlic powder**
- **⅛ teaspoon cayenne pepper**
- **Dash salt**

1. In a small skillet, cook bacon over medium heat until crisp. Remove to paper towels. Cut each into four pieces.
2. Cut eggs in half lengthwise. Remove yolks; set whites aside. In a small bowl, mash yolks. Add the mayonnaise, guacamole, cilantro and seasonings; mix well. Stuff or pipe into egg whites. Garnish with bacon. Refrigerate until serving.

ULTIMATE OSCAR PARTY!

HOST A WINNING OSCAR BASH AT HOME WITH OUR EASY MOVIE-THEMED TAPAS MENU

Lights! Camera! Action! Once a year, the stars come out for a night of true Hollywood glamour. This year, why not join all the beautiful people and invite a few film-buff friends over for the ultimate red carpet affair? Our winning appetizer menu is simple, smart and inexpensive, so you're guaranteed to win the best food award. And our no-fuss decor ideas and keep-the-night-moving tips let you go glitzy with ease. Place the TV so all can see—the show is about to begin!

American Beauty

The perfect signature drink for your soiree, this is surprisingly smooth, so it'll go down easy. But be careful: Too many of these and you'll go from American Beauty to Sleeping Beauty!
—TASTE OF HOME TEST KITCHEN

PREP/TOTAL TIME: 5 MIN. **MAKES:** 1 SERVING

- **Ice cubes**
- **½ ounce dry vermouth**
- **½ ounce orange juice**
- **½ ounce brandy**
- **½ ounce grenadine syrup**
- **¼ teaspoon clear creme de menthe**
- **1 teaspoon port wine**

1. Fill a shaker three-fourths full with ice. Add the vermouth, orange juice, brandy, grenadine and creme de menthe; cover and shake for 10-15 seconds or until condensation forms on the outside of shaker. Strain into a chilled cocktail glass; top with port wine.

Sausage Ratatouille

You'll feel like Ratatouille's great chef, Remy, when you serve this veggie-packed dish guests will rave about. Don't let the ingredient list fool you—pantry staples and an easy-cook method make this recipe a cinch.
—JANINE FREEMAN BLAINE, WASHINGTON

PREP: 20 MIN. **COOK:** 25 MIN. **MAKES:** 24 SERVINGS

- **2 pounds sweet Italian sausage links, cut into ½-inch slices**
- **½ pound fresh green beans, trimmed and cut into 2-inch pieces**
- **2 medium green peppers, julienned**
- **1 large onion, chopped**
- **5 shallots, chopped**
- **2 garlic cloves, minced**
- **2 tablespoons butter**
- **2 tablespoons olive oil**
- **4 medium zucchini, quartered and sliced**
- **5 roma tomatoes, chopped**
- **½ teaspoon sugar**
- **½ teaspoon salt**
- **¼ teaspoon pepper**
- **¼ teaspoon crushed red pepper flakes**
- **⅛ teaspoon ground allspice**
- **¼ cup minced fresh parsley**
- **⅓ cup grated Parmesan cheese**
- **Hot cooked rice**

1. In a large skillet, cook sausage over medium heat until no longer pink; drain. Remove and keep warm.
2. In the same skillet, cook the beans, green peppers, onion, shallots and garlic in butter and oil over medium heat until tender. Stir in the zucchini, tomatoes, sugar, salt, pepper, pepper flakes and allspice. Cook and stir for 6-8 minutes or until vegetables are tender.
3. Stir in sausage and parsley; heat through. Sprinkle with cheese. Serve with rice.

Keep the party exciting! Play Oscar bingo (find cards at oscars.org) & check out imdb.com for fun movie facts and trivia!

Gump's Shrimp & Grits

As Forrest Gump would say, shrimp and grits go together like peas and carrots in this appetizer. You'll love the rich sauce, the touch of heat and the refreshing citrus flavor.

—**GENE PETERS** EDWARDSVILLE, ILLINOIS

PREP: 30 MIN. **BAKE:** 15 MIN. **MAKES:** 16 APPETIZERS

- **2¼ cups water**
- **1½ teaspoons Creole seasoning, divided**
- **½ cup uncooked old-fashioned grits**
- **¾ cup shredded smoked Gouda cheese**
- **½ cup butter, melted**
- **¼ cup olive oil**
- **4 garlic cloves, minced**
- **1 teaspoon dried oregano**
- **⅛ teaspoon plus ¼ teaspoon cayenne pepper, divided**
- **1 medium lemon, quartered**
- **16 uncooked jumbo shrimp, deveined**
- **2 cups chopped baby portobello mushrooms**
- **5 bacon strips, finely chopped**
- **2 tablespoons chopped shallot**
- **½ cup white wine**
- **2 cups chopped fresh spinach**
- **1 cup half-and-half cream**

1. In a large saucepan, bring water and 1/2 teaspoon Creole seasoning to a boil. Slowly stir in grits. Reduce heat. Cover and cook for 12-14 minutes or until thickened, stirring occasionally. Add cheese; cook and stir for 2-3 minutes or until melted. Set aside and keep warm.
2. Place butter, oil, garlic, oregano, 1/8 teaspoon cayenne and remaining Creole seasoning in a 13-in. x 9-in. baking dish. Squeeze juice from lemon into dish; add lemon quarters. Bake, uncovered, at 400° for 4-6 minutes or until hot. Add shrimp; bake 10-12 minutes longer or until shrimp turn pink, stirring once.
3. Meanwhile, in a large skillet, cook the mushrooms, bacon, shallot and remaining cayenne over medium heat until bacon is crisp. Add wine, stirring to loosen browned bits from pan. Bring to a boil; cook until liquid is evaporated. Reduce heat; stir in spinach and cream.
4. Peel shrimp, leaving tails on. Spoon grits onto serving dishes; top each with sauce mixture and a shrimp.

Editor's Note: *The following spices may be substituted for 1 teaspoon Creole seasoning: 1/4 teaspoon each salt, garlic powder and paprika; and a pinch each of dried thyme, ground cumin and cayenne pepper.*

Gladiator Chicken Skewers

A mild, creamy sauce with hints of cilantro and lime balances the cayenne kick in these hearty skewers. Serve with extra napkins to help little gladiators keep their party clothes clean.

—**SUSAN SEYMOUR** VALATIE, NEW YORK

PREP/TOTAL TIME: 30 MIN. **MAKES:** 6 SKEWERS (1 CUP SAUCE)

- **1 pound boneless skinless chicken breasts, cut into thin strips**
- **¼ cup dry bread crumbs**
- **1 tablespoon chili powder**
- **½ teaspoon salt**
- **½ teaspoon pepper**
- **¼ teaspoon cayenne pepper**
- **2 tablespoons butter**

SAUCE

- **1 container (8 ounces) sour cream**
- **3 tablespoons minced fresh cilantro**
- **2 teaspoons lime juice, optional**
- **⅛ teaspoon salt**

1. Thread chicken onto six metal or soaked wooden skewers. In a shallow bowl, combine the bread crumbs, chili powder, salt, pepper and cayenne. Coat chicken with crumb mixture. In a large skillet, brown chicken in batches in butter. Place skewers on a greased baking sheet.
2. Bake, uncovered, at 400° for 8-10 minutes or until a meat thermometer reads 170°.
3. Meanwhile, in a small bowl, combine the sour cream, cilantro, lime juice if desired and salt. Serve with chicken skewers.

123 MAKE IT SIMPLE

Short on time? Choose one or two of these recipes to make, and round out the menu with chips and salsa, store-bought fruit or cheese trays and other easy nibbles. Guests will enjoy the bites and you'll enjoy the time to mingle with friends.

MOVIE MUNCHIES

TO JAZZ UP 3 QTS. PLAIN POPCORN, DRIZZLE WITH ¼ CUP MELTED BUTTER COMBINED WITH FLAVORINGS.

You'll never want regular buttered popcorn again! For Buttery Cajun-Style Popcorn, stir melted butter with 2 Tbsp. lime juice and 4½ tsp. Cajun seasoning. Sprinkle with ¼ cup grated Parmesan cheese. For Nacho Popcorn, stir melted butter with 4 tsp. dried parsley, ½ tsp. each garlic salt and chili powder and 3 drops hot pepper sauce. Sprinkle with 4 tsp. grated Parmesan cheese.

Rocky Road Freezer Pie

Whip up this easy chocolaty pie the night before, and you'll feel like a champ when you serve it on party day.

—**ADDRENNE ROTH** DONNA, TEXAS

PREP: 15 MIN. + FREEZING **MAKES:** 16 SERVINGS

- **1½ cups half-and-half cream**
- **1 package (3.9 ounces) instant chocolate pudding mix**
- **1 carton (8 ounces) frozen whipped topping, thawed**
- **⅓ cup semisweet chocolate chips**
- **⅓ cup miniature marshmallows**
- **⅓ cup chopped pecans**
- **1 graham cracker crust (9 inches)**

1. In a large bowl, whisk cream and pudding mix for 2 minutes. Fold in whipped topping. Stir in the chocolate chips, marshmallows and pecans. Transfer to pie crust. Freeze until firm, about 6 hours. Remove from the freezer 10 minutes before serving.

Godfather Crostini

We're going to make you an offer you can't refuse: Spend just a few minutes in the kitchen to serve up an elegant, restaurant quality appetizer that's a fun twist on BLTs. You can't go wrong. Capiche?

—**KENDRA ALLANSON** FRONT ROYAL, VIRGINIA

PREP/TOTAL TIME: 30 MIN. **MAKES:** 16 APPETIZERS

- **1 loaf (8 ounces) French bread, cut into 16 slices**
- **2 tablespoons plus 1 teaspoon olive oil, divided**
- **8 bacon strips, halved**
- **⅓ cup mayonnaise**
- **2 tablespoons minced chives**
- **2 teaspoons lemon juice**
- **16 fresh basil leaves**
- **16 oil-packed sun-dried tomatoes**
- **¼ cup prepared pesto**
- **2 tablespoons shredded Parmesan cheese**

1. Brush bread slices with 2 tablespoons oil and place on an ungreased baking sheet. Bake at 400° for 5-6 minutes on each side or until lightly browned.
2. Meanwhile, in a large skillet, cook bacon over medium heat until crisp. Remove to paper towels to drain.
3. In a small bowl, combine the mayonnaise, chives, lemon juice and remaining oil; spread over toast. Top each with a basil leaf, tomato, pesto and a piece of bacon. Sprinkle with cheese.

Tara's Happy
Orange Turkey

Holiday & Seasonal Pleasers

"Here's the perfect centerpiece for your Thanksgiving feast. Champagne and oranges flavor this special entree. One of my guests called it 'the best turkey recipe ever!'"

TARA BAIER MENOMONIE, WISCONSIN
Happy Orange Turkey, page 265

Crown Roast with Spring Rice Pilaf

Family and friends will feel like royalty when you serve this gorgeous roast.

—TASTE OF HOME TEST KITCHEN

PREP: 30 MIN. **BAKE:** 2 HOURS + STANDING
MAKES: 12 SERVINGS

- **2 medium lemons**
- **1 jar (10 ounces) cherry spreadable fruit**
- **1 envelope Lipton savory herb with garlic soup mix**
- **1 pork crown roast (12 ribs and about 8 pounds)**

RICE PILAF

- **1 cup chopped sweet onion**
- **1 cup sliced fresh mushrooms**
- **¼ cup butter, cubed**
- **2 cups cut fresh asparagus (1-inch pieces)**
- **3 cups chicken broth**
- **½ cup slivered almonds, toasted**
- **½ cup golden raisins**
- **¼ teaspoon pepper**
- **3 cups uncooked instant rice**

SAUCE

- **1 jar (10 ounces) cherry spreadable fruit**
- **6 tablespoons chicken broth**
- **¼ teaspoon salt**

1. Finely grate peel from lemons. Juice lemons, reserving 1 teaspoon for sauce. In a small microwave-safe bowl, combine the spreadable fruit, soup mix, lemon peel and juice. Microwave, uncovered, on high for 30-60 seconds or until heated through.

2. Place roast on a rack in a large shallow roasting pan. Brush fruit mixture over roast. Cover rib ends with foil. Bake, uncovered, at 350° for 1½ hours.

3. Meanwhile, in a large skillet, saute onion and mushrooms in butter until tender. Add asparagus; cook 1-2 minutes longer or until asparagus is crisp-tender. Add the broth, almonds, raisins and pepper. Bring to a boil. Stir in rice. Cover and remove from the heat; let stand for 5 minutes. Fluff with a fork.

4. Carefully spoon stuffing into center of roast. Bake 30-45 minutes longer or until a thermometer reads 145°.

5. Meanwhile, in a small microwave-safe dish, combine the sauce ingredients and reserved lemon juice. Microwave, uncovered, on high for 30-60 seconds or until heated through.

6. Transfer roast to a serving platter. Let stand for 10-15 minutes. Remove foil. Cut between ribs to serve. Serve with sauce.

HESS
SELECT
CABERNET
SAUVIGNON

Elegant Spring Salad

Dried cranberries and grapes add fruity flavor to this lovely and colorful six-ingredient salad.

—**DANELLE MONTEVAGO** HANOVER, MARYLAND

PREP/TOTAL TIME: 15 MIN. **MAKES:** 12 SERVINGS

- **2 packages (5 ounces each) spring mix salad greens**
- **3 cups green grapes, halved**
- **1½ cups dried cranberries**
- **1½ cups pistachios, roasted and salted**
- **1¼ cups (5 ounces) crumbled Gorgonzola cheese**
- **⅔ cup reduced-fat raspberry walnut vinaigrette**

1. In a large bowl, combine the salad greens, grapes, cranberries, pistachios and cheese. Add vinaigrette; toss to coat.

Shhh! SIMPLE SECRET

To prepare ahead of time, wash and halve the green grapes for the Elegant Spring Salad. Store the halved grapes in a resealable plastic bag or tightly sealed container in the refrigerator.

Green Onion Rolls

Better double the batch, because these savory, elegant rolls will disappear fast!

—**JANE KROEGER** KEY LARGO, FLORIDA

PREP: 30 MIN. + RISING **BAKE:** 20 MIN. **MAKES:** 1 DOZEN

- **2 bunches green onions, sliced**
- **1 tablespoon butter**
- **1 loaf (1 pound) frozen bread dough, thawed**
- **½ cup shredded part-skim mozzarella cheese**
- **⅓ cup grated Parmesan cheese**
- **½ teaspoon pepper**
- **¾ teaspoon garlic salt, optional**

1. In a small skillet, saute onions in butter. Roll dough into a 12-in. x 8-in. rectangle. Spread with onion mixture. Sprinkle with cheeses, pepper and garlic salt if desired.

2. Roll up jelly-roll style, starting with the long side; pinch seams to seal. Cut into 12 slices. Place each slice in a greased muffin cup. Cover and let rise in a warm place until doubled, about 30 minutes.

3. Bake at 375° for 18-20 minutes or until golden brown. Cool for 5 minutes before removing to a wire rack. Serve warm.

Brandy-Glazed Carrots

Dress up your carrots with a light brandy sauce for this beautiful side dish with mass appeal.

—**TAMMY LANDRY** SAUCIER, MISSISSIPPI

PREP/TOTAL TIME: 30 MIN. **MAKES:** 12 SERVINGS

- **3 pounds fresh baby carrots**
- **½ cup butter, cubed**
- **½ cup honey**
- **¼ cup brandy**
- **¼ cup minced fresh parsley**
- **½ teaspoon salt**
- **¼ teaspoon pepper**

1. In a large skillet, bring ½ in. of water to a boil. Add carrots. Cover and cook for 5-9 minutes or until crisp-tender. Drain; remove carrots and set aside. In the same skillet, cook butter and honey over medium heat until butter is melted; stir in brandy. Bring to a boil; cook until liquid is reduced to about ½ cup. Add the carrots, parsley, salt and pepper; heat through.

Wow! That's what you'll hear when you bring this showstopping tart to the table. With a hint of mint and lime, luscious blueberries, pleasant ginger and a buttery crust, it's tough to stop at just one slice. —KAREN HICKS MABELVALE, ARKANSAS

Blueberry & Ginger Tart

PREP: 30 MIN. **BAKE:** 40 MIN. + COOLING
MAKES: 14 SERVINGS

- **1¾ cups all-purpose flour**
- **¾ cup packed brown sugar**
- **¾ cup cold butter, cubed**
- **2 tablespoons lime juice, divided**
- **⅔ cup sugar**
- **4 teaspoons cornstarch**
- **1½ teaspoons minced fresh gingerroot**
- **1 teaspoon minced fresh mint**
- **3½ cups fresh or frozen blueberries, thawed**
- **Whipped cream**

1. In a food processor, combine the flour, brown sugar and butter; cover and pulse until mixture resembles coarse crumbs. Remove and set aside 1 cup for topping. Stir 1 tablespoon lime juice into remaining pastry. Press onto the bottom and up the sides of a greased 11-in. fluted tart pan with removable bottom.

2. In a large bowl, combine the sugar, cornstarch, ginger and mint. Add blueberries and remaining lime juice; toss to coat. Transfer to crust. Sprinkle with reserved topping.

3. Bake at 400° for 40-45 minutes or until filling is bubbly and topping is golden brown. Cover edges with foil during the last 15 minutes to prevent overbrowning if necessary. Cool completely on a wire rack. Serve with whipped cream.

It's a good idea to take inventory of your pans before you start this Easter feast. Make sure you have a large shallow roasting pan with a rack for the pork roast, an 11-in. fluted tart pan with a removable bottom for the blueberry tart and a standard-size muffin pan for the rolls.

Grilled Fajita Rolled Steak

My family was tired of eating the same old fajitas, so I whipped up this new recipe. I like it with chipotle, but a black pepper marinade also works well.

—CRYSTAL BRUNS ILIFF, COLORADO

PREP: 20 MIN. **GRILL:** 20 MIN. **MAKES:** 4 SERVINGS

- **1 beef sirloin tip steak (1 inch thick and 1 pound)**
- **1 cup chipotle marinade**
- **1 package (14 ounces) frozen pepper strips**
- **1 tablespoon canola oil**
- **2 ounces cream cheese, softened**

1. Flatten steak to 1/4-in. thickness. Pour marinade into a large resealable plastic bag; add steak. Seal bag and turn to coat; refrigerate for 4 hours or overnight, turning occasionally.
2. In a large skillet, saute pepper strips in oil until tender. Remove from the heat. Drain and discard marinade from steak. Spread cream cheese over steak to within 1 in. of edges. Top with half of the peppers. Roll up jelly-roll style, starting with a long side; tie with kitchen string.
3. Grill, covered, over medium heat for 20-25 minutes or until meat reaches desired doneness (for medium-rare, a thermometer should read 145°; medium, 160°; well-done, 170°), turning occasionally. Let stand for 10 minutes before slicing. Discard toothpicks. Serve with remaining pepper strips.

Southwest Rice Pilaf

I like to combine the starch and vegetable in my sides. This one is nice because it blends the tastes of tacos and fajitas—two of my family's favorite dishes.

—MARTHA ULFELDER SOUTHBOROUGH, MASSACHUSETTS

PREP/TOTAL TIME: 30 MIN. **MAKES:** 6 SERVINGS

- **2 cups uncooked instant rice**
- **1 can (11 ounces) Mexicorn, drained**
- **1/3 cup minced fresh cilantro**
- **2 tablespoons butter**
- **1/2 teaspoon salt**

1. Cook rice according to package directions. Stir in the Mexicorn, cilantro, butter and salt.

Carnitas Tacos

The house smells fantastic all day long when I'm slow-simmering this. The tacos have so much flavor, you'd never guess they use just five ingredients. And I love that they're ready when you need them at the end of the day.

—MARY WOOD MAIZE, KANSAS

PREP: 5 MIN. **COOK:** 6 HOURS **MAKES:** 12 SERVINGS

- **1 boneless pork shoulder butt roast (3 to 4 pounds)**
- **1 envelope taco seasoning**
- **1 can (10 ounces) diced tomatoes and green chilies, undrained**
- **12 flour tortillas (8 inches), warmed**
- **2 cups (8 ounces) shredded Colby-Monterey Jack cheese**
- **Sour cream, optional**

1. Cut roast in half; place in a 4- or 5-qt. slow cooker. Sprinkle with taco seasoning. Pour tomatoes over top. Cover and cook on low for 6-8 hours or until meat is tender.
2. Remove meat from slow cooker; shred with two forks. Skim fat from cooking juices. Return meat to slow cooker; heat through. Using a slotted spoon, place 1/2 cup on each tortilla; top with cheese. Serve with sour cream if desired.

Cerveza Margaritas

One sip of this refreshing drink and you'll picture sand, sea and blue skies that stretch for miles. It's like a vacation in a glass, and you can mix it up in moments. What are you waiting for?

—CHRISTINA BREMSON PARKVILLE, MISSOURI

PREP/TOTAL TIME: 10 MIN. **MAKES:** 5 SERVINGS

- **Lime slices and kosher salt, optional**
- **1 can (12 ounces) lemon-lime soda, chilled**
- **1 bottle (12 ounces) beer**
- **1 can (12 ounces) frozen limeade concentrate, thawed**
- **3/4 cup tequila**
- **Crushed ice**

1. If desired, use lime slices to moisten the rims of five margarita or cocktail glasses. Sprinkle salt on a plate; dip rims in salt. Set glasses aside.
2. In a pitcher, combine the soda, beer, limeade concentrate and tequila. Serve in prepared glasses over crushed ice.

Grilled Peaches & Pound Cake

Brush up on grilling dessert with fresh peaches and pound cake. Store-bought cake makes it quick to prepare, and the caramelized flavor will make it disappear fast!

—**JOY PENDLEY** ORTONVILLE, MICHIGAN

PREP/TOTAL TIME: 20 MIN. **MAKES:** 6 SERVINGS

- **3 medium peaches, sliced**
- **1 tablespoon balsamic vinegar**
- **1 loaf (10¾ ounces) frozen pound cake, thawed**
- **¼ cup packed brown sugar**
- **2 tablespoons butter, melted**
- **6 scoops vanilla ice cream**

1. Brush peaches with vinegar and place in a grill wok or basket. Grill, uncovered, over medium heat for 10-12 minutes or until tender, stirring frequently.
2. Cut pound cake into six slices. In a small bowl, combine brown sugar and butter; brush over both sides of cake slices. Grill, uncovered, over medium heat for 1-2 minutes on each side or until light golden brown. Place cake slices on serving plates and top with peaches and ice cream.

Editor's Note: *If you do not have a grill wok or basket, use a disposable foil pan. Poke holes in the bottom of the pan with a meat fork to allow liquid to drain.*

Beer Can Chicken

PREP: 20 MIN. **GRILL:** 1¼ HOURS + STANDING
MAKES: 4 SERVINGS

- **4 teaspoons chicken seasoning**
- **2 teaspoons sugar**
- **2 teaspoons chili powder**
- **1½ teaspoons paprika**
- **1¼ teaspoons dried basil**
- **¼ teaspoon pepper**
- **1 broiler/fryer chicken (3 to 4 pounds)**
- **1 tablespoon canola oil**
- **2 lemon slices**
- **1 can (12 ounces) beer or nonalcoholic beer**

1. In a small bowl, combine the first six ingredients. Gently loosen skin from the chicken. Brush chicken with oil. Sprinkle 1 teaspoon of spice mixture into cavity. Rub the remaining spice mixture over and under the skin. Place lemon slices in neck cavity. Tuck wing tips behind the back.
2. Prepare grill for indirect heat, using a drip pan. Pour out half of the beer, reserving for another use. Poke additional holes in top of the can with a can opener. Holding the chicken with legs pointed down, lower chicken over the can so it fills the body cavity.
3. Place chicken over drip pan; grill, covered, over indirect medium heat for 1¼ to 1½ hours or until a thermometer reads 180°. Remove chicken from grill; cover and let stand for 10 minutes. Remove chicken from can.

Editor's Note: *This recipe was tested with McCormick's Montreal Chicken Seasoning. Look for it in the spice aisle.*

Green Bean & Balsamic Salad

Fresh and crisp, this summery salad just begs to be taken to picnics and potlucks. Tossed with vinaigrette, it's a smart side dish for outdoor meals.

—**AMANDA SMITH** LEXINGTON, TENNESSEE

PREP/TOTAL TIME: 30 MIN. **MAKES:** 6 SERVINGS

- **¾ pound fresh green beans, trimmed**
- **3 cups cherry tomatoes, quartered**
- **1¾ cups quartered English cucumber**
- **6 tablespoons olive oil**
- **3 tablespoons balsamic vinegar**
- **1½ teaspoons ground mustard**
- **½ teaspoon salt**
- **½ teaspoon pepper**
- **¼ teaspoon sugar**
- **¼ teaspoon garlic powder**

1. Place beans in a large saucepan and cover with water. Bring to a boil. Cover and cook for 3 minutes. Drain and immediately place beans in ice water. Drain and pat dry.
2. In a large bowl, combine the tomatoes, cucumber and beans. In a small bowl, whisk the remaining ingredients. Pour over vegetables; toss to coat.

"This is a stand-up chicken that you'll be proud to serve at any family gathering. Treated to a savory rub, then roasted over a beer can for added moisture, it's so tasty you'll want to call dibs on the leftovers now!"

—**SHIRLEY WARREN** THIENSVILLE, WISCONSIN

Gourmet Caramel Apples

These drizzled confections look gorgeous and taste over-the-top yummy. With peanut butter flavor and a salty burst, they'll be the treats you can't wait to make every autumn.

—TASTE OF HOME TEST KITCHEN

PREP: 20 MIN. + STANDING
MAKES: 4 SERVINGS

- **4 large tart apples**
- **4 Popsicle sticks**
- **1 cup milk chocolate chips**
- **1 cup semisweet chocolate chips**
- **4½ ounces white candy coating, coarsely chopped**
- **1 teaspoon shortening**
- **1 package (11 ounces) Kraft caramel bits**
- **2 tablespoons water**
- **4 pretzel rods, coarsely crushed**
- **½ cup Reese's pieces**

1. Line a baking sheet with waxed paper and grease the paper; set aside. Wash and thoroughly dry apples. Insert a Popsicle stick into the top of each; set aside.
2. Place chocolate chips in separate microwave-safe bowls. Heat in a microwave until melted; stir until smooth. In another microwave-safe bowl, melt candy coating and shortening; stir until smooth.
3. Combine caramels and water in another microwave-safe bowl. Heat in a microwave until melted; stir until smooth. Dip apples into caramel; turn to coat. Immediately press pretzels and Reese's pieces into sides of apples. Drizzle melted chocolate and candy coating over tops. Place on prepared pan; let stand until set.

No-Fail Dipping

Before you start, grease or spray the waxed paper on which you'll place the freshly dipped fruit. Otherwise the warm caramel will stick to the paper. If you're planning on double-dipping fruit, dip fruit in caramel and let it set. Use a small knife to remove any residual caramel rings before dipping the fruit again.

Ghost Caramel Pears

Whip up some double-dipped pear ghosts so simple it's scary! Display them on your table for a fun Halloween centerpiece—the whimsical faces will make them the life of any party.

—TASTE OF HOME TEST KITCHEN

PREP: 30 MIN. + STANDING **MAKES:** 4 SERVINGS

- **4 medium ripe Bosc pears**
- **4 Popsicle sticks**
- **1 package (11 ounces) Kraft caramel bits**
- **2 tablespoons water**
- **1 pound white candy coating, coarsely chopped**
- **1 tablespoon shortening**
- **Red and black shoestring licorice, blanched almonds and miniature semisweet chocolate chips**

1. Line a baking sheet with waxed paper and grease the paper; set aside. Wash and thoroughly dry pears; insert a Popsicle stick into the top of each.
2. Melt caramels and water in a microwave; stir until smooth. Dip each pear into caramel; turn to coat. Place on prepared pan and let stand until set.
3. Melt candy coating and shortening at 50% power for 1 minute; stir. Microwave at additional 20- to 30-second intervals, stirring until smooth. Dip pears into coating; allow excess to drip off. Decorate faces as desired; return to pan and let stand until set.

Salted Caramel & Dark Chocolate Figs

Here's a special appetizer that won't last long! Fruit, caramel and rich dark chocolate add a wonderfully sweet touch to this grown-up dipped fruit.

—TASTE OF HOME TEST KITCHEN

PREP: 30 MIN. + STANDING **MAKES:** 1 DOZEN

- **12 large toothpicks**
- **12 dried figs**
- **4 ounces fresh goat cheese**
- **1 teaspoon honey**
- **1 teaspoon balsamic vinegar**
- **1 package (11 ounces) Kraft caramel bits**
- **2 tablespoons water**
- **1/3 cup finely chopped almonds**
- **1 1/2 cups dark chocolate chips, melted**
- **Coarse sea salt**

1. Line a baking sheet with waxed paper and grease the paper; set aside.
2. Insert a toothpick into each fig. Make a 1/2-in. cut on the side of each fig. Combine the cheese, honey and vinegar in a small bowl. Transfer to a heavy-duty resealable plastic bag; cut a small hole in a corner of bag. Pipe cheese mixture into figs.
3. Melt caramels and water in a microwave; stir until smooth. Dip each fig into caramel; turn to coat. Place on prepared pan; let stand until set.
4. Place almonds in a small shallow bowl. Dip bottom third of each fig into melted chocolate; allow excess to drip off. Dip into almonds and sprinkle with salt. Return to pan; let stand until set.

Trick-or-Treat Cake

When we were kids, my younger sisters and I always went trick-or-treating together. Once we had our loot, we'd come home, throw it on the floor and start sorting. Recalling those fun times, I came up with the idea for this easy cake shaped like a treat bag with lots of yummy candy spilling out of it.

—**AMY MCCOY** HUNTINGTON BEACH, CALIFORNIA

PREP: 30 MIN. **BAKE:** 35 MIN. + COOLING **MAKES:** 12 SERVINGS

- **1 package (18 1/4 ounces) chocolate cake mix**
- **2 cans (16 ounces each) vanilla frosting**
- **1 tube each black, orange and green decorating gel**
- **Assorted candies**

1. Prepare and bake cake according to package directions, using a greased and floured 13-in. x 9-in. baking pan. Cool for 10 minutes before removing from pan to a wire rack to cool completely.
2. Transfer the cake to a 20-in. x 17-in. covered board. Create a zigzag pattern on one short end of cake to resemble the top of a treat bag. Spread top and sides of cake with frosting; decorate, as desired, with gels and candies.

Chocolate and orange are always delicious, but add gooey caramel and the result is scrumptious! Let kids help paint the leaves with candy coating for a memorable fall treat.
—TASTE OF HOME TEST KITCHEN

Chocolate Caramel Oranges

PREP: 50 MIN. + CHILLING
MAKES: 4 SERVINGS

- **½ cup each yellow, green, orange and red candy coating disks**
- **16 to 20 small lemon, rose or mint leaves**
- **2½ cups dark chocolate chips**
- **2 tablespoons shortening**
- **4 Popsicle sticks**
- **4 large navel oranges, peeled**
- **1 package (11 ounces) Kraft caramel bits**
- **2 tablespoons water**

1. Place candy coatings in separate microwave-safe bowls. Heat in a microwave until melted; stir until smooth. With a small new paint brush, brush candy coating in a thin layer on the underside of each leaf. Refrigerate until set, about 10 minutes.

2. Apply a second layer of candy coating to leaves; refrigerate for at least 15 minutes or overnight. Gently peel leaves from coating.

3. Line a baking sheet with waxed paper and grease the paper; set aside. In a microwave, melt chocolate chips and shortening; stir until smooth. Dip ends of Popsicle sticks into chocolate and insert into oranges. Let stand until chocolate is set.

4. Melt caramels and water in a microwave; stir until smooth. Dip oranges into caramel; turn to coat. Place on prepared pan and let stand until set.

5. Remelt chocolate if necessary. Dip oranges into chocolate; allow excess to drip off. Attach leaves as desired. Return to pan; refrigerate until serving. Cut with a serrated knife.

Tara's Happy
Orange Turkey

Happy Orange Turkey

Here's the perfect centerpiece for your Thanksgiving feast. Champagne and oranges flavor this special entree. One of my guests called it "the best turkey recipe ever!"

—**TARA BAIER** MENOMONIE, WISCONSIN

PREP: 30 MIN. **BAKE:** 3¾ HOURS + STANDING **MAKES:** 14 SERVINGS

- 3 **medium oranges**
- ½ **cup butter, softened**
- 1 **turkey (14 to 16 pounds)**
- 1 **tablespoon garlic powder**
- 1 **teaspoon salt**
- ½ **teaspoon pepper**
- 2 **tablespoons butter, melted**
- 1 **small onion, cut into wedges**
- 4 **fresh rosemary sprigs**
- 2 **fresh thyme sprigs**
- 2 **tablespoons all-purpose flour**
- **Turkey-size oven roasting bag**
- 1½ **cups Champagne**
- ½ **cup orange juice**

1. Finely grate peel from oranges. Cut the fruit into wedges. Combine softened butter and orange peel. With fingers, carefully loosen skin from the turkey; rub butter mixture under the skin.

2. Pat turkey dry. Combine the garlic powder, salt and pepper; rub over the outside and inside of turkey. Drizzle with melted butter. Place the oranges, onion, rosemary and thyme inside the cavity. Skewer turkey openings; tie drumsticks together.

3. Place flour in oven bag and shake to coat. Place oven bag in a roasting pan. Place turkey, breast side up, in bag. Pour Champagne and orange juice over turkey. Cut six 1/2-in. slits in top of bag; close bag with tie provided.

4. Bake at 325° for 3¾ to 4¼ hours or until a thermometer inserted in thigh reads 180°. Remove turkey to a serving platter and keep warm. Let stand for 20 minutes before carving. If desired, thicken pan drippings for gravy.

Grandma's Turkey Gravy

This stress-free recipe will impress Grandma herself! Seasonings and a shallot add wonderful flavor to the velvety gravy, which tastes just as good the next day.

—**JESSE KLAUSMEIER** BURBANK, CALIFORNIA

PREP/TOTAL TIME: 20 MIN. **MAKES:** 2 CUPS

- **Roasted turkey drippings**
- **Reduced-sodium chicken broth**
- 1 **shallot, finely chopped**
- ¼ **cup all-purpose flour**
- ½ **teaspoon salt**
- ¼ **teaspoon onion powder**
- ¼ **teaspoon poultry seasoning**
- ¼ **teaspoon pepper**

1. Pour drippings into a 2-cup measuring cup. Skim fat, reserving 1/4 cup. Add enough broth to the drippings to measure 2 cups.

2. Saute shallot in reserved fat in a small saucepan. Stir in the flour, salt, onion powder, poultry seasoning and pepper until blended; cook and stir for 2 minutes or until browned (do not burn). Gradually add broth. Bring to a boil; cook and stir for 2 minutes or until thickened.

TAKING SHORTCUTS

SHORTCUTS ARE OK! IF YOU PLAN TO MAKE THE WHOLE MEAL, CONSIDER THESE POINTERS.

- Picking up cheese and sausage, fruit or veggie platters or fresh shrimp and dip appetizers.
- Buying ready-made dinner rolls or purchasing a bakery pie.
- Roasting the turkey in a roasting bag. Choose a roasting pan that's at least 2 inches deep and large enough to allow room for the bag to expand in cooking without touching any racks, heating elements or oven walls.
- Using the slow cooker for sides or hot drinks.

Chive Smashed Potatoes

No need to peel the potatoes—in fact, this is the only way we make mashed potatoes anymore. They're chunky, tasty and attractive. And the flavored cream cheese is a delightful twist!

—BEVERLY NORRIS EVANSTON, WYOMING

PREP/TOTAL TIME: 30 MIN. **MAKES:** 12 SERVINGS (⅔ CUP EACH)

- **4 pounds red potatoes, quartered**
- **2 teaspoons chicken bouillon granules**
- **1 carton (8 ounces) spreadable chive and onion cream cheese**
- **½ cup half-and-half cream**
- **¼ cup butter, cubed**
- **1 teaspoon salt**
- **¼ teaspoon pepper**

1. Place potatoes and bouillon in a Dutch oven and cover with 8 cups water. Bring to a boil. Reduce heat; cover and cook for 15-20 minutes or until tender.
2. Drain and return to pan. Mash potatoes with cream cheese, cream, butter, salt and pepper.

Spiced Eggnog Pumpkin Pie

With its 10-minute prep time and lovely blend of mild eggnog flavor and spices, this is a busy hostess' dream dessert! It's a staple for Thanksgiving and Christmas. In fact, my grown kids request it whenever they come to visit.

—PATTI LEAKE COLUMBIA, MISSOURI

PREP: 10 MIN. **BAKE:** 45 MIN. + COOLING **MAKES:** 8 SERVINGS

- **Pastry for single-crust pie (9 inches)**
- **1 can (15 ounces) solid-pack pumpkin**
- **1¼ cups eggnog**
- **¾ cup sugar**
- **2 eggs**
- **1 teaspoon ground cinnamon**
- **½ teaspoon salt**
- **½ teaspoon ground ginger**
- **¼ teaspoon ground cloves**
- **¼ teaspoon ground nutmeg**

1. Roll out pastry to fit a 9-in. pie plate. Transfer pastry to pie plate. Trim pastry to ½ in. beyond edge of plate; flute edges.
2. Place the remaining ingredients in a large bowl; beat just until smooth. Pour into pastry.
3. Bake at 425° for 15 minutes. Reduce heat to 350°; bake 30-35 minutes longer or until a knife inserted near the center comes out clean. (Cover edges with foil during the last 15 minutes to prevent overbrowning if necessary.) Cool completely on a wire rack. Store in the refrigerator.

Editor's Note: *This recipe was tested with commercially prepared eggnog.*

Pan Gravy

Use this basic recipe to prepare gravy from meats and poultry that have been roasted in an uncovered roasting pan.

—TASTE OF HOME TEST KITCHEN

PREP/TOTAL TIME: 15 MIN. **MAKES:** 2 CUPS

- **Roasted meat drippings**
- **¼ cup all-purpose flour**
- **Chicken broth or water**
- **Salt, pepper and browning sauce, optional**

1. Pour pan drippings into a measuring cup. Loosen the browned bits from the roasting pan and add to the drippings. Skim fat.
2. Reserve ¼ cup fat and transfer to a small saucepan; whisk in flour until smooth. Add enough broth or water to pan drippings to measure 2 cups. Gradually stir into flour mixture in saucepan. Bring to a boil; cook and stir for 2 minutes or until thickened. Season with salt, pepper and browning sauce if desired.

Orange Tarragon Turkey Gravy: *Skim fat from drippings and discard. Add enough water to turkey drippings to measure 1½ cups. Combine flour and ½ cup orange juice until smooth. Stir in drippings, 1 teaspoon chicken bouillon granules, ¼ teaspoon dried tarragon and ⅛ teaspoon white pepper. Proceed as directed.*
Yield: *2 cups.*

Patti's Spiced
Eggnog
Pumpkin Pie

Pomegranate Orange Salsa

Pomegranates give this salsa a wonderful, sweet-tart flavor.

—NANCEE MAYNARD BOX ELDER, SOUTH DAKOTA

PREP: 10 MIN. + CHILLING **MAKES:** 4 CUPS

1 can (15 ounces) mandarin oranges
3⅓ cups pomegranate seeds
¼ cup minced fresh cilantro
2 jalapeno peppers, seeded and finely chopped
Tortilla chips

1. Drain oranges, reserving 2 tablespoons juice. Cut oranges in half; transfer to a large bowl. Add the pomegranate seeds, cilantro, jalapenos and reserved juice. Cover and refrigerate for 2 hours. Serve with tortilla chips.

Editor's Note: *Wear disposable gloves when cutting hot peppers; the oils can burn skin. Avoid touching your face.*

Reuben Dip

Men love this rich, cheesy dip. It comes together so quickly, you can make it just before guests arrive. I often serve it with rye bread wedges, too.

—MARY JO HAGEY GLADWIN, MICHIGAN

PREP/TOTAL TIME: 15 MIN. **MAKES:** 2½ CUPS

1 tablespoon butter
2 green onions, chopped
1½ cups (6 ounces) shredded Muenster cheese
4 ounces cream cheese, cubed
2 tablespoons ketchup
2 teaspoons Dijon mustard
¼ teaspoon pepper
½ pound cooked corned beef, chopped
1 cup sauerkraut, rinsed and well drained
Assorted crackers

1. Place butter in a small microwave-safe bowl and microwave on high for 20 seconds or until melted. Add onions; cover and cook 1 minute longer.
2. Stir in the cheeses, ketchup, mustard and pepper. Cover and cook on high for 1 minute; stir. Cook 45 seconds longer. Stir in beef.
3. Place sauerkraut in a microwave-safe 1-qt. dish; top with beef mixture. Cover and microwave on high for 2-3 minutes or until heated through. Serve with crackers.

Editor's Note: *This recipe was tested in a 1,100-watt microwave.*

Chocolate Rum Fondue

Who needs a fancy fondue restaurant when you can whip up a chocolate sensation like this in just 10 minutes? You'll love the hint of rum flavor.

—ANGIE SAMPLES MAYSVILLE, GEORGIA

PREP/TOTAL TIME: 10 MIN. **MAKES:** 1½ CUPS

3 milk chocolate Toblerone candy bars (3.52 ounces each), coarsely chopped
⅔ cup heavy whipping cream
4 teaspoons rum or ½ teaspoon rum extract
Pear slices, cubed cake, large marshmallows and/or macaroon cookies

1. In a small heavy saucepan, combine candy bars and cream. Cook and stir over medium-low heat until blended. Remove from the heat; stir in rum.
2. Transfer to a small fondue pot and keep warm. Serve with dippers of your choice.

Beef & Onion Cheese Ball

You've seen cheese balls in the cheese and deli department at the supermarket, but did you know they were this easy to make?

—CHRISSY LESZCZYNSKI MADISON, WISCONSIN

PREP: 10 MIN. + CHILLING **MAKES:** 1⅔ CUPS

1 package (8 ounces) cream cheese, softened
1 package (2 ounces) thinly sliced deli beef, chopped
1 bunch green onions, chopped
1 tablespoon prepared horseradish
1 cup chopped walnuts
Assorted crackers and vegetables

1. In a small bowl, combine the cream cheese, beef, onions and horseradish. Cover and refrigerate for 15 minutes. Shape into a ball, then roll in walnuts. Wrap tightly in plastic wrap.
2. Cover and refrigerate until serving. Serve with crackers and vegetables.

Warm Christmas Punch

Red-hot candies add rich color and spiciness to this festive punch, and the cranberry juice gives it a little tang.

—JULIE STERCHI JACKSON, MISSOURI

PREP: 5 MIN. **COOK:** 2 HOURS **MAKES:** 8 SERVINGS (2 QUARTS)

- **1 bottle (32 ounces) cranberry juice**
- **5 cans (6 ounces each) unsweetened pineapple juice**
- **⅓ cup red-hot candies**
- **1 cinnamon stick (3½ inches)**
- **Additional cinnamon sticks, optional**

1. In a 3-qt. slow cooker, combine juices, red-hots and cinnamon stick. Cover and cook on low for 2-5 hours. Discard cinnamon stick before serving. Use additional cinnamon sticks as stirrers if desired.

Pomegranate Cosmo

Every soiree needs a signature drink. Sugar dresses up this simple cosmo that lets you enjoy a cozy evening with friends and still shake things up.

—TASTE OF HOME TEST KITCHEN

PREP/TOTAL TIME: 10 MIN. **MAKES:** 1 SERVING

- **1 tablespoon coarse red sugar**
- **Ice cubes**
- **1½ ounces lemon-lime soda**
- **1½ ounces pomegranate liqueur or cranberry juice**
- **1 ounce X-Rated fusion liqueur**
- **1 ounce cranberry-pomegranate juice**
- **½ ounce Triple Sec**
- **1 lemon peel strip**
- **1 fresh cranberry**

1. Sprinkle sugar on a plate. Moisten the rim of a cocktail glass with water; hold glass upside down and dip rim into sugar.

2. Fill a shaker three-fourths full with ice. Add the soda, liqueurs, juice and Triple Sec; cover and shake for 10-15 seconds or until condensation forms on outside of shaker. Strain into prepared glass. Garnish with lemon peel strip and cranberry.

Peppered Pork with Asti Cream Sauce

Asti Spumante—a sparkling white wine often served as a dessert wine—lends a splash of sweetness to the silky sauce in this celebratory dish.

—TASTE OF HOME TEST KITCHEN

PREP/TOTAL TIME: 30 MIN. **MAKES:** 4 SERVINGS

- **1 pork tenderloin (1 pound), cut into ¾-inch slices**
- **3½ teaspoons coarsely ground pepper**
- **2¾ teaspoons paprika**
- **1 teaspoon garlic powder**
- **2 tablespoons canola oil, divided**
- **1½ cups sliced fresh mushrooms**
- **1 green onion, sliced**
- **¾ cup reduced-sodium beef broth**
- **⅔ cup Asti Spumante**
- **½ cup heavy whipping cream**

1. Flatten pork to ½-in. thickness. In a large resealable plastic bag, combine pepper, paprika and garlic powder. Add pork, a few pieces at a time, and shake to coat.

2. In a large skillet over medium-high heat, cook pork in 1 tablespoon oil in batches for 3-4 minutes on each side or until a meat thermometer reads 160°. Set aside and keep warm.

3. In the same skillet, saute the mushrooms and onion in remaining oil until tender. Add broth and Asti Spumante. Bring to a boil; cook until liquid is reduced by half, about 8 minutes. Stir in cream. Bring to boil; cook for 3-5 minutes or until thickened. Return pork to pan and heat through.

Caramel Coconut Stars

My grandma always used to bake her holiday cookies with coconut, and these crisp homemade treats remind me of her. They're a fun, simple twist on sugar cookie cutouts.

—**LIZ DELIA** OSWEGO, NEW YORK

PREP: 30 MIN. + CHILLING **BAKE:** 10 MIN./BATCH + COOLING
MAKES: 3½ DOZEN

- **1 cup butter, softened**
- **1½ cups sugar**
- **2 eggs**
- **3 teaspoons vanilla extract**
- **2¾ cups all-purpose flour**
- **2 teaspoons baking powder**
- **¼ teaspoon salt**
- **1 package (11 ounces) Kraft caramel bits**
- **2 tablespoons water**
- **1 cup flaked coconut, toasted**

1. Cream butter and sugar in a large bowl until light and fluffy. Beat in eggs and vanilla. Combine the flour, baking powder and salt; gradually add to creamed mixture and mix well.
2. Divide dough in half. Shape each into a ball, then flatten into a disk. Wrap in plastic wrap and refrigerate for 1 hour.
3. Roll one portion of dough to 1/8-in. thickness on a lightly floured surface. Cut with a floured 3-in. star-shaped cookie cutter. Place 2 in. apart on greased baking sheets. Repeat with remaining dough.
4. Bake at 375° for 6-8 minutes or until edges begin to brown. Remove to wire racks to cool completely.
5. Melt caramel bits and water in a microwave; stir until smooth. Working with a few cookies at a time, spread caramel over cookies and immediately sprinkle with coconut. Let stand until set.

Crème de Menthe Cheesecake Cookies

Some say these are the best cookies they've ever had! Such a cinch to put together with just five ingredients, and so easy to vary. Stir in your favorite baking chips and change up the decorations to suit any holiday. See why they're the best?

—**SHEILA SPORN** HOUSTON, TEXAS

PREP: 15 MIN. **BAKE:** 10 MIN./BATCH + COOLING
MAKES: 4 DOZEN

- **1 tube (16½ ounces) refrigerated sugar cookie dough**
- **1 package (8 ounces) cream cheese, softened**
- **1 egg**
- **1⅓ cups Andes creme de menthe baking chips**
- **Green candy coating disks and sprinkles, optional**

1. Let cookie dough stand at room temperature for 5 minutes to soften. In a large bowl, beat cream cheese until fluffy. Add egg and cookie dough; beat until combined. Add baking chips and mix well. Drop by tablespoonfuls 2 in. apart onto ungreased baking sheets.
2. Bake at 350° for 9-12 minutes or until lightly browned. Cool for 2 minutes before removing from pans to wire racks to cool completely.
3. If decoration is desired, melt candy coating in a microwave. Transfer melted coating to a pastry or plastic bag; cut a small hole in the corner. Pipe designs onto cookies and decorate with sprinkles.

Honey-Nut Christmas Cookies

My sons, Aaron and Zach, adore these at Christmastime and like to warm them in the microwave before they eat them. The treats are well worth the time they take.

—**GLENDA HERZ** LAWRENCE, NEBRASKA

PREP: 30 MIN. **BAKE:** 20 MIN./BATCH **MAKES:** ABOUT 3½ DOZEN

- **2 cups all-purpose flour**
- **1 cup cold butter, cubed**
- **1 package (8 ounces) cream cheese, softened**
- **¼ cup sugar**
- **1½ cups chopped pecans, divided**
- **⅓ cup plus ¼ cup honey, divided**
- **1 teaspoon butter, melted**
- **½ teaspoon ground cinnamon**

1. Place the flour in a large bowl. Cut in cold butter and cream cheese until mixture resembles coarse crumbs. Shape into two disks; wrap in plastic wrap. Refrigerate for 2 hours or until easy to handle.
2. Place sugar and 1 cup pecans in a food processor; cover and process until pecans are finely chopped. Transfer to a small bowl; stir in 1/3 cup honey, butter and cinnamon.
3. On a lightly floured surface, roll one portion of dough to 1/8-in. thickness. Cut with a floured 2-in. round cookie cutter. Place a teaspoonful of filling on the center of half of the circles; top with remaining circles. Press edges with a fork to seal. Repeat with remaining dough.
4. Transfer to greased baking sheets. Brush with remaining honey and sprinkle with remaining pecans. Bake at 325° for 18-22 minutes or until golden brown. Remove to wire racks to cool.

Chocolate Candy Cane Cookies

These cookies are so simple, even children can help prepare them. They taste delicious and look so festive on cookie trays.

—**AGNES WARD** STRATFORD, ONTARIO

PREP: 25 MIN. + CHILLING **BAKE:** 10 MIN./BATCH + STANDING
MAKES: 4 DOZEN

- **¾ cup butter, softened**
- **1 package (8 ounces) cream cheese, softened**
- **1 cup sugar**
- **4 ounces semisweet chocolate, melted and cooled**
- **2 teaspoons vanilla extract**
- **2½ cups all-purpose flour**
- **½ teaspoon baking soda**
- **6 ounces white baking chocolate**
- **⅔ cup crushed spearmint candies**

1. Cream the butter, cream cheese and sugar in a large bowl until light and fluffy. Beat in melted chocolate and vanilla. Combine flour and baking soda; gradually add to creamed mixture and mix well. Refrigerate for 1 hour.
2. Divide dough into 48 pieces; shape each into a 3-in. rope. Place 2 in. apart on greased baking sheets; curve the top of each cookie to form the handle of a candy cane. Bake at 350° for 8-10 minutes or until set. Cool for 1 minute before removing to wire racks to cool completely.
3. Melt white chocolate in a microwave; stir until smooth. Drizzle over the cookies and sprinkle with candies. Let stand until set.

Salted Caramel Fudge Drops

These cookies, which start with a mix, are unbelievably decadent! I like to use caramel-filled Dove chocolates. It's a nice dough to make ahead, roll into balls and freeze for up to 3 months. Then just bake the cookies as you need them.

—**CAROLE HOLT** MENDOTA HEIGHTS, MINNESOTA

PREP: 20 MIN. **BAKE:** 10 MIN./BATCH **MAKES:** 4 DOZEN

- **6 ounces unsweetened chocolate**
- **⅓ cup butter, cubed**
- **1 package (17½ ounces) sugar cookie mix**
- **1 egg**
- **1 can (14 ounces) sweetened condensed milk**
- **1 teaspoon vanilla extract**
- **48 caramel-filled chocolate candies**
- **Coarsely ground sea salt**

1. Melt unsweetened chocolate and butter in a microwave; stir until smooth. Cool slightly. In a large bowl, beat the cookie mix, egg, milk, vanilla and chocolate mixture. Drop by tablespoonfuls 2 in. apart on ungreased baking sheets.

2. Bake at 350° for 8-10 minutes or until edges are set. Press a candy into the center of each cookie. Let stand for 2 minutes. Sprinkle with salt. Remove from pans to wire racks to cool completely.

Snowman Cutouts

As the song goes, "Frosty the snowman was a jolly, happy soul," and you will be, too, when you whip up this easy recipe! Kids of all ages will love rolling out the dough and mixing and matching pieces to make their very own snowmen.

—**TASTE OF HOME TEST KITCHEN**

PREP: 35 MIN.
BAKE: 10 MIN./BATCH + COOLING
MAKES: 2 SNOWMEN

- **1 tube (16½ ounces) refrigerated sugar cookie dough**
- **½ cup all-purpose flour**
- **½ teaspoon almond extract**
- **1 can (16 ounces) vanilla frosting**
- **Food coloring of your choice**

1. Let cookie dough stand at room temperature for 5-10 minutes to soften. In a small bowl, beat the cookie dough, flour and extract until combined.

2. On a lightly floured surface, roll out dough to 1/4-in. thickness. With a floured 4 1/2-in. round cookie cutter, cut out two circles. Repeat with 3 1/2-in. and 3-in. round cookie cutters. Cut out six 1-in. circles, four 1¾-in. mittens and two 2 1/4-in. carrots.

3. On waxed paper, draw a top hat, 3 1/2 in. wide x 2 1/2 in. tall, and a pipe, 3 1/4 in. wide x 1¾ in. tall; cut out. Re-roll dough scraps if necessary. Using patterns, cut out two hats and two pipes.

4. Transfer pieces to greased baking sheets. Bake at 350° for 6-11 minutes or until edges are lightly browned. Remove to wire racks to cool completely.

5. Tint frosting as desired; frost over cookie pieces. Let stand until set. Store in an airtight container.

Do It Yourself

When cookies require canned vanilla frosting, and you don't have any on hand, it's easy to make your own. To make about 2 cups buttercream: Cream ½ cup butter, softened. Beat in 4 cups confectioners' sugar and 1 tsp. vanilla extract. Add 4 to 6 Tbsp. milk until the frosting reaches the desired consistency.

Peppermint S'more Tassies

PREP: 25 MIN.
BAKE: 10 MIN./BATCH + COOLING
MAKES: 3 DOZEN

Graham cracker cookie cups brim with a luscious peppermint-milk chocolate filling, sweet marshmallow creme and crushed peppermint candies. Santa (and his elves) will look forward to these! —EDWINA GADSBY HAYDEN, IDAHO

- **1 package (17½ ounces) sugar cookie mix**
- **½ cup graham cracker crumbs**
- **½ cup butter, softened**
- **1 egg**
- **1 cup milk chocolate chips**
- **⅓ cup heavy whipping cream**
- **½ teaspoon peppermint extract**
- **½ cup marshmallow creme**
- **¼ cup crushed peppermint candies**

1. Place the cookie mix, cracker crumbs, butter and egg in a large bowl; beat until well mixed. Shape into 36 balls; press onto the bottoms and up the sides of greased miniature muffin cups.

2. Bake at 375° for 9-10 minutes or until golden brown. Cool for 30 minutes before removing from pans to wire racks.

3. Meanwhile, place chocolate chips in a small bowl. In a small saucepan, bring cream just to a boil. Pour over chocolate; whisk until smooth. Stir in extract. Let stand for 15 minutes or until cooled. Spoon 2 teaspoons chocolate mixture into each cup.

4. Place marshmallow creme in a small microwave-safe bowl. Microwave at 50% power for 15 seconds or just until softened. Spoon a dollop of marshmallow cream onto each cup; sprinkle with candies.

Shhh! SIMPLE SECRET

To make the Peppermint S'more Tassies ahead of time, bake and cool the cookie cups as directed. Freeze them for up to 1 month. When ready, finish cookies as directed several hours before serving.

Frosted Anise Cookies

I love anise flavoring, and my nana loved sugar cookies, so I put them together. These have a soft, from-scratch texture and are so good, it's hard to stop at just one!

—**RACHELE ANGELONI** NORTH PROVIDENCE, RHODE ISLAND

PREP: 30 MIN. **BAKE:** 10 MIN./BATCH + COOLING
MAKES: 3½ DOZEN

- **1 cup butter, softened**
- **1½ cups sugar**
- **1 egg**
- **1 teaspoon anise extract**
- **2¾ cups all-purpose flour**
- **1 teaspoon baking soda**
- **½ teaspoon baking powder**
- **1 can (16 ounces) vanilla frosting**
- **Holiday sprinkles**

1. Cream the butter and sugar in a large bowl until light and fluffy. Beat in the egg and extract. Combine the flour, baking soda and baking powder; gradually add to the creamed mixture and mix well.
2. Drop by tablespoonfuls 2 in. apart onto ungreased baking sheets. Bake at 375° for 9-11 minutes or until golden brown. Remove to wire racks to cool completely.
3. Spread cookies with frosting and decorate with sprinkles. Let stand until set. Store in an airtight container.

Hot Chocolate Peppermint Cookies

This is a variation of the cookies my mother made when I was growing up. Now my 13-year-old daughter and I bake them together. They're always a huge hit! The taste is like rich hot chocolate baked into a scrumptious cookie.

—**LARRY PIKLOR** JOHNSBURG, ILLINOIS

PREP: 30 MIN. **BAKE:** 10 MIN./BATCH + COOLING
MAKES: 3½ DOZEN

- **1 cup butter, softened**
- **1 cup sugar**
- **1 egg**
- **1 teaspoon peppermint extract**
- **2⅓ cups all-purpose flour**
- **⅓ cup baking cocoa**
- **1 teaspoon salt**
- **1 teaspoon baking soda**
- **1 package (11½ ounces) milk chocolate chips**
- **1 cup marshmallow creme**
- **1 cup finely crushed peppermint candies**

1. Cream butter and sugar in a large bowl until light and fluffy. Beat in the egg and extract. Combine the flour, cocoa powder, salt and baking soda; gradually add to creamed mixture and mix well.
2. Drop by tablespoonfuls 2 in. apart onto greased baking sheets. Bake at 375° for 10-12 minutes or until tops are cracked. Remove to wire racks to cool completely.
3. Melt chocolate chips in a microwave; stir until smooth. Drop a teaspoonful of marshmallow creme into the center of each cookie. Dip half of each cookie into melted chocolate; allow excess to drip off. Immediately sprinkle with candies. Place on waxed paper and let stand until set. Store in an airtight container.

Christmas Elf Cake Pops

Don't you just want to kiss these adorable elves? They are sure to be pop-ular with anyone who loves the taste of PB&J.

—TASTE OF HOME FOOD STYLING TEAM
GREENDALE, WISCONSIN

PREP: 1 HOUR **BAKE:** 35 MIN. + FREEZING
MAKES: 4 DOZEN

- **1 package (18¼ ounces) yellow cake mix**
- **½ cup seedless strawberry jam**
- **48 lollipop sticks**
- **1 can (16 ounces) vanilla frosting**
- **¼ cup creamy peanut butter**
- **1½ cups canned chocolate fudge frosting**
- **Additional vanilla frosting, red paste food coloring and dark chocolate and candy cane-flavored kisses**

1. Prepare and bake cake according to package directions, using a greased 13-in. x 9-in. baking pan. Cool completely on a wire rack.
2. Crumble cake into a large bowl. Add jam and mix well. Shape into 1½-in. balls. Place on baking sheets; insert sticks. Freeze for at least 2 hours or refrigerate for at least 3 hours or until cake balls are firm and easy to handle.
3. Insert cake pops into a Styrofoam block to stand. In a microwave, warm vanilla frosting and peanut butter; stir until smooth. Spoon over cake pops.
4. Tint desired amount of additional vanilla frosting red. Using fudge, vanilla and red frostings, pipe hair and faces; top each with a chocolate or candy cane-flavored kiss hat. Let stand until set.

Candy Coating

Not familiar with candy coating? Also known as confectionery coating, this specialty product is ready for melting and sets up quickly at room temperature. It's available in blocks or disks in grocery stores and comes in white, milk chocolate and dark chocolate varieties.

Snowman Cake Pops

Turn that frosting into Frosty! This is one of our favorite ways to build a snowman—indoors!
—TASTE OF HOME FOOD STYLING TEAM GREENDALE, WISCONSIN

PREP: 1 HOUR + FREEZING **BAKE:** 30 MIN. + COOLING **MAKES:** 3 DOZEN

- **1 package (18¼ ounces) chocolate cake mix**
- **½ cup plus 1 can (16 ounces) cream cheese frosting, divided**
- **36 lollipop sticks**
- **Sprinkles, M&M's minis and red Fruit by the Foot fruit rolls**

1. Prepare and bake cake according to package directions, using a greased 13-in. x 9-in. baking pan. Cool completely on a wire rack.
2. Crumble cake into a large bowl. Add ½ cup frosting and mix well. Shape mixture into thirty-six ¾-in. balls and thirty-six 1-in. balls. Place on baking sheets. Freeze for at least 2 hours or refrigerate for at least 3 hours or until cake balls are firm and easy to handle.
3. To assemble snowmen, insert a lollipop stick into a large cake ball and then a small cake ball. Insert cake pops into a foam block to stand. In a microwave, warm remaining frosting; stir until smooth. Spoon frosting over each pop.
4. Using sprinkles, add faces and buttons to snowmen. Add earmuffs and scarves with M&M's and pieces of fruit rolls. Let stand until set.

Fun & Festive Cake Pops

Pop goes the party! No worries on who's cutting the cake; just serve and watch them disappear!

—**TASTE OF HOME FOOD STYLING TEAM** GREENDALE, WISCONSIN

PREP: 1 HOUR **BAKE:** 35 MIN. + FREEZING **MAKES:** 4 DOZEN

- **1 package (18¼ ounces) cake mix of your choice**
- **1 cup prepared frosting of your choice**
- **48 lollipop sticks**
- **2½ pounds dark chocolate, milk chocolate or white candy coating, coarsely chopped**
- **Optional toppings: crushed peppermint candies, finely chopped cashews, unsweetened coconut, assorted sprinkles, finely chopped crystallized ginger, crushed gingersnap cookies, melted caramels and coarse sea salt**

1. Prepare and bake cake mix according to package directions, using a greased 13-in. x 9-in. baking pan. Cool completely on a wire rack.

2. Crumble cake into a large bowl. Add frosting and mix well. Shape into 1½-in. balls. Place on baking sheets; insert sticks. Freeze for at least 2 hours or refrigerate for at least 3 hours or until cake balls are firm.

3. In a microwave, melt candy coating. Dip each cake ball in coating; allow excess to drip off. Roll, sprinkle or drizzle with toppings of your choice. Insert cake pops into a Styrofoam block to stand. Let stand until set.

Present Cake Pops

If only all wrapping paper tasted this sweet. We used cut strips of Fruit Roll-Ups for ribbon, but the pop-sibilities are endless!

—**TASTE OF HOME FOOD STYLING TEAM** GREENDALE, WISCONSIN

PREP: 1 HOUR **BAKE:** 25 MIN. + FREEZING **MAKES:** 4 DOZEN

- **1 package (18¼ ounces) yellow cake mix**
- **½ cup plus 1 can (16 ounces) vanilla frosting, divided**
- **48 lollipop sticks**
- **Fruit by the Foot fruit rolls**

1. Prepare and bake cake according to package directions, using a greased 13-in. x 9-in. baking pan. Cool completely on a wire rack.

2. Crumble cake into a large bowl. Add ½ cup frosting and mix well. Press cake mixture into silicone ice cube trays; insert a lollipop stick into each. Freeze for at least 2 hours or until cake cubes are firm.

3. Run a small spatula around the edge of each cake cube to loosen; remove from trays. In a microwave, warm remaining vanilla frosting; stir until smooth. Dip pops in frosting. Insert cake pops into a foam block to stand. Form ribbons and bows with strips of fruit rolls. Let stand until set.

Shhh! SIMPLE SECRET

If you have a little frosting left over after decorating the cake pops, use it to make more sweet treats. Spread some of the frosting over a graham cracker or the flat side of a cookie, such as a vanilla wafer or gingersnap, then top with another cookie or cracker.

280
288
290

Easy Odds & Ends

"Pork chops are a great economical cut of meat and cook up quickly, making them ideal for busy weeknight meals. But turning out tender chops can be tricky. Browning them first, then finishing them in this tangy, slightly sweet sauce results in perfectly cooked chops."

SUSAN BENTLEY BURLINGTON, NEW JERSEY
Pork Chops in a Honey-Mustard Sauce, page 295

CONDIMENTS & LIGHT DRESSINGS

Honey-Mustard Salad Dressing

This delicious dressing has only four ingredients, but it's big on flavor. My family loves the thick, tangy golden topping over a mixture of fresh greens and mushrooms.
—**JOANNE HOF** LOS ALAMOS, NEW MEXICO

PREP/TOTAL TIME: 10 MIN. **MAKES:** 1 CUP

- **3 tablespoons honey**
- **2 tablespoons Dijon mustard**
- **¼ cup cider vinegar**
- **½ cup canola oil**

1. In a small bowl, combine honey and mustard. Add vinegar; whisk until blended. Gradually whisk in oil. Store in an airtight container in the refrigerator.

Tangy Barbecue Sauce

This sweet and tangy basting sauce came from my husband's family. With just four ingredients, it's simple to stir up. A speedy alternative to bottled sauce, it can be brushed on chicken, ribs, brisket, pork or even turkey.
—**JENINE SCHMIDT** STOUGHTON, WISCONSIN

PREP/TOTAL TIME: 5 MIN. **MAKES:** 1⅓ CUPS

- **1 cup ketchup**
- **⅔ cup packed brown sugar**
- **2 teaspoons prepared mustard**
- **½ teaspoon ground nutmeg**

1. In a bowl, whisk all ingredients. Use as a basting sauce for grilled meat.

Classic Tartar Sauce

You'll never buy tartar sauce again once you've tasted this super-easy homemade version!
—**MICHELLE STROMKO** DARLINGTON, MARYLAND

PREP/TOTAL TIME: 10 MIN. **MAKES:** 1 CUP

- **⅔ cup chopped dill pickles**
- **½ cup mayonnaise**
- **3 tablespoons finely chopped onion**
- **Dash pepper**

1. In a small bowl, combine all ingredients. Cover and refrigerate until serving.

Classic Pesto

This versatile pesto boasts a perfect basil flavor. Pair it with pasta and you've got a classic Italian dinner!
—**IOLA EGLE** BELLA VISTA, ARKANSAS

PREP/TOTAL TIME: 10 MIN. **MAKES:** 1 CUP

- **4 cups loosely packed basil leaves**
- **½ cup grated Parmesan cheese**
- **2 garlic cloves, halved**
- **¼ teaspoon salt**
- **½ cup pine nuts, toasted**
- **½ cup olive oil**

1. Place basil, cheese, garlic and salt in a food processor; cover and pulse until chopped. Add nuts; cover and process until blended. While processing, gradually add oil in a steady stream.

Chili Seafood Sauce

My husband and I like to treat ourselves to a shrimp appetizer. This sauce goes wonderfully with breaded jumbo butterfly shrimp.
—**ALYCE WYMAN** PEMBINA, NORTH DAKOTA

PREP/TOTAL TIME: 5 MIN. **MAKES:** 1 CUP

- **½ cup ketchup**
- **½ cup chili sauce**
- **1 tablespoon lemon juice**
- **1 tablespoon prepared horseradish**
- **⅛ teaspoon hot pepper sauce**

1. In a small bowl, combine the ketchup, chili sauce, lemon juice, horseradish and pepper sauce. Cover and refrigerate until serving.

Tangy Barbecue Sauce
Honey-Mustard Salad Dressing

Blue Cheese Dressing

No one will ever guess that this chunky salad dressing is low in fat.
—CAROLYN STEELE MARATHON SHORES, FLORIDA

PREP/TOTAL TIME: 15 MIN. **MAKES:** ABOUT ¾ CUP

- **½ cup fat-free mayonnaise**
- **2 tablespoon 1% milk**
- **1 tablespoon lemon juice**
- **½ teaspoon sugar**
- **¼ teaspoon garlic powder**
- **¼ teaspoon ground mustard**
- **½ cup crumbled blue cheese**
- **Salad greens**

1. In a small bowl, combine the first six ingredients; blend until smooth. Add blue cheese; mix well. Serve over greens. Cover and refrigerate any extra dressing.

Citrus-Marmalade Vinaigrette

Add this fresh-tasting splash of citrus to a wide variety of salad mixings.
—SARAH VASQUES MILFORD, NEW HAMPSHIRE

PREP/TOTAL TIME: 10 MIN. **MAKES:** ¾ CUP

- **⅓ cup olive oil**
- **3 tablespoons lemon juice**
- **2 tablespoons orange marmalade**
- **4 teaspoons minced fresh thyme**
- **1 tablespoon Dijon mustard**
- **2 teaspoons grated lemon peel**
- **⅛ teaspoon salt**

1. In a small bowl whisk all ingredients. Chill until serving.

ON THE LIGHT SIDE

IF YOU'RE COUNTING CALORIES AND GRAMS OF FAT, THERE'S NO NEED TO SACRIFICE FLAVOR!

Five of the dressings on these pages and the next are light: the Blue Cheese and Balsamic are less than 50 calories per 2 tablespoons (with 2 grams or less of saturated fat), the Makeover Honey French and Light Green Goddess are less than 100 calories per 2 tablespoons (with 1 gram of saturated fat or less) and the Citrus-Marmalade is 128 calories per 2 tablespoons (with 2 grams of saturated fat). So, if you're watching calories, no need to fret about adding a little extra dressing to your favorite salad. We've got you covered!

Makeover Honey French Dressing

This makeover recipe has half the fat, about 40% fewer calories and a third less sodium than regular, but still adds gusto to salads!
—TASTE OF HOME TEST KITCHEN

PREP/TOTAL TIME: 5 MIN. **MAKES:** 2 CUPS

- **½ cup ketchup**
- **½ cup honey**
- **½ cup chopped onion**
- **⅓ cup cider vinegar**
- **¼ cup apricot nectar**
- **3 garlic cloves, minced**
- **1 teaspoon paprika**
- **½ teaspoon celery seed**
- **¼ teaspoon salt**
- **⅓ cup canola oil**

1. In a blender or food processor, combine the first nine ingredients; cover and process until blended. While processing, add oil in a steady stream. Process until thickened. Store in the refrigerator.

Greens with Balsamic Vinaigrette

Even when there are just two at the table, I always see to it that the dinner salads are well-dressed. And I always keep a bottle of this light dressing in the fridge.
—**SANDY HUNT** RACINE, WISCONSIN

PREP/TOTAL TIME: 5 MIN. **MAKES:** ⅔ CUP

- **1 tablespoon Dijon mustard**
- **¼ cup water**
- **2 tablespoons olive oil**
- **¼ cup balsamic vinegar**
- **1 tablespoon minced fresh basil**
- **½ teaspoon pepper**
- **Salad greens and vegetables of your choice**

1. In a jar with a tight-fitting lid, combine the first six ingredients; shake well. Serve over salad.

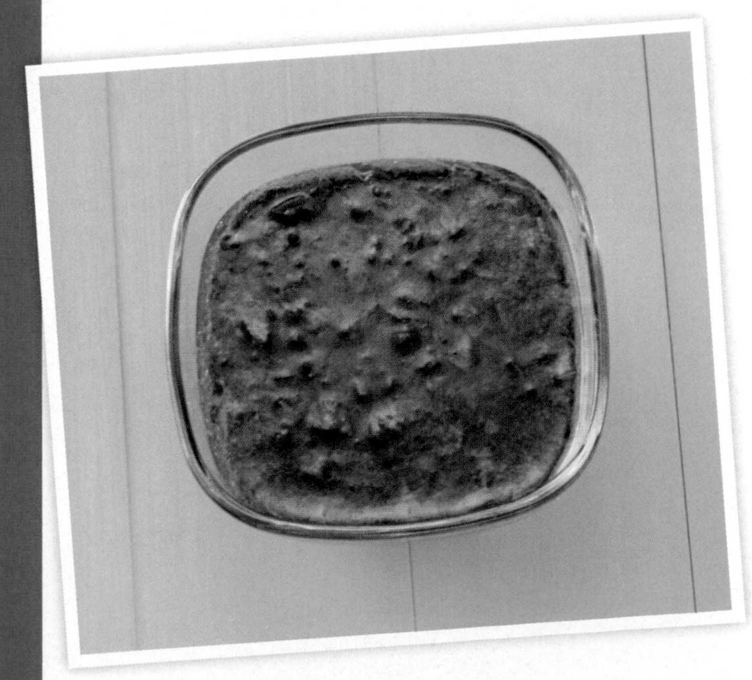

Light Green Goddess Salad Dressing

Here's a do-it-yourself version of a popular salad dressing that's lower in calories and fat, but with all the fabulous flavor.
—**PAGE ALEXANDER** BALDWIN CITY, KANSAS

PREP/TOTAL TIME: 10 MIN. **MAKES:** 2 CUPS

- **1 cup reduced-fat mayonnaise**
- **½ cup reduced-fat sour cream**
- **¼ cup chopped green pepper**
- **¼ cup packed fresh parsley sprigs**
- **3 anchovy fillets**
- **2 tablespoons lemon juice**
- **2 green onion tops, coarsely chopped**
- **1 garlic clove, peeled**
- **¼ teaspoon pepper**
- **⅛ teaspoon Worcestershire sauce**

1. Place all ingredients in a blender; cover and process until smooth. Transfer to a bowl or jar; cover and store in the refrigerator.

Finnegan House Dry Rub

I came across this recipe for a dry rub and tweaked it to make it my own. I store it in a sealed container so I always have it on hand. The rub is full of flavor and goes great with chicken, pork, beef and ribs. For extra punch, add 1-2 tablespoons of cayenne pepper.
—**LISA FINNEGAN** FORKED RIVER, NEW JERSEY

PREP/TOTAL TIME: 10 MIN. **MAKES:** 1⅓ CUPS

- **½ cup paprika**
- **⅓ cup pepper**
- **¼ cup kosher salt**
- **¼ cup packed brown sugar**
- **¼ cup ground cumin**
- **¼ cup chili powder**
- **3 tablespoons sugar**

1. In a small bowl, combine all ingredients. Store in an airtight container in a cool dry place for up to 6 months. Rub over meat or poultry before grilling or broiling.

THRILL OF THE GRILL

The King's Crowned Filets

Guests will feel like royalty when you present this tender filet with a lightly breaded horseradish topping. Best of all, it grills in just 15 minutes, giving you more time to visit.

—**TONYA BURKHARD** DAVIS, ILLINOIS

PREP: 10 MIN. + CHILLING **GRILL:** 15 MIN. **MAKES:** 4 SERVINGS

- **¼ cup butter, softened**
- **3 tablespoons dry bread crumbs**
- **1 tablespoon prepared horseradish**
- **¼ teaspoon coarsely ground pepper**
- **⅛ teaspoon crushed red pepper flakes**
- **Dash salt**
- **Dash dried thyme**
- **4 beef tenderloin steaks (8 ounces each)**
- **2 teaspoons Montreal steak seasoning**

1. In a small bowl, combine the first seven ingredients; shape into four ovals. Place on a baking sheet. Refrigerate for 30 minutes or until firm.

2. Sprinkle steaks with steak seasoning. Grill, covered, over medium heat or broil 4 in. from the heat for 6-8 minutes on each side or until meat reaches desired doneness (for medium-rare, a thermometer should read 145°; medium, 160°; well-done, 170°).

3. Place a butter piece on each steak. Broil 4 in. from the heat for 2-3 minutes or until topping is golden brown.

Orange BBQ Baby Back Ribs

I avoid long and complicated recipes during the hot summer months (when I'd rather be out by the pool with my family!), so I came up with this easy citrus barbecue. The orange juice and peel add a subtle, deliciously fresh flavor. I also use this sauce when I make chicken fondue.

—**KELLIE SEAMANS** CHANDLER, ARIZONA

PREP: 2¼ HOURS **GRILL:** 15 MIN. **MAKES:** 4 SERVINGS

- **4 pounds pork baby back ribs**
- **1 bottle (18 ounces) honey barbecue sauce**
- **1 cup orange juice**
- **2 tablespoons grated orange peel**

1. Place ribs bone side down on a rack in a shallow roasting pan. Cover and bake at 325° for 2 to 2½ hours or until tender; drain.

2. In a small bowl, combine barbecue sauce, orange juice and peel; set aside 1 cup for serving. Moisten a paper towel with cooking oil; using long-handled tongs, lightly coat grill rack.

3. Place ribs over direct heat; baste with some of the sauce. Grill, covered, over medium heat for 15-20 minutes or until browned, turning and basting occasionally. Serve with reserved sauce.

Parmesan-Onion Potato Packets

This fun twist on the baked potato is great for summer cookouts because the potatoes can be added to the grill while the meat is cooking. Because each potato is individually wrapped in foil, it also makes an excellent take-along side dish. And it's easy to double or triple the recipe if needed.

—**JODI BEVEVINO** WARREN, PENNSYLVANIA

PREP: 25 MIN. **GRILL:** 10 MIN. **MAKES:** 5 SERVINGS

- **1½ pounds medium potatoes**
- **2 tablespoons water**
- **2 tablespoons butter, melted**
- **2 tablespoons grated Parmesan cheese**
- **2 tablespoons onion soup mix**
- **⅛ teaspoon pepper**

1. Scrub potatoes; cut into 1-in. cubes. Place potatoes and water in a large microwave-safe bowl. Cover and microwave on high for 3-4 minutes or until crisp-tender, stirring once. Drain. Add the remaining ingredients; toss to coat.
2. Place on a double thickness of heavy-duty foil (about 18 in. square). Fold foil around potato mixture and seal tightly.
3. Grill, covered, over medium heat for 8-10 minutes or until potatoes are tender. Open foil carefully to allow steam to escape.

Basil-Mint Chicken Thighs

You're going to love plunging fork first into this juicy grilled chicken! It's just bursting with flavors of cilantro, basil, mint and chili pepper. Toss any leftovers in tacos or salads for quick meals.

—KAREN NAIHE EWA BEACH, HAWAII

PREP: 15 MIN. + MARINATING **GRILL:** 10 MIN. **MAKES:** 6 SERVINGS

- **6 boneless skinless chicken thighs (4 ounces each)**
- **4½ teaspoons lemon juice**
- **4½ teaspoons olive oil**
- **1 tablespoon reduced-sodium soy sauce**
- **1 teaspoon chili powder**
- **½ teaspoon salt**
- **½ teaspoon pepper**
- **½ cup fresh mint leaves**
- **¼ cup fresh basil leaves**
- **4 garlic cloves, minced**
- **1 tablespoon fresh cilantro leaves**

1. Place chicken thighs in large resealable plastic bag. In a blender, combine the remaining ingredients. Cover and process until pureed. Add to bag. Seal and turn to coat. Refrigerate overnight.
2. Moisten a paper towel with cooking oil; using long-handled tongs, lightly coat the grill rack. Grill chicken, covered, over medium heat or broil 4-6 inches from the heat for 3-4 minutes on each side or until a thermometer reads 180°.

Steakhouse Strip Steaks With Chimichurri

Chilies and lime juice give this version of chimichurri sauce a zesty Southwest flair that's dynamite with the cumin-rubbed steaks.

—GILDA LESTER MILLSBORO, DELAWARE

PREP: 30 MIN. **GRILL:** 10 MIN. **MAKES:** 4 SERVINGS

- **4 boneless beef top loin steaks (8 ounces each)**
- **1 tablespoon olive oil**
- **2 teaspoons ground cumin**
- **1 teaspoon salt**
- **1 teaspoon coarsely ground pepper**

CHIMICHURRI

- **2½ cups chopped green onions**
- **3 garlic cloves, minced**
- **5 tablespoons olive oil, divided**
- **1 cup packed fresh parsley sprigs**
- **½ cup fresh cilantro leaves**
- **½ cup loosely packed basil leaves**
- **2 tablespoons canned chopped green chilies**
- **¼ teaspoon salt**
- **¼ teaspoon coarsely ground pepper**
- **¼ cup reduced-sodium chicken broth**
- **3 tablespoons lime juice**
- **Lime wedges**

1. Brush steaks with oil. Combine the cumin, salt and pepper. Rub over steaks; set aside.
2. In a large skillet, saute onions and garlic in 2 tablespoons oil until tender. Cool slightly.
3. In a food processor, combine the onion mixture, herbs, chilies, salt and pepper; cover and process until finely chopped. Add broth and lime juice. While processing, gradually add remaining oil in a steady stream.
4. Grill steaks, covered, over medium heat or broil 4 in. from the heat for 5-7 minutes on each side or until meat reaches desired doneness (for medium-rare, a thermometer should read 145°; medium 160°; well-done 170°). Serve with chimichurri and lime wedges.

Editor's Note: *Top loin steak may be labeled as strip steak, Kansas City steak, New York strip steak, ambassador steak or boneless club steak in your region.*

Swordfish with Fennel and Tomatoes

Step aside, marinara. There's a new sauce in town, and it's blissfully fresh with fennel and basil. TV-inspired and husband-adored, it would be a crime not to share this one.

—**LAUREL DALZELL** MANTECA, CALIFORNIA

PREP/TOTAL TIME: 25 MIN. **MAKES:** 4 SERVINGS

- **1 medium onion, halved and thinly sliced**
- **1 fennel bulb, halved and thinly sliced**
- **3 tablespoons olive oil**
- **1 garlic clove, minced**
- **1 can (28 ounces) whole tomatoes, drained**
- **2 tablespoons chicken broth**
- **2 tablespoons white wine**
- **¾ teaspoon pepper**
- **½ teaspoon kosher salt**
- **½ cup loosely packed basil leaves, thinly sliced**
- **1 tablespoon butter**

FISH

- **4 swordfish steaks (8 ounces each)**
- **2 tablespoons olive oil**
- **½ teaspoon kosher salt**
- **¼ teaspoon pepper**

1. In a large skillet, saute onion and fennel in oil until tender. Add garlic; cook 1 minute longer. Stir in the tomatoes, broth, wine, pepper and salt. Bring to a boil. Reduce heat; simmer, uncovered, for 5 minutes. Stir in basil and butter. Remove from the heat and set aside.

2. Brush steaks with oil; sprinkle with salt and pepper. Using long-handled tongs, moisten a paper towel with cooking oil and lightly coat the grill rack. Grill swordfish, covered, over medium-hot heat or broil 4 in. from the heat for 5-7 minutes on each side or until fish just turns opaque. Serve with tomato mixture.

Grilled Pork Chops With Peach Sauce

My girlfriend wanted to find a use for the succulent peaches from her peach tree besides pie, cobbler or canning. Now my family begs for these savory chops!

—**TRICIA GOSS** TUCSON, ARIZONA

PREP/TOTAL TIME: 30 MIN.
MAKES: 4 SERVINGS

- **2 cups frozen unsweetened sliced peaches, thawed and chopped**
- **2 tablespoons apple jelly**
- **1½ teaspoons minced fresh tarragon or ½ teaspoon dried tarragon**
- **1 teaspoon white wine vinegar**
- **¼ teaspoon crushed red pepper flakes**
- **4 bone-in pork loin chops (7 ounces each and ¾-inch thick)**
- **¼ teaspoon salt**
- **¼ teaspoon pepper**

1. In a small saucepan, combine the first five ingredients. Cook and stir over medium heat for 3-4 minutes or until jelly is melted. Remove from the heat and set aside.

2. Sprinkle chops with salt and pepper. Grill, covered, over medium heat for 4-5 minutes on each side or until a thermometer reads 145°. Let stand for 5 minutes before serving. Serve with peach sauce.

Grilled Romaine With Swiss

Although this dish may sound unusual, you won't believe how delicious it is.

—**TASTE OF HOME TEST KITCHEN**

PREP/TOTAL TIME: 15 MIN.
MAKES: 4 SERVINGS

- **2 romaine hearts, halved lengthwise**
- **1 tablespoon olive oil**
- **⅛ teaspoon salt**
- **⅛ teaspoon pepper**
- **⅓ cup prepared raspberry vinaigrette**
- **½ cup shredded Swiss cheese**
- **½ cup dried cherries**
- **⅓ cup chopped walnuts**

1. Brush romaine with oil and sprinkle with salt and pepper.

2. Using long-handled tongs, moisten a paper towel with cooking oil and lightly coat the grill rack. Grill the romaine, covered, over medium heat for 30 seconds on each side or until heated through. Transfer to a platter; drizzle with vinaigrette. Sprinkle with cheese, cherries and walnuts.

SLOW COOKER

Slow Cooker Golombki

Just like Mom's? Well, sort of! I simplify my mother's traditional recipe by using the slow cooker. My family loves the addition of spaghetti sauce with the tomato soup, and I like the fact that you don't have to precook the cabbage in this fuss-free remake.

—MARY WALKER CLERMONT, FLORIDA

PREP: 25 MIN. **COOK:** 6 HOURS **MAKES:** 8 SERVINGS

- **1 pound ground beef**
- **1 small onion, chopped**
- **1 cup uncooked converted rice**
- **¾ teaspoon salt**
- **¼ teaspoon pepper**
- **1 jar (24 ounces) meatless spaghetti sauce**
- **2 cans (10¾ ounces each) condensed tomato soup, undiluted**
- **1 cup water**
- **½ teaspoon sugar**
- **1 medium head cabbage, chopped**

1. In a large skillet, cook beef and onion over medium heat until meat is no longer pink; drain. Stir in the rice, salt and pepper. In a large bowl, combine the spaghetti sauce, soup, water and sugar.

2. In a 5-qt. slow cooker, layer one third of the sauce, half of the beef mixture and one third of the cabbage. Repeat layers; top with remaining sauce and cabbage.

3. Cover and cook on low for 6-8 hours or until cabbage and rice are tender.

Mushroom Steak

Usually, I'd make this dish in the oven. But when I knew I wouldn't have time for it to bake one night, I let it simmer all day in the slow cooker and had great results. The leftovers are wonderful!

—SANDY PETTINGER LINCOLN, NEBRASKA

PREP: 20 MIN. **COOK:** 7 HOURS **MAKES:** 6 SERVINGS

- **⅓ cup all-purpose flour**
- **½ teaspoon salt**
- **½ teaspoon pepper, divided**
- **1 beef top round steak (2 pounds), cut into 1½-inch strips**
- **2 cups sliced fresh mushrooms**
- **1 small onion, cut into thin wedges**
- **1 can (10¾ ounces) condensed golden mushroom soup, undiluted**
- **¼ cup sherry or beef broth**
- **½ teaspoon dried oregano**
- **¼ teaspoon dried thyme**
- **Hot cooked egg noodles**

1. In a large resealable plastic bag, combine the flour, salt and 1/4 teaspoon pepper. Add beef, a few pieces at a time, and shake to coat.

2. In a 3-qt. slow cooker combine the mushrooms, onion and beef. Combine the soup, sherry, oregano, thyme and remaining pepper; pour over top. Cover and cook on low for 7-9 hours or until beef is tender. Serve with noodles.

Lemon Chicken Breasts with Veggies

Why bake chicken when this slow-cooked version is so fuss-free? Flecked with herbs, these chicken breasts are nestled with crisp-tender veggies in a subtle lemon sauce. The recipe is hearty and comforting with everything you need for a satisfying meal.

—AMBER OTIS MORRIS, OKLAHOMA

PREP: 25 MIN. **COOK:** 8 HOURS **MAKES:** 6 SERVINGS

- 1 pound fresh baby carrots
- 3 cups cubed red potatoes
- 1 package (14 ounces) frozen pearl onions, thawed
- 2 celery ribs, thinly sliced
- 6 bone-in chicken breast halves (10 ounces each), skin removed
- 1 can (10¾ ounces) condensed cream of chicken soup, undiluted
- ½ cup water
- ½ cup lemon juice
- 1 teaspoon dried parsley flakes
- 1 teaspoon dried thyme
- ½ teaspoon pepper
- ¼ teaspoon salt

1. In a 5- or 6-qt. slow cooker, combine the carrots, potatoes, onions and celery. Top with chicken. In a small bowl, combine the soup, water, lemon juice, parsley, thyme, pepper and salt. Pour the soup mixture over chicken and vegetables. Cover and cook on low for 8-9 hours or until a thermometer reads 170°.

Citrus-Herb Pork Roast

The genius combination of seasonings and citrus for this tender roast reminds us why we cherish tasty recipes.

—**LAURA BRODINE** COLORADO SPRINGS, COLORADO

PREP: 25 MIN. **COOK:** 8 HOURS **MAKES:** 8 SERVINGS

- 1 boneless pork sirloin roast (3 to 4 pounds)
- 1 teaspoon dried oregano
- ½ teaspoon ground ginger
- ½ teaspoon pepper
- 2 medium onions, cut into thin wedges
- 1 cup plus 3 tablespoons orange juice, divided
- 1 tablespoon sugar
- 1 tablespoon white grapefruit juice
- 1 tablespoon steak sauce
- 1 tablespoon reduced-sodium soy sauce
- 1 teaspoon grated orange peel
- ½ teaspoon salt
- 3 tablespoons cornstarch
- Hot cooked egg noodles

1. Cut roast in half. In a small bowl, combine the oregano, ginger and pepper; rub over pork. In a large nonstick skillet coated with cooking spray, brown roast on all sides. Transfer to a 4-qt. slow cooker; add onions.

2. In a small bowl, combine 1 cup orange juice, sugar, grapefruit juice, steak sauce and soy sauce; pour over top. Cover and cook on low for 8-10 hours or until a meat is tender. Remove meat and onions to a serving platter; keep warm.

3. Skim fat from cooking juices; transfer to a small saucepan. Add orange peel and salt. Bring to a boil. Combine cornstarch and the remaining orange juice until smooth. Gradually stir into the pan. Bring to a boil; cook and stir for 2 minutes or until thickened. Serve with pork and noodles.

Best Ever Roast Beef

This roast beef is the best I've ever tasted, and it's great for family dinners! Cube leftover meat and save any extra sauce; they'll add new flavor to basic fried rice.

—**CAROLINE FLYNN** TROY, NEW YORK

PREP: 15 MIN. **COOK:** 7 HOURS **MAKES:** 6 SERVINGS

- 1 boneless beef chuck roast (4 pounds), trimmed
- 1 large sweet onion, chopped
- 1⅓ cups plus 3 tablespoons water, divided
- 1 can (10½ ounces) condensed French onion soup
- 1 cup packed brown sugar
- ⅓ cup reduced-sodium soy sauce
- ¼ cup cider vinegar
- 6 garlic cloves, minced
- 1 teaspoon ground ginger
- ¼ teaspoon pepper
- 3 tablespoons cornstarch

1. Cut roast in half. Transfer to a 5-qt. slow cooker; add onion and 1⅓ cups water. In a small bowl, combine the soup, brown sugar, soy sauce, vinegar, garlic, ginger and pepper; pour over top. Cover and cook on low for 7-8 hours or until meat is tender.

2. Remove meat to a serving platter and keep warm. Skim fat from cooking juices; transfer to a small saucepan. Bring liquid to a boil. Combine cornstarch and remaining water until smooth; gradually stir into the pan. Bring to a boil; cook and stir for 2 minutes or until thickened. Serve with roast.

FREEZER PLEASERS

Italian Enchiladas

I created this Italian spin on enchiladas one night when I wanted an easy oven meal and had extra tortillas on hand.

—YVONNE OPP GREENVILLE, PENNSYLVANIA

PREP: 30 MIN. **BAKE:** 35 MIN.
MAKES: 2 CASSEROLES (6 SERVINGS EACH)

- **2 cans (14½ ounces each) diced tomatoes, undrained**
- **1 can (6 ounces) tomato paste**
- **4 teaspoons sugar**
- **2 teaspoons dried basil**
- **1½ teaspoons dried oregano**
- **½ teaspoon salt**
- **½ teaspoon onion powder**
- **½ teaspoon garlic powder**
- **1 pound bulk spicy pork sausage**
- **1 cup chopped fresh mushrooms**
- **1 package (3½ ounces) sliced pepperoni**
- **3 cups (12 ounces) shredded provolone cheese**
- **1 cup chopped ripe olives**
- **12 flour tortillas (6 inches)**
- **⅓ cup shredded Parmesan cheese**

1. In a large saucepan, combine the first eight ingredients. Bring to a boil. Reduce heat; simmer, uncovered, for 5-10 minutes or until thickened, stirring occasionally.
2. In a large skillet, cook pork and mushrooms over medium heat until meat is no longer pink; drain.
3. Spread ⅓ cup sauce on the bottom of each of two greased 11-in. x 7-in. baking dishes. Place 4 pepperoni slices, ¼ cup sausage mixture, 2 tablespoons provolone cheese and 1 heaping tablespoonful olives down the center of each tortilla. Roll up and place seam side down in prepared baking dishes. Pour remaining sauce over the top; sprinkle with Parmesan and remaining provolone cheese.

4. Cover and bake one casserole at 350° for 30 minutes. Uncover; bake 5-10 minutes longer or until heated through and cheese is melted. Cover and freeze remaining casserole for up to 3 months.
To use frozen casserole: *Thaw in the refrigerator overnight. Remove from the refrigerator 30 minutes before baking. Cover and bake at 350° for 30 minutes. Uncover; bake 5-10 minutes longer or until heated through and cheese is melted.*

Homemade Meatless Spaghetti Sauce

When my garden tomatoes ripen, the first two things I make are BLTs and this homemade spaghetti sauce.

—SONDRA BERGY LOWELL, MICHIGAN

PREP: 20 MIN. **COOK:** 3¼ HOURS **MAKES:** 2 QUARTS

- **4 medium onions, chopped**
- **½ cup canola oil**
- **12 cups chopped peeled fresh tomatoes**
- **4 garlic cloves, minced**
- **3 bay leaves**
- **4 teaspoons salt**
- **2 teaspoons dried oregano**
- **1¼ teaspoons pepper**
- **½ teaspoon dried basil**
- **2 cans (6 ounces each) tomato paste**
- **⅓ cup packed brown sugar**
- **Hot cooked spaghetti**

1. In a Dutch oven, saute onions in oil until tender. Add the tomatoes, garlic, bay leaves, salt, oregano, pepper and basil. Bring to a boil. Reduce heat; cover and simmer for 2 hours, stirring occasionally.
2. Add tomato paste and brown sugar; simmer, uncovered, for 1 hour. Discard bay leaves. Serve with spaghetti.
Editor's Note: *Browned ground beef or Italian sausage can be added to the cooked sauce if desired. The sauce also freezes well.*

Chipotle Mac & Cheese

Beefy and bubbly, this Southwestern pasta bake heats up the dinner hour with a peppery bite.

—CYNDY GERKEN NAPLES, FLORIDA

PREP: 35 MIN. **BAKE:** 30 MIN.
MAKES: 2 CASSEROLES (8 SERVINGS EACH)

- **1 package (16 ounces) spiral pasta**
- **2 pounds ground beef**
- **2 large onions, chopped**
- **2 large green peppers, chopped**
- **3 garlic cloves, minced**
- **1 can (28 ounces) crushed tomatoes**
- **1 can (10¾ ounces) condensed cheddar cheese soup, undiluted**
- **½ cup 2% milk**
- **1 chipotle pepper in adobo sauce, chopped**
- **2 tablespoons chili powder**
- **1 tablespoon ground cumin**
- **1 teaspoon cayenne pepper**
- **1 teaspoon dried oregano**
- **½ teaspoon salt**
- **¼ teaspoon pepper**
- **2 cups (8 ounces) shredded Monterey Jack cheese**
- **2 tablespoons minced fresh cilantro, optional**

1. Cook pasta according to package directions to al dente. Meanwhile, in a Dutch oven, cook the beef, onions, green peppers and garlic over medium heat until meat is no longer pink. Drain.
2. Stir in the tomatoes, soup, milk, chipotle pepper and seasonings. Bring to a boil. Reduce heat; cover and simmer for 15 minutes or until thickened.
3. Drain pasta; stir into meat mixture. Divide between two greased 8-in. square baking dishes; sprinkle with cheese and cilantro if desired.
4. Cover and freeze one casserole for up to 3 months. Cover and bake the remaining casserole at 350° for 20 minutes. Uncover; bake 8-10 minutes longer or until bubbly and cheese is melted.

To use frozen casserole: Thaw in the refrigerator overnight. Remove from the refrigerator 30 minutes before baking. Cover and bake at 350° for 60 minutes. Uncover; bake 8-10 minutes longer or until bubbly and cheese is melted.

Taco Shepherd's Pie

This family-pleasing entree is one for the front of your recipe files!
—**SANDRA PARKER** GLEN BURNIE, MARYLAND

PREP: 30 MIN. **BAKE:** 40 MIN. **MAKES:** 2 PIES (6 SERVINGS EACH)

- **1 package (14.1 ounces) refrigerated pie pastry**
- **6 large potatoes, peeled and cut into chunks**
- **2 pounds lean ground beef (90% lean)**
- **14 green onions, chopped (white portion only)**
- **1¼ cups water**
- **2 envelopes taco seasoning**
- **1 cup 2% milk**
- **¼ cup butter**
- **2 teaspoons garlic powder**
- **¼ teaspoon salt**
- **¼ teaspoon pepper**
- **2 cups (8 ounces) shredded sharp cheddar cheese**
- **2 cups (8 ounces) shredded pepper jack cheese**

1. Roll out pastry to fit two 9-in. deep-dish pie plates. Transfer pastry to pie plates; flute edges. Line unpricked pastry with a double thickness of heavy-duty foil. Fill with dried beans, uncooked rice or pie weights.
2. Bake at 450° for 8 minutes. Remove foil and weights; bake 5 minutes longer. Cool on a wire rack.
3. Place potatoes in a Dutch oven and cover with water. Bring to a boil. Reduce heat; cover and cook for 15-20 minutes or until tender.
4. Meanwhile, in a large skillet, cook beef and onions over medium heat until meat is no longer pink; drain. Stir in water and taco seasoning. Bring to a boil; cook until liquid is evaporated. Spoon into pastry shells.
5. Drain potatoes and place in a large bowl. Add the milk, butter, garlic powder, salt and pepper; mash until smooth. Spread over meat mixture.
6. Sprinkle one pie with half of the cheeses. Cover and freeze for up to 3 months. Bake remaining pie, uncovered, at 350° for 35 minutes. Sprinkle with remaining cheeses. Bake 5-10 minutes longer or until heated through and cheese is melted.

To use frozen pie: *Thaw in the refrigerator overnight. Remove from the refrigerator 30 minutes before baking. Cover and bake at 350° for 1½ hours. Uncover; bake 10-15 minutes longer or until heated through.*

Editor's Note: *Let pie weights cool before storing. Beans and rice may be reused for pie weights, but not for cooking.*

Chicken and Sausage Penne

Gather the clan for a comfy-cozy dinner filled with two types of meat and a garlic-cream sauce. It's versatile, too. Sub in whatever cream soup or cheese you have on hand.
—**SANDRA PERRIN** NEW IBERIA, LOUISIANA

PREP/TOTAL TIME: 30 MIN. **MAKES:** 8 SERVINGS

- **1 package (16 ounces) penne pasta**
- **1 pound boneless skinless chicken breasts, cubed**
- **¾ pound smoked Polish sausage or fully cooked bratwurst links, cubed**
- **1 medium onion, chopped**
- **1 medium sweet red pepper, chopped**
- **1 medium green pepper, chopped**
- **2 tablespoons olive oil**
- **6 garlic cloves, minced**
- **2 jars (16 ounces each) Parmesan Alfredo sauce**
- **1 can (10¾ ounces) condensed cream of mushroom soup, undiluted**
- **½ teaspoon pepper**
- **¼ teaspoon salt**
- **2 cups (8 ounces) shredded cheddar cheese**

1. Cook pasta according to package directions. Meanwhile, in a Dutch oven, cook the chicken, sausage, onion and red and green peppers in oil over medium heat for 6-8 minutes or until chicken is no longer pink. Add garlic; cook and stir 1 minute longer.
2. Stir in the Alfredo sauce, soup, pepper and salt. Bring to a boil. Reduce heat; simmer, uncovered, for 2 minutes. Stir in cheese. Drain pasta; add to chicken mixture and toss to coat.
3. Serve desired amount immediately. Cool remaining mixture; transfer to freezer containers. Freeze for up to 3 months.

To use frozen pasta: *Thaw in the refrigerator overnight. Transfer to a large skillet; cook and stir over medium heat for 10-12 minutes or until heated through.*

To microwave frozen pasta: *Thaw in the refrigerator overnight. Transfer to a microwave-safe dish. Cover and microwave on high for 10-12 minutes or until heated through, stirring once.*

COOKING TECHNIQUE DEEP FRYING

FRY FOODS AT 375°. IF THE OIL IS TOO HOT, THE FOOD WILL BROWN TOO FAST BUT BE UNCOOKED IN THE CENTER. IF THE OIL IS NOT HOT ENOUGH, THE FOOD WILL ABSORB OIL AND TASTE GREASY. YOU'LL HAVE BETTER RESULTS IF YOU FRY IN SMALL BATCHES.

Crispy Beer Battered Fish

A local restaurant made a similar breading for shrimp po' boys, but we think this version's better. I serve it with a ranch dressing and hot sauce mixture as a dip.

—JENNY WENZEL GULFPORT, MISSISSIPPI

PREP: 25 MIN. **COOK:** 5 MIN./BATCH
MAKES: 4 SERVINGS

- **½ cup cornstarch**
- **1½ teaspoons baking powder**
- **¾ teaspoon salt**
- **½ teaspoon Creole seasoning**
- **¼ teaspoon paprika**
- **¼ teaspoon cayenne pepper**
- **1 cup all-purpose flour, divided**
- **½ cup 2% milk**
- **⅓ cup beer or nonalcoholic beer**
- **2 cups crushed unsalted top saltines (about 40)**
- **4 cod fillets (6 ounces each)**
- **Oil for deep-fat frying**

1. In a shallow bowl, combine the cornstarch, baking powder, salt, creole seasoning, paprika, cayenne and ½ cup flour. Stir in milk and beer until smooth. Place crackers and remaining flour in separate shallow bowls. Coat fillets with flour, then dip in batter and coat with crackers.

2. In an electric skillet or deep-fat fryer, heat oil to 375°. Fry fish in batches for 2-3 minutes on each side or until golden brown. Drain on paper towels.

Editor's Note: *The following spices may be substituted for 1 teaspoon Creole seasoning: ¼ teaspoon each salt, garlic powder and paprika; and a pinch each of dried thyme, ground cumin and cayenne pepper.*

SIMPLE SWAP

You can easily change the spices in the Crispy Beer Battered Fish, depending on what you like or have on hand. Unsalted-top saltines are some of the best crackers to use, because they don't make the recipe too salty.

COOKING TECHNIQUE ROUX

WHEN FLOUR AND FAT ARE COMBINED TO BE USED AS A THICKENER, IT'S A CALLED A "ROUX" (FRENCH, PRONOUNCED "RUE"). THE MIXTURE SHOULD BE COMBINED IN A SAUCEPAN, THEN COOKED UNTIL THE RAW FLOUR TASTE IS NO LONGER DETECTED.

Crispy Scallops with Tarragon Cream

You'll flip for these tender, crisp-coated scallops. The ridiculously easy, creamy tarragon sauce truly makes this dish a star. Utterly brilliant!

—KAREN KUEBLER DALLAS, TEXAS

PREP/TOTAL TIME: 25 MIN.
MAKES: 4 SERVINGS

- **1 egg**
- **2 teaspoons water**
- **⅔ cup Italian-style panko (Japanese) bread crumbs**
- **⅓ cup mashed potato flakes**
- **1 pound sea scallops**
- **¼ cup olive oil**
- **2 tablespoons butter**
- **1 tablespoon all-purpose flour**
- **¼ teaspoon salt**
- **⅛ teaspoon pepper**
- **¾ cup heavy whipping cream**
- **2 tablespoons minced fresh tarragon or 2 teaspoons dried tarragon**

1. In a shallow bowl, whisk egg and water. In another shallow bowl, combine bread crumbs and potato flakes. Dip scallops in egg mixture, then coat with crumb mixture.

2. Heat oil in a large skillet over medium-high heat. Cook scallops in batches for 2 minutes on each side or until golden brown.

3. Meanwhile, in a small saucepan, melt butter. Stir in the flour, salt and pepper until smooth; gradually add cream. Bring to a boil; cook and stir for 1-2 minutes or until thickened. Stir in tarragon. Serve with scallops.

COOKING TECHNIQUE SAUTEEING

THIS COOKING METHOD COOKS FOOD (THIN SLICES OR FILLETS OF MEAT, FISH OR VEGETABLES) QUICKLY. COMPARED TO FRYING, A SMALL AMOUNT OF OIL IS USED. BE SURE THE PAN ISN'T TOO CROWDED OR THE FOOD WILL STEAM RATHER THAN BROWN.

Pork and Waffles with Maple-Pear Topping

Maple and Dijon mustard flavors come through beautifully in these upscale, crowd-pleasing waffles.

—TASTE OF HOME TEST KITCHEN

PREP/TOTAL TIME: 25 MIN. **MAKES:** 4 SERVINGS

- **½ cup seasoned bread crumbs**
- **1 teaspoon dried thyme**
- **1 pork tenderloin (1 pound), cut into 12 slices**
- **2 tablespoons olive oil**
- **2 medium pears, thinly sliced**
- **½ cup maple syrup**
- **2 tablespoons Dijon mustard**
- **½ teaspoon salt**
- **8 frozen waffles, toasted**
- **2 tablespoons minced chives**

1. In a large resealable plastic bag, combine bread crumbs and thyme. Add pork, a few pieces at a time, and shake to coat. In a large skillet, cook pork in oil in batches over medium heat for 2-4 minutes on each side or until tender. Remove from the pan and keep warm.
2. Add the pears, syrup, mustard and salt to the skillet; cook and stir for 1-2 minutes or until pears are tender. Serve pork slices and pear mixture over waffles. Sprinkle with chives.

Microwaved Chicken Kiev

As a technique, microvowave cooking is a true time saver. I fix these easy microwave-easy chicken breasts all the time!

—DOROTHY LACOMBE HAMBURG, NEW YORK

PREP/TOTAL TIME: 30 MIN. **MAKES:** 4 SERVINGS

- **5 tablespoons butter, softened, divided**
- **½ teaspoon minced chives**
- **¼ teaspoon garlic powder**
- **¼ teaspoon white pepper**
- **4 boneless skinless chicken breast halves (6 ounces each)**
- **⅓ cup cornflake crumbs**
- **1 tablespoon grated Parmesan cheese**
- **½ teaspoon dried parsley flakes**
- **¼ teaspoon paprika**

1. In a small bowl, combine 3 tablespoons butter, chives, garlic powder and pepper; shape into four cubes. Cover and freeze until firm, about 10 minutes.
2. Meanwhile, flatten chicken breast halves to ¼-in. thickness. Place a butter cube in the center of each. Fold long sides over butter; fold ends up and secure with a toothpick.
3. In a shallow bowl, combine the cornflakes, cheese, parsley and paprika. Melt remaining butter. Dip chicken into butter; coat evenly with cornflake mixture. Place seam side down in a microwave-safe dish.
4. Microwave, uncovered, on high for 5-6 minutes or until chicken juices run clear and a thermometer reads 170°. Remove toothpicks. Drizzle chicken with pan drippings.
Editor's Note: *This recipe was tested in a 1,100-watt microwave.*

COOKING TECHNIQUE DEGLAZING & PAN SAUCE

ADDING WATER, BROTH OR WINE TO A PAN AFTER SAUTEEING CUTS OF MEAT HELPS TO REMOVE THE BITS FROM THE BOTTOM OF THE PAN. THE LIQUID AND FLAVORFUL BITS ARE THE BEGINNINGS OF A PAN SAUCE, AS DIRECTED IN THE RECIPE BELOW.

Pork Chops in a Honey-Mustard Sauce

Pork chops are a great economical cut of meat and cook up quickly, making them ideal for busy weeknight meals. But turning out tender chops can be tricky. Browning them first, then finishing them in this tangy, slightly sweet sauce results in perfectly cooked chops.

—SUSAN BENTLEY
BURLINGTON, NEW JERSEY

PREP/TOTAL TIME: 30 MIN.
MAKES: 4 SERVINGS

- **¾ teaspoon garlic powder, divided**
- **½ teaspoon salt**
- **¼ teaspoon pepper**
- **4 boneless pork loin chops (6 ounces each)**
- **1 tablespoon olive oil**
- **½ cup white wine or chicken broth**
- **¼ cup chicken broth**
- **2 tablespoons Dijon mustard**
- **1 tablespoon honey**
- **½ cup heavy whipping cream**

1. Combine 1/2 teaspoon garlic powder, salt and pepper; sprinkle over pork chops. In a large skillet, brown pork chops in oil. Remove and keep warm.
2. Remove skillet from heat and add wine, stirring to loosen browned bits from pan. Bring to a boil; cook until liquid is reduced by half. Reduce heat to medium. Whisk in the broth, mustard, honey and remaining garlic powder; cook and stir for 1 minute. Whisk in cream; cook and stir for 4-6 minutes or until thickened.
3. Return pork chops and juices to the skillet. Cover and cook for 3-5 minutes or until a thermometer reads 145°. Let stand for 5 minutes before serving.

Advice for On-the-Go Cooks

Every busy cook can use help with menu planning, shopping and baking tips. Here, our Test Kitchen experts offer up their best advice to maximize time spent at the grocery store and in the kitchen.

THE COMPLETE GUIDE TO MENU PLANNING

FIND EVERYTHING YOU NEED TO MAKE MEALTIME EASIER WITH OUR SIMPLE GUIDE

Looking for something—anything, really—to simplify your week? For on-the-go families, coming up with meal ideas can be a hassle. In fact, it's probably the No. 1 struggle today's home cooks complain about. But, as daunting and time-consuming as the task can seem, planning weekly menus in advance is the single best suggestion for any busy family. To tell the truth: You'll have to make an initial investment of time. But the rewards are worth it—more money in your pocket, less scrambling during the dinner hour, a more enjoyable and exciting cooking experience, and often, healthier eating.

It's time to set your table for nourishing meals you and your family will look forward to eating! On the following pages, you'll learn great tips for creating a weekly menu plan and grocery list with ingredients you have on hand, as well as secrets for preparing quick suppers using up what you buy. We're also sharing hints on how to create appealing meals that will have everyone running to the table. And we're hoping that our sample menu with dinner recipes and preparation tips will give you the information you need to put your newfound skills to work. Let's get started!

HOW TO GET STARTED

Do the words "menu planning" overwhelm you? Don't let them! In its simplest form, menu planning is just deciding what you want to cook and eat over a period of time. To start, keep it easy and plan no more than a week ahead. Why? The food you'll have on hand will be fresher; you'll have more flexibility to take advantage of sales on perishables and seasonal items, and it will be easier to adjust if your plans change. Here's how to create a menu:

☒ **MAKE A LIST OF THE DAYS AND TIMES YOU NEED MEALS.**
Review your family's calendar and think about which meals you'll have time to cook and which ones you'll need to make ahead. Remember to include breakfast, lunch, dinner and snacks between meals.

☒ **TAKE INVENTORY OF YOUR GROCERIES.**
Make note of what's in your pantry, fridge and freezer, and don't forget spices. This list will save you time and money later.

☒ **FILL IN MEAL IDEAS.**
What does your family like to eat? Do you already have some favorite recipes? If so, consider adding them to your list.

Think about both nutrition and the foods that suit your family's taste. Build meals with a variety of lean meats, vegetables and fruit, whole grains and low-fat dairy products.

Also keep in mind, it's not necessary to prepare a recipe or cook for every meal of the day. For instance, one of our food editors typically only cooks dinner because that works for her. She fills in the rest of the day with simple store-bought items. For example, during the week, her family eats hot or cold cereal or toast and eggs, fruit, juice and coffee for breakfast. Lunch might be a sandwich or salad with a protein, fresh veggies and fruit, or dinner leftovers. Snacks include string cheese, nuts, popcorn and low-fat yogurt. She rotates these foods often and may change up the ingredients, but mainly she plans the same types of foods because they're easy for her to prepare. Doing this saves time and money, because her family is eating what she's buying, and she's not spending a lot on ingredients to make several different meals.

When planning dinner, think about how much time you'll have to cook each night, and consider foods that cook quickly. (Our 30-Minute Meals, p.8, offer great solutions for busy nights.) Or add a slow-cooked entree to the rotation (see p. 288 for ideas).

If you have extra time one night, double a recipe that freezes well, so you can cook once and eat twice. Don't forget to refer to the pantry list you created. Are there recipes you could fix easily? If so, decide what days to prepare those dishes and add them to your plan. Pay attention to how excited you feel about what you're planning. Are you looking forward to the meals? If not, find a new recipe.

☒ **DRAW UP A GROCERY LIST.**
After checking recipes against ingredients in your pantry, jot down what you still need. Write these items alongside your menu. After shopping, use the list to remind you of the meals you've planned.

For ease at the store, group ingredients by grocery aisle, such as produce, deli, meat, dairy and pantry. Along with items you need for recipes, remember to add basics, such as cereal, bread and eggs.

It's also helpful to clip coupons and attach them to this list.

MAKE THE MOST OF GROCERIES

Planning a menu and grocery shopping with a list are the secrets to eliminating frivolous spending on food you might not eat before it expires. Use these smart strategies to spend less at the store:

- Choose recipes with ingredients that are on sale or in season, or make substitutions.
- Select recipes with ingredients in common to help you use up larger quantities of fresh produce and other perishables. For example, do you need a bag of fresh carrots for a soup on Monday? Find a recipe that finishes off the carrots later in the week.
- If you only need a small amount of fresh veggies for a recipe, simply visit the store's salad bar so you can get just what you need or consider frozen produce.
- Check store ads when buying meat. The butcher and deli departments can be terrific assets when shopping for specific portions, but sometimes buying meat in bulk is less expensive. In those cases, divide meat into family-size portions and freeze it.

When you get home from the store, get a head start on upcoming meals:

- Prep and cook parts of recipes in advance. For example, clean and cut veggies before the workweek starts. Keep in mind that delicate ingredients or fruits and veggies that brown easily, such as herbs, potatoes, tomatoes and avocados, can't be prepared ahead. Prep these foods as you add them to your finished recipe.
- Brown ground meats and cook larger cuts or several smaller cuts, like chicken breasts, ahead of time to use in future recipes. When the workweek starts, you'll be better prepared to come home and start cooking at the end of the day.

STOCK UP!

Do you marvel at cooks who can throw together a meal in a matter of minutes? Their secret is most likely a well-stocked pantry. Menu planning and preparation are easier when you have staple ingredients at your fingertips. Here's why:

▶ **YOU SAVE TIME,** because you avoid last-minute trips to the grocery store.
▶ **YOU ELIMINATE FRUSTRATION,** because you have ingredients on hand when you want to cook.
▶ **YOU SAVE MONEY,** because you can take advantage of sales to stock up on things you'll eventually need to buy.

To avoid a huge grocery bill, build up your pantry gradually. Buy items when you have a coupon or when they're on sale.

Remember, the term "pantry" doesn't refer only to dry and canned goods, but to a supply of basic refrigerated and frozen foods, too. Keep a running list of items you need so it's easier to restock them. Also, rotate items stored in your pantry so you use them up before they expire. Refer to the list, at right, to see which pantry items we recommend keeping on hand.

AVOID RUTS

Readers often say that one of the challenges with sticking to a menu plan is that it's easy to get into a rut. It's true: The same food prepared the same way time after time can be boring. Looking forward to delicious meals is one way to stay out of dinnertime ruts, so we can't encourage you enough to keep the excitement alive by adding new recipes and cooking techniques to your repertoire. Don't add a recipe to your menu plan that you're not excited about making and that your family wouldn't be excited about eating. Just like at a restaurant, trying a new recipe is fun!

Prepare meals that not only taste good but look good, too. A friend always says, "People eat with their eyes first." Attractive dishes send a message from the eyes to the brain that tasty food is on the way. To prepare meals that look good, think like an artist: Vary colors, flavors, textures and shapes.

Look for opportunities to make each plate a work of art. Add color with bright fruits and vegetables; layer flavors with different herbs and spices; add textures by stirring in toasted nuts for crunch, for example; or serve foods with different shapes and sizes together for interest. These small changes will bring more pleasure and fun to your meals and enhance your dining experience.

On the next page, you'll find hints on how to add flavor to recipes using herbs and spices. These no-fuss flavor profiles will help you create new meals any night, whether you have a recipe to work from or not.

We hope this simple plan gives you the tools you need to shop on the weekend, avoid after-work chaos and get a jump start on those weeknight meals. With the tips and ideas you'll learn on the next two pages, you'll have everything you need to feed your family new quality meals at home any night. Turn the page to see how!

PACK THE PANTRY

KEEP THESE ITEMS STOCKED TO EASILY FIX QUICK MEALS!

- ☐ all-purpose flour
- ☐ balsamic vinegar
- ☐ barbecue sauce
- ☐ beef broth
- ☐ butter
- ☐ canned beans
- ☐ canned tomatoes and tomato paste
- ☐ chicken broth
- ☐ cider vinegar
- ☐ condensed cream soups
- ☐ corn or flour tortillas
- ☐ dried bread crumbs
- ☐ dried herbs and spices (allspice, basil, cayenne pepper, chili powder, cinnamon, cloves, cumin, curry powder, dill weed, garlic powder and garlic salt, ginger, Italian seasoning, mustard powder, nutmeg, onion salt, oregano, paprika, parsley flakes, pepper, red pepper flakes, poppy seeds, rosemary, sage, salt, sesame seeds, seasoned salt and thyme)
- ☐ eggs
- ☐ frozen vegetables
- ☐ instant rice
- ☐ ketchup
- ☐ mayonnaise
- ☐ milk
- ☐ onions
- ☐ pastas
- ☐ pizza crust
- ☐ prepared pesto
- ☐ preserves
- ☐ salad dressings
- ☐ spaghetti sauce

BUILD FLAVOR

Feeling stumped on how to choose recipes for meals? Just as certain wines pair well with beefy steak, certain herbs and spices fit seamlessly together to create flavor profiles. A secret to cooking tasty meals with ease is knowing how to blend different flavors. Once you are familiar with how ingredients work together, you can start combining them to create your own recipes!

Use the lists below as a tool when you don't know where to start, especially when you don't have a recipe—or if you're searching online for one that includes certain items you already have on hand. Keep a few of your favorite ingredients in your pantry, and you'll always be armed with ideas.

FOR ITALIAN FLAVOR:

- ☐ fresh or dried basil
- ☐ fresh or dried oregano
- ☐ fresh or dried rosemary
- ☐ fresh or dried thyme
- ☐ garlic cloves
- ☐ Italian seasoning
- ☐ olive oil
- ☐ Parmesan cheese

FOR MEXICAN/ SOUTHWESTERN FLAVOR:

- ☐ cayenne pepper and/or crushed red pepper flakes
- ☐ chili powder
- ☐ dried oregano
- ☐ fresh cilantro
- ☐ ground cumin
- ☐ paprika
- ☐ taco seasoning mix

FOR MEDITERRANEAN/ GREEK FLAVOR:

- ☐ dried basil
- ☐ dried oregano
- ☐ feta cheese
- ☐ fresh mint
- ☐ lemon juice
- ☐ olive oil

FOR ASIAN FLAVOR:

- ☐ brown sugar
- ☐ chili sauce
- ☐ garlic cloves
- ☐ ground ginger or fresh gingerroot
- ☐ hoisin and/or plum sauce
- ☐ reduced-sodium soy sauce

FOR AMERICAN COMFORT-FOOD FLAVOR:

- ☐ canola oil
- ☐ dill weed
- ☐ garlic powder
- ☐ onion powder
- ☐ prepared mustard
- ☐ rubbed sage
- ☐ shredded cheddar cheese
- ☐ Worcestershire sauce

OTHER HINTS:

- ▶ To start, try adding one or several of the ingredients listed in small amounts. Taste frequently to avoid overseasoning. For example, to prepare an Italian side dish without a recipe: Toss raw cut veggies with a little olive oil, basil, oregano, salt and pepper, then roast the veggies. After roasting, taste to see if they need more seasoning. If they do, add more, or sprinkle them with some Parmesan cheese to boost the flavor.
- ▶ Remember, it's usually less expensive to buy dried herbs, and they last longer than fresh. If you decide to purchase fresh, plan another recipe with that ingredient to use it up later in the week.
- ▶ If you don't have a seasoning on hand, choose another in the same family. To save time, substitute or go without instead of running to the store.
- ▶ These seasonings work well with beef, fish or seafood, poultry, pork and meatless dishes. You can also try them in salads, sides, sandwiches, soups, casseroles and pastas, stir-fries, burgers and meat loaves, as a rub on meats and stirred into marinades.
- ▶ Use these ingredients to search for recipes at *tasteofhome.com*. Scroll over Recipes in the menu bar, then select Advanced Search from the drop-down menu. Enter the ingredients you'd like to search for in the Ingredients to Include section and click Get Recipes at the bottom of the screen.

TIME TO GET STARTED!

Changing the way you plan meals and buy groceries may take some time. For ease, we've put together a sample weekly menu plan for dinners. We've selected Saturday as shopping day. The plan shows you how to dovetail ingredients and prep parts of meals ahead; it also uses the slow cooker and incorporates leftovers. A cinch for weeknights, most of these recipes start with everyday ingredients, so they're easy on your wallet, too.

SATURDAY:
Shop for ingredients you'll need for these meals. Don't forget to double-check your pantry, fridge and freezer to see what you have on hand.

SUNDAY'S DINNER:
Old-World Pizza Meat Loaf (p. 90) + Orzo with Peppers & Spinach (p. 202)

SUNDAY:
Whisk milk, soups, wine and ranch salad dressing mix; cover and refrigerate for Creamy Onion Pork Chops on Monday morning.

Cube and refrigerate two slices of Old-World Pizza Meat Loaf for Wednesday night.

MONDAY'S DINNER:
Soccer practice and haircut; no time to cook. Use the slow cooker. Creamy Onion Pork Chops (p. 65) + Zucchini & Tomato Saute (p. 26)

MONDAY MORNING:
Whisk the soup mixture just before pouring over the pork chops. Start the slow cooker.

MONDAY NIGHT:
Combine honey mustard, apricot preserves, ginger, salt and pepper; cover and refrigerate for Apricot-Honey Chicken on Tuesday night.

TUESDAY'S DINNER:
Apricot-Honey Chicken (p. 25) + Mushroom Salad (p. 25) + store-bought dinner rolls

SHOPPING TIP FOR THIS MEAL:
Buy torn mixed salad greens and sliced mushrooms to save time when preparing the Mushroom Salad. Also, pick up an extra tomato or two and salad dressing for the Whatever's Left Side Salad on Wednesday night.

TUESDAY NIGHT:
Cook the green pepper, sausage, mushrooms and onion for Sausage Alfredo. Cool, cover and refrigerate for Thursday night.

WEDNESDAY'S DINNER:
Next Day Meat Loaf Pie (p. 90) + Whatever's Left Side Salad

WEDNESDAY PREP TIP:
Next Day Meat Loaf Pie uses leftover meat loaf from Sunday's dinner. The Whatever's Left Side Salad uses any leftover salad ingredients from side dishes earlier in the week.

WEDNESDAY NIGHT:
Remember: Company's coming on Friday. Call the neighbors to discuss dinner plans.

THURSDAY'S DINNER:
Sausage Alfredo (p. 26) + Herbed Corn and Carrots (p. 26)

THURSDAY PREP TIP: Cook pasta. Reheat the sausage mixture and add Alfredo sauce to the entree. Continue as the recipe directs.

THURSDAY NIGHT:
Pick up fresh cod for Friday night.

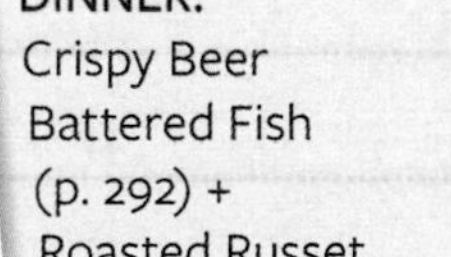

FRIDAY'S DINNER:
Crispy Beer Battered Fish (p. 292) + Roasted Russet & Sweet Potato Wedges (p. 141)

SATURDAY'S LUNCH:
Clean-out-your-fridge pizza. It's grocery shopping day again!

25 WAYS TO BE A *SAVVY SHOPPER*

Illustrations by Tom Bachtell

GET SMART WITH YOUR CART AND STOP BEING FOOLED BY MARKETING TRICKS

Even if saving money didn't make your top 10 list of New Year's resolutions, it's not too late to start making a few changes that will ultimately thicken your wallet. The trick is not to get tricked.

Tapping into the minds of two experts—Erin Chase, author of *The $5 Dinner Mom Cookbook*, and renowned food reporter Phil Lempert, also known as the "supermarket guru"—not only helped gather the best advice for smarter grocery shopping, it revealed some intriguing secrets of marketing strategy. With their help, we disclose 25 ways to avoid grocery store traps, save your sanity and help you be the best shopper you can be.

LET'S START SAVING!

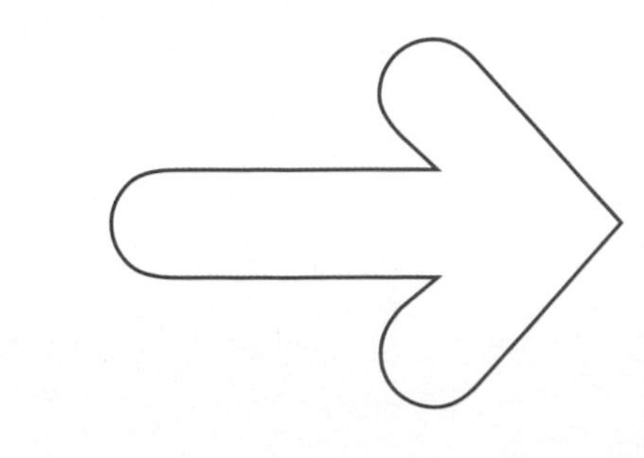

PAY ATTENTION TO YOUR MOOD. YOU'VE HEARD THIS BEFORE: DON'T GO SHOPPING WHEN YOU'RE HUNGRY OR CRANKY. YOU'LL LIKELY SPEND MORE ON IMPULSE ITEMS. BUT AS LEMPERT POINTS OUT, THE SAME IS TRUE FOR SHOPPING IN A GREAT MOOD. BE AWARE OF HOW YOUR MIND-SET MAY HAVE AN INFLUENCE ON YOUR BUYING DECISIONS.

KNOW BEFORE YOU GO. BEING AN INTELLIGENT SHOPPER STARTS AT HOME. A FEW SIMPLE HABITS WILL PREPARE YOU TO SHOP SMART.

PICK YOUR DAY. Decide when you like to shop best. If crowded markets freak you out, avoid shopping on Friday, Saturday or Sunday. According to Lempert, the slowest days are Monday and Tuesday.

TAKE INVENTORY. Be smarter than the average shopper, who, as Lempert points out, tends to buy what she already has at home. Keep track of what you have in stock. There are several sites with printable templates, but we like the easy-to-customize version at *organizedhome.com/printable/household-notebook/pantry-inventory*. You can also categorize your own list by store deparments.

CREATE A MUST-STOCK LIST. Cross-check your inventory with common pantry staples and note which ones you're missing and where you're running low. Having a well-stocked pantry eases meal planning so that you always have dinner on hand.

GO SLOW TO GO CHEAP! When creating your weekly menu, use your slow cooker to cook inexpensive meats. "I try to incorporate a slow-cooker meal at least once a week. It saves my time, my sanity, my dishes and my money," says Chase.

ORGANIZE A MEAL PLAN. FOR CHASE, HABITS ARE KEY. AT THE BEGINNING OF EACH WEEK, FIGURE OUT WHEN YOU'LL NEED MEALS AND WHAT YOUR FAMILY LIKES TO EAT. MAKE A SHOPPING LIST BASED ON THOSE MEALS.

KEEP IMPULSES IN CHECK. Shopping with children can be hazardous to your shopping bill. Combat the impulse purchases kids often beg you to make by including two child-friendly snack and cereal options on your list. Once in the store, let the kids decide between the two. They'll feel as though they're participating, which may limit their begging.

COUPON ALERT! Before you go shopping, attach applicable coupons to your list to remind you which brands to buy. (See Coupon Myths on page 309.)

BRING YOUR OWN BAGS. Better yet, start keeping several reusable shopping bags in your car. Some stores knock a few cents off the bill if you bring your own.

GO TEAM! Before entering the store, give yourself a parking lot pep talk. Repeat this three times to yourself: "I will stick to the list." People who don't have a list on hand typically spend 40 percent more, Lempert reports.

IS THE FISH FRESH? READ THE SIGNS AT THE SEAFOOD COUNTER CAREFULLY. MOST FISH WILL SAY "PREVIOUSLY FROZEN." ACCORDING TO LEMPERT, BUYING FROZEN FISH INSTEAD OF FRESH COULD SAVE YOU NEARLY 40 PERCENT.

WHAT'S THE DEAL? GET MORE BARGAINS FOR YOUR BUCK WITH SIMPLE TIPS & TRICKS

WATCH THE CHEESE! Cheese with a Protected Designation of Origin (PDO) stamp or label typically costs 20 to 50 percent more than similar cheeses without it, notes Lempert. These labels, required by the European Union, specify where and how an item is made. A label for cheese, for example, might indicate that the cheese was made in a particular region from unpasteurized milk produced by a specific breed.

We found this to be the case during a recent trip to the cheese counter in a local market. A 6-ounce wedge of PDO-stamped Parmigiano-Reggiano cost $16.99. Similar cheeses produced outside this region of Italy may be legally sold under the generic name Parmesan—for a much lower price.

TRY SOMETHING NEW. Are your habits costing you? In 2010, total U.S. bottled water consumption reached 8.75 billion gallons. That's an average of 28.3 gallons per American. If you're worried about contaminants, invest in a water filter pitcher (about $30), and pocket the savings.

Along those lines, how much are you paying for coffee? If your daily commute includes a $2 coffee, your habit is costing you something like $500 a year. Buying a pound of coffee once every two weeks and brewing it at home could save you about $300 annually.

VISIT THE BULK BARGAINS.

THE BULK SECTION IS HANDY FOR BUYING SMALL AMOUNTS OF KEY ITEMS. THINK CANDY FOR CAKE DECORATING, SPECIALTY FLOURS AND DRIED FRUITS.

DO THE MATH. Look for the unit cost of an item. It's typically found on the price tag attached to the shelf and represents the cost per liter, gram, pound, ounce, etc. Ask your store manager if you don't see it. Otherwise, do the math yourself.

FOR EXAMPLE:

A 10.8-ounce can of ground coffee costs $4.69.

Divide the price by units.
$4.69/10.8 = 43¢ per ounce

Now compare that to an 11.3-ounce can of ground coffee at $5.69.

You might assume you're getting a better deal by buying the bigger can, but check this out:

$5.69/11.3 = 50¢ per ounce

Selecting the bigger can will cost 7¢ extra per ounce of coffee.

START SAVING. Do you grocery shop regularly? If so, ask a clerk or store manager about the savings card program. Most supermarkets offer store-specific deals when you use the discount card, which is typically free.

GENERIC VS. BRAND NAME. IS THE STORE BRAND ALWAYS CHEAPER? NOPE.

FOR EXAMPLE:
During a recent trip to the store, editors compared a 21.7-ounce box of Kellogg's Apple Jacks to a 12.2-ounce box of the store brand.

KELLOGG'S APPLE JACKS
21.7-ounce box = $5.29

STORE BRAND
12.2-ounce box = $3.39

OUNCE FOR OUNCE, Kellogg's was the better deal:

$5.29/21.7 =
24¢ per ounce

$3.39/12.2 =
28¢ per ounce

HEAD TO THE SALAD BAR. You might assume that buying food from the salad bar is tossing your money away, but that's not always true. At a $5.99-per-pound bar, you may find that chicken strips, feta cheese, nuts and fresh spinach are cheaper per pound than they are on store shelves. The salad bar is also helpful for picking up veggies you need in small amounts. Make smart use of prepared ingredients with the salad bar recipe **Ham & Pea Fettuccine**, below.

HAM & PEA FETTUCCINE

PREP/TOTAL TIME: 20 MIN. **MAKES:** 3 **COST:** $1.11/SERVING

Cook 4 oz. uncooked **fettuccine** according to package directions. Saute 1 cup cubed fully cooked **ham**; ¾ cup frozen **peas**, thawed; ¼ cup chopped **walnuts**; 1 **green onion**, chopped; ¼ tsp. dried **thyme**; and ¼ tsp. **pepper** in 2 Tbsp. **olive oil** in a large skillet until heated through. Drain fettuccine. Add to ham mixture; toss to coat. Add ⅓ cup shredded **cheddar cheese**; cover for 1 minute or until cheese is melted.

—**WILLIE DEWAARD** CORALVILLE, IOWA

THE DAIRY DEBATE. SOME EXPERTS ARGUE THAT BASIC ITEMS, SUCH AS MILK, ARE LOCATED IN THE BACK OF THE STORE TO GET YOU TO WALK THROUGH THE AISLES. OTHERS SAY IT'S BECAUSE OF THE LOGISTICS OF LOADING AND UNLOADING PERISHABLES FROM THE DOCKS BEHIND THE STORE. WHATEVER THE REASON, IF YOU'RE JUST RUNNING IN FOR MILK, PUT ON YOUR BLINDERS AND GET IN AND OUT QUICKLY.

GROCERY STORE GEOGRAPHY. STORES ARE HELPFULLY DESIGNED TO GET YOU TO BUY MORE. A SAVVY SHOPPER UNDERSTANDS THE CONCEPT OF SENSORY OVERLOAD, CHASE NOTES. BE MINDFUL OF HOW YOUR SIGHT, SMELL, TASTE, HEARING AND TOUCH ARE BEING AFFECTED AS YOU NAVIGATE A STRATEGICALLY LAID OUT MARKET.

COUPON MYTHS. Erin Chase, author of *The $5 Dinner Mom Cookbook*, helps debunk common misconceptions about coupons.

YOU CAN GET ONLY ONE PRODUCT EVEN IF YOU HAVE TWO IDENTICAL COUPONS. The wording "Limit one coupon per purchase" on many coupons is misleading. "Per purchase" means "per item," so you can use two coupons to buy two items.

YOU CAN PRINT ONLY ONE COUPON. Most coupon sites allow shoppers to print two of the same coupon.

COUPONS TAKE TOO LONG. Online coupon sites, smartphone applications and email alerts bring the savings to you. Check out these websites for smart deals:

coupons.com
smartsource.com
redplum.com
hotcouponworld.com
slickdeals.net
couponmom.com

DON'T EAT WITH YOUR EYES. Grocery stores take advantage of visual appeal by welcoming shoppers with a bright and bountiful produce department. You may also notice tempting seasonal displays and other enticements, such as blooming bouquets and delicious baked goods. Enjoy the eye candy—but don't let it tempt you into buying things you don't need. In other words: Stick to your list.

FREE SAMPLE? Don't mind if I do. Just remember, there's no obligation to buy. Unless it's something you really need—and there's a substantial coupon—you're better off with the eat-and-run method.

PAY ATTENTION TO SOUNDS. The familiar tunes you hear pumping through the speakers are the supermarket's way of buttering you up to buy. It's OK to sing along, but try replacing the words with "Stick to the list, stick to the list."

NOTICE TRICKY PLACEMENTS. Watch out for what's within child's reach. Use the kid-friendly options on your list when you notice your little ones reaching for the sugar-laden cereals and snacks that just so happen to be on the lower shelves—conveniently placed at their eye level.

And keep in mind that aisle tricks aren't just for kids. Chase has found that some companies pay a premium to get their products displayed at your eye level, too. When you're looking for the best deal on ingredients you need, remember to reach high and low.

MIND THE ENDS! End caps are the shelves at the end of aisles used to display popular sale items. The prices on end cap products, however, are not always the best. As Chase recommends, it's worth a trip down the aisle to scout for cheaper selections.

PASS THE SMELL TEST. FRESH BAKED BREAD, BREWING COFFEE, THE POPCORN MACHINE DOING ITS THING: WHEN YOU SMELL THESE AROMAS, IT'S EASY TO MAKE AN UNPLANNED PURCHASE. REMIND YOURSELF THAT WHEN YOU COMPLETE YOUR MISSION, YOU'LL HAVE THE SUPPLIES YOU NEED TO MAKE THESE ITEMS AT HOME.

ABOUT THE EXPERTS

PHIL LEMPERT is the food trends editor and correspondent for NBC News' *Today* show, where he reports on consumer trends, food safety, money-saving tips and new products. He has appeared often on The View, The Oprah Winfrey Show, 20/20, CNN, CNBC and MSNBC as well as on local TV throughout the country. Find him at *supermarketguru.com*.

ERIN CHASE is the creator of *5dollardinners.com* and has appeared on Rachael Ray. She is the author of *The $5 Dinner Mom Cookbook*, a collection of shopping tips and more than 150 recipes costing $5 or less.

OUR 25 BEST BAKING TIPS

BE A BETTER BAKER WITH TIPS AND TRICKS FROM THE PROS

Do you know what's causing your cookies to spread? How can you tell if your baking soda is still good? Why does a Bundt cake need to cool in the pan? And why, oh why, won't those quick breads behave?

Our Test Kitchen pros put on their oven mitts to answer some of the burning questions that come up when you're baking. Here we bring you their best advice, along with tips and secrets to solve any rising dilemmas. Preheat the oven, pull out the rolling pin and stand that mixing bowl at attention. It's time to bake like a pro!

Measurements That Count

When it comes to baking, measurements really do count! Here are some tips and techniques to keep your recipes from overreacting.

1 **It may sound like a "duh" thing to say, but using proper tools to measure ingredients can prevent baking flops.** Choose glass liquid measuring cups for all liquids. When measuring, place the cup on a level surface so you can view it at eye level. Spoon dry ingredients into a dry measuring cup until it overflows, then level it with a metal spatula or knife. Spoon bulkier ingredients, such as nuts or chocolate chips, into the cup until they're level with the rim.

2 **In a nutshell, if the word "chopped" comes before the ingredient, chop it before measuring.** If it's listed after the ingredient, chop after measuring.

3 **If you've suddenly been inspired to bake (and good for you!), your flour's likely been left alone awhile.** When seldom used, flour can settle and compact, so it's easy to measure more than you need. To keep it loose, aerate it with a wire whisk. You can also place a sieve over a bowl and sift the flour through the sieve, then spoon it into a dry measuring cup.

Do's and Doughs

Nothing's worse than seeing cookies or breads you've slaved over come out shapeless or flat. For the perfect shape and texture, consider your dough's needs and mixing methods.

4 **Biscuit dough isn't as needy as you think.** After you cut in shortening, add the liquids all at once and mix until just combined. The dough might not be smooth, but that's OK—it won't affect the outcome.

Knead dough as your recipe directs, just until it holds together. Extra kneading makes dough tough. If dough is very soft, pat it to the proper thickness before cutting, or gently roll it with a lightly floured rolling pin.

5 **Take a lesson from Grandma: To knead bread dough by hand, turn it onto a lightly floured surface.** Lightly flour your hands and shape the dough into a ball. Fold the top toward you. With your palms, push it with a rolling motion away. After each push, give the dough a quarter turn and fold it toward you again. As you knead, add flour to the surface only as needed to keep dough from sticking. Continue kneading in this manner until the dough is smooth and elastic, typically about 6 to 8 minutes.

For less of an arm workout, use a stand mixer with a dough hook. Knead on low speed for 3 minutes, or until it clings to the hook and cleans the sides of the bowl. Continue to knead the dough 3-4 minutes longer, or until it's smooth and elastic. Check it often to prevent overmixing, which can result in hard, doughy bread.

QUICK FIX: To save time, use your food processor to knead dough. Check the manufacturer's directions for more information.

6 **Frozen bread dough can help you to turn out beautiful breads in less time.** Thawed bread dough should be soft, warm and pliable before it's rolled out. If it springs back when rolled, cover and let it rest 15 minutes longer. You can also hold the dough in place for a few seconds when rolling to help it retain the shape you want.

7 **Stop feeding the trash can faulty bread when you bake your favorite quick breads.** To prevent a disappointing loaf next time, use the simple method that's just right for quick bread: Mix wet and dry ingredients separately and combine them only until moist. (Don't worry about any small lumps; they will disappear while baking.)

Also check your oven with an oven thermometer. A cool oven may produce an undercooked center. And for best results, use heavy, good-quality loaf pans. Disposable baking pans may cause the bread's exterior to bake faster than the interior.

8 **Cookies, while sweet, are sensitive creatures.** Here's how you can soften or shape them up.

For softer cookies: Measure flour carefully; too much may make cookies firm, dry and tough. Avoid overmixing the dough, and check for doneness at the minimum baking time, baking longer if needed. Also try a recipe with brown sugar or honey instead of white sugar—which produces a crisper cookie.

Cookies spreading too much? If your recipe contains a lot of fat, such as butter or oil, your greased cookie sheet may be to blame. Instead, top your baking sheets with parchment paper or Teflon liners to help prevent cookies from turning out flat.

Having trouble with butter? Butter melts faster than margarine, giving cookies more time to spread before they set up. For plump cookies, try placing dough on cooled baking sheets before baking; chill soft dough to keep butter cold; use a recipe with less sugar (undissolved sugar and fat melt during baking, causing cookies to spread); and measure carefully—cookies are sensitive to small ingredient differences.

9 Waiting for butter to come to room temperature is like waiting for water to boil. To soften 1/2 cup cold butter quickly, place an unwrapped stick on a microwave-safe plate. In an 1,100-watt microwave, heat at 30 percent power for 15-20 seconds or until softened.

10 Let's dish this out: Baking pans are made of metal. Baking dishes are made of ovenproof glass or ceramic. We prefer to bake in metal pans with dull finishes; they produce foods with an even, golden surface. Pans with dark finishes hold more heat, so they may cook and brown foods faster. Glass dishes bake even faster than baking pans.

If substituting a glass baking dish for a metal baking pan, reduce the oven temperature by 25 degrees to avoid overbaking and overbrowning.

To Swap or Not

Baking is part art and part science, but as anyone who's tried to substitute one ingredient for another and watched a cake flop knows, it's also a tricky business. Use these hints to make accurate swaps.

11 Yes, quick-rise and regular active dry yeast can be substituted for each other in recipes, but remember: Quick-rise yeast doesn't need to be dissolved in water before mixing, and it requires only one rise. In place of the first rise, let dough rest, covered, for 10 minutes before shaping. Once shaped, the dough's rise should take about half the time listed in a recipe that calls for active dry yeast.

12 In the case of light brown vs. dark brown sugar, the choice is yours, sugar! But keep in mind, light brown sugar has a subtle, delicate taste. If you like a more intense molasses flavor in baked goods, use dark brown instead.

13 Quick-cooking oats and old-fashioned oats can be interchanged in baked goods, but old-fashioned oats add more texture, so you may notice a difference without 'em.

14 You can use unsalted butter without adding more salt to the recipe. Salted butter has only about 1/8 teaspoon salt per stick; the salt acts as a preservative for the butter.

15 Soy much for milk! Soy milk can be swapped for dairy milk in equal parts and is an excellent alternative for anyone with a milk allergy. Soy milk does have a tendency to curdle when mixed with an acidic ingredient, such as lemon juice or wine, so use with care.

16 Here's a sweet substitute: Evaporated skim milk can replace whipping cream in many recipes. Baking with reduced-fat evaporated milk? There may be some changes in texture and flavor from the full-fat version. **QUICK FACTS:** What's the difference between evaporated milk and sweetened condensed milk? Sweetened condensed milk is a mixture of whole milk and sugar from which 60 percent of the water has been removed. Unsweetened condensed milk, known as evaporated milk, comes in whole, reduced-fat and fat-free forms.

17 Baking soda and baking powder are both leaveners that cause baked goods to rise and give them a light texture. But—and this is a big but—baking soda neutralizes acidic ingredients (buttermilk, lemon juice, molasses or cream of tartar), tenderizing baked goods; baking powder does not. Batters and doughs that use only baking soda as a leavening agent should be baked immediately to keep the texture light and ensure proper rise.

18 Bonus tip! Much success with baked goods depends on your baking powder and baking soda's freshness. The shelf life for these products is about 6 months, but here's how to test to be sure they're active:

For baking powder, mix 1 teaspoon with 1/3 cup hot water. For baking soda, mix 1/4 teaspoon with 2 teaspoons vinegar.

If active bubbling occurs, the products are still fresh and fine to use. If not, they should be replaced. When buying new, remember to check for an expiration date.

Keep It Cool

It might be worth risking a burned mouth for a taste of treats straight from the oven, but most of the time it's better to let them cool. Knowing when to chill out and how to use freezing to your advantage comes in handy when prepping for special occasions.

19 **Unless a recipe states otherwise, cakes baked in fluted tube pans should cool for 10-15 minutes before you move them to a wire rack to cool completely.** Removing a cake too soon can cause it to crack, break or stick to the pan. Leaving a cake in the pan too long, however, can cause moisture to form between the cake and the pan. So keep an eye on that timer.

20 **Most cookie doughs may be refrigerated or frozen, then baked later.** When placed in airtight wrapping, unbaked cookie doughs can be refrigerated for a week or frozen for up to 3 months.

We like to freeze cookie dough by dropping tablespoonfuls onto baking sheets. Cover and freeze until firm. When the dough's frozen, transfer the dough balls to resealable plastic freezer bags. To use frozen cookie dough: Place dough balls 2 in. apart on greased or ungreased baking sheets. Bake as the recipe directs, until the cookies are lightly browned.

21 **Unfrosted butter cakes and ones iced with buttercream frosting freeze well.** Place individual cake layers on a baking sheet and freeze. Once frozen, place in heavy-duty resealable plastic freezer bags. Unfrosted butter cakes can be frozen for up to 4 months; frosted butter cakes, up to 2 months. (Not all frostings freeze well.) Thaw cakes in the fridge.

Both quick breads and yeast breads also freeze well. Freeze completely cooled bread in heavy-duty resealable plastic freezer bags for up to 3 months.

Cookies can be wrapped in plastic wrap, stacked in an airtight container and sealed for 1 to 3 months in your freezer. Thaw wrapped cookies and breads at room temperature. Always allow cookies to cool completely before freezing.

When Looks Matter

We eat with our eyes first. Here's how to make goodies look as special as they taste.

22 **To keep a pie crust's tender edges from burning, fold a 12-in. square of foil into quarters.** Make a mark on the two folded sides about 3¾ in. from the closed corner. Holding the closed corner in one hand, use scissors to cut an arc from one mark to the other. Discard the center. Unfold the remaining foil.

When the crust's edges are nicely browned, place the foil shield over the pie, crimping it around the edges. Then return the pie to the oven to finish baking.

23 **There's more than one way to curl chocolate for a decadent adornment to cakes or pies.**

If you have a solid block of chocolate, use a vegetable peeler to peel off curls, allowing them to fall gently onto a plate in a single layer. (If you get only shavings, warm the chocolate slightly.)

Or, melt chocolate chips, confectionery coating or bars and pour chocolate onto the back of an inverted cookie sheet. Spread until you have a thin smooth layer. Let cool until firm and pliable but not brittle. With a metal spatula or pancake turner, using even pressure, scrape up a thin layer of chocolate. It will curl as you go. The slower you scrape, the wider the curls. Slide a toothpick or wooden skewer through each curl to carefully lift it onto the cake, and arrange as desired.

24 **Decorating cookies with piped frosting gives them a festive look.** But holding the pastry bag with one hand while using the other hand to fill it can be tricky. Instead, do this:

Secure the frosting tip and coupler on the pastry bag. Place the bag's tip into a tall empty glass. Fold the bag's wide opening halfway over the glass. Use a spoon to transfer frosting to the bag. When it's three-fourths full, pull the bag's sides up over the frosting. Lift it out of the glass, twist the open end to close and apply pressure to the bag as you happily pipe away.

25 **If you don't think the mess is half the fun of frosting a cake, try this method:** Before transferring cooled cake layers to the plate, cut waxed paper into narrow strips and place around the plate's edges. Center the cake on the plate over strips. When you're finished frosting, carefully remove the waxed paper by pulling out one piece at a time from underneath the cake. Voilà! You'll have a beautifully frosted cake, and a clean serving plate, too!

Substitutions & Equivalents

EQUIVALENT MEASURES

3 teaspoons	=	1 tablespoon	**16 tablespoons**	=	1 cup
4 tablespoons	=	1/4 cup	**2 cups**	=	1 pint
5-1/3 tablespoons	=	1/3 cup	**4 cups**	=	1 quart
8 tablespoons	=	1/2 cup	**4 quarts**	=	1 gallon

FOOD EQUIVALENTS

GRAINS

Macaroni	1 cup (3-1/2 ounces) uncooked	=	2-1/2 cups cooked
Noodles, Medium	3 cups (4 ounces) uncooked	=	4 cups cooked
Popcorn	1/3 to 1/2 cup unpopped	=	8 cups popped
Rice, Long Grain	1 cup uncooked	=	3 cups cooked
Rice, Quick-Cooking	1 cup uncooked	=	2 cups cooked
Spaghetti	8 ounces uncooked	=	4 cups cooked

CRUMBS

Bread	1 slice	=	3/4 cup soft crumbs, 1/4 cup fine dry crumbs
Graham Crackers	7 squares	=	1/2 cup finely crushed
Buttery Round Crackers	12 crackers	=	1/2 cup finely crushed
Saltine Crackers	14 crackers	=	1/2 cup finely crushed

FRUITS

Bananas	1 medium	=	1/3 cup mashed
Lemons	1 medium	=	3 tablespoons juice, 2 teaspoons grated peel
Limes	1 medium	=	2 tablespoons juice, 1-1/2 teaspoons grated peel
Oranges	1 medium	=	1/4 to 1/3 cup juice, 4 teaspoons grated peel

VEGETABLES

Cabbage	1 head	=	5 cups shredded	**Green Pepper**	1 large	=	1 cup chopped
Carrots	1 pound	=	3 cups shredded	**Mushrooms**	1/2 pound	=	3 cups sliced
Celery	1 rib	=	1/2 cup chopped	**Onions**	1 medium	=	1/2 cup chopped
Corn	1 ear fresh	=	2/3 cup kernels	**Potatoes**	3 medium	=	2 cups cubed

NUTS

Almonds	1 pound	=	3 cups chopped	**Pecan Halves**	1 pound	=	4-1/2 cups chopped
Ground Nuts	3-3/4 ounces	=	1 cup	**Walnuts**	1 pound	=	3-3/4 cups chopped

EASY SUBSTITUTIONS

When you need...		Use...
Baking Powder	1 teaspoon	1/2 teaspoon cream of tartar + 1/4 teaspoon baking soda
Buttermilk	1 cup	1 tablespoon lemon juice or vinegar + enough milk to measure 1 cup (let stand 5 minutes before using)
Cornstarch	1 tablespoon	2 tablespoons all-purpose flour
Honey	1 cup	1-1/4 cups sugar + 1/4 cup water
Half-and-Half Cream	1 cup	1 tablespoon melted butter + enough whole milk to measure 1 cup
Onion	1 small, chopped (1/3 cup)	1 teaspoon onion powder or 1 tablespoon dried minced onion
Tomato Juice	1 cup	1/2 cup tomato sauce + 1/2 cup water
Tomato Sauce	2 cups	3/4 cup tomato paste + 1 cup water
Unsweetened Chocolate	1 square (1 ounce)	3 tablespoons baking cocoa + 1 tablespoon shortening or oil
Whole Milk	1 cup	1/2 cup evaporated milk + 1/2 cup water

Cooking Terms

Here's a quick reference for some of the cooking terms used in *Taste of Home* recipes:

BASTE To moisten food with melted butter, pan drippings, marinades or other liquid to add more flavor and juiciness.

BEAT To combine ingredients with a rapid movement using a fork, spoon, wire whisk or electric mixer.

BLEND To combine ingredients until *just* mixed.

BOIL To heat liquids until bubbles form that cannot be "stirred down." In the case of water, the temperature will reach 212°.

BONE To remove all meat from the bone before cooking.

CREAM To beat ingredients together to a smooth consistency, usually in the case of butter and sugar for baking.

DASH A small amount of seasoning, less than 1/8 teaspoon. If using a shaker, a dash would be a quick flip of the container.

DREDGE To coat foods with flour or other dry ingredients. Most often done with pot roasts and stew meat before browning.

FOLD To incorporate several ingredients by careful and gentle turning with a spatula. Used generally with beaten egg whites or whipped cream when mixing into the rest of the ingredients to keep the batter light.

JULIENNE To cut foods into long thin strips much like matchsticks. Used most often for salads and stir-fry dishes.

MARINATE To tenderize and/or flavor foods, usually meat or raw vegetables, by placing in a liquid mixture of oil, vinegar, wine, lime or lemon juice, herbs and spices.

MINCE To cut into very fine pieces. Used often for garlic or fresh herbs.

PARBOIL To cook partially, usually used in the case of chicken, sausages and vegetables.

PARTIALLY SET Describes the consistency of gelatin after it has been chilled for a short amount of time. Mixture should resemble the consistency of egg whites.

PUREE To process foods to a smooth mixture. Can be prepared in an electric blender, food processor, food mill or sieve.

SAUTE To fry quickly in a small amount of fat, stirring almost constantly. Most often done with onions, mushrooms and other chopped vegetables.

SCORE To cut slits partway through the outer surface of foods. Often used with ham or flank steak.

STIR-FRY To cook meats and/or vegetables with a constant stirring motion in a small amount of oil in a wok or skillet over high heat.

General Recipe Index

This handy index lists every recipe by food category, major ingredient and/or cooking method, so you can easily locate recipes to suit your needs.

✓Recipe includes Nutrition Facts and Diabetic Exchanges

ALFREDO

Alfredo Creamed Spinach, 52
Chicken and Sausage Penne, 291
Chicken Fajita Alfredo, 180
Salmon Fettuccine Alfredo, 98
Sausage Alfredo, 26
Stuffed Alfredo Pork Chops, 96
Turkey Alfredo Tetrazzini, 64

APPETIZERS & SNACKS (also see Beverages; Breads & Rolls)

Cold Appetizers

Chicks-on-the-Ranch Deviled Eggs, 242
Curry On Deviled Eggs, 245
Dazzling Dirty Martini Deviled Eggs, 245
Dill-icious Deviled Eggs, 242
Hoisin-It-Nice Deviled Eggs, 245
Hop-To-It Deviled Eggs, 242
Lil' Devil Eggs, 244
Little Italy Deviled Eggs, 244
Lone Star Deviled Eggs, 244
Roast Beef Aioli Bundles, 238
Salmon Mousse Tartlets, 41
Salsa Dipper Deviled Eggs, 244
Savory Corn Bread Pops, 130
Tater Salad Deviled Eggs, 244
Tortellini & Shrimp Skewers with Sun-Dried Tomato Sauce, 239
West Coaster Deviled Eggs, 245

Dips & Spreads

Cheese-Trio Artichoke & Spinach Dip, 126
Chili con Queso El Dorado, 131
Reuben Dip, 268
Sun-Dried Tomato and Parmesan Spread, 130

Hot Appetizers

Balsamic-Glazed Chicken Wings, 42
Creamy Cranberry Meatballs, 129
Family-Favorite Turkey Egg Rolls, 126
Gladiator Chicken Skewers, 248
Godfather Crostini, 249
Gump's Shrimp & Grits, 248
Italian Dipping Sticks, 72
Maple Jalapenos, 133
Panko Chicken with Fresh Marinara, 135
Peanut Chicken Wings, 127
Pinwheel Pizza Snacks, 79
Sweet & Spicy Chicken Wings, 129

Snacks

Chicken Nachos for One, 135
Chocolate Butterscotch Tartlets, 131
Crispy Mexican Truffles, 132
Jazzed-Up French Bread, 41
Peanut Butter-Graham Snack Mix, 78

APPLES

Apple Almond Salad, 55
Apple-Balsamic Pork Chops, 13
Apple Spiced Tea, 130
Caramel-Apple Pork Chops, 111
Cinnamon Apple Shakes, 135
Gourmet Caramel Apples, 261
Slow-Cooked Fruited Oatmeal with Nuts, 118

APRICOTS

Apricot Cream Biscuits, 117
Apricot Crisp, 222
Apricot-Honey Chicken, 25
Desert Oasis Chicken, 172
Sacher Bars, 228
Summer's Best Spinach Salad, 145

ARTICHOKES

Cheese-Trio Artichoke & Spinach Dip, 126
Jazzy Spaghetti Sauce, 102
Mediterranean Tuna Linguine, 101
Pepperoni-Artichoke Pasta Salad, 143
Rustic Antipasto Tart, 238
The Bistro Baked Potato, 240

ASPARAGUS

Asparagus Mushroom Quiche, 114
✓Asparagus Salad with Grilled Salmon, 204
Balsamic Broiled Asparagus, 17
Orange Beef and Asparagus Stir-Fry, 92
Parmesan Roasted Asparagus, 18
Roast Beef Aioli Bundles, 238

AVOCADO

Coconut Shrimp Chowder, 157
Green Breakfast Smoothie, 121
Ham & Cheese Bagels, 122
Mexican Couscous, 49
Summer Salads with Mandarin Oranges, 142
Summer's Best Spinach Salad, 145

BACON

Alfredo Creamed Spinach, 52
Bacon Cheeseburger Rice, 75
Bacon-Gouda Stuffed Onions, 42
Bacon-Parmesan Brussels Sprouts, 47
BLT Catfish Sandwiches, 157
Blue Cheese Quiche with Caramelized Pears, 119
Breadstick Pizza, 58
Caramel-Apple Pork Chops, 111
Chicken & Bacon Tart, 101
Chicken & Shrimp Fettuccine, 109
Garlic Chicken & Bacon Pizza, 47
Godfather Crostini, 249
Gump's Shrimp & Grits, 248
Hawaiian Barbecue Beans, 50
Hungry Man's Baked Potatoes, 241
Loaded Breakfast Potatoes, 121
Maple Jalapenos, 133
Slow Cooker Hula Chicken, 65
The Elvis Ice Cream Sandwich, 225
West Coaster Deviled Eggs, 245

BANANAS

Nutty Waffle Sandwiches, 116
Teddy Bear Sandwiches, 72

BARLEY

Vegetable Beef & Barley Soup, 83

BARS & BROWNIES

Million Dollar Pecan Bars, 221
Peanut Butter-Hazelnut Brownies, 229
Quick Crisp Snack Bars, 77
Sacher Bars, 228
Triple-Layer Pretzel Brownies, 221

BEANS

Beef & Bean Tacos, 97
Black Bean & Corn Salsa, 146
Cajun Beef and Beans, 89
Chicken Chimichangas, 84
Chicken Nachos for One, 135
Fiesta Rice and Bean Salad, 149
Hawaiian Barbecue Beans, 50
Kielbasa Spinach Soup, 165
Loaded Mexican Pizza, 194
Mexican Tater-Topped Casserole, 89
Skillet Cassoulet, 168
Southwest Chicken Pockets, 102
✓Tuna with Tuscan White Bean Salad, 206
Vegetarian Potato au Gratin, 103
White Bean and Spinach Salads, 142

BEEF & CORNED BEEF (also see Ground Beef)

Appetizers

Beef & Onion Cheese Ball, 268
Lone Star Deviled Eggs, 244
Reuben Dip, 268
Roast Beef Aioli Bundles, 238

Main Dishes

Best Ever Roast Beef, 289
Caramelized Onion Chuck Roast, 83
Chili-Beer Glazed Steaks, 41
Country Chuck Roast with Mushroom Gravy, 168
Family-Favorite Spaghetti Sauce, 77
Grilled Fajita Rolled Steak, 257
Grilled Ribeyes with Blue Cheese Butter, 92
Layered Potato Beef Casserole, 85
✓Makeover Beef Stroganoff, 211
Mexican Fiesta Steak Stir-Fry, 173
Mushroom Steak, 288
Orange Beef and Asparagus Stir-Fry, 92
Philly Cheesesteak Pizza, 188
Philly-Style Barbecue Pizza, 64
Roast Beef Potpie, 66
Rueben Strata, 91
Sirloin Stir-Fry with Ramen Noodles, 177
Slow-Cooked Corned Beef, 91
Smothered Burritos, 49
Steakhouse Strip Steaks with Chimichurri, 285
Sweet & Tender Beef Ribs, 185
The Bistro Baked Potato, 240
The King's Crowned Filets, 284

Sandwiches

Beef Gyros, 165
Deli Roast Beef Sandwiches with Mashed Potatoes, 58
Italian Shredded Beef Sandwiches, 162
Philadelphia Beef Sandwich, 161
Sweet & Savory Slow-Cooked Beef, 159

Soups & Stew

Chilly Night Beef Stew, 85
Vegetable Beef & Barley Soup, 83

BEVERAGES

American Beauty, 246
Apple Spiced Tea, 130
Bella Basil Raspberry Tea, 132
Berry Delicious Smoothies, 127
Blackberry Beer Cocktail, 45
Blueberry-Oat Smoothies, 117
Cerveza Margaritas, 257
Champagne Fruit Punch, 236
Cinnamon Apple Shakes, 135
Green Breakfast Smoothie, 121
Lemon Mint Spritzer, 129
Mocha Cappuccino Punch, 130
Pineapple Colada Shake, 133
Pomegranate Cosmo, 269
Sunny Breakfast Smoothies, 73
Super Mango Smoothies, 129
Warm Christmas Punch, 269

BISCUITS

Apricot Cream Biscuits, 117
Cheddar Garlic Biscuits, 58
Jalapeno Cheddar Biscuits, 22

BLACKBERRIES

Berry Delicious Smoothies, 127
Blackberry Beer Cocktail, 45

BLUEBERRIES

✓Almond Berry Pancakes, 201
Berry-Cherry Peach Sauce, 215
Berry Delicious Smoothies, 127
Blueberry & Ginger Tart, 255
Blueberry-Lemon Ice Cream Sandwiches, 44
Blueberry-Oat Smoothies, 117
Blueberry-Rhubarb Crisp, 222

BREADS & ROLLS (also see Biscuits; Corn Bread & Cornmeal; Pizza)

Cheddar Bread Twists, 21
Chimichurri Monkey Bread, 63
Easy Cinnamon Rolls, 116
Farmhouse Barbecue Muffins, 73
Green Onion Rolls, 254
Hearty Sausage-Stuffed Loaf, 61
Italian Dipping Sticks, 72
Italian-Style Croissants, 55
Jazzed-Up French Bread, 41
Mini Caramel Rolls, 114
Spinach Salmon Bundles, 63
Spiral Stromboli, 60
Sun-Dried Tomato Garlic Bread, 10
Turkey-Brie Stromboli, 61

BREAKFAST & BRUNCH (also see Breads & Rolls; Eggs; Pancakes; Quiche & Savory Tarts; Waffles)

✓Almond Berry Pancakes, 201
Apricot Cream Biscuits, 117
Asparagus Mushroom Quiche, 114
Best Scrambled Eggs, 114
Blue Cheese Quiche with Caramelized Pears, 119
Blueberry-Oat Smoothies, 117
✓Cardamom Sour Cream Waffles, 198
Chocolate Challah French Toast, 121
Coconut-Pecan Coffee Cake, 118
Cranberry Pancakes, 122
Cream Cheese & Chive Omelet, 117
Easy Cinnamon Rolls, 116
Green Breakfast Smoothie, 121
Ham & Cheese Bagels, 122
✓Herb Breakfast Frittata, 201
Loaded Breakfast Potatoes, 121
Maple & Chipotle Sausages, 122
Mini Caramel Rolls, 114
Nutty Waffle Sandwiches, 116
✓Sausage & Salsa Breakfast Burritos, 199
Slow-Cooked Fruited Oatmeal with Nuts, 118
Yogurt & Honey Fruit Cups, 122

BROCCOLI

Broccoli Salad with Cucumber, 138
Broccoli with Orange Browned Butter, 25
Creamy Salmon Linguine, 87
Pasta & Broccoli Sausage Simmer, 180
Pasta Primavera, 176
Salmon Fettuccine Alfredo, 98
Sirloin Stir-Fry with Ramen Noodles, 177
Zesty Broccoli, 146

BRUSSELS SPROUTS

Bacon-Parmesan Brussels Sprouts, 47
Garlic Brussels Sprouts, 30
Maple-Dijon Sausage & Sprouts, 110

BUTTER

Broccoli with Orange Browned Butter, 25
Brown Butter Spice Cookies, 232
Buttered Noodles, 13
Chicken with Rosemary Butter Sauce for 2, 29
Grilled Ribeyes with Blue Cheese Butter, 92

CABBAGE & COLESLAW MIX

Baja Fish Tacos, 175
Cajun Fish Tacos, 105
Family-Favorite Turkey Egg Rolls, 126
Golombki, 192
Honey Mustard Coleslaw, 138
Rueben Strata, 91
Slow Cooker Golombki, 288
Teriyaki Chicken and Vegetables, 106
Vegetarian Reubens, 152
Warm Pecan Cabbage Slaw, 34

CAKES, CHEESECAKES & CUPCAKES

Bride and Groom Cupcakes, 237
Cake with Lemon Sauce, 226
Chocolate Cake in a Mug, 214
Christmas Elf Cake Pops, 276
Coconut-Pecan Coffee Cake, 118
Crème de Menthe Cheesecake Cookies, 271
Dark Chocolate Carrot Cake, 231
Fun & Festive Cake Pops, 277
Grilled Peaches & Pound Cake, 258
Lion and Lamb Cupcakes, 74
Pineapple Orange Cheesecake, 226
Present Cake Pops, 277
Snowman Cake Pops, 276
Strawberry Cheesecake Pops, 78
Trick-or-Treat Cake, 262

CANDY & CONFECTIONS

Alligator Cookie Pops, 79
Candy Craze Ice Cream Sandwiches, 70
Candy-Licious Fudge, 233
Chocolate Candy Cane Cookies, 271
Chocolate Caramel Oranges, 263
Christmas Elf Cake Pops, 276
Crispy Mexican Truffles, 132
Fun & Festive Cake Pops, 277
Ghost Caramel Pears, 261
Gourmet Caramel Apples, 261
Hot Chocolate Peppermint Cookies, 275
Nutter Butter Truffles, 238
Peppermint S'more Tassies, 274
Present Cake Pops, 277
Salted Caramel & Dark Chocolate Figs, 262
Salted Caramel Fudge Drops, 272
Snowman Cake Pops, 276

CARAMEL

Caramel Coconut Stars, 271
Caramel-Pecan Ice Cream Sandwiches, 225
Chocolate Caramel Oranges, 263
Cinnamon Apple Shakes, 135
Ghost Caramel Pears, 261
Gourmet Caramel Apples, 261
Mini Caramel Rolls, 114
Salted Caramel & Dark Chocolate Figs, 262
Salted Caramel Fudge Drops, 272

CARROTS

Balsamic Pork Stir-Fry, 179
Brandy-Glazed Carrots, 254
Dark Chocolate Carrot Cake, 231
Herbed Corn and Carrots, 26
Indian Baked Chicken, 186

Rosemary Carrots, 33
Savory Peas and Carrots, 13
✓Sweet Onion & Carrot Medley, 203

CASSEROLES (also see Breakfast & Brunch; Oven Entrees; Quiche & Savory Tarts)
Baked Rigatoni & Sausage, 55
Baked Spaghetti, 194
Buffalo Chicken Pasta Bake, 185
Cajun Beef Casserole, 99
Cajun Chicken Pasta Bake, 193
Chicken and Sausage Penne, 291
Chicken Madeira Pastry, 192
Chipotle Mac & Cheese, 290
Crab Imperial Casserole, 186
Easy Cheddar Chicken Potpie, 184
Ham & Noodle Bake, 86
Layered Potato Beef Casserole, 85
Mexican Tater-Topped Casserole, 89
Mom's Turkey Tetrazzini, 192
Next Day Meat Loaf Pie, 90
Philly-Style Mac and Cheese, 191
Roast Beef Potpie, 66
Rueben Strata, 91
Sausage Florentine Potpie, 66
Sloppy Joe Veggie Casserole, 189
Stacked Vegetables and Ravioli, 107
Taco Shepherd's Pie, 291
Turkey Alfredo Tetrazzini, 64
Turkey Potpie Cups, 67
Vegetarian Potato au Gratin, 103

CEREAL
Cereal & Milk Ice Cream Sandwiches, 71
Peanut Butter-Graham Snack Mix, 78
Quick Crisp Snack Bars, 77

CHEESE (also see Cream Cheese)
Appetizers
Beef & Onion Cheese Ball, 268
Cheese-Trio Artichoke & Spinach Dip, 126
Chili con Queso El Dorado, 131
Rustic Antipasto Tart, 238
Sun-Dried Tomato and Parmesan Spread, 130
Breads
Cheddar Bread Twists, 21
Cheddar Garlic Biscuits, 58
Jalapeno Cheddar Biscuits, 22
Main Dishes
Baked Spaghetti, 194
Blue Cheese Quiche with Caramelized Pears, 119
Chicken and Sausage Penne, 291
Chipotle Mac & Cheese, 290
Creamy Chicken Lasagna Roll-Ups, 188
Easy Cheddar Chicken Potpie, 184
Italian Enchiladas, 290
Layered Potato Beef Casserole, 85
✓Makeover Macaroni and Cheese, 211
Philly Cheesesteak Pizza, 188
Philly-Style Barbecue Pizza, 64
Philly-Style Mac and Cheese, 191
Stacked Chicken Cordon Bleu, 169
Taco Shepherd's Pie, 291
Tuscan Parmesan Pork Chops, 48
Sandwiches
Ham & Cheese Bagels, 122
Hearty Sausage-Stuffed Loaf, 61
Philadelphia Beef Sandwich, 161
Spiral Stromboli, 60
Turkey-Brie Stromboli, 61
Vegetarian Reubens, 152
Side Dishes & Salads
Chicken & Brie Salad, 147
Fiesta Corn Chip Salad, 145
Grilled Romaine with Swiss, 286
Parmesan-Onion Potato Packets, 284
Poutine, 64
Scalloped Potatoes & Ham, 144
Spinach & Gorgonzola Salad, 10
Soups
Cream of Potato & Cheddar Soup, 158

CHERRIES
Berry-Cherry Peach Sauce, 215
Berry Delicious Smoothies, 127
Cherry Cordial Cookies, 218
Sicilian Ice Cream Sandwiches, 224

CHICKEN (also see Sausage)
Appetizer
Balsamic-Glazed Chicken Wings, 42
Chicken Nachos for One, 135
Gladiator Chicken Skewers, 248
Panko Chicken with Fresh Marinara, 135
Peanut Chicken Wings, 127
Sweet & Spicy Chicken Wings, 129
Main Dishes
Apricot-Honey Chicken, 25
Baked Peanut Chicken, 62
Balsamic Chicken Fettucine, 99
Basil-Mint Chicken Thighs, 285
Beer Can Chicken, 258
Blushing Angel Hair Pasta with Chicken, 62
Buenos Dias Baked Potatoes, 241
Buffalo Chicken Pasta Bake, 185
Cajun Chicken Pasta Bake, 193
Chicken & Bacon Tart, 101
Chicken and Sausage Penne, 291
Chicken & Shrimp Fettuccine, 109
Chicken Chimichangas, 84
Chicken Madeira Pastry, 192
Chicken Rellenos with Cilantro-Lime Cream Sauce, 174
Chicken Strips Milano, 33

CHICKEN (continued)

Chicken Taco Rice, 181
Chicken with Caramelized Pears, 98
Chicken with Rosemary Butter Sauce for 2, 29
Creamy Chicken Lasagna Roll-Ups, 188
Curry Citrus Chicken, 34
Desert Oasis Chicken, 172
Easy Cheddar Chicken Potpie, 184
Garlic Chicken & Bacon Pizza, 47
Gnocchi Chicken Skillet, 173
Herbed Chicken and Rice, 30
Honey & Spice Baked Chicken, 84
Honey Roasted Chicken, 51
Indian Baked Chicken, 186
Lemon & Sage Roasted Chicken, 82
Lemon Chicken Breasts with Veggies, 288
Microwaved Chicken Kiev, 294
Nutty Oven-Fried Chicken, 184
Pan-Fried Chicken Athena, 14
Pan-Fried Chicken with Hoisin Cranberry Sauce, 108
Parmesan Chicken Couscous, 82
Philly-Style Barbecue Pizza, 64
Red Pepper-Curry Chicken, 17
Root Beer Glazed Chicken, 23
Rosemary-Orange Roasted Chicken, 190
Sizzling Chicken Lo Mein, 179
Slow Cooker Hula Chicken, 65
Southwest Chicken Pockets, 102
Spicy Asian Noodle Bowls, 171
Spinach Stuffed Chicken with Linguine, 105
Stacked Chicken Cordon Bleu, 169
Super-Stuffed Mexican Potatoes, 71
Teriyaki Chicken and Vegetables, 106

Salads

Chicken & Brie Salad, 147
✓Chicken & Fruit Spinach Salads, 207

Sandwiches

Pecan-Crusted Chicken Waffle Sandwiches, 59
Sesame Chicken Wraps, 160

Soups & Chili

Chunky Chicken Noodle Soup, 152
Hearty Chicken & Wild Rice Soup, 164

CHOCOLATE

Brown Butter Spice Cookies, 232
Candy-Licious Fudge, 233
Chocolate Butterscotch Tartlets, 131
Chocolate Cake in a Mug, 214
Chocolate Candy Cane Cookies, 271
Chocolate Caramel Oranges, 263
Chocolate Challah French Toast, 121
Chocolate Chip Ice Cream Pie, 51
Chocolate Lover's Cream Pie, 226
Chocolate Mint Parfaits, 218
Chocolate Rum Fondue, 268
Chocolate-Peanut Butter Cup Cookies, 231
Crispy Mexican Truffles, 132
Dark Chocolate Carrot Cake, 231
Hazelnut Chocolate Mousse, 38
Hot Chocolate Peppermint Cookies, 275
Mocha Cappuccino Punch, 130
Nutter Butter Truffles, 238
Outrageous Chocolate Mint Cookies, 229
Peanut Butter-Chocolate Ice Cream Torte, 223
Peanut Butter-Hazelnut Brownies, 229
Rocky Road Freezer Pie, 249
Sacher Bars, 228
Salted Caramel & Dark Chocolate Figs, 262
Sicilian Ice Cream Sandwiches, 224
Triple Chip Cookies, 215
Triple-Layer Pretzel Brownies, 221

COCONUT

Almond Macaroons, 218
Caramel Coconut Stars, 271
Coconut Fruit Salad, 146
Coconut-Pecan Coffee Cake, 118
Coconut Shrimp Chowder, 157

COFFEE

After Hours Ice Cream Sandwiches, 225
Macadamia-Coffee Bean Cookies, 52
Mocha Cappuccino Punch, 130

CONDIMENTS (also see Gravy)

Black Bean & Corn Salsa, 146
Chili Seafood Sauce, 280
Classic Pesto, 280
Classic Tarter Sauce, 280
Finnegan House Dry Rub, 282
Pomegranate Orange Salsa, 268
Tangy Barbecue Sauce, 280

COOKIES

Alligator Cookie Pops, 79
Almond Macaroons, 218
Brown Butter Spice Cookies, 232
Caramel Coconut Stars, 271
Cherry Cordial Cookies, 218
Chocolate Candy Cane Cookies, 271
Chocolate-Peanut Butter Cup Cookies, 231
Crème de Menthe Cheesecake Cookies, 271
Frosted Anise Cookies, 275
Gingerbread Fruitcake Cookies, 214
Honey-Nut Christmas Cookies, 271
Hot Chocolate Peppermint Cookies, 275
Macadamia-Coffee Bean Cookies, 52
Outrageous Chocolate Mint Cookies, 229
Peppermint S'more Tassies, 274
Salted Caramel Fudge Drops, 272
Snowman Cutouts, 272
Triple Chip Cookies, 215
Whoopie Cookies, 38

CORN (also see Corn Bread & Cornmeal)

Black Bean & Corn Salsa, 146
Country Corn, 138

Fiesta Corn Chip Salad, 145
Fiesta Rice and Bean Salad, 149
Grilled Corn Medley, 41
Herbed Corn and Carrots, 26
Sweet and Sour Shrimp in a Hurry, 179
Zucchini Corn Medley, 140

CORN BREAD & CORNMEAL
Cajun Beef Casserole, 99
Savory Corn Bread Pops, 130
Super-Fast Corn Bread, 21

COUSCOUS
Lemon Date Couscous, 147
Maple-Dijon Sausage & Sprouts, 110
Mexican Couscous, 49
Pan-Fried Chicken with Hoisin Cranberry Sauce, 108
Parmesan Chicken Couscous, 82
Tomato-Basil Couscous Salad, 45

CRANBERRIES & CRANBERRY JUICE
Apple Almond Salad, 55
Cranberry Pancakes, 122
Cranberry Sweet-and-Sour Pork, 177
Creamy Cranberry Meatballs, 129
Pan-Fried Chicken with Hoisin Cranberry Sauce, 108
Pork Medallions with Cranberry Sauce, 18
Slow-Cooked Fruited Oatmeal with Nuts, 118
Warm Christmas Punch, 269

CREAM CHEESE (also see Cakes, Cheesecakes & Cupcakes)
Beef & Onion Cheese Ball, 268
Cake with Lemon Sauce, 226
Cheese-Trio Artichoke & Spinach Dip, 126
Chocolate Candy Cane Cookies, 271
Chocolate Lover's Cream Pie, 226
Cream Cheese & Chive Omelet, 117
Crème de Menthe Cheesecake Cookies, 271
Crispy Mexican Truffles, 132
Nutter Butter Truffles, 238
Pineapple Orange Cheesecake, 226
Salmon Mousse Tartlets, 41
Savory Corn Bread Pops, 130
Sun-Dried Tomato and Parmesan Spread, 130
Tortellini & Shrimp Skewers with Sun-Dried Tomato Sauce, 239

DESSERTS (also see Bars & Brownies; Cakes, Cheesecakes & Cupcakes; Candy & Confections; Chocolate; Cookies; Ice Cream & Ice Cream Toppings; Pies & Tarts)
Apricot Crisp, 222
Blueberry-Rhubarb Crisp, 222
Chocolate Cake in a Mug, 214
Chocolate Mint Parfaits, 218
Chocolate Rum Fondue, 268
Crunchy Amaretto Peach Cobbler, 228
Grilled Peaches & Pound Cake, 258
Hazelnut Chocolate Mousse, 38
Mango Sorbet Dessert, 217
Rhubarb Sundaes, 233
Strawberry Tarragon Crumble, 232
White Chocolate Berry Parfaits, 222

EGGS (also see Breakfast & Brunch; Casseroles)
Asparagus Mushroom Quiche, 114
Best Scrambled Eggs, 114
Blue Cheese Quiche with Caramelized Pears, 119
Chicks-on-the-Ranch Deviled Eggs, 242
Cream Cheese & Chive Omelet, 117
Curry On Deviled Eggs, 245
Dazzling Dirty Martini Deviled Eggs, 245
Deli-Style Potato Salad, 139
Dill-icious Deviled Eggs, 242
✓Herb Breakfast Frittata, 201
Hoisin-It-Nice Deviled Eggs, 245
Hop-To-It Deviled Eggs, 242
Lil' Devil Eggs, 244
Little Italy Deviled Eggs, 244
Lone Star Deviled Eggs, 244
Salsa Dipper Deviled Eggs, 244
✓Sausage & Salsa Breakfast Burritos, 199
Sausage Breakfast Hash, 59
Tater Salad Deviled Eggs, 244
West Coaster Deviled Eggs, 245

FIGS
Salted Caramel & Dark Chocolate Figs, 262
Sweet & Savory Ice Cream Sandwiches, 224

FISH & SEAFOOD
Appetizers
Gump's Shrimp & Grits, 248
Hoisin-It-Nice Deviled Eggs, 245
Salmon Mousse Tartlets, 41
Tortellini & Shrimp Skewers with Sun-Dried Tomato Sauce, 239
Main Dishes
Asian Snapper with Capers, 22
Baja Fish Tacos, 175
✓Basil Crab Cakes, 208
✓Blackened Halibut, 208
Bombay Rice with Shrimp, 110
Cajun Fish Tacos, 105
Caramel Glazed Salmon, 18
Chicken & Shrimp Fettuccine, 109
Citrus-Spice Glazed Salmon, 50
Crab Imperial Casserole, 186
Creamy Salmon Linguine, 87
Creole Shrimp Pasta, 174

FISH & SEAFOOD

Main Dishes (continued)

Creole Shrimp Pasta, 174
Crispy Beer Battered Fish, 292
Crispy Scallops with Tarragon Cream, 293
Herb-Crusted Perch Fillets with Pea Puree, 175
Logan's Fried Catfish, 65
Maple Baked Salmon, 47
✓Mediterranean Shrimp Linguine, 198
Mediterranean Tuna Linguine, 101
✓Parsley-Crusted Cod, 200
Pasta with Shrimp & Basil, 10
✓Peking Shrimp, 203
Pesto Grilled Salmon, 87
Salmon Fettuccine Alfredo, 98
✓Salmon with Tangy Raspberry Sauce, 209
Scallops with Chipotle-Orange Sauce, 33
Sesame Dill Fish, 34
Sesame Salmon with Wasabi Mayo, 193
Shrimp Piccata, 17
Spinach Salmon Bundles, 63
Summer Fish Skillet, 107

Sweet and Sour Shrimp in a Hurry, 179
Swordfish with Fennel and Tomatoes, 286
Tilapia & Lemon Sauce, 30
✓Tropical Tilapia, 209
Tuna Cakes with Mustard Mayo, 103
✓Tuna with Tuscan White Bean Salad, 206
✓Zucchini Pesto with Shrimp and Farfalle, 207

Salads & Sandwiches

✓Asparagus Salad with Grilled Salmon, 204
BLT Catfish Sandwiches, 157
Cajun Popcorn Shrimp Sandwiches, 162
Crab Sandwiches, 77
✓Hot Shrimp Salad, 210
Shrimp & Spinach Salad, 144

Soups

Coconut Shrimp Chowder, 157

FRUIT (also see specific kinds)

Champagne Fruit Punch, 236
✓Chicken & Fruit Spinach Salads, 207
Coconut Fruit Salad, 146
Desert Oasis Chicken, 172
Gingerbread Fruitcake Cookies, 214
Mandarin Watermelon Salad, 149
✓Tropical Tilapia, 209
Watermelon Shark, 70
Yogurt & Honey Fruit Cups, 122

GARLIC

Cheddar Garlic Biscuits, 58
Garlic Brussels Sprouts, 30
Garlic Chicken & Bacon Pizza, 47
Pasta with Garlic Oil, 168
Sun-Dried Tomato Garlic Bread, 10

GRAVY

Grandma's Turkey Gravy, 265
Pan Gravy, 266

GREEN BEANS

Green Bean & Balsamic Salad, 258
Green Beans with Shallots, 14
✓Lemon Beans with Prosciutto, 202
Sausage Ratatouille, 246
Snappy Green Beans, 140

GRILLED RECIPES

Appetizers

Jazzed-Up French Bread, 41

Desserts

Grilled Peaches & Pound Cake, 258
Grilled Pineapple & Maple Sundaes, 43

Main Dishes

✓Asparagus Salad with Grilled Salmon, 204
Basil-Mint Chicken Thighs, 285
Beer Can Chicken, 258
Chili-Beer Glazed Steaks, 41
Grilled Chicken Sausages with Harvest Rice, 52
Grilled Fajita Rolled Steak, 257
Grilled Pork Chops with Peach Sauce, 286
Grilled Ribeyes with Blue Cheese Butter, 92
✓Mustard Turkey Cutlets, 202
Orange BBQ Baby Back Ribs, 284
Pesto Grilled Salmon, 87
Red Pepper-Curry Chicken, 17
✓Salmon with Tangy Raspberry Sauce, 209
Steakhouse Strip Steaks with Chimichurri, 285
Swordfish with Fennel and Tomatoes, 286
The Bistro Baked Potato, 240
The King's Crowned Filets, 284
✓Tuna with Tuscan White Bean Salad, 206
Very Veggie Baked Potatoes, 241
Walsh Family Grilled Pork Tenderloins, 88

Sandwiches & Side Dishes

BLT Catfish Sandwiches, 157
Grilled Corn Medley, 41
Grilled Romaine with Swiss, 286
Parmesan-Onion Potato Packets, 284
Portobello Burger with Muffuletta Topping, 162
Spicy Cajun Salsa Burgers, 156

GROUND BEEF

Hamburgers

Spicy Cajun Salsa Burgers, 156

Main Dishes

Bacon Cheeseburger Rice, 75
Baked Spaghetti, 194

Beef & Bean Tacos, 97
Beef Tostadas, 176
Cajun Beef and Beans, 89
Cajun Beef Casserole, 99
Chili Hash, 100
Chipotle Mac & Cheese, 290
Family-Favorite Spaghetti Sauce, 77
Farmhouse Barbecue Muffins, 73
Golombki, 192
Greek Ravioli Skillet, 106
Italian-Style Salisbury Steaks, 13
Jazzy Spaghetti Sauce, 102
Mexican Tater-Topped Casserole, 89
Moist & Savory Meat Loaf, 188
Next Day Meat Loaf Pie, 90
Old-World Pizza Meat Loaf, 90
Sloppy Joe Veggie Casserole, 189
Smothered Burritos, 49
Taco Shepherd's Pie, 291
Tasty Tacos, 71
That's Amore Baked Potatoes, 241

Salad, Sandwiches, Soup & Chili

Hearty Pita Spinach Salad, 104
Slow Cooker Golombki, 288

HAM & PROSCIUTTO

Best Scrambled Eggs, 114
Bourbon-Glazed Ham, 191
Ham & Cheese Bagels, 122
Ham & Noodle Bake, 86
Ham & Noodles with Veggies, 58
Ham & Pea Fettuccine, 171
Heavenly Citrus Ham, 86
✓Lemon Beans with Prosciutto, 202
Loaded Breakfast Potatoes, 121
Scalloped Potatoes & Ham, 144
Skillet Cassoulet, 168
Spiral Stromboli, 60
Stacked Chicken Cordon Bleu, 169

ICE CREAM & ICE CREAM TOPPINGS

After Hours Ice Cream Sandwiches, 225
All-Star Ice Cream Sandwiches, 70
Berry-Cherry Peach Sauce, 215
Blueberry-Lemon Ice Cream Sandwiches, 44
Candy Craze Ice Cream Sandwiches, 70
Caramel-Pecan Ice Cream Sandwiches, 225
Cereal & Milk Ice Cream Sandwiches, 71
Chocolate Chip Ice Cream Pie, 51
Cinnamon Apple Shakes, 135
Cool & Creamy Ice Cream Sandwiches, 224
Frozen Lime Cake, 48
Grilled Pineapple & Maple Sundaes, 43
Mango Sorbet Dessert, 217
Mocha Cappuccino Punch, 130
Peanut Butter-Chocolate Ice Cream Torte, 223
Rhubarb Sundaes, 233
Rocky Road Freezer Pie, 249
Sicilian Ice Cream Sandwiches, 224
Strawberry Cheesecake Pops, 78
Sweet & Savory Ice Cream Sandwiches, 224
The Elvis Ice Cream Sandwich, 225

LAMB

Mediterranean Rack of Lamb, 191

LEMONS

Blueberry-Lemon Ice Cream Sandwiches, 44
Cake with Lemon Sauce, 226
Hint of Lemon Squash Saute, 18
Lemon & Sage Roasted Chicken, 82
✓Lemon Beans with Prosciutto, 202
Lemon Chicken Breasts with Veggies, 288
Lemon Date Couscous, 147
Lemon Mint Spritzer, 129
Tilapia & Lemon Sauce, 30

LIMES

Chicken Rellenos with Cilantro-Lime Cream Sauce, 174
Frozen Lime Cake, 48

MANGOES

Mango Sorbet Dessert, 217
Super Mango Smoothies, 129

MAPLE

Grilled Pineapple & Maple Sundaes, 43
Maple & Chipotle Sausages, 122

Maple Baked Salmon, 47
Maple-Dijon Sausage & Sprouts, 110
Maple Jalapenos, 133
Pork and Waffles with Maple-Pear Topping, 294

MARSHMALLOWS

Caramel-Pecan Ice Cream Sandwiches, 225
Hot Chocolate Peppermint Cookies, 275
Peppermint S'more Tassies, 274
Rocky Road Freezer Pie, 249
Whoopie Cookies, 38

MEAT LOAF & MEATBALLS

Creamy Cranberry Meatballs, 129
Moist & Savory Meat Loaf, 188
Next Day Meat Loaf Pie, 90
Old-World Pizza Meat Loaf, 90
Salisbury Meatballs, 26
Vegetable Meatball Soup, 164

MUSHROOMS

✓Asian Spaghetti, 200
Asparagus Mushroom Quiche, 114
Chicken Fajita Alfredo, 180
Country Chuck Roast with Mushroom Gravy, 168

MUSHROOMS (continued)

Crab Imperial Casserole, 186
Gump's Shrimp & Grits, 248
Italian Enchiladas, 290
Mom's Turkey Tetrazzini, 192
Mushroom Salad, 25
Mushroom Steak, 288
Peppered Portobello Penne, 38
Pesto Portobello Pizzas, 44
Pork Medallions with Brandy Cream Sauce, 181
Portobello Burger with Muffuletta Topping, 162
Sausage Florentine Potpie, 66
Squash and Mushroom Medley, 23
Vegetarian Reubens, 152

NUTS (also see Peanut Butter)

✓Almond Berry Pancakes, 201
Almond Macaroons, 218
Apple Almond Salad, 55
Baked Peanut Chicken, 62
Candy-Licious Fudge, 233
Caramel-Pecan Ice Cream Sandwiches, 225
Coconut-Pecan Coffee Cake, 118
Crunchy Amaretto Peach Cobbler, 228
Gingerbread Fruitcake Cookies, 214
Hazelnut Chocolate Mousse, 38
Honey-Nut Christmas Cookies, 271
Macadamia-Coffee Bean Cookies, 52
Million Dollar Pecan Bars, 221
Nutty Oven-Fried Chicken, 184
Pecan-Crusted Chicken Waffle Sandwiches, 59
Quick Crisp Snack Bars, 77
Rocky Road Freezer Pie, 249
Sicilian Ice Cream Sandwiches, 224
Slow-Cooked Fruited Oatmeal with Nuts, 118
Teddy Bear Sandwiches, 72
Warm Pecan Cabbage Slaw, 34

ONIONS

Bacon-Gouda Stuffed Onions, 42
Beef & Onion Cheese Ball, 268
Caramelized Onion Chuck Roast, 83
Creamy Onion Pork Chops, 65
Green Onion Rolls, 254
Parmesan-Onion Potato Packets, 284
✓Sweet Onion & Carrot Medley, 203

ORANGES

BBQ Pork Salad, 147
Broccoli with Orange Browned Butter, 25
✓Chicken & Fruit Spinach Salads, 207
Chocolate Caramel Oranges, 263
Citrus-Herb Pork Roast, 289
Happy Orange Turkey, 265
Heavenly Citrus Ham, 86
Mandarin Watermelon Salad, 149
Orange BBQ Baby Back Ribs, 284
Orange Beef and Asparagus Stir-Fry, 92
Pineapple Orange Cheesecake, 226
Pomegranate Orange Salsa, 268
Rosemary-Orange Roasted Chicken, 190
Scallops with Chipotle-Orange Sauce, 33
Summer Salads with Mandarin Oranges, 142

OVEN ENTREES (also see Breakfast & Brunch; Casseroles; Pizza)

Beef & Ground Beef

Country Chuck Roast with Mushroom Gravy, 168
Golombki, 192
Moist & Savory Meat Loaf, 188
Old-World Pizza Meat Loaf, 90
Philly Cheesesteak Pizza, 188
Smothered Burritos, 49
Sweet & Tender Beef Ribs, 185
That's Amore Baked Potatoes, 241
The Bistro Baked Potato, 240

Chicken

Apricot-Honey Chicken, 25
Baked Peanut Chicken, 62
Buenos Dias Baked Potatoes, 241
Creamy Chicken Lasagna Roll-Ups, 188
Honey & Spice Baked Chicken, 84
Honey Roasted Chicken, 51
Indian Baked Chicken, 186
Lemon & Sage Roasted Chicken, 82
Nutty Oven-Fried Chicken, 184
Rosemary-Orange Roasted Chicken, 190
Southwest Chicken Pockets, 102
Spinach Stuffed Chicken with Linguine, 105

Fish & Seafood

Bombay Rice with Shrimp, 110
Cajun Popcorn Shrimp Sandwiches, 162
Caramel Glazed Salmon, 18
Citrus-Spice Glazed Salmon, 50
Italian Pesto Pizzas, 189
Maple Baked Salmon, 47
✓Parsley-Crusted Cod, 200
Sesame Salmon with Wasabi Mayo, 193
Spinach Salmon Bundles, 63

Lamb

Mediterranean Rack of Lamb, 191

Meatless

Asparagus Mushroom Quiche, 114
Loaded Mexican Pizza, 194
Very Veggie Baked Potatoes, 241

Pork

Bourbon-Glazed Ham, 191
Chili-Spiced Pork Chops, 186
Crown Roast with Spring Rice Pilaf, 252
Heavenly Citrus Ham, 86
Hungry Man's Baked Potatoes, 241
Italian Enchiladas, 290
Queso Pork Enchiladas, 93
Tuscan Parmesan Pork Chops, 48

Turkey

Blue Cheese Quiche with Caramelized Pears, 119
Happy Orange Turkey, 265

PANCAKES

✓Almond Berry Pancakes, 201
Cranberry Pancakes, 122

PASTA & NOODLES (also see Couscous)

Main Dishes

✓Asian Spaghetti, 200
Baked Rigatoni & Sausage, 55
Baked Spaghetti, 194
Balsamic Chicken Fettucine, 99
Blushing Angel Hair Pasta with Chicken, 62
Buffalo Chicken Pasta Bake, 185
Cajun Chicken Pasta Bake, 193
Chicken and Sausage Penne, 291
Chicken & Shrimp Fettuccine, 109
Chicken Fajita Alfredo, 180
Chicken Strips Milano, 33
Chipotle Mac & Cheese, 290
Citrus-Herb Pork Roast, 289
Crab Imperial Casserole, 186
Creamy Chicken Lasagna Roll-Ups, 188
Creamy Salmon Linguine, 87
Creole Shrimp Pasta, 174
Garden Vegetable Primavera, 172
Gnocchi Chicken Skillet, 173
Greek Ravioli Skillet, 106
Ham & Noodle Bake, 86
Ham & Noodles with Veggies, 58
Ham & Pea Fettuccine, 171
Homemade Meatless Spaghetti Sauce, 290
Jazzy Spaghetti Sauce, 102
✓Makeover Beef Stroganoff, 211
✓Makeover Macaroni and Cheese, 211
✓Mediterranean Shrimp Linguine, 198
Mediterranean Tuna Linguine, 101
Mom's Turkey Tetrazzini, 192
Mushroom Steak, 288
Pasta & Broccoli Sausage Simmer, 180
Pasta Primavera, 176
Pasta with Garlic Oil, 168
Pasta with Shrimp & Basil, 10
Peppered Portobello Penne, 38
Pepperoni Penne Carbonara, 179
Philly-Style Mac and Cheese, 191
Pork & Vegetable Skillet, 111
Pork Medallions with Brandy Cream Sauce, 181
Salmon Fettuccine Alfredo, 98
Sausage Alfredo, 26
Shrimp Piccata, 17
Sirloin Stir-Fry with Ramen Noodles, 177
Sizzling Chicken Lo Mein, 179
Speedy Stovetop Spaghetti, 171
Spicy Asian Noodle Bowls, 171
Spinach Stuffed Chicken with Linguine, 105
Stacked Vegetables and Ravioli, 107
Turkey Alfredo Tetrazzini, 64
Zippy Zucchini Pasta, 21
✓Zucchini Pesto with Shrimp and Farfalle, 207

Salads

Italian Linguini Salad, 141
Pepperoni-Artichoke Pasta Salad, 143
Tortellini Tossed Salad, 149

Side Dishes

Buttered Noodles, 13
✓Garden Orzo Risotto, 204
✓Orzo with Peppers & Spinach, 202

Soups

Chunky Chicken Noodle Soup, 152

PEACHES

Berry-Cherry Peach Sauce, 215
Berry Delicious Smoothies, 127
Crunchy Amaretto Peach Cobbler, 228
Ginger-Peach Pork Skillet, 88
Grilled Peaches & Pound Cake, 258
Grilled Pork Chops with Peach Sauce, 286
Raspberry Peach Pie, 217
Sunny Breakfast Smoothies, 73

PEANUT BUTTER

Candy Craze Ice Cream Sandwiches, 70
Candy-Licious Fudge, 233
Chocolate-Peanut Butter Cup Cookies, 231
Christmas Elf Cake Pops, 276
Nutty Waffle Sandwiches, 116
Peanut Butter-Chocolate Ice Cream Torte, 223
Peanut Butter-Graham Snack Mix, 78
Peanut Butter-Hazelnut Brownies, 229
Peanut Chicken Wings, 127
Quick Crisp Snack Bars, 77
Teddy Bear Sandwiches, 72
The Elvis Ice Cream Sandwich, 225
Triple-Layer Pretzel Brownies, 221

PEARS

Blue Cheese Quiche with Caramelized Pears, 119
Chicken with Caramelized Pears, 98
Deconstructed Pear Pork Chops, 97
Ghost Caramel Pears, 261
Green Breakfast Smoothie, 121
Pork and Waffles with Maple-Pear Topping, 294

PEAS

✓Asian Spaghetti, 200
Gingered Snow Peas, 33
Ham & Pea Fettuccine, 171
Herb-Crusted Perch Fillets with Pea Puree, 175
Pasta Primavera, 176
Savory Peas and Carrots, 13
Snow Pea Medley, 29
Sweet and Sour Shrimp in a Hurry, 179
✓Sweet Onion & Carrot Medley, 203

PEPPERONI

Best-Ever Pepperoni Pizza, 74
Italian Enchiladas, 290
Pepperoni-Artichoke Pasta Salad, 143
Pepperoni Penne Carbonara, 179
Pizza on a Stick, 75
Rustic Antipasto Tart, 238
That's Amore Baked Potatoes, 241

PEPPERS & CHILIES

Buenos Dias Baked Potatoes, 241
Chicken Rellenos with Cilantro-Lime Cream Sauce, 174
Chili con Queso El Dorado, 131
Chipotle Mac & Cheese, 290
Cool & Creamy Ice Cream Sandwiches, 224
Fiesta Rice and Bean Salad, 149
Grilled Fajita Rolled Steak, 257
Jalapeno Cheddar Biscuits, 22
Maple & Chipotle Sausages, 122
Maple Jalapenos, 133
Mexican Fiesta Steak Stir-Fry, 173
Mexican Tater-Topped Casserole, 89
✓Orzo with Peppers & Spinach, 202
Roast Beef Aioli Bundles, 238
Sausage Ratatouille, 246

PESTO

Classic Pesto, 280
Godfather Crostini, 249
Italian Pesto Pizzas, 189
Italian-Style Croissants, 55
Pesto Grilled Salmon, 87
Pesto Portobello Pizzas, 44
✓Zucchini Pesto with Shrimp and Farfalle, 207

PHYLLO & PUFF PASTRY

Blue Cheese Quiche with Caramelized Pears, 119
Cheddar Bread Twists, 21
Chicken & Bacon Tart, 101
Chicken Madeira Pastry, 192
Chocolate Butterscotch Tartlets, 131
Salmon Mousse Tartlets, 41
Sausage Florentine Potpie, 66
Southwest Chicken Pockets, 102

PIES & TARTS (for savory pies and tarts, see Breakfast & Brunch; Casseroles; Quiche & Savory Tarts)

Blueberry & Ginger Tart, 255
Chocolate Chip Ice Cream Pie, 51
Chocolate Lover's Cream Pie, 226
Raspberry Peach Pie, 217
Rocky Road Freezer Pie, 249
Spiced Eggnog Pumpkin Pie, 266
Toffee Cream Pie, 231

PINEAPPLE

Cranberry Sweet-and-Sour Pork, 177
Grilled Pineapple & Maple Sundaes, 43
Hawaiian Barbecue Beans, 50
Pineapple Colada Shake, 133
Pineapple Orange Cheesecake, 226
Sausage Pineapple Lettuce Wraps, 161
Slow Cooker Hula Chicken, 65
Super Mango Smoothies, 129

PIZZA

Best-Ever Pepperoni Pizza, 74
Breadstick Pizza, 58
Chicken & Bacon Tart, 101
Garlic Chicken & Bacon Pizza, 47
Italian Pesto Pizzas, 189
Loaded Mexican Pizza, 194
Pesto Portobello Pizzas, 44
Philly Cheesesteak Pizza, 188
Philly-Style Barbecue Pizza, 64
Pinwheel Pizza Snacks, 79
Pizza on a Stick, 75

POMEGRANATE

Pomegranate Cosmo, 269
Pomegranate Orange Salsa, 268

PORK (also see Bacon; Ham & Prosciutto; Pepperoni; Sausage)

Apple-Balsamic Pork Chops, 13
Balsamic-Glazed Pork Chops, 25
Balsamic Pork Stir-Fry, 179
BBQ Pork Salad, 147
Bistro Herb-Rubbed Pork Tenderloin, 172
Caramel-Apple Pork Chops, 111
Carnitas Tacos, 257
Chili-Spiced Pork Chops, 186
Citrus-Herb Pork Roast, 289
Cranberry Sweet-and-Sour Pork, 177
Creamy Onion Pork Chops, 65
Crown Roast with Spring Rice Pilaf, 252
Deconstructed Pear Pork Chops, 97
Elegant Pork Marsala, 14
Ginger-Peach Pork Skillet, 88
Grilled Pork Chops with Peach Sauce, 286
Hungry Man's Baked Potatoes, 241
Moist & Savory Meat Loaf, 188
Orange BBQ Baby Back Ribs, 284
Peppered Pork with Asti Cream Sauce, 269
Philly-Style Barbecue Pizza, 64
Pork & Vegetable Skillet, 111
Pork and Waffles with Maple-Pear Topping, 294
Pork Chops in a Honey-Mustard Sauce, 295
Pork Medallions with Brandy Cream Sauce, 181
Pork Medallions with Cranberry Sauce, 18
✓Pork Medallions with Raspberry-Balsamic Sauce, 199
Queso Pork Enchiladas, 93
Slow Cooked BBQ Pork Ribs, 93
Southern Skillet Chops, 21

Southwest Pulled Pork, 160
Stuffed Alfredo Pork Chops, 96
Tuscan Parmesan Pork Chops, 48
Walsh Family Grilled Pork Tenderloins, 88

POTATOES
Buenos Dias Baked Potatoes, 241
Cheesy Chive Potatoes, 14
Chili Hash, 100
Chilly Night Beef Stew, 85
Chive Smashed Potatoes, 266
Cream of Potato & Cheddar Soup, 158
Deli Roast Beef Sandwiches with Mashed Potatoes, 58
Deli-Style Potato Salad, 139
Gnocchi Chicken Skillet, 173
✓Herb Breakfast Frittata, 201
Herbed Potato Soup, 152
Herby Potatoes with Sour Cream, 143
Hungry Man's Baked Potatoes, 241
Indian Baked Chicken, 186
Layered Potato Beef Casserole, 85
Lemon & Sage Roasted Chicken, 82
Loaded Breakfast Potatoes, 121
Mexican Tater-Topped Casserole, 89
Next Day Meat Loaf Pie, 90
Parmesan-Onion Potato Packets, 284
Poutine, 64
Roasted Russet & Sweet Potato Wedges, 141
Sausage Breakfast Hash, 59
Scalloped Potatoes & Ham, 144
Seasoned Oven Fries, 149
Slow-Cooked Corned Beef, 91
Super-Stuffed Mexican Potatoes, 71
Taco Shepherd's Pie, 291
Tater Salad Deviled Eggs, 244
That's Amore Baked Potatoes, 241
The Bistro Baked Potato, 240
Vegetarian Potato au Gratin, 103
Very Veggie Baked Potatoes, 241

PUMPKIN
Autumn Pumpkin Chili, 155
Spiced Eggnog Pumpkin Pie, 266

QUICHE & SAVORY TARTS
Asparagus Mushroom Quiche, 114
Blue Cheese Quiche with Caramelized Pears, 119
Chicken & Bacon Tart, 101
Rustic Antipasto Tart, 238

RASPBERRIES
✓Almond Berry Pancakes, 201
Bella Basil Raspberry Tea, 132
Berry Delicious Smoothies, 127
Cake with Lemon Sauce, 226
Champagne Fruit Punch, 236
Mango Sorbet Dessert, 217
✓Pork Medallions with Raspberry-Balsamic Sauce, 199
Raspberry Peach Pie, 217
✓Salmon with Tangy Raspberry Sauce, 209

RHUBARB
Blueberry-Rhubarb Crisp, 222
Rhubarb Sundaes, 233

RICE
Bacon Cheeseburger Rice, 75
Baked Peanut Chicken, 62
Balsamic Pork Stir-Fry, 179
Bombay Rice with Shrimp, 110
Chicken Taco Rice, 181
Crown Roast with Spring Rice Pilaf, 252
Curry Rice Pilaf, 17
Fiesta Rice and Bean Salad, 149
✓Garden Orzo Risotto, 204
Ginger-Peach Pork Skillet, 88
Golombki, 192
Grilled Chicken Sausages with Harvest Rice, 52
Hearty Chicken & Wild Rice Soup, 164
Herbed Chicken and Rice, 30
Mexican Fiesta Steak Stir-Fry, 173
Parsleyed Rice Pilaf, 22
Sausage Ratatouille, 246
Slow Cooker Golombki, 288
Southwest Rice Pilaf, 257
Stuffed Alfredo Pork Chops, 96
Summer Fish Skillet, 107
Sweet and Sour Shrimp in a Hurry, 179
Teriyaki Chicken and Vegetables, 106
Zucchini Rice Pilaf, 34

SALADS & SALAD DRESSING
Coleslaw
Honey Mustard Coleslaw, 138
Dressing
Blue Cheese Dressing, 281
Citrus-Marmalade Vinaigrette, 281
Greens with Balsamic Vinaigrette, 282
Honey-Mustard Salad Dressing, 280
Light Green Goddess Salad Dressing, 282
Makeover Honey French Dressing, 282
The-Best-of-Both Worlds Dressing, 141
Fruit Salads
Apple Almond Salad, 55
Coconut Fruit Salad, 146
Mandarin Watermelon Salad, 149
Green Salads
Elegant Spring Salad, 254
Grilled Romaine with Swiss, 286
Spinach & Gorgonzola Salad, 10
Summer Salads with Mandarin Oranges, 142
Summer's Best Spinach Salad, 145
Tortellini Tossed Salad, 149
Tossed Salad, 145
White Bean and Spinach Salads, 142
Main-Dish Salads
✓Asparagus Salad with Grilled Salmon, 204
BBQ Pork Salad, 147
Chicken & Brie Salad, 147
✓Chicken & Fruit Spinach Salads, 207
Hearty Pita Spinach Salad, 104
✓Hot Shrimp Salad, 210
Shrimp & Spinach Salad, 144

SALADS & SALAD DRESSING (continued)

Pasta, Potato & Couscous Salads

Deli-Style Potato Salad, 139
Italian Linguini Salad, 141
Lemon Date Couscous, 147
Pepperoni-Artichoke Pasta Salad, 143
Tomato-Basil Couscous Salad, 45

Vegetable Salads

Broccoli Salad with Cucumber, 138
Fiesta Corn Chip Salad, 145
Green Bean & Balsamic Salad, 258
Mushroom Salad, 25

SANDWICHES & WRAPS

Cold Sandwiches

BLT Catfish Sandwiches, 157
Crab Sandwiches, 77
Deli Sandwich Spread, 156
Teddy Bear Sandwiches, 72

Hot Sandwiches

Beef Gyros, 165
Cajun Popcorn Shrimp Sandwiches, 162
Deli Roast Beef Sandwiches with Mashed Potatoes, 58
Ham & Cheese Bagels, 122
Hearty Sausage-Stuffed Loaf, 61
Italian Shredded Beef Sandwiches, 162
Pecan-Crusted Chicken Waffle Sandwiches, 59
Philadelphia Beef Sandwich, 161
Portobello Burger with Muffuletta Topping, 162
Southwest Pulled Pork, 160
Spicy Cajun Salsa Burgers, 156
Spiral Stromboli, 60
Sweet & Savory Slow-Cooked Beef, 159
Toasted Sausage Cacciatore Sammies, 109
Turkey-Brie Stromboli, 61
Vegetarian Reubens, 152

Wraps

Asian Turkey Lettuce Wraps, 155
Sausage Pineapple Lettuce Wraps, 161
Sesame Chicken Wraps, 160

SAUSAGE (also see Pepperoni)

Breakfast & Brunch

Maple & Chipotle Sausages, 122
✓Sausage & Salsa Breakfast Burritos, 199
Sausage Breakfast Hash, 59

Main Dishes

Baked Rigatoni & Sausage, 55
Chicken and Sausage Penne, 291
Family-Favorite Spaghetti Sauce, 77
Grilled Chicken Sausages with Harvest Rice, 52
Italian Enchiladas, 290
Maple-Dijon Sausage & Sprouts, 110
Pasta & Broccoli Sausage Simmer, 180
Pizza on a Stick, 75
Sausage Alfredo, 26
Sausage Florentine Potpie, 66
Sausage Ratatouille, 246
Speedy Stovetop Spaghetti, 171

Soups, Chili & Sandwiches

Hearty Sausage-Stuffed Loaf, 61
Kielbasa Spinach Soup, 165
Sausage Pineapple Lettuce Wraps, 161
Toasted Sausage Cacciatore Sammies, 109

SIDE DISHES (also see Condiments; Gravy; Salads & Salad Dressing)

Alfredo Creamed Spinach, 52
Bacon-Gouda Stuffed Onions, 42
Bacon-Parmesan Brussels Sprouts, 47
Balsamic Broiled Asparagus, 17
Brandy-Glazed Carrots, 254
Broccoli with Orange Browned Butter, 25
Buttered Noodles, 13
Cheesy Chive Potatoes, 14
Chive Smashed Potatoes, 266
Country Corn, 138
Curry Rice Pilaf, 17
Fiesta Rice and Bean Salad, 149
✓Garden Orzo Risotto, 204
Garlic Brussels Sprouts, 30
Gingered Snow Peas, 33
Green Beans with Shallots, 14
Grilled Corn Medley, 41
Hawaiian Barbecue Beans, 50
Herbed Corn and Carrots, 26
Herby Potatoes with Sour Cream, 143
Hint of Lemon Squash Saute, 18
Mexican Couscous, 49
Parmesan-Onion Potato Packets, 284
Parmesan Roasted Asparagus, 18
Parsleyed Rice Pilaf, 22
Poutine, 64
Ribboned Vegetables, 29
Roasted Russet & Sweet Potato Wedges, 141
Rosemary Carrots, 33
Savory Peas and Carrots, 13
Scalloped Potatoes & Ham, 144
Seasoned Oven Fries, 149
Snappy Green Beans, 140
Snow Pea Medley, 29
Southwest Rice Pilaf, 257
Squash and Mushroom Medley, 23
Vegetable Trio, 30
Warm Pecan Cabbage Slaw, 34
Zesty Broccoli, 146
Zucchini & Tomato Saute, 26
Zucchini Corn Medley, 140
Zucchini Rice Pilaf, 34

SLOW COOKER RECIPES

Appetizers & Beverages
Cheese-Trio Artichoke & Spinach Dip, 126
Creamy Cranberry Meatballs, 129
Sweet & Spicy Chicken Wings, 129
Warm Christmas Punch, 269

Main Dishes
Best Ever Roast Beef, 289
Caramelized Onion Chuck Roast, 83
Carnitas Tacos, 257
Citrus-Herb Pork Roast, 289
Creamy Onion Pork Chops, 65
Egg Drop Soup, 155
Family-Favorite Spaghetti Sauce, 77
Lemon Chicken Breasts with Veggies, 288
Mushroom Steak, 288
Slow Cooked BBQ Pork Ribs, 93
Slow-Cooked Corned Beef, 91
Slow-Cooked Fruited Oatmeal with Nuts, 118
Slow Cooker Hula Chicken, 65

Sandwiches
Italian Shredded Beef Sandwiches, 162
Southwest Pulled Pork, 160
Sweet & Savory Slow-Cooked Beef, 159

Side Dishes
Hawaiian Barbecue Beans, 50
Scalloped Potatoes & Ham, 144

Soups, Stews & Chili
Autumn Pumpkin Chili, 155
Chilly Night Beef Stew, 85
Cream of Potato & Cheddar Soup, 158
Slow Cooker Golombki, 288

SOUPS, STEWS & CHILI
Autumn Pumpkin Chili, 155
Chili-Basil Tomato Soup, 22
Chilly Night Beef Stew, 85
Chunky Chicken Noodle Soup, 152
Coconut Shrimp Chowder, 157
Cream of Potato & Cheddar Soup, 158
Egg Drop Soup, 155
Hearty Chicken & Wild Rice Soup, 164
Herbed Potato Soup, 152
Kielbasa Spinach Soup, 165
Vegetable Beef & Barley Soup, 83
Vegetable Meatball Soup, 164

SPINACH
Alfredo Creamed Spinach, 52
Cheese-Trio Artichoke & Spinach Dip, 126
✓Chicken & Fruit Spinach Salads, 207
✓Garden Orzo Risotto, 204
Green Breakfast Smoothie, 121
Hearty Pita Spinach Salad, 104
Hearty Sausage-Stuffed Loaf, 61
Kielbasa Spinach Soup, 165
✓Orzo with Peppers & Spinach, 202
Sausage Florentine Potpie, 66
Shrimp & Spinach Salad, 144
Spinach & Gorgonzola Salad, 10
Spinach Salmon Bundles, 63
Spinach Stuffed Chicken with Linguine, 105
Summer's Best Spinach Salad, 145
The Bistro Baked Potato, 240
Vegetarian Reubens, 152
White Bean and Spinach Salads, 142

STOVETOP ENTREES (also see Sandwiches; Soups, Stews & Chili)

Beef & Ground Beef
Bacon Cheeseburger Rice, 75
Beef Gyros, 165
Beef Tostadas, 176
Cajun Beef and Beans, 89
Chili Hash, 100
Country Chuck Roast with Mushroom Gravy, 168
Greek Ravioli Skillet, 106
Italian-Style Salisbury Steaks, 13
Jazzy Spaghetti Sauce, 102
✓Makeover Beef Stroganoff, 211
Mexican Fiesta Steak Stir-Fry, 173
Orange Beef and Asparagus Stir-Fry, 92
Philadelphia Beef Sandwich, 161
Salisbury Meatballs, 26
Sirloin Stir-Fry with Ramen Noodles, 177
Tasty Tacos, 71
Vegetable Meatball Soup, 164

Chicken
Balsamic Chicken Fettucine, 99
Blushing Angel Hair Pasta with Chicken, 62
Chicken and Sausage Penne, 291
Chicken Chimichangas, 84
Chicken Fajita Alfredo, 180
Chicken Rellenos with Cilantro-Lime Cream Sauce, 174
Chicken Strips Milano, 33
Chicken Taco Rice, 181
Chicken with Caramelized Pears, 98
Chicken with Rosemary Butter Sauce for 2, 29
Chunky Chicken Noodle Soup, 152
Desert Oasis Chicken, 172
Gnocchi Chicken Skillet, 173
Hearty Chicken & Wild Rice Soup, 164
Herbed Chicken and Rice, 30
Pan-Fried Chicken Athena, 14
Pan-Fried Chicken with Hoisin Cranberry Sauce, 108
Parmesan Chicken Couscous, 82
Red Pepper-Curry Chicken, 17
Root Beer Glazed Chicken, 23
Sizzling Chicken Lo Mein, 179
Spicy Asian Noodle Bowls, 171
Stacked Chicken Cordon Bleu, 169
Teriyaki Chicken and Vegetables, 106

Fish & Seafood
Asian Snapper with Capers, 22
Baja Fish Tacos, 175
✓Basil Crab Cakes, 208
✓Blackened Halibut, 208
Chicken & Shrimp Fettuccine, 109
Coconut Shrimp Chowder, 157
Creamy Salmon Linguine, 87
Creole Shrimp Pasta, 174
Crispy Beer Battered Fish, 292
Crispy Scallops with Tarragon Cream, 293
Herb-Crusted Perch Fillets with Pea Puree, 175
✓Hot Shrimp Salad, 210
✓Mediterranean Shrimp Linguine, 198
Mediterranean Tuna Linguine, 101
Pasta with Shrimp & Basil, 10
✓Peking Shrimp, 203
Salmon Fettuccine Alfredo, 98
Scallops with Chipotle-Orange Sauce, 33
Sesame Dill Fish, 34
Shrimp Piccata, 17
Summer Fish Skillet, 107

Sweet and Sour Shrimp in a Hurry, 179
Tilapia & Lemon Sauce, 30
✓Tropical Tilapia, 209
Tuna Cakes with Mustard Mayo, 103
✓Zucchini Pesto with Shrimp and Farfalle, 207

Meatless
✓Asian Spaghetti, 200
Garden Vegetable Primavera, 172
Herbed Potato Soup, 152
Homemade Meatless Spaghetti Sauce, 290
✓Makeover Macaroni and Cheese, 211
Pasta Primavera, 176
Pasta with Garlic Oil, 168
Peppered Portobello Penne, 38
Vegetarian Reubens, 152
Zippy Zucchini Pasta, 21

Pork
Apple-Balsamic Pork Chops, 13
Balsamic-Glazed Pork Chops, 25
Balsamic Pork Stir-Fry, 179
Bistro Herb-Rubbed Pork Tenderloin, 172
Caramel-Apple Pork Chops, 111
Cranberry Sweet-and-Sour Pork, 177
Deconstructed Pear Pork Chops, 97
Elegant Pork Marsala, 14
Ginger-Peach Pork Skillet, 88
Ham & Noodles with Veggies, 58
Ham & Pea Fettuccine, 171
Peppered Pork with Asti Cream Sauce, 269
Pork & Vegetable Skillet, 111
Pork and Waffles with Maple-Pear Topping, 294
Pork Chops in a Honey-Mustard Sauce, 295
Pork Medallions with Brandy Cream Sauce, 181
Pork Medallions with Cranberry Sauce, 18
✓Pork Medallions with Raspberry-Balsamic Sauce, 199
Skillet Cassoulet, 168
Southern Skillet Chops, 21
Stuffed Alfredo Pork Chops, 96

Sausage
Kielbasa Spinach Soup, 165
Maple-Dijon Sausage & Sprouts, 110
Pasta & Broccoli Sausage Simmer, 180
Sausage Alfredo, 26
Sausage Pineapple Lettuce Wraps, 161
Sausage Ratatouille, 246
Speedy Stovetop Spaghetti, 171

Turkey
Asian Turkey Lettuce Wraps, 155
Pepperoni Penne Carbonara, 179
Skillet Cassoulet, 168
Turkey Scallopini, 29

STRAWBERRIES
Berry Delicious Smoothies, 127
✓Chicken & Fruit Spinach Salads, 207
Cool & Creamy Ice Cream Sandwiches, 224
Nutty Waffle Sandwiches, 116
Strawberry Cheesecake Pops, 78
Strawberry Tarragon Crumble, 232
White Chocolate Berry Parfaits, 222

SUMMER SQUASH (also see Zucchini)
Chicken Fajita Alfredo, 180
Hint of Lemon Squash Saute, 18
Ribboned Vegetables, 29
Squash and Mushroom Medley, 23
Stacked Vegetables and Ravioli, 107
Summer Fish Skillet, 107
Teriyaki Chicken and Vegetables, 106
Very Veggie Baked Potatoes, 241

SWEET POTATOES
Hungry Man's Baked Potatoes, 241
Roasted Russet & Sweet Potato Wedges, 141

TOMATOES
BLT Catfish Sandwiches, 157
Chili-Basil Tomato Soup, 22
Family-Favorite Spaghetti Sauce, 77
✓Garden Orzo Risotto, 204
Garden Vegetable Primavera, 172
Homemade Meatless Spaghetti Sauce, 290
Panko Chicken with Fresh Marinara, 135

Sun-Dried Tomato and Parmesan Spread, 130
Sun-Dried Tomato Garlic Bread, 10
Swordfish with Fennel and Tomatoes, 286
Tomato-Basil Couscous Salad, 45
Tortellini & Shrimp Skewers with Sun-Dried Tomato Sauce, 239
Zucchini & Tomato Saute, 26

TURKEY (also see Pepperoni; Sausage)

Appetizers

Family-Favorite Turkey Egg Rolls, 126

Main Dishes

Blue Cheese Quiche with Caramelized Pears, 119
Grandma's Turkey Gravy, 265
Happy Orange Turkey, 265
Mom's Turkey Tetrazzini, 192
✓Mustard Turkey Cutlets, 202
Skillet Cassoulet, 168
Turkey Alfredo Tetrazzini, 64
Turkey Potpie Cups, 67
Turkey Scallopini, 29

Salad & Sandwiches

Asian Turkey Lettuce Wraps, 155
Turkey-Brie Stromboli, 61

Soup & Chili

Autumn Pumpkin Chili, 155

VEGETABLES (also see specific kinds)

Breadstick Pizza, 58
Easy Cheddar Chicken Potpie, 184
✓Garden Orzo Risotto, 204
Garden Vegetable Primavera, 172
Ginger-Peach Pork Skillet, 88
Ham & Noodles with Veggies, 58
Italian Pesto Pizzas, 189
Lemon Chicken Breasts with Veggies, 288
Loaded Mexican Pizza, 194
Pasta Primavera, 176
Pork & Vegetable Skillet, 111
Ribboned Vegetables, 29
Roast Beef Potpie, 66
Sausage Ratatouille, 246
Sirloin Stir-Fry with Ramen Noodles, 177
Sizzling Chicken Lo Mein, 179
Sloppy Joe Veggie Casserole, 189
Stacked Vegetables and Ravioli, 107
Summer Fish Skillet, 107
✓Sweet Onion & Carrot Medley, 203
Teriyaki Chicken and Vegetables, 106
Turkey Potpie Cups, 67
Vegetable Beef & Barley Soup, 83
Vegetable Meatball Soup, 164
Vegetable Trio, 30
Very Veggie Baked Potatoes, 241

WAFFLES

✓Cardamom Sour Cream Waffles, 198
Nutty Waffle Sandwiches, 116
Pecan-Crusted Chicken Waffle Sandwiches, 59
Pork and Waffles with Maple-Pear Topping, 294

WINTER SQUASH (also see Pumpkin)

Grilled Chicken Sausages with Harvest Rice, 52

YOGURT

Berry Delicious Smoothies, 127
Blueberry-Oat Smoothies, 117
Yogurt & Honey Fruit Cups, 122

ZUCCHINI (also see Summer Squash)

✓Garden Orzo Risotto, 204
Garden Vegetable Primavera, 172
Greek Ravioli Skillet, 106
Grilled Corn Medley, 41
Ribboned Vegetables, 29
Sausage Ratatouille, 246
Squash and Mushroom Medley, 23
Stacked Vegetables and Ravioli, 107
Very Veggie Baked Potatoes, 241
Zippy Zucchini Pasta, 21
Zucchini & Tomato Saute, 26
Zucchini Corn Medley, 140
✓Zucchini Pesto with Shrimp and Farfalle, 207
Zucchini Rice Pilaf, 34

Alphabetical Recipe Index

This handy index lists every recipe in alphabetical order so you can easily find your favorites.

A

After Hours Ice Cream Sandwiches, 225
Alfredo Creamed Spinach, 52
All-Star Ice Cream Sandwiches, 70
Alligator Cookie Pops, 79
Almond Berry Pancakes, 201
Almond Macaroons, 218
American Beauty, 246
Apple Almond Salad, 55
Apple-Balsamic Pork Chops, 13
Apple Spiced Tea, 130
Apricot Cream Biscuits, 117
Apricot Crisp, 222
Apricot-Honey Chicken, 25
Asian Snapper with Capers, 22
Asian Spaghetti, 200
Asian Turkey Lettuce Wraps, 155
Asparagus Mushroom Quiche, 114
Asparagus Salad with Grilled Salmon, 204
Autumn Pumpkin Chili, 155

B

Bacon Cheeseburger Rice, 75
Bacon-Gouda Stuffed Onions, 42
Bacon-Parmesan Brussels Sprouts, 47
Baja Fish Tacos, 175
Baked Peanut Chicken, 62
Baked Rigatoni & Sausage, 55
Baked Spaghetti, 194
Balsamic Broiled Asparagus, 17
Balsamic Chicken Fettucine, 99
Balsamic-Glazed Chicken Wings, 42
Balsamic-Glazed Pork Chops, 25
Balsamic Pork Stir-Fry, 179
Basil Crab Cakes, 208
Basil-Mint Chicken Thighs, 285
BBQ Pork Salad, 147
Beef & Bean Tacos, 97
Beef & Onion Cheese Ball, 268
Beef Gyros, 165
Beef Tostadas, 176
Beer Can Chicken, 258
Bella Basil Raspberry Tea, 132
Berry-Cherry Peach Sauce, 215
Berry Delicious Smoothies, 127
Best-Ever Pepperoni Pizza, 74
Best Ever Roast Beef, 289
Best Scrambled Eggs, 114
Bistro Herb-Rubbed Pork Tenderloin, 172
Black Bean & Corn Salsa, 146
Blackberry Beer Cocktail, 45
Blackened Halibut, 208
BLT Catfish Sandwiches, 157
Blue Cheese Dressing, 281
Blue Cheese Quiche with Caramelized Pears, 119
Blueberry & Ginger Tart, 255
Blueberry-Lemon Ice Cream Sandwiches, 44
Blueberry-Oat Smoothies, 117
Blueberry-Rhubarb Crisp, 222
Blushing Angel Hair Pasta with Chicken, 62
Bombay Rice with Shrimp, 110
Bourbon-Glazed Ham, 191
Brandy-Glazed Carrots, 254
Breadstick Pizza, 58
Bride and Groom Cupcakes, 237
Broccoli Salad with Cucumber, 138
Broccoli with Orange Browned Butter, 25
Brown Butter Spice Cookies, 232
Buenos Dias Baked Potatoes, 241
Buffalo Chicken Pasta Bake, 185
Buttered Noodles, 13

C

Cajun Beef and Beans, 89
Cajun Beef Casserole, 99
Cajun Chicken Pasta Bake, 193
Cajun Fish Tacos, 105
Cajun Popcorn Shrimp Sandwiches, 162
Cake with Lemon Sauce, 226
Candy Craze Ice Cream Sandwiches, 70
Candy-Licious Fudge, 233
Caramel-Apple Pork Chops, 111
Caramel Coconut Stars, 271
Caramel Glazed Salmon, 18
Caramel-Pecan Ice Cream Sandwiches, 225
Caramelized Onion Chuck Roast, 83
Cardamom Sour Cream Waffles, 198
Carnitas Tacos, 257
Cereal & Milk Ice Cream Sandwiches, 71
Cerveza Margaritas, 257
Champagne Fruit Punch, 236
Cheddar Bread Twists, 21
Cheddar Garlic Biscuits, 58
Cheese-Trio Artichoke & Spinach Dip, 126
Cheesy Chive Potatoes, 14
Cherry Cordial Cookies, 218
Chicken & Bacon Tart, 101
Chicken & Brie Salad, 147
Chicken & Fruit Spinach Salads, 207
Chicken and Sausage Penne, 291
Chicken & Shrimp Fettuccine, 109
Chicken Chimichangas, 84
Chicken Fajita Alfredo, 180
Chicken Madeira Pastry, 192
Chicken Nachos for One, 135
Chicken Rellenos with Cilantro-Lime Cream Sauce, 174

Chicken Strips Milano, 33
Chicken Taco Rice, 181
Chicken with Caramelized Pears, 98
Chicken with Rosemary Butter Sauce for 2, 29
Chicks-on-the-Ranch Deviled Eggs, 242
Chili-Basil Tomato Soup, 22
Chili-Beer Glazed Steaks, 41
Chili con Queso El Dorado, 131
Chili Hash, 100
Chili Seafood Sauce, 280
Chili-Spiced Pork Chops, 186
Chilly Night Beef Stew, 85
Chimichurri Monkey Bread, 63
Chipotle Mac & Cheese, 290
Chive Smashed Potatoes, 266
Chocolate Butterscotch Tartlets, 131
Chocolate Cake in a Mug, 214
Chocolate Candy Cane Cookies, 271
Chocolate Caramel Oranges, 263
Chocolate Challah French Toast, 121
Chocolate Chip Ice Cream Pie, 51
Chocolate Lover's Cream Pie, 226
Chocolate Mint Parfaits, 218
Chocolate-Peanut Butter Cup Cookies, 231
Chocolate Rum Fondue, 268
Christmas Elf Cake Pops, 276
Chunky Chicken Noodle Soup, 152
Cinnamon Apple Shakes, 135
Citrus-Herb Pork Roast, 289
Citrus-Marmalade Vinaigrette, 281
Citrus-Spice Glazed Salmon, 50
Classic Pesto, 280
Classic Tartar Sauce, 280
Coconut Fruit Salad, 146
Coconut-Pecan Coffee Cake, 118
Coconut Shrimp Chowder, 157
Cool & Creamy Ice Cream Sandwiches, 224
Country Chuck Roast with Mushroom Gravy, 168
Country Corn, 138
Crab Imperial Casserole, 186
Crab Sandwiches, 77
Cranberry Pancakes, 122
Cranberry Sweet-and-Sour Pork, 177
Cream Cheese & Chive Omelet, 117
Cream of Potato & Cheddar Soup, 158
Creamy Chicken Lasagna Roll-Ups, 188
Creamy Cranberry Meatballs, 129
Creamy Onion Pork Chops, 65
Creamy Salmon Linguine, 87
Crème de Menthe Cheesecake Cookies, 271
Creole Shrimp Pasta, 174
Crispy Beer Battered Fish, 292
Crispy Mexican Truffles, 132
Crispy Scallops with Tarragon Cream, 293
Crown Roast with Spring Rice Pilaf, 252
Crunchy Amaretto Peach Cobbler, 228
Curry Citrus Chicken, 34
Curry On Deviled Eggs, 245
Curry Rice Pilaf, 17

D

Dark Chocolate Carrot Cake, 231
Dazzling Dirty Martini Deviled Eggs, 245
Deconstructed Pear Pork Chops, 97
Deli Roast Beef Sandwiches with Mashed Potatoes, 58
Deli Sandwich Spread, 156
Deli-Style Potato Salad, 139
Desert Oasis Chicken, 172
Dill-icious Deviled Eggs, 242

E

Easy Cheddar Chicken Potpie, 184
Easy Cinnamon Rolls, 116
Egg Drop Soup, 155
Elegant Pork Marsala, 14
Elegant Spring Salad, 254

F

Family-Favorite Spaghetti Sauce, 77
Family-Favorite Turkey Egg Rolls, 126
Farmhouse Barbecue Muffins, 73
Fiesta Corn Chip Salad, 145
Fiesta Rice and Bean Salad, 149
Finnegan House Dry Rub, 282
Frosted Anise Cookies, 275
Frozen Lime Cake, 48
Fun & Festive Cake Pops, 277

G

Garden Orzo Risotto, 204
Garden Vegetable Primavera, 172
Garlic Brussels Sprouts, 30
Garlic Chicken & Bacon Pizza, 47
Ghost Caramel Pears, 261
Ginger-Peach Pork Skillet, 88
Gingerbread Fruitcake Cookies, 214
Gingered Snow Peas, 33
Gladiator Chicken Skewers, 248

Gnocchi Chicken Skillet, 173
Godfather Crostini, 249
Golombki, 192
Gourmet Caramel Apples, 261
Grandma's Turkey Gravy, 265
Greek Ravioli Skillet, 106
Green Bean & Balsamic Salad, 258
Green Beans with Shallots, 14
Green Breakfast Smoothie, 121
Green Onion Rolls, 254
Greens with Balsamic Vinaigrette, 282
Grilled Chicken Sausages with Harvest Rice, 52
Grilled Corn Medley, 41
Grilled Fajita Rolled Steak, 257
Grilled Peaches & Pound Cake, 258
Grilled Pineapple & Maple Sundaes, 43
Grilled Pork Chops with Peach Sauce, 286
Grilled Ribeyes with Blue Cheese Butter, 92
Grilled Romaine with Swiss, 286
Gump's Shrimp & Grits, 248

H

Ham & Cheese Bagels, 122
Ham & Noodle Bake, 86
Ham & Noodles with Veggies, 58
Ham & Pea Fettuccine, 171
Happy Orange Turkey, 265
Hawaiian Barbecue Beans, 50
Hazelnut Chocolate Mousse, 38
Hearty Chicken & Wild Rice Soup, 164
Hearty Pita Spinach Salad, 104
Hearty Sausage-Stuffed Loaf, 61
Heavenly Citrus Ham, 86
Herb Breakfast Frittata, 201
Herb-Crusted Perch Fillets with Pea Puree, 175
Herbed Chicken and Rice, 30
Herbed Corn and Carrots, 26
Herbed Potato Soup, 152
Herby Potatoes with Sour Cream, 143
Hint of Lemon Squash Saute, 18
Hoisin-It-Nice Deviled Eggs, 245
Homemade Meatless Spaghetti Sauce, 290
Honey & Spice Baked Chicken, 84
Honey Mustard Coleslaw, 138
Honey-Mustard Salad Dressing, 280
Honey-Nut Christmas Cookies, 271
Honey Roasted Chicken, 51
Hop-To-It Deviled Eggs, 242
Hot Chocolate Peppermint Cookies, 275
Hot Shrimp Salad, 210
Hungry Man's Baked Potatoes, 241

I

Indian Baked Chicken, 186
Italian Dipping Sticks, 72
Italian Enchiladas, 290
Italian Linguini Salad, 141
Italian Pesto Pizzas, 189
Italian Shredded Beef Sandwiches, 162
Italian-Style Croissants, 55
Italian-Style Salisbury Steaks, 13

J

Jalapeno Cheddar Biscuits, 22
Jazzed-Up French Bread, 41
Jazzy Spaghetti Sauce, 102

K

Kielbasa Spinach Soup, 165

L

Layered Potato Beef Casserole, 85
Lemon & Sage Roasted Chicken, 82
Lemon Beans with Prosciutto, 202
Lemon Chicken Breasts with Veggies, 288
Lemon Date Couscous, 147
Lemon Mint Spritzer, 129
Light Green Goddess Salad Dressing, 282
Lil' Devil Eggs, 244
Lion and Lamb Cupcakes, 74
Little Italy Deviled Eggs, 244
Loaded Breakfast Potatoes, 121
Loaded Mexican Pizza, 194
Logan's Fried Catfish, 65
Lone Star Deviled Eggs, 244

M

Macadamia-Coffee Bean Cookies, 52
Makeover Beef Stroganoff, 211
Makeover Honey French Dressing, 282
Makeover Macaroni and Cheese, 211
Mandarin Watermelon Salad, 149
Mango Sorbet Dessert, 217
Maple & Chipotle Sausages, 122
Maple Baked Salmon, 47
Maple-Dijon Sausage & Sprouts, 110
Maple Jalapenos, 133
Mediterranean Rack of Lamb, 191
Mediterranean Shrimp Linguine, 198
Mediterranean Tuna Linguine, 101

Mexican Couscous, 49
Mexican Fiesta Steak Stir-Fry, 173
Mexican Tater-Topped Casserole, 89
Microwaved Chicken Kiev, 294
Million Dollar Pecan Bars, 221
Mini Caramel Rolls, 114
Mocha Cappuccino Punch, 130
Moist & Savory Meat Loaf, 188
Mom's Turkey Tetrazzini, 192
Mushroom Salad, 25
Mushroom Steak, 288
Mustard Turkey Cutlets, 202

N

Next Day Meat Loaf Pie, 90
Nutter Butter Truffles, 238
Nutty Oven-Fried Chicken, 184
Nutty Waffle Sandwiches, 116

O

Old-World Pizza Meat Loaf, 90
Orange BBQ Baby Back Ribs, 284
Orange Beef and Asparagus Stir-Fry, 92
Orzo with Peppers & Spinach, 202
Outrageous Chocolate Mint Cookies, 229

P

Pan-Fried Chicken Athena, 14
Pan-Fried Chicken with Hoisin Cranberry Sauce, 108
Pan Gravy, 266
Panko Chicken with Fresh Marinara, 135
Parmesan Chicken Couscous, 82
Parmesan-Onion Potato Packets, 284
Parmesan Roasted Asparagus, 18
Parsley-Crusted Cod, 200
Parsleyed Rice Pilaf, 22
Pasta & Broccoli Sausage Simmer, 180
Pasta Primavera, 176
Pasta with Garlic Oil, 168
Pasta with Shrimp & Basil, 10
Peanut Butter-Chocolate Ice Cream Torte, 223
Peanut Butter-Graham Snack Mix, 78
Peanut Butter-Hazelnut Brownies, 229
Peanut Chicken Wings, 127
Pecan-Crusted Chicken Waffle Sandwiches, 59
Peking Shrimp, 203
Peppered Pork with Asti Cream Sauce, 269
Peppered Portobello Penne, 38
Peppermint S'more Tassies, 274
Pepperoni-Artichoke Pasta Salad, 143
Pepperoni Penne Carbonara, 179
Pesto Grilled Salmon, 87
Pesto Portobello Pizzas, 44
Philadelphia Beef Sandwich, 161
Philly Cheesesteak Pizza, 188
Philly-Style Barbecue Pizza, 64
Philly-Style Mac and Cheese, 191
Pineapple Colada Shake, 133
Pineapple Orange Cheesecake, 226
Pinwheel Pizza Snacks, 79
Pizza on a Stick, 75
Pomegranate Cosmo, 269
Pomegranate Orange Salsa, 268
Pork & Vegetable Skillet, 111
Pork and Waffles with Maple-Pear Topping, 294
Pork Chops in a Honey-Mustard Sauce, 295
Pork Medallions with Brandy Cream Sauce, 181
Pork Medallions with Cranberry Sauce, 18
Pork Medallions with Raspberry-Balsamic Sauce, 199
Portobello Burger with Muffuletta Topping, 162
Poutine, 64
Present Cake Pops, 277

Q

Queso Pork Enchiladas, 93
Quick Crisp Snack Bars, 77

R

Raspberry Peach Pie, 217
Red Pepper-Curry Chicken, 17
Reuben Dip, 268
Rhubarb Sundaes, 233
Ribboned Vegetables, 29
Roast Beef Aioli Bundles, 238
Roast Beef Potpie, 66
Roasted Russet & Sweet Potato Wedges, 141
Rocky Road Freezer Pie, 249
Root Beer Glazed Chicken, 23
Rosemary Carrots, 33
Rosemary-Orange Roasted Chicken, 190
Rueben Strata, 91
Rustic Antipasto Tart, 238

S

Sacher Bars, 228
Salisbury Meatballs, 26
Salmon Fettuccine Alfredo, 98
Salmon Mousse Tartlets, 41
Salmon with Tangy Raspberry Sauce, 209
Salsa Dipper Deviled Eggs, 244
Salted Caramel & Dark Chocolate Figs, 262
Salted Caramel Fudge Drops, 272
Sausage Alfredo, 26
Sausage & Salsa Breakfast Burritos, 199
Sausage Breakfast Hash, 59
Sausage Florentine Potpie, 66
Sausage Pineapple Lettuce Wraps, 161
Sausage Ratatouille, 246
Savory Corn Bread Pops, 130
Savory Peas and Carrots, 13
Scalloped Potatoes & Ham, 144
Scallops with Chipotle-Orange Sauce, 33
Seasoned Oven Fries, 149
Sesame Chicken Wraps, 160
Sesame Dill Fish, 34
Sesame Salmon with Wasabi Mayo, 193

Shrimp & Spinach Salad, 144
Shrimp Piccata, 17
Sicilian Ice Cream Sandwiches, 224
Sirloin Stir-Fry with Ramen Noodles, 177
Sizzling Chicken Lo Mein, 179
Skillet Cassoulet, 168
Sloppy Joe Veggie Casserole, 189
Slow Cooked BBQ Pork Ribs, 93
Slow-Cooked Corned Beef, 91
Slow-Cooked Fruited Oatmeal with Nuts, 118
Slow Cooker Golombki, 288
Slow Cooker Hula Chicken, 65
Smothered Burritos, 49
Snappy Green Beans, 140
Snow Pea Medley, 29
Snowman Cake Pops, 276
Snowman Cutouts, 272
Southern Skillet Chops, 21
Southwest Chicken Pockets, 102
Southwest Pulled Pork, 160
Southwest Rice Pilaf, 257
Speedy Stovetop Spaghetti, 171
Spiced Eggnog Pumpkin Pie, 266
Spicy Asian Noodle Bowls, 171
Spicy Cajun Salsa Burgers, 156
Spinach & Gorgonzola Salad, 10
Spinach Salmon Bundles, 63
Spinach Stuffed Chicken with Linguine, 105
Spiral Stromboli, 60
Squash and Mushroom Medley, 23
Stacked Chicken Cordon Bleu, 169
Stacked Vegetables and Ravioli, 107
Steakhouse Strip Steaks with Chimichurri, 285
Strawberry Cheesecake Pops, 78
Strawberry Tarragon Crumble, 232
Stuffed Alfredo Pork Chops, 96
Summer Fish Skillet, 107
Summer Salads with Mandarin Oranges, 142
Summer's Best Spinach Salad, 145
Sun-Dried Tomato and Parmesan Spread, 130
Sun-Dried Tomato Garlic Bread, 10
Sunny Breakfast Smoothies, 73
Super-Fast Corn Bread, 21
Super Mango Smoothies, 129
Super-Stuffed Mexican Potatoes, 71
Sweet & Savory Ice Cream Sandwiches, 224
Sweet & Savory Slow-Cooked Beef, 159
Sweet and Sour Shrimp in a Hurry, 179
Sweet & Spicy Chicken Wings, 129
Sweet & Tender Beef Ribs, 185
Sweet Onion & Carrot Medley, 203
Swordfish with Fennel and Tomatoes, 286

T

Taco Shepherd's Pie, 291
Tangy Barbecue Sauce, 280
Tasty Tacos, 71
Tater Salad Deviled Eggs, 244
Teddy Bear Sandwiches, 72
Teriyaki Chicken and Vegetables, 106
That's Amore Baked Potatoes, 241
The-Best-of-Both Worlds Dressing, 141
The Elvis Ice Cream Sandwich, 225
The King's Crowned Filets, 284
Tilapia & Lemon Sauce, 30
Toasted Sausage Cacciatore Sammies, 109
Toffee Cream Pie, 231
Tomato-Basil Couscous Salad, 45
Tortellini & Shrimp Skewers with Sun-Dried Tomato Sauce, 239
Tortellini Tossed Salad, 149
Tossed Salad, 145
Trick-or-Treat Cake, 262
Triple Chip Cookies, 215
Triple-Layer Pretzel Brownies, 221
Tropical Tilapia, 209
Tuna Cakes with Mustard Mayo, 103
Tuna with Tuscan White Bean Salad, 206
Turkey Alfredo Tetrazzini, 64
Turkey-Brie Stromboli, 61
Turkey Potpie Cups, 67
Turkey Scallopini, 29
Tuscan Parmesan Pork Chops, 48

V

Vegetable Beef & Barley Soup, 83
Vegetable Meatball Soup, 164
Vegetable Trio, 30
Vegetarian Potato au Gratin, 103
Vegetarian Reubens, 152
Very Veggie Baked Potatoes, 241

W

Walsh Family Grilled Pork Tenderloins, 88
Warm Christmas Punch, 269
Warm Pecan Cabbage Slaw, 34
Watermelon Shark, 70
West Coaster Deviled Eggs, 245
White Bean and Spinach Salads, 142
White Chocolate Berry Parfaits, 222
Whoopie Cookies, 38

Y

Yogurt & Honey Fruit Cups, 122

Z

Zesty Broccoli, 146
Zippy Zucchini Pasta, 21
Zucchini & Tomato Saute, 26
Zucchini Corn Medley, 140
Zucchini Pesto with Shrimp and Farfalle, 207
Zucchini Rice Pilaf, 34